OVID AND THE MODERNS

Giorgio de Chirico, *The Joys and Enigmas of a Strange Hour.* 1913. Oil on canvas, 33 × 51 inches (84 × 129 cm). Private collection. Courtesy of Massimo Martino Fine Arts & Projects, Mendrisio, Switzerland.

OVID AND THE MODERNS

THEODORE ZIOLKOWSKI

CORNELL UNIVERSITY PRESS
ITHACA AND LONDON

First published 2005 by Cornell University Press

Printed in the United States of America

Library of Congress Cataloging-in-Publication Data

Ziolkowski, Theodore.
    Ovid and the moderns / Theodore Ziolkowski.
        p.   cm.
    Includes bibliographical references and index.
    ISBN 0-8014-4274-5 (alk. paper)
    1. Ovid, 43 B.C.–17 or 18 A.D.—Criticism and interpretation—
History—20th century. 2. Ovid, 43 B.C.–17 or 18 A.D.—Translations—
History and criticism.   3. Ovid, 43 B.C.–17 or 18 A.D—In literature.
4. Ovid, 43 B.C.–17 or 18 A.D.—Appreciation.   5. Ovid, 43 B.C.–17 or 18
A.D.—Influence.   6. Literature, Modern—Roman influences. I. Title
    PA6537.Z56 2004
    871′.01—dc   2004017452

Cornell University Press strives to use environmentally responsible suppliers
and materials to the fullest extent possible in the publishing of its books.
Such materials include vegetable-based, low-VOC inks and acid-free
papers that are recycled, totally chlorine-free, or partly composed of
nonwood fibers. For further information, visit our website at
www.cornellpress.cornell.edu.

Cloth printing   10 9 8 7 6 5 4 3 2 1

WILFRIED BARNER

viro doctissimo
collegae humanissimo
amico fidelissimo

CONTENTS

PREFACE

I began the study of Latin in the years immediately following World War II when Ovid's works were still regarded as suitable at best for school and college anthologies but hardly worthy of serious critical attention. Later, trained in the New Criticism of the early 1950s, we young scholars did not deign to concern ourselves with a poet whose writings, as we confidently knew from our teachers and handbooks, were superficial, trivial, and even immoral. It took several years, in the wake of the bimillennial celebrations of 1957–58, before I realized that the authorities I had trusted were wrong—that Ovid was not only a superb poet and a fascinating figure but that his popularity and powerful influence over the centuries alternated in an almost predictable rhythm with that of the older Augustans.

This rhythm became apparent to me during the 1980s while I was working on a book that later appeared under the title *Virgil and the Moderns* (1993). Pursuing that insight, a few years later I wrote an article titled "Modern Metamorphoses of Ovid" (*Classical and Modern Literature* 17 [1997]: 341–66), which surveyed several poems, plays, and novels treating the life of Ovid, and notably his exile, in European literature since World War II. In the years since that writing several more novels about Ovid have appeared in different languages, a volume of poeticized tales by an English Poet Laureate, an international collection of short stories based on Ovid's life and works, and an ecstatically acclaimed Broadway production revolving around tales from the *Metamorphoses*. At least two websites in this country are devoted to Ovid. *The Ovid Project* at the University of Vermont (www.uvm.edu/~hag/ovid/) went online in 1994, and *Pagina Amicorum Nasonis* (www3.baylor.edu/~Alden_Smith/) at Baylor University in 1998. In 2003, my local Barnes & Noble bookstore carried translations of Ovid's erotic poems, his *Heroides,* his poems from exile, and no fewer than four different modern renditions of the *Metamorphoses* as well as a reprint of the classic Golding translation of 1567—more editions by far than for Homer, Virgil, Dante, Milton, Goethe, or most other representatives of the classic canon of world literature. The *New Yorker* noted the revival in a column titled "Change Will Do You Good" (16 September 2002), and *Newsweek* hailed "The Return of Ovid" (2 December 2002), observing that "From stage to page, the master of change is everywhere."

The revival is not limited to the United States. In autumn 2002 Dussmann, a vast "cultural department store" located in the heart of Berlin, offered in addition to Ovid's love poems three translations of the *Metamorphoses* published in major series (DTV, Goldmann, Insel)—not on the shelves for classics or poetry, but in general fiction. As early as 1987 the internationally acclaimed stage designer Achim Freyer, with the composer Dieter Schnebel, produced a celebrated adaptation of scenes from the *Metamorphoses* at Vienna's Burgtheater. The distinguished German Ovid scholar Michael von Albrecht collaborated with his wife, Ruth von Albrecht, on a volume titled *Ovid für Liebende* [Ovid for lovers] (Gerlingen: Lambert Schneider, 1998) containing translations of relevant passages from Ovid's poems along with illustrations from world art. Almost in response, a popular soft-cover series brought out an anthology of epigrams called *Ovid für Verliebte* [Ovid for those in love] (Frankfurt am Main: Insel, 1999). A year later Gerhard Fink published an abridgment of the *Metamorphoses* in a paperback series called Masterpieces Briefly and Succinctly (Munich: Piper, 2000). The Humboldt University in Berlin supports an "Ovid Homepage" called *Kirke—tenerorum lusor amorum* (www.kirke.hu-berlin.de/ovid/start.html). Such developments as these encouraged the Munich classicist Niklas Holzberg in 1998 to conjecture that we are entering a new "Age of Ovid" (see *Ovid: The Poet and His Works,* trans. G. M. Goshgarian [Ithaca: Cornell University Press, 2002]).

This striking phenomenon, even if it does not justify the claim to another *aetas Ovidiana,* suggests at the very least that the reasons for the conspicuous popularity of the Roman poet—his life as well as his works—at the turn of the new millennium bear investigation. To this end I shall consider the background of Ovidianism throughout the twentieth century and the various transformations that the poet's life and works have undergone. In the opening lines of his *Metamorphoses* Ovid outlined the project of his world-poem: *In nova fert animus mu-*

tatas dicere formas / corpora ("My mind inspires me to speak of [ideal] forms changed into new bodies"). By analogy, the project of this book is to speak of the new bodies assumed in the twentieth century by the poems and tales to which Ovid gave their classic form—including prominently the account of his own life, which has been hailed by many writers of our time as the archetype of exile.

My aim in part is to expose unexplored dimensions of meaning in the various twentieth-century works discussed—though not in Ovid's Latin poetry, which I approach not as a classicist but as a student of modern literature. In the literature from our own time the focus on Ovid often yields surprising results. The contextualization of individual works helps us to understand that they belong to a larger tradition rather than being unique, as is sometimes assumed. It does not diminish the stature of Christoph Ransmayr's international bestseller *The Last World* to compare it, say, to Jacek Bocheński's *Nazo poeta* or Marin Mincu's *Il diario di Ovidio;* but it reminds us that Ransmayr's novel is not the only brilliant fictionalization of Ovid in recent decades. By analogy, we see Eliot's *Waste Land* with different eyes when we reread it together with major poems by Rilke and Mandelstam from the same year. I have not aspired to bibliographical completeness: an important new work may appear next month, or may already be present in a language unknown to me. I hope simply to adduce enough representative examples in each category to justify a certain degree of generalization.

Beyond the interpretation of individual works, I intend to suggest some of the reasons for Ovid's appeal to different writers and different generations. In that enterprise representative scholarly works on Ovid themselves become material for observation. In every case it can be revealing to ask whether the focus is Ovid's life or his works. If the former, then is it the life prior to or during his years of exile that has captured the writer's interest? In the latter case, which Ovidian works attract the modern author? And why, at certain historical junctures, has Ovid given way in public attention and esteem to Virgil?

In recent decades the theme of metamorphosis has become a critical and academic shibboleth. I am concerned here not with "metamorphosis" generally but only insofar as a specific connection to Ovid can be established, as in the case of the writers treated in Chapters 5 and 10. By analogy, I deal with individual mythological themes—Ariadne, Lycaon, Actaeon, Daphne, Philomela, Orpheus, and others—only to the extent that Ovid can be identified as their specific source. This book is about the reception of Ovid—his life and his works—and not about metamorphosis or mythological themes that occur more broadly in classical literature. A vast bibliography of studies on both of those topics already exists.

Because my groupings of texts, and my argument concerning the reasons for those groupings, depend on familiarity with the works treated, and because some of these works are not widely known and often not easily accessible, I have taken the liberty in certain instances of recapitulating: not Joyce's *Portrait* but Bocheński's *Nazo poeta,* not Eliot's *Waste Land* but Benn's "Orpheus' Tod." Similarly, since many nonspecialist readers are not familiar with the classical background, I have provided an introductory overview of Ovid's life and the premodern reception of his works—material with which the scholar of Latin literature will already be well acquainted.

I have generally cited Ovid according to the six-volume edition in the conveniently available Loeb Classical Library. In a few cases (obvious misprints or useful variants) I have consulted the Teubner edition of *Metamorphoses,* edited by Rudolf Ehwald (Leipzig, 1928), and notably the new Oxford Classical Text of the *Metamorphoses,* edited by R. J. Tarrant (Oxford, 2004). All translations, unless otherwise noted, are my own. I have preferred literal prose renditions to any attempt to reproduce the poetic form of the originals; these normally follow the quoted text. Occasionally, for stylistic reasons, I have offered a close paraphrase, sometimes changing the first person of the original to the third; such paraphrases, indicated by quotation marks, precede the quoted text.

I have incurred numerous debts along the way to my rediscovery of Ovid. I am grateful to M. J. Fitzgerald for helping me to locate several of her provocative stories based on the *Metamorphoses,* and to Robin Robertson for assisting me in my quest for permissions to reprint lines from his witty poem. Bernhard Kendler of Cornell University Press has followed the progress of this book with gratifying interest and encouragement. I am indebted to Carole Newlands for her meticulous, thoughtful, and critical reading of my manuscript. My text has again benefited from Jane Dieckmann's fine editorial eye. I continue to appreciate the friendly professionalism of the staff at Cornell University Press, and notably Teresa Jesionowski. As always, my family have offered me the benefit of their expertise in many areas: Margaret Ziolkowski in Russian literature; Jan M. Ziolkowski in medieval Latin literature; Eric J. Ziolkowski in the history of religion; and my son-in-law Robert Thurston in modern European history. My wife Yetta has listened to my ideas since the beginning—after a performance of *Ariadne auf Naxos* in Berlin, at the exhibition of de Chirico's Ariadne-paintings in Philadelphia, on my often excited return from the Staatsbibliothek in Berlin or Firestone Library here in Princeton—and has responded with her usual critical acumen and provocative suggestions, not to mention her genial findings on the Internet. Notwithstanding my love of Ovid's works and my affection for the man, the warm support that surrounds me has never allowed me to identify with his tragic experience of exile.

THEODORE ZIOLKOWSKI

Princeton, New Jersey

ACKNOWLEDGMENTS

The image of de Chirico's painting "The Joys and Enigmas of a Strange Hour" is reproduced from a private collection, courtesy of Massimo Martino Fine Arts & Projects, Mendrisio (Switzerland).

I thank the following individuals and publishers for permission to reprint:

Lines from "Orpheus' Tod" by Gottfried Benn. *Statische Gedichte.* Edited by Paul Raabe. © 1948, 2000 by Arche Verlag AG, Zürich-Hamburg. Reprinted by courtesy of Arche Verlag.

Lines from *Elegien aus dem Nachlass des Ovid* by Ernst Fischer, © Insel Verlag 1963. Reprinted by courtesy of Insel Verlag.

"Ovid in the Third Reich" from *New & Collected Poems 1952–1992,* by Geoffrey Hill. Copyright © 1994 by Geoffrey Hill. Reprinted by permission of Houghton Mifflin Company. All rights reserved. And from *Collected Poems* by Geoffrey Hill (first published in *King Log* 1968 by Andre Deutsch, Penguin Books, 1985). Copyright © Geoffrey Hill, 1968.

Excerpt from *Tales of Ovid* by Ted Hughes. Copyright © 1997 by Ted Hughes. Reprinted by permission of Farrar, Straus and Giroux, LLC, and of Faber and Faber Ltd.

Lines from "Ovid in Tomis" by Derek Mahon. By kind permission of the author and The Gallery Press, Loughcrew, Oldcastle, Country Meath, Ireland. From *Collected Poems* (1999); and by permission of Wake Forest University Press. From *The Hunt by Night* (1983).

Poem No. 80 from Osip Mandelstam's *Tristia*. Reprinted by permission from *Complete Poetry of Osip Mandelstam* translated by Burton Raffel and Alla Burago, the State University of New York Press. © 1973 State University of New York. All rights reserved.

Extracts from *Letter from Pontus* by John Masefield. By courtesy of The Society of Authors, literary representative of the Estate of John Masefield.

Excerpt from *A Painted Field,* copyright © 1997 by Robin Robertson, reprinted by courtesy of the author and by permission of Harcourt, Inc., and of Pan Macmillan Ltd., London, UK.

Lines from Slavitt, David R., trans. *The Metamorphoses of Ovid,* pp. ix, x, xii, 1, 50, 72, 73, 135, 183, 184–185, 188. © 1994. Reprinted with permission of The Johns Hopkins University Press.

Lines from Tracy, Robert, trans. *Osip Mandelstam's Stone.* Copyright © 1981 by Princeton University Press. Reprinted by permission of Princeton University Press.

Excerpt from "The Hotel Normandie Pool" from *Collected Poems 1948–1984* by Derek Walcott. Copyright © 1986 by Derek Walcott. Reprinted by permission of Farrar, Straus and Giroux, LLC, and of Faber and Faber Ltd.

The editors of *Classical and Modern Literature* have graciously permitted me to reprint and otherwise use material from my article "Modern Metamorphoses of Ovid" (17 [1997]: 341–66).

INTRODUCTION

◢ 1 ◣

THE LURE OF ARIADNE

ARIADNE IN STONE

In 1912–13 the twenty-four-year-old Giorgio de Chirico executed a series of eight paintings, as well as a small, rough plaster sculpture, revolving around the mythological figure of Ariadne.[1] These works, shown together at an exhibition in the artist's studio in October 1913 and subsequently displayed at the Salon d'Automne (1914) and the Salon des Indépendants (1915), were praised in the reviews of Guillaume Apollinaire and first brought the ambitious young artist to the attention of a larger public. De Chirico's fascination with Ariadne was not exhausted by the works of a single year. He returned obsessively to the theme over the course of his long career, which ended only with his death in 1978 at the age of ninety—notably in over one hundred works (carried out mainly in the 1950s) known as the *Piazza d'Italia* paintings. Yet the basic characteristics of these scores of paintings are evident from the earliest ones on.

All of them, as exemplified in *The Joys and Enigmas of a Strange Hour* (1913), feature a reclining female figure in marble on a plinth situated in an empty piazza with distorted perspectives and weirdly shadowed by surrounding arcades while, in the background behind a low wall, a train puffs by. Often a tower rises in the background, and sometimes two diminutive and unidentifiable figures are standing in the distance. Regardless of variations, the basic pattern is instantly recognizable to museum visitors all over the world as the work of de Chirico.[2]

The central figure is most often portrayed, as in *The Joys and Enigmas of a Strange Hour*, in the classic attitude—reclining with lightly crossed legs, her face propped on one hand with the other arm thrown loosely over her head. The pose of thoughtful melancholy, identified since the early nineteenth century with Ariadne, has been familiar in modern Europe since the early sixteenth century from such works as the Roman copy of a lost Hellenistic sculpture in the Museo Pio-Clementino of the Vatican or the second-century *Sleeping Ariadne* in the Villa Corsini in Florence.[3] Subsequently it was imitated in dozens of paintings and sculptures down to the early twentieth century, when "Ariane couchée" achieved formal iconographic status in such textbooks as Salomon Reinach's five-volume *Répertoire de la statuaire grecque et romaine* (Paris, 1897–1910), a manual that de Chirico studied and used.[4] De Chirico was therefore drawing on a familiar convention in art history when he adapted the Ariadne theme for his own purposes.[5]

What were those purposes? Since antiquity Ariadne has traditionally embodied abandonment and exile. As recounted in various classical sources and widely represented on ancient vases and in paintings, the Cretan princess was smitten by love for Theseus when he arrived in Knossos to liberate Athens from the tribute exacted every nine years by King Minos.[6] Fearful for his safety, she provided him with a ball of thread that enabled him to find his way back out of the labyrinth after slaying her half brother, the Minotaur. In return, Theseus promised love and marriage, but soon deserted Ariadne as she lay sleeping on the desolate island of Naxos (known earlier as Dia). Her plaintive lament was poeticized by Catullus in his epyllion (*Carmen* 64) and by Ovid in the tenth of his *Heroides* (representing an epistle from Ariadne to Theseus). In his early series it was principally the abandoned and exiled Ariadne that appealed to de Chirico—not the Ariadne subsequently rescued and married by Bacchus, as painted by a succession of artists since Titian in his *Bacchus and Ariadne* (1523–24) and that same year by Lovis Corinth in his *Ariadne auf Naxos* (1913). At this point in his life and career de Chirico also had every reason to regard himself as an exile.

Giorgio de Chirico was born in 1888 in Volos, the coastal capital of Thessaly in Greece. His father was a Dalmatian nobleman employed as an engineer in the construction of the Thessalian railway system, and his mother was descended from a Greek-Italian family in Smyrna.[7] Educated privately at home and briefly at the Liceo Leonino, a Jesuit seminary for the Italian colony in Athens, in 1900 de Chirico enrolled for art courses at the Polytechnic Institute in Athens. In 1906, after his father's death, his mother moved with her two sons to Munich, so that Giorgio could pursue his studies at the distinguished Academy of Fine Arts while his musically gifted brother Andrea (who later assumed the pseudonym Alberto Savinio) studied composition with Max Reger. Two years later, unhappy in Bavaria, de Chirico moved to Italy, where he first joined his mother and brother in Milan and then accompanied his brother to Florence, where at the Impressionist exhibition of 1910 the young artist was first exposed to works by Cézanne, Gauguin, Matisse, and Van Gogh. He was excited by the avant-garde developments in France, which differed so sharply from the German Romantic tradition in which he had been trained in Munich—notably Arnold Böcklin, whom he admired and imitated in his earliest works. In the summer of 1911 de Chirico moved with his mother to Paris, even though he had been conscripted by the Italian military. Declared a deserter, he was located by the authorities and ordered, in March 1912, to report for duty in Turin. After only a few days, however, he fled back to Paris, again charged with desertion, and dedicated himself to his painting. He associated initially with the circle of Greek exiles from the haute bourgeoisie, to whom he had access through his father's noble lineage. Soon he met Guillaume Apollinaire and was included in the cénacle of young experimental poets and painters of Paris who came together every Saturday in the poet-critic's apartment.

De Chirico, in sum, had every reason to consider himself an outsider—a pose he cultivated throughout his life and depicted in the hero of his novel *Hebdomeros*[8]—and an exile: first during his boyhood, as an Italian in Greece;[9] later as a disgruntled foreigner in Munich; and most recently as an Italian deserter in Paris, where he moved back and forth between the community of Greek exiles and his new friends from the French artistic avant-garde. During this same period his feelings of exile were intensified by the First Balkan War (Oct. 1912 to May 1913), in which an alliance of Serbia, Montenegro, Bulgaria, and Greece recaptured territory controlled by the Ottoman Empire—events that de Chirico and his Greek friends followed with passionate interest. (As a boy in Volos de Chirico had personally experienced the war between the Greeks and Turks in 1897.)[10] Under these circumstances it is hardly surprising that the figure of the isolated Ariadne contemplating her destiny, whose statue the young art student would have seen in Rome or Florence—held for de Chirico a uniquely personal appeal absent among the many other painters and sculptors who over the centuries had been attracted to the theme for essentially aesthetic reasons.

A further factor motivating his adaptation of the Ariadne figure is related to his obsession with Friedrich Nietzsche, whose works he had discovered in Munich in 1906 and in whose writing he sensed "the strong and mysterious feeling" that dominates his own painting: "the melancholy of beautiful autumn days, afternoons in Italian cities."[11] (In his self-portrait of 1911 de Chirico consciously depicted himself in the pose assumed by Nietzsche in the widely recognized photograph of 1882: in full profile with his face propped on a hand and gazing meditatively into the distance.) It is well known that the philosopher's thought and works are permeated by the figure of Ariadne. In his own life Nietzsche often identified Ariadne with Richard Wagner's wife Cosima, with whom he was infatuated and to whom at the onset of his madness in Turin (January 1889) he addressed a note reading "Ariadne, I love you" and signed it Dionysus.[12] But the identification becomes meaningful only in the larger context of Nietzsche's thought, in which Ariadne is a recurrent theme.[13]

Ariadne entered Nietzsche's imagination in her association with the figure of Dionysus, whose spontaneity and rapturous exuberance ever since *The Birth of Tragedy* (1872) he had set in opposition to the order and rationality represented by Apollo.[14] For Nietzsche, who saw himself as the herald of the Dionysian, Ariadne exemplified the soul vacillating between the poles of the Apollonian and the Dionysian, just as the mythic Ariadne was torn between her love for Theseus, who as king of Athens, the city of Artemis and her brother Apollo, represented the Apollonian, and Dionysus, who rescued her from Naxos. In 1887 Nietzsche contemplated a project that he called "the perfect book" and that would have included short dialogues among Theseus, Dionysus, and Ariadne.[15] The section of *Thus Spoke Zarathustra* titled "On the Great Longing" ("Von der großen Sehnsucht") and which is addressed throughout to "my soul," was originally called "Ariadne." And his *Dionysos Dithyrambs* include "Ariadne's Lament" ("Klage der Ariadne"). But here, other than in the laments by Catullus and Ovid, Ariadne is not addressing the departed Theseus; rather, the abandoned soul cries out to the coming Dionysus, who tells her in the last line that "I am your labyrinth." On the basis of these and many other mentions in his writings Nietzsche felt fully justified, in *Ecce homo* (section 8 of the chapter on *Thus Spoke Zarathustra*), in exclaiming: "Who apart from me knows what Ariadne is!"

Clearly de Chirico's ideas during these years, and specifically his image of Ariadne, were deeply indebted to Nietzsche. His friend Apollinaire argued in his book *Les peintres cubistes* (1913) that Nietzsche's writings had motivated modern artists in their move from the classical model toward "works which are more cerebral than sensual."[16] De Chirico, whose paintings of those years are known as "metaphysical," was a profoundly philosophical artist. He was intensively studying Nietzsche at the very time when the figure of Ariadne initially appeared in his paintings, and he continued for the remainder of his life to read and discuss the thinker whom he characterized as "the most profound of all poets."[17] In *Thus Spoke Zarathustra* he recognized the quality of "surprise" and "strangeness" toward which he felt all art must aspire.[18] Moreover, "transformation" of an ethical-aesthetic nature can be seen as the principal theme of Nietzsche's thought from Zarathustra's opening speech "On the Three Transformations" ("Von den drei Verwandlungen"), to the "transvaluation of all values" that permeates his later works.[19] But Nietzsche represented for de Chirico not simply the encouragement toward "metaphysical" painting generally or toward "artistry" and "transformation"; he provided more specifically the impetus for the young de Chirico's appropriation of Ariadne as the most suitable image for his own situation of exile. (For the mature artist of the *Piazza d'Italia* she offered a more hopeful image of the soul, abandoned by Theseus in his puffing locomotive but dreaming of Dionysus, whose coming is suggested in some of the paintings by the sails of an approaching boat.)[20]

We can only speculate about de Chirico's sources for his acquaintance with the myth of Ariadne.[21] De Chirico knew his Latin: several of his early paintings bear Latin inscriptions,[22] and his writings during these years contain frequent quotations from Horace, Cicero, and other classical works.[23] It seems likely that a Jesuit-trained Italian would have encountered the story in the two best-known and most extensive Latin accounts: the laments of Catullus (*Car.* 64) and Ovid (*Her.* 10).[24] Both poets describe the heroine awakening from a deep sleep to find herself deserted:

> utpote fallaci quae tunc primum excita somno
> desertam in sola miseram se cernat harena.
> (*Car.* 64.56–57)

> (when, first awakened from deceitful sleep, she
> finds herself abandoned and wretched on the
> lonely sand.)

For Ovid she wakes up on "the shore on which my sleep, and you, so badly betrayed me" (*litore . . . in quo me somnusque meus male prodidit et tu; Her.* 10.3–5). Both texts, moreover, contain phrases that at least hint at a transformation into stone. Catullus's Ariadne stands amid the seaweed on the shore, staring at the departing Theseus with her hair and clothes in disarray "like the stone image of a bacchante" (*saxea ut effigies bacchantis, Car.* 64.61). Ovid's Ariadne in her grief also rages wildly like a bacchantic reveler, but she sits on a stone high on a cliff, "I myself as much stone as the stone on which I sat" (*quamque lapis sedes, tam lapis ipsa fui; Her.* 10.50).

But several further reasons speak for the likelihood that Ovid was chief source for de Chirico's specific themes and images, apart from the general principle that Ovid's treatment in the *Heroides* has provided the most frequent channel for the story from the Middle Ages down to modern times.[25] In the first place, transformation of human beings—into birds, beasts, fish, water, flowers, trees, and not least stones—is the main theme of the *Metamorphoses,* which was still widely read as a school text and familiar to every schoolchild. De Chirico is the first artist who represents Ariadne in such a petrification (which of course does not happen to her in the *Metamorphoses,* though her jeweled crown is transformed into a constellation). The many earlier paintings portrayed her as alive and either sleeping or welcoming the arrival of Bacchus. In the second place, just as Ariadne is the poetic embodiment of abandonment, Ovid is the classic poet of exile—the Roman citizen relegated to end his life in the remote corner of the empire, the Sarmatian town of Tomis on the western shores of the Black Sea (Constanța in present-day Romania).

If the themes of transformation, abandonment, and exile, as represented in Ovid's works and his own life, and the influence of Nietzsche go far to explain de Chirico's obsession with Ariadne, and if the long artistic tradition helps us to understand the iconography of her pose, why has de Chirico—unlike the scores of earlier painters and sculptors—placed her in a modern setting? It is widely agreed that the empty piazzas and mysterious arcades that invariably constitute the background—from the early Ariadne series to the late *Piazza d'Italia* paintings—were inspired by de Chirico's brief exposure to the vast statue-populated piazzas and celebrated arcades of Turin. He had spent four days in March 1912 there awaiting his military assignment; moreover, the city was meaningful to him as the place where Nietzsche had suffered his final breakdown a little over two decades earlier. The emptiness of the piazzas emphasizes the abandonment of Ariadne on her lonely shore. (The conjunction of classical statues and arcades is reminiscent also of the halls of the European art academies—e.g., the Academy in Munich and the École des Beaux Arts in Paris—in which the plaster casts used as models were often stored and displayed.)[26]

The omnipresent train, in turn, recalls the profession of de Chirico's father as an engineer for the Greek railway system—the father whom the artist admiringly loved and then lost at an early age.[27] (De Chirico's painting of 1913 entitled *The Anxious Journey* suggests that the train is laden with a certain psychological cargo of travel anxiety.) More relevant, as the exemplary modern mode of transportation the train represents a contemporary equivalent to the ship that bore Theseus away from the sleeping Ariadne. In other words, through a radical juxtaposition of past and present, classic and modern, myth and reality, timelessness (the statue) and time (the moving train and often the clock on the railway station), the artist has created a startlingly vivid image of human alienation, loneliness, abandonment, and exile—an alienation so total that it has objectified the once living and loving Ariadne into a marble sculpture. The mythic and timeless Ariadne has been violently transported into the modern world of railway timetables and reduced to a stock figure in a traditional pose. The metaphor of Ovid's poetry (*lapis ipsa fui*) has been reified through the painting.

This is the shocking modernity of de Chirico's Ariadne paintings, which sets them apart from the scores of earlier treatments of the theme.

ARIADNE IN SONG

Almost simultaneously with de Chirico in Paris, and with a'similar obsessiveness, Hugo von Hofmannsthal in Vienna was working on the libretto for a one-act opera entitled *Ariadne auf Naxos*. The theme was no greater novelty in European opera than it was in European art. Since Monteverdi's *Arianna* (1608), whose "lament" ("Lasciatemi morire") became the most popular musical piece of its day, almost a hundred operas, ballets, *Singspiele* and travesties filled the stages of Europe,[28] and Hofmannsthal could take it for granted that the audience would be familiar with the story. Unlike de Chirico, Hofmannsthal (1874–1929) was no novice: the author of several earlier adaptations of classical myths (*Alkestis*, 1894; *Elektra*, 1903; *Ödipus und die Sphinx*, 1906), he had already collaborated with Richard Strauss on *Elektra* (1909) and *Der Rosenkavalier* (1911). *Ariadne auf Naxos*, however, was the first libretto that he conceived expressly as an opera; both of the earlier texts had been written originally for the stage. The opera, as it premiered in Stuttgart in October 1912, was little more than an appendage to Hofmannsthal's adaptation of Molière's play *Le bourgeois gentilhomme*. (In the original Hofmannsthal/Strauss version, the short opera *Ariadne auf Naxos* took the place of the *Ballet des nations*, set by Jean-Baptiste Lully, with which Molière's comedy concluded.) Since the first version, lasting altogether with intermissions some four hours, was a conspicuous failure, the poet and composer drastically altered the script, reducing Molière's play to a brief *Vorspiel* or prelude. The resulting two-hour opera, which premiered in 1916, is the form in which *Ariadne auf Naxos* has become an acclaimed standard in the opera houses of the world.[29]

The striking parallels between the opera of the Austrian/German collaborators and the paintings of the young Greco-Italian artist may not be immediately apparent. The *Vorspiel* revolves around a dispute between the music teacher, whose protégé has composed an opera seria about *Ariadne auf Naxos*, and the dancing master, who manages an opera buffa featuring Zerbinetta and her four commedia dell'arte companions.[30] Commissioned by one of the wealthiest men in eighteenth-century Vienna for the entertainment of his guests, the opera was to be followed for comic relief by the lighter *Singspiel*. At the last minute, however, the majordomo informs the musicians that the lord of the manor has changed his mind: in view of the fireworks display scheduled for nine o'clock sharp, the two works must be performed simultaneously. The composer, whose figure Hofmannsthal based on his conception of the passionate and uncompromising young Beethoven, is indignantly and unalterably opposed to any such trivialization of his music, which he regards as the most sacred of the arts, and finally rushes out in despair. The dancing master, contemptuous of the pretensions of any self-styled higher art, points out that Zerbinetta and her troupe are skilled at improvisation and can easily adapt themselves to the plot of the opera. The music teacher, whose sense of practicality overcomes his artistic scruples, is prepared to compromise. At this point the opera proper of *Ariadne auf Naxos* begins, and we are to imagine, as Hofmannsthal emphasizes in his stage directions (48) that it is a play within a play: that is, that the eighteenth-century audience is watching the performance from loggias on the stage.

The opera itself falls into three parts: two dramatic scenes divided by a comic intermezzo. As it opens, Ariadne is reclining before her cave on the desolate island, weeping in her sleep and observed by three nymphs (Najade, Dryade, and Echo). Expressing her grief over the betrayal by her beloved Theseus, she is so distraught that she can scarcely remember her own name, so closely interwoven was it with that of Theseus.

> Ein Schönes war, hieß Theseus-Ariadne
> Und ging im Licht und freute sich des Lebens!
>
> . . . .
>
>   ja, dies muß ich finden:
> das Mädchen, das ich war!
> Jetzt hab' ich's—Götter! daß ich's nur behalte!
> Den Namen nicht—der Name ist verwachsen
> mit einem anderen Namen, ein Ding wächst
> So leicht ins andere, wehe!
>   (27–28)

> (There was a lovely thing called Theseus-Ariadne
> and walked in the light and rejoiced in life.
>
> . . . .
>
>   yes, that's what I must find:
> the girl that I was.
> Now I have it—Gods! if only I can hold on to it.
> Not the name—the name has grown together
> with a different name. One thing grows
> so easily into the other, alas.)

Even Zerbinetta and her entourage (Harlekin, Scaramuccio, Truffaldin, and Brighella), watching from the wings, are moved to pity by her lament. The frivolous Zerbinetta, incapable of comprehending the depth of Ariadne's grief, believes that the princess will quickly find another lover and that she can be cheered up in the meantime by the songs and dances of the comic troupe. But Ariadne, convinced after Theseus's betrayal that purity and loyalty cannot be found in this world, directs her longing toward death.

> Es gibt es Reich, wo alles rein ist:
> Es hat auch einen Namen: Totenreich.
> (29)

> (There is a realm where all is pure:
> It also has a name: Realm of Death.)

Ignoring Zerbinetta and the comedians, who try to amuse her with their song and dance, Ariadne covers her face in grief. As Zerbinetta sings a ditty in which she speaks of her own frequent betrayal by faithless men and her subsequent recovery through ever new love affairs, Ariadne retreats into her cave. Zerbinetta dances flirtatiously from one to the next of her four companions, visually enacting her flighty conception of love.

This comic intermezzo is interrupted by the reappearance of the three nymphs excitedly announcing the arrival of the young Bacchus, whose ship has just appeared. They report that he has come from the isle of Circe, who unsuccessfully sought through her magic to transform him into an animal, as she had often done with other men. Ariadne, attracted by the music heralding Bacchus, emerges from her cave as Bacchus appears, singing of his escape from Circe. Ariadne, who has had nothing but death in her mind, mistakes him for Hermes, the god of death, for whom she has been single-mindedly longing.

> O Todesbote! süß ist deine Stimme!
> Balsam ins Blut, und Schlummer in die Seele!
> (43)

> (O Messenger of Death! sweet is your voice!
> Balm to the blood and slumber to the soul!)

Believing that she is going to embark on a ship to the underworld, she yields to his invitation to accompany him. Bacchus, however, smitten by her beauty and realizing that she is not simply another sorceress like Circe, is genuinely enchanted. Succumbing each to the other, they are both transformed spiritually. Ariadne is awakened by the god's love from her spiritual death to a new life:

> Lag nicht die Welt auf meiner Brust? hast du,
> Hast du sie fortgeblasen?
>
> (46)

> (Did not the world lie upon my breast? have you,
> have you blown it away?)

Bacchus, in turn, having resisted Circe's enticement to bestiality, is elevated by his love to an understanding of his divinity and thereby transforms her cave of grief into a pleasure dome:

> Ich bin ein anderer, als ich war!
> Der Sinn des Gottes ist wach in mir,
> Dein herrlich Wesen ganz zu fassen!
> Die Glieder reg' ich in göttlicher Lust!
> Die Höhle da! Laß mich, die Höhle deiner Schmerzen
> Zieh' ich zur tiefsten Lust um dich und mich!
>
> (46)

> (I am another than I was!
> The sense of the god has awakened in me
> to grasp fully your splendid being.
> I stir my limbs in divine desire.
> The cave there! Allow me. The cave of your pain
> I shall draw around you and me for our deepest pleasure.)

Zerbinetta, for whom transformation means nothing loftier than a change of lovers, is incapable of understanding this dual process and sees in Bacchus at most a temporary new paramour, a nobler Harlekin, come to console Ariadne for a time. The opera ends as Bacchus announces that he has been enriched by his experience of Ariadne's human grief and thereby elevated to divine status.

> Deiner hab ich um alles bedurft!
> Nun bin ich ein anderer, als ich war,
> Durch deine Schmerzen bin ich reich,
> Nun reg' ich die Glieder in göttlicher Lust!
> Und eher sterben die ewigen Sterne,
> Eh' denn du stürbest aus meinen Armen!
>
> (47)

(I needed you for everything!
Now I am another than I was.
Through your grief I am enriched,
Now I stir my limbs in divine desire!
And the eternal stars shall die out
before you die from my arms.)

At this point we begin to make out the similarities to de Chirico's Ariadne paintings. Once again we are dealing with a work whose theme is transformation—a word that occurs a dozen times in the last few pages of the libretto. Indeed, one early critic maintained that this is the first "crystallization of that psychological-philosophical problem that throughout his life was *the* problem of Hugo von Hofmannsthal."[31] But here, rather than a physical transformation into stone, metamorphosis is a spiritual process. (To be sure, at one point Zerbinetta remarks that Ariadne sits before her cave as proud and motionless "as though you were the statue on your own crypt" [32].) As the composer explains his noble conception of the opera in the *Vorspiel:* "She yields to death—is no longer there—wiped away—plunges into the mystery of transformation—is born anew—arises again in his arms!—Thereby he becomes a god. How else in the world could anyone become a god other than through this experience?" (22).

Hofmannsthal expounded his ideas in a letter that he sent during the composition (summer 1911) to Richard Strauss—a difficult concept of transformation, he concedes, that can be expressed more powerfully through music than in words alone. "It is a question of a simple and immense life problem: the problem of loyalty. To cling to what has been lost, to persist forever unto death—or to live, to live on, to get over it, to transform oneself, to give up the unity of the soul and yet preserve oneself in transformation, to remain a human being, not sink down to a memoryless animal."[32] As he later developed his thoughts in a revision of the letter for publication in the *Almanach für die Musikalische Welt* (1913), "Transformation [*Verwandlung*] is the life of life, the essential mystery of creative nature; persistence is paralysis and death. Whoever wishes to live must transcend himself, must transform himself: he must forget."[33] But there is an inherent contradiction, Hofmannsthal continues, for all human dignity depends on loyalty and fidelity. Zerbinetta, a creature wholly without loyalty, dances frenetically from man to man. But Ariadne is capable of belonging to one man only and, following his loss, resigns herself to death. It is the miracle of metamorphosis that she can be reborn through her new love. "When Ariadne in the presence of her transformed Self sees even the cave of her grief transformed to a temple of joy . . . and the island changed from a prison cell into Elysium—

what else is she confessing other than that she loves and lives." This process of reciprocal transformation for which Hofmannsthal coined the term "allomatic" (i.e., activated by and for the other)[34] is, as he continues, a paradigmatic "allegory of the social." "The path to the social" leads by way of self-sacrifice to oneself.[35]

While Hofmannsthal had no personal experience of alienation and abandonment analogous to de Chirico's and, in any case, scrupulously avoided the autobiographical in his works, his interest in the theme of Ariadne was intensified by his close friendship with Ottonie Degenfeld, a young woman who after a brief marriage had lost her husband and suffered grievous doubts about existence.[36] But primarily the identification of Ariadne with his vision of "the social" accounted for his obsession with the theme. This identification also assists us in specifying Hofmannsthal's principal source for his libretto. We can take it for granted that Hofmannsthal, who acquired a solid knowledge of the classics in school and later earned his doctorate in Romance languages, knew the principal sources in the original. Walter Jens, a scholar of classical literature, singled out Hesiod, Catullus, and Tintoretto's painting as the most probable sources.[37] Daviau and Buelow added Ovid's *Heroides* and *Amores* to Jens's suggestions.[38] Manfred Hoppe, the editor of the new standard edition, narrowed it down to Catullus's epyllion and Ovid's four different treatments. But we can go even further.

Ovid is mentioned frequently in Hofmannsthal's works whereas Catullus is cited only three times in passing.[39] In Hofmannsthal's original adaptation of Molière's play, for instance, the philosopher reminds his listeners that the image of the maiden in love has often been depicted. "Catullus, Tibullus, Propertius, but above all Ovid have sketched it with a master's hand."[40] Moreover, only Ovid portrays Ariadne in a scene that prefigures the clowning of Zerbinetta and her entourage: in the *Ars amatoria* (1.541–48) he depicts the arrival of Silenus accompanied by the satyrs, so inebriated that he can scarcely cling to his donkey and, as he pursues the laughing bacchantes, finally tumbling drunkenly to the ground. (Catullus, in contrast [*Car.* 64.254–64], mentions only the ecstatic orgies of the revelers.) A few years later, in his appreciation of the Austrian *Volksstück* playwright Ferdinand Raimund (1920), Hofmannsthal wrote: "From time to time individuals emerge in whom a social whole fatefully and, one might say, effortlessly comes to bloom: such a figure was Goldoni; such a figure was Ovid."[41] And most emphatically in his sketches (1917/18) for a never-written drama "Die beiden Götter" (The two deities) he speaks of "my affinity [*Verwandtschaft*] with Ovid, who takes myth socially."[42]

While the central themes of transformation and the social, as well as his own avowal, link Hofmannsthal more closely to Ovid than to any other classical source, other factors reveal his close affinity to de Chirico. Both the opera and the paintings exploit a radical juxtaposition of past and present. In Hofmannsthal's libretto, in fact, the juxtaposition is doubled: first by the audience watching the performance; and then, within the opera, by the intrusion of Zerbinetta and the four commedia dell'arte characters into the tragedy of Ariadne. The impatience of the elegant onlookers with the opera and their arrogant dismissal of art parallel the insouciance of the background figures in de Chirico's paintings. The clash of opera seria and *Singspiel,* of myth and commedia dell'arte, produces precisely the same alienation effect, the same sense of "surprise" and "strangeness" created by the juxtaposition of statue and locomotive.[43] But Hofmannsthal, in contrast to de Chirico's dour cultural pessimism, has a more positive view of the intertwining of past and present.[44] They are not mutually exclusive; Zerbinetta and Harlekin are simply comic variations of Ariadne and Bacchus.

For Hofmannsthal, as much as for de Chirico, Ariadne becomes a central image: as the idealistic composer puts it, "the symbol of human loneliness" (19). When we first see her in her grief she expresses the same human despair and abandonment that Ariadne embodies in de Chirico's early paintings. But in the course of the opera she transcends her grief and through "allomatic" transformation achieves a spiritual renewal, not unlike the Ariadnes in the later paintings of *Piazza d'Italia,* whose repose symbolizes the dream of redemption through the Dionysian art professed by Nietzsche.

That Hofmannsthal was able to achieve this vision can be attributed to the same inspiration that motivated de Chirico: the writings of Nietzsche. The precocious Hofmannsthal began reading Nietzsche in 1890, when he was sixteen years old, and in 1892−93 attended a course on Nietzsche's aesthetics.[45] In particular *The Birth of Tragedy* impressed the young poet-dramatist, and he alludes to that book frequently in his letters from those years. In his notes and journals from the period 1890−95 he observes, for instance: "The basic myth of tragedy: the world disaggregated into individuals longs for unity; Dionysus Zagreus wants to be reborn."[46] It is precisely such a rebirth that Bacchus experiences in the opera through his allomatic encounter with Ariadne—a symbiosis of the two individuals that symbolizes the integrity that Hofmannsthal praises as "social." It goes without saying that Hofmannsthal encountered the ideal collaborator for his Nietzschean libretto in the musician who had earlier composed the symphonic poem *Thus Spoke Zarathustra* (1896). Together they accomplished the ultimate metamorphosis of Ariadne—her sublimation into pure song.

We can more fully appreciate the boldness of the adaptations by de Chirico and Hofmannsthal/Strauss, and at the same time the revived popularity of the Ovidian theme, if we contrast their works with three other "Ariadnes" that appeared about the same time. Maurice Hewlett's verse drama *Ariadne in Naxos,* which constitutes the central part of his "Trilogy of God and Man" *The Agonists,* was written as early as 1895–97. But the work was not published until 1911, which suggests the author's sense of timing: the public was ready for an Ariadne drama, but it still favored the explicitly Victorian and Wagnerian poetic style that Hewlett cultivated.[47] In his introduction the author tells us that his trilogy, containing also *Minos King of Crete* and *The Death of Hippolytus,* was meant as a Christian effort to expose "the fallacies which underlay the ancient conceptions of Godkind and Mankind" (viii). His *Ariadne in Naxos* features Dionysus as its protagonist, the god whose tragedy is that "he had Power over men, but could not win their Love" (viii). Dionysus, filled with desire for Ariadne, is already waiting in Naxos when Theseus arrives. Tempting Theseus with promises of glory, he sends him on his way back to Athens. But Ariadne, tainted by the curse of her mother Pasiphaë, realizes that she has sinned by submitting to Dionysus and chooses a voluntary death to end her sorrow. Dionysus, who has sought out Artemis to beg pity and forgiveness for his new love, is left behind in "the chill remoteness" of the sterile ancient gods—"starved, pitiless, unpitied, feared and shunned" (167).

The following year Robert Calverley Trevelyan published his music drama *The Bride of Dionysus* (1912), an utterly conventional dramatization in blank verse, which recapitulates the familiar story from Theseus's arrival at the court of Minos to Ariadne's rescue and transfiguration by Dionysus.[48] The classicizing operatic setting by Donald Francis Tovey simply underscores the distance of his collaboration with Trevelyan vis-à-vis that of Hofmannsthal/Strauss. That same year, finally, the popular German novelist and dramatist Paul Ernst (1866–1933) produced a three-act *Ariadne auf Naxos* in blank verse.[49] While the style is conventionally neoclassical, Ernst inverts the plot: his Theseus is deeply in love with Ariadne and wants to remain with her in Naxos, where he hopes to bring law and civilization to the barbaric islanders. But Theseus is killed by a mob when they learn that Ariadne poisoned her father back in Knossos. Ariadne is rescued by Dionysos, who at the end elevates her into heaven and divinity. None of these three contemporary works, in sum, features the themes of transformation and abandoned exile that mark de Chirico and Hofmannsthal/Strauss as quintessentially modern.

We have seen, then, how two epoch-making works on the theme of Ariadne were created on the eve of World War I: a startling series of paintings by a young Greek-Italian artist, and a bold operatic venture by an Austrian poet and a German composer. Inspired in both cases by Nietzsche's conception of a new art and by his vision of Ariadne, the creators almost certainly went back directly to

Ovid, and specifically to the *Metamorphoses* and the *Heroides,* for their themes and images. In their presentation of Ovid's mythic heroine as the symbol of loneliness, abandonment, and exile, they anticipated the reception of Ovid by many subsequent writers from James Joyce to the literally exiled intellectuals in the second half of the twentieth century. In their fascination with the theme of metamorphosis they foreshadowed another group of writers from Franz Kafka to the authors of the recent cluster of postmodern poems, plays, and novels revolving around the *Metamorphoses.* And in their radical experimentation—notably the juxtaposition of past and present, myth and reality—they prefigured the inventive treatment of Ovid's life and his poems that has permeated the twentieth century.

◂ 2 ▸

TRANSITIONS

That de Chirico and Hofmannsthal should have turned to Ovid as their source about 1912 was by no means inevitable. Although the *Metamorphoses* and *Heroides* were still widely read in classrooms in Europe and the United States, the poet himself was not highly regarded by scholars at the turn of the century. While grudging respect was accorded to his artistry, his morals were sternly censured by the strict standards of Victorian England and Wilhelmine Germany. According to one contemporary history of Roman literature in Germany, Ovid was a superficial man whom "not even the passion of love gripped; his songs are addressed to lifeless shadows"; and his "heart clung to life's fleeting froth and glitter."[1] Another accused him of "misusing his virtuosity and talent through a lack of self-criticism," with the result that his *Amores* contain much that is simply "schoolboyish" while his *Epistulae ex Ponto* belong to the most "devoid of content" in all Roman literature.[2] The voices from England were only slightly less severe, calling him, in a work widely consulted in American schools and colleges, an "incorrigibly immoral but inexpressibly graceful poet" whose poems are "elegant but lascivious" and whose "idea of the desolate and lovelorn Ariadne writing a letter from the barren isle of Naxos is in itself ridiculous."[3] The representative scholarly view of the times was summed up in 1910 by the author of a standard history of Roman literature widely consulted in Germany and abroad.

[Ovid] remains a rhetorician even in his poetry, playing with thoughts and themes, mirroring himself in the reflection of his figures und witty turns of expression; without seriousness, higher goals and character; heedless without regard to the demands and questions of life; but clever, piquant, and original; of unexcelled mastery in all formal aspects and of inimitable lightness, agility, and grace.[4]

While Ovid was condemned for his offenses against conventional moral standards, he was also—in an age of at least surface piety—censured for his religious skepticism, in contrast to such Roman poets as Virgil, whose fourth Eclogue was acclaimed as a herald of Christianity. And in countries with an imperial agenda, such as England, France, and Germany, Ovid's social criticism and his political exile gained him few supporters.[5] It had not always been so.

TENERORUM LUSOR AMORUM

Early in his career Ovid enjoyed a popular success rarely matched among poets of the ancient world: *notaque non tarde facta Thalia mea est* ("and my Muse was not slow to become known"; *Tr.* 4.10.56), he tells us. He thanks his Muse for "giving him while still alive something quite rare—a lofty name that fame normally bestows only after death."

> tu mihi, quod rarum est, vivo sublime dedisti
> nomen, ab exequiis quod dare fama solet.
> (*Tr.* 4.10.121–22)

Ever since the publication of his *Ars amatoria* he had been Rome's most celebrated poet: his bust decorated villas, his image was engraved on seal-rings worn by fashionable ladies, and his works were collected in the public libraries.[6] His poems were performed in the theaters, where they were recited to the accompaniment of music and dance. And his reputation blazed with a lively flame for several centuries following his death.[7] Despite Quintilian's censure in his *Institutio oratoria* (10.1.88)—*lascivus quidem in herois quoque Ovidius et nimium amator ingenii sui* ("Ovid was playful even in epic and too much in love with his own brilliance")—Ovid was the most influential force among poets of the Silver Age. His works, first taken as models in the schools of rhetoric and later adapted as school texts, remained canonical until displaced by Virgil in the eighth century. Even his poems from exile enjoyed a special relevance—perhaps, it has been suggested, for the paradoxical reason that his exile on the Black Sea exposed him to conditions and circumstances that foreshadowed life in the early Middle Ages and thus made him seem more of a contemporary than other poets of Augustan Rome.[8]

No ancient "Life" of Ovid is extant of the sort that Suetonius provided for Terence, Horace, and Lucan or of the kind that resembles the detailed biography of Virgil which has come down to us under the name *vita Donatiana*. Instead we have something even more unusual: the first poetic autobiography in world literature, a Wordsworthian *Prelude avant la lettre,* which Ovid composed as one of his elegies from exile. No doubt it is thanks to his exile that he was driven to create such a document, for in remote Tomis—away from his family, his friends, and the stimulating cultural life of his beloved Rome, with few books at his disposal, and with no one with whom to converse in his native language—Ovid was thrown back almost entirely upon his inner resources and his memories. Accordingly the five books of his *Tristia* (especially book 2) and the four books of *Epistulae ex Ponto* are teeming with facts about his life, which is systematically recounted as autobiography in the 132 verses of *Tristia* 4.10. There is considerable scholarly debate as to what extent that life amounts to an authentic biography and to what extent it reflects a poetic *persona* projected to suit the author's immediate psychological and political needs. For our purposes we can regard it as the document of Ovid's life because, from the time of his death down to our own day, writers concerned with his life and works have not been distracted by the quarrels of the scholars but have taken Ovid at his word.

Ovid, who introduces himself in the first line of his autobiography as *tenerorum lusor amorum* ("the playful poet of tender loves")—a designation, as he instructed his wife (*Tr.* 3.3.73–76), he wished to have engraved on his tomb—was born in Sulmo (today's Sulmona), a fertile locale some ninety miles east of Rome.[9] He came into the world, according to his own precise indications, on 20 March 43 BCE, descended from an old line of equestrian rank and exactly a year to the day after the birth of his older brother. He therefore belonged to the second generation living during the long reign of Augustus (31 BCE–14 CE)—a generation that came to maturity after the fourteen years of civil war following the assassination of Julius Caesar and that thus lacked the sense of political engagement and appreciation that characterized such elders as Virgil and Horace.[10]

At an early age the boys were sent by their ambitious father to Rome, where they were instructed in the basic liberal arts—notably rhetoric and the skills of *controversiae* and *suasoriae*—by the city's most distinguished teachers (*imus ad insignes Urbis ab arte viros*). While his brother excelled in forensic oratory, Ovid, seduced by his Muse, turned to the arts. His father, alarmed by this turn, asked him why he was pursuing such useless studies and reminded him that even Homer died penniless. The dutiful son, stirred by these words, tried to give up poetry and, as he put it, to write sentences without rhythm; but whatever he wrote turned willy-nilly into verse (*et quod temptabam scribere versus erat*). When he and his brother at about age sixteen assumed the toga with the broad purple stripe of the senatorial class, they embarked on the *cursus honorum* that normally led smoothly upward through the ranks of the Roman political hierarchy. After his brother died at twenty, Ovid bravely embarked on the first stage and became a member of the *tresviri*, the Board of Three that decided cases of murder, theft, and arson. Later, as he reminded Augustus elsewhere (*Tr.* 2.93–95) he served as a judge in the *centumviri* (Board of One Hundred) and successfully handled several private cases of law. However, suited to a public career neither by body nor by disposition, he soon renounced any political ambitions (along with the senatorial stripe) and turned to the private life of cultural leisure that he had longed for, traveling to Greece and the cities of the Near East with his friend Pompeius Macer.

Ovid, now in his twenties, was the last of the great poets of the Augustan Age. When he came to poetic maturity, Lucretius, Catullus, and Gallus were already dead. Virgil (died 19 BCE) he only saw, nor did fate allow him time for friendship with Tibullus (who died the same year). But he heard Horace (died 8 BCE) recite his poetry, he was acquainted with the aged didactic poet Macer, and, above all, was a friend of Propertius (died 2 CE), who "often recited his own fiery verses" (*saepe suos solitus recitare Propertius ignes*). When he first presented his own poems publicly, Ovid tells us further, his beard had been trimmed only once or twice, but his erotic elegies about the mistress he praised under the name Corinna were already being sung throughout the city, and he was soon taken under the protective wing of Messalla Corvinus, who like Maecenas sponsored promising young poets.

There is considerable uncertainty about the dates of Ovid's works. He wrote his love elegies—short poems in the tradition of Tibullus, Gallus, and Propertius—which revolve around his affair with the fictionally composite Corinna, in his twenties and first collected them about 13–12 BCE in an edition of five books, which some four years later he reduced to three and published as the *Amores* as they have come down to us. Sometime near the beginning of the new era he wrote the dazzlingly witty and irreverent *Ars amatoria*—a manual of seduction for men (bks. 1–2) and women (bk. 3)—which titillated the sophisticated public but subsequently became a major factor in his exile. It should be stressed that the *Ars* is anything but pornographic; indeed, Ovid emphasizes the role of *cultus* (bodily care, spiritual culture, and good breeding—all the hallmarks of civilization) as essential to any true love affair. Related to these works are two further books: the *Remedia amoris,* a sequel to the *Ars amatoria,* in which Ovid seeks with tongue in cheek to undo the mischief caused by the wiles of love and thus to counteract the disapproval aroused in the emperor by the "art of love"; and the fragmentarily extant *De medicamine faciei,* a guide to cosmetics and personal hygiene for women. At some point during these years he also wrote his fifteen *Heroides:* monologic epistles allegedly addressed to their lovers by heroines famous in mythology. (He later added six letters exchanged by three mixed couples). His ambition and insight into the psychology of women led him to write the now lost drama *Medea,* which was regarded by Tacitus (*Dialogus de oratoribus,* 12) as one of the "illustrious" Roman tragedies. The years following 1 BCE/1 CE saw the composition of his *Metamorphoses* in fifteen books, which through recitations and piecemeal circulation in manuscript form became familiar to the Roman public before their publication. At the same time he completed at least the first six books of his other great collective project, *Fasti,* a poem explaining the Roman calendar and the origin of its religious festivals.

Ovid was married three times. While still little more than a boy, he was wed briefly to a woman he calls "unworthy" (*nec digna*). For unspecified reasons a second marriage to an irreproachable woman did not last much longer. But the third union, to which his wife brought a stepdaughter and which produced another daughter, lasted to the end of his life. Twice a grandfather and with his daughter well married (to a senator), he also enjoyed the company of his parents until his father was ninety. He owned a town house in Rome, a villa in the suburbs, and a family estate in Sulmo. Then at age fifty, at the peak of fame, prosperity, and personal happiness, as his hair was just beginning to gray, disaster struck. Suddenly and without warning, toward the end of 8 CE Ovid was sent into exile to Tomis on the Black Sea at the most remote reaches of the empire, where three cultures met and intermingled: the indigenous Getic population, the Greeks who colonized the town, and the Romans who later conquered it.

The precise reasons for Ovid's exile are unclear still today.[11] He tells us repeatedly that he was punished for "two crimes, a poem and a mistake" (*duo crimina, carmen et error, Tr.* 2.207). The *carmen* clearly refers to the *Ars amatoria,* which, for all its popular success, had aroused the emperor's wrath (*principis ira, Tr.* 4.10.48). As a manual for extramarital sex it certainly amounted to a provocation of Augustus's strict marriage laws by this *obsceni doctor adulterii* ("obscene professor of adultery," *Tr.* 2.212). And the work seemed anti-Augustan for other reasons as well. It added poetic insult to moral injury by presenting Ovid's advice on erotic love in a form that was obviously a parodic inversion of such serious and revered didactic works as Virgil's *Georgics* and Lucretius's *De rerum natura.* And to illustrate his teachings he made what more sober readers may well have regarded as a frivolous use of myth. (For example, he illustrated the harmfulness of jealousy and seemed humorously to justify adultery by telling the story of Venus and Mars, caught in the act by her husband Vulcan [*Ars* 2.535–600].)

As for the *error*, Ovid refused to the end of his life to be more specific, saying at times that the matter was common knowledge (*Tr.* 4.10.99–100) and at other times that he had no wish further to aggrieve Augustus by reminding him of a painful incident (*Tr.* 2.208–10). Scholars have speculated for centuries about the nature of this mistake.[12] The most likely explanation is that he witnessed some palace indiscretion or scandal—perhaps an illicit liaison of Augustus's granddaughter Julia, who enjoyed a certain sexual notoriety.

> nec breve nec tutum, quo sint mea, dicere, casu
> lumina funesti conscia facta mali.
>
> (*Tr.* 3.6.27–28)

(It is neither quick nor safe to tell by what chance my eyes became aware of the disastrous evil.)

For this reason, in any case, Ovid felt a poignant affinity for the tale of Actaeon, who was torn apart by his own hounds because he accidentally saw Diana unclad (*Tr.* 2.105). Whatever the provocation, Ovid had to be removed from the Rome where he had been feted for some twenty years and in whose sophisticated culture he thrived as a celebrity.

Technically, Ovid's punishment was not exile but *relegatio* (*Tr.* 2.137), which meant that he was permitted to retain his citizenship and his personal property. But his books were banned and removed from the public libraries. As he bitterly complains, he was promptly betrayed by many "friends" and even by personal servants afraid of offending the emperor (*Tr.* 1.8). Some acquaintances went even further, libeling Ovid in his absence (*Tr.* 3.11, 5.8). But he wrote fondly and gratefully to other loyal friends who supported him in his misery. Meanwhile, his wife Fabia, who was related to the imperial family, stayed behind in Rome to care for Ovid's estate and to make appeals on his behalf to Augustus.

To no avail. Ovid was destined to remain until his death in Tomis, the place identified in Greek tradition as the spot where Medea cut up her brother Absyrtus and strewed the body parts on the sea to distract her pursuing father. Those ten years produced the five books of *Tristia* and the four books of *Epistulae ex Ponto,* which contain in addition to numerous autobiographical details a vivid depiction of life among the Getae and Sarmatians on the remote Black Sea coast just south of the Danube delta, the region of Romania known today as Dobrudja. Ovid also occupied himself with several lesser projects, notably the Hellenistic curse poem against the enemy he called "Ibis" and the fragmentary work on ichthyology and angling titled *Halieutica.*

The elegies of the *Tristia,* addressed to friends unnamed (for reasons of their security), describe his departure from Rome, the perilous journey across the seas and Thrace to Tomis, and his initially appalled reaction to the barbaric peoples among whom he was condemned to spend the rest of his life. He wrote about the dangers from the savage tribes who shot poisoned arrows into the fortified town, complained about the frustrations of a poet dwelling among people who speak no Latin and know nothing of his poetry or Roman culture, and repeatedly expressed his hopes for exoneration and a return to Rome or at least to a gentler place of exile. What he did not put into the letters, which might have been read by his wife or the emperor, are any hints about his possible erotic experiences in Tomis or any mention of the new religious ideas he probably encountered among the monotheistic Getae—ideas that would have been sharply at odds with the official state religion in Rome.[13]

The later letters sound a more resigned note as Ovid discovers the virtues of the Black Sea peoples, is made an honorary citizen of Tomis, and even begins to write poems in their language, always aware that the poet is free in his imagination to journey through measureless lands (*illa per immensas spatiatur libera terras; Tr.* 4.2.59). Ovid died in 17 or 18 CE and was buried in Tomis despite his fervent pleas that his "bones not be crushed by Scythian soil" (*ossa nec a Scythia nostra premantur humo; Ex Ponto* 1.2.108). A constant theme running through all the elegies from exile is Ovid's concern for his poetic survival and for his enduring reputation, which in fact was not eclipsed by Virgil and Horace until the Carolingian Renaissance of the eighth and ninth centuries.

OVIDIAN AGES

In a famous phrase coined by the German classicist Ludwig Traube, an *aetas Ovidiana* in the twelfth and thirteenth centuries succeeded the Virgilian and Horatian Ages that had marked the preceding four centuries.[14] During that period Ovid's works were not only the most widely used for teaching Latin style and rhetoric, his *Heroides* were praised as models for poetic epistles, the first book of the *Metamorphoses* was a popular authority for cosmogony and cosmology, and his *Remedia amoris* was consulted for medical advice. As a result they were among the most frequently cited and anthologized works of the period;[15] the *Metamorphoses* amounted to what Ernst Robert Curtius has labeled the mythological *Who's Who* of the Middle Ages;[16] and forgeries under Ovid's name, such as the thirteenth-century romance *De vetula* ("The Hag"), enjoyed enormous popularity. In sharp contrast to the morally rigorous scholars of the nineteenth and early twentieth centuries, the medieval *scholastici* regarded Ovid as an authority on ethics, extracting moral precepts from his works.[17] Johannes de Garlandia in his mid-thirteenth-century *Integumenta Ovidii* offered a moral exegesis of the poet's works, while the anonymous early-fourteenth-century *Ovide moralisé* in the course of its 72,000 lines thoroughly Christianized the *Metamorphoses* by means of allegory.[18] Following a recapitulation of the story of Daphne and Apollo, for instance, the "historical" explanation suggests that Daphne was in reality a girl who died defending her virtue and was then buried beneath a laurel tree; the "allegorical" interpretation goes on to present her as an emblem of Christian morality. By analogy, Echo represents true virtue while Narcissus embodies merit lost out of vanity. In the tale of Hero and Leander, Hero can be taken and read as divine wisdom ("Par Hero puis prendre et gloser / Cele devine sapience," 4.3665–66), while Leander can be rightly understood as mankind generally ("Par Leander puis droitement / Entendre home ou humain lignage," 4.3669–70), and "the narrow but deep sea" through which he swims "is our mortal life where we have no other vessel than our body to bear us toward the joy of our heavenly reward":

> Par la mer estroite et parfonde
> Puis noter ceste mortel vie,
> Ou nous n'avons autre navie
> Que les cors pour tendre a la joie
> De la celestrial monjoie.

Ovid's tomb at Tomis and his houses in Rome and in his hometown of Sulmona became centers of cultic celebration and legend.[19] The sixteen tales from Ovid engraved on the bronze doors of St. Peter's in Rome in 1445 attest to both his Christianization and his popularity.[20]

This popularization had a profound effect upon the literature of the *aetas Ovidiana*.[21] In the mid-twelfth century Chrétien de Troyes wrote a *Philomena* based on Ovid, and by 1210 Albrecht von Halberstadt had translated the entire *Metamorphoses* for the first time into vernacular verse (Middle High German).[22] It has been estimated that some ten percent of the 22,000 lines of the thirteenth-century *Roman de la rose* (begun by Guillaume de Lorris and completed by Jean de Meun) are translated or paraphrased from Ovid.[23] Early in his *Divina Commedia* Dante lists Ovid among the four members of "la bella scola" of poetry led by Homer and including Horace and Lucan (*Inferno* 4.88–90).[24] Chaucer in *The House of Fame* (c. 1380) describes a copper image of "Venus clerk, Ovyde" seated next to Virgil and, in his *Legend of Good Women* (c. 1380), relates the stories of nine women taken mostly from Ovid's *Heroides* and *Metamorphoses* (Thisbe, Hypsipyle, Medea, Ariadne, Philomela, Hypermnestra).[25] Chaucer's friend John Gower, in his *Confessio amantis* (c. 1390), recounts Ovid's enduringly popular tale of Pyramus and Thisbe.

The Renaissance brought a second *aetas Ovidiana* or at least a revival of Ovid's medieval popularity.[26] Although Petrarch deplored the lasciviousness of the *Ars amatoria,* he numbered Ovid's other poems among his favorites. In his early works, notably *Fiametta,* Boccaccio drew extensively on the *Heroides* as well as the *Metamorphoses,* which provided the familiar tale of Pyramus and Thisbe. In the Latin scholarly works of his later life—*De genealogia deorum* and *De claris mulieribus*—he relied heavily on the mythology of Ovid's *Metamorphoses.* The neo-Latin poetry of the Renaissance was thoroughly Ovidian and took as its model in particular the love elegies.[27] In the Netherlands, Joost van den Vondel's translation of the *Metamorphoses* (*Herscheppinge,* 1671) transformed Ovid's work into what amounted to a national classic.[28]

Ovid's impact in England is difficult to overestimate.[29] Arthur Golding's translation of the *Metamorphoses* (1567) remained influential from Shakespeare to Ezra Pound and continues to be reprinted today.[30] The Roman poet is omnipresent in Spenser's *The Faerie Queene,* and Marlowe's *Hero and Leander* draws directly upon the *Heroides* (18–19). Above all, Shakespeare's works are conspicuously Ovidian.[31] In the early tragedy *Titus Andronicus* a copy of the *Metamorphoses* plays a central role in the plot: by pointing to the story of Philomela (*Met.* 4.424–674) Lavinia identifies the attackers who raped her and then cut out her tongue and amputated her hands; that same episode prefigures the revenge that Titus Andronicus takes upon the Gothic queen Tamora by serving her two sons to her in a pie. The still popular tale of Pyramus and Thisbe is prominently featured in *A Midsummer Night's Dream,* and three Ovidian myths—the abduction of Proserpina, the tale of Orpheus and Eurydice, and the story of Pygmalion—are intertwined productively in *The Winter's Tale.*[32] Ovid provides both the Latin motto (*Amores* 1.15.35–36) and the plot (*Met.* 10.519–59 and 708–39) for Shakespeare's *Venus and Adonis.* It has been argued that the dramatic monologues of the *Metamorphoses* exerted a pronounced influence upon the speeches in Shakespeare's dramas while Ovid's images and ideas permeate the sonnets.[33] In 1680 John Dryden published translations of the Epistles (*Heroides*) by divers hands, with a preface extolling those poems as "the most perfect pieces of Ovid."[34] As late as 1717 a collective translation of the *Metamorphoses* edited by Samuel Garth featured such contributors as John Dryden, Joseph Addison, John Gay, Alexander Pope, and other neoclassicists.

Ovid was so pervasive in sixteenth- and seventeenth-century French literature—among the authors of the Pléiade, as well as La Fontaine, and Racine, who in 1661 planned (but never carried out) a drama on "Les amours d'Ovide"—that it has been called "another *aetas Ovidiana*."[35] Montaigne, who was educated with Latin as his mother tongue, tells us in his *Essays* that Ovid's *Metamorphoses*, which he read as a boy of seven or eight, gave him his first taste for books and that he would steal away from other pastimes to read them.[36] This veneration inevitably produced a reaction in the form of such travesties as Charles Dassousy's popular *Ovide en belle humeur* and his comic musical *Les amours d'Apollon et de Daphné* (both 1650) and Louis Richer's *Ovide bouffon, ou les Metamorphoses travesties en vers burlesques* (1662).[37] But like all parody, these too imply a widespread familiarity with the original.

By the end of the eighteenth century, however, various factors combined to turn literary sentiment against Ovid's playfulness, wit, and urbanity. The new values of spontaneity, originality, feeling, and sincerity that entered the European consciousness with the French Revolution, the German *Sturm und Drang*, and English Romanticism rejected any literature that smacked of the order and elegance of prerevolutionary absolutist Europe and its detested Rococo culture and that, like Ovid's works, struck these young revolutionaries as mythological compendia rather than expressions of genius.[38]

This late-eighteenth-century turn against Ovid was most pronounced in Germany, as a direct result of what has been called "the tyranny of Greece over Germany."[39] Christoph Martin Wieland wrote two cantos of "Anti-Ovid or the Art of Loving" ("Anti-Ovid oder die Kunst zu lieben," 1752), in which Ovid is depicted as "the master of impudent arts" ("der Meister loser Künste") who teaches impertinence and ignores breeding and innocence.[40] Immanuel Kant, whose rationality had little patience with fantastic transformations, termed the *Metamorphoses* "grotesques" ("Fratzen").[41] Johann Gottlieb Herder, given his insistence on the priority of "nature" and popular culture over what he regarded as the artificiality of civilization, had nothing but contempt for Ovid's urbane wit. In his autobiography Goethe recalls how, about 1770, Herder almost spoiled the pleasure in the *Metamorphoses* which Goethe had enjoyed from his earliest childhood. No matter how Goethe defended his favorite poet, the sober Herder maintained that "there is no true and immediate truth in these poems; here there is neither Greece nor Italy, neither a primal world nor a cultivated one; rather, everything is an imitation of what was already there and a mannered representation of the sort that might be expected from an overcultivated mind."[42] Added to this chorus of vituperation were the voices of the neoclassicist aestheticians. Winckelmann rejected art representing metamorphosis—e.g., Bernini's sculpture *Apollo and Daphne*—as "caricatures" that distorted the classical ideal of human beauty. Hegel argued in his *Aesthetics* that Ovid's metamorphoses constitute "degradations" and "humiliations of the human" because, as punishment for one transgression or another, they transform human beings into lower forms of nature.[43]

The poets were more generous in their assessment. Schiller's early poems are filled with allusions to Ovid: his *Anthologie auf das Jahr 1782* contains, in addition to a motto from the *Metamorphoses* and frequent mythological allusions, a two-scene "lyrical operetta" on the theme of "Semele" (*Met.* 3.253–315). Goethe reacted to the experience of Herder's defamation by sharpening his own appreciation of Ovid as a pure poet.[44] When he left Rome in April 1788, as he tells us on the last page of his *Italian Journey,* he experienced a sensation that he called "heroic-elegiac" and recited to himself the lines in which Ovid recalled his forced departure from Rome (*Tristia* 1.3.1–4 and 27–30). "In such a moment how should my memory not recall the elegy of Ovid, who, likewise exiled, had to leave Rome on a moonlit night." The idea of metamorphosis is central to Goethe's theory of science, as evidenced in his poems *Metamorphose der Pflanzen* and *Metamorphose der Tiere.* And among the Ovidian stories that he reworked in his own poetry, none is more typical than the radical re-vision of Philemon and Baucis, which occurs close to the end of *Faust II* and where the elderly couple is killed and their hut burned down by Mephistopheles and his henchmen. Friedrich Schlegel, in his history of European literature (1803–4), concluded: "If an easy style, an equally easily flowing fantasy and a nimble feeling constitute a poet, then Ovid was such to the highest degree. He excels all other Roman poets in grace, elegance, ease, and fluidity of language and representation."[45] More charming and brilliant than Horace, Virgil, and Propertius, he is also more original than they. Schlegel's brother August Wilhelm, himself the author of Ovidian elegies,[46] called the *Metamorphoses* "the most complete example that we have of a mythic didactic poem" ("mythisches Lehrgedicht").[47] But Mme de Staël, summing up the view of most readers at the beginning of the nineteenth century, sniffed contemptuously that Ovid "recalls the bad taste of the century of Louis XIV."[48] And across the channel Macaulay became "heartily tired" of Ovid, whom he regarded as "rather a rhetorician than a poet."[49]

There were occasional exceptions to the general neglect. Søren Kierkegaard almost predictably refers to Ovid in his *Diary of the Seducer* (in *Either/Or,* 1843), quoting directly from the *Ars amatoria* as well as the *Remedia amoris* and alluding to several of the tales from the *Metamorphoses* (Phaethon, Ariadne, Echo). In the 1880s and 1890s Auguste Rodin, who read Ovid in Latin and French, created several sculptures based on themes from the *Metamorphoses:* among others, *La Danaïde, La chute d'Icare, Orphée et Eurydice,* and the entwined double-figure entitled *Les métamorphoses d'Ovide.* It has been suggested that the sense of inchoateness in many of Rodin's representations of figures emerging from stone is justified by Ovid's notion of metamorphosis, which dominated the sculptor's imagination.[50]

Yet despite the interest of alienated and isolated writers and artists, Ovid was largely displaced, at least in the public mind, by Virgil, who was gloriously enhanced on the occasion of the nineteenth centenary of his death.[51] The volume of international tributes published by the Accademia Virgiliana of Mantua, the poet's birthplace, for the grand commemoration in September 1882 contains contributions in six different languages by writers who hailed Virgil as the most appropriate poet for the age. In his ode *To Virgil,* Tennyson noted Virgil's melancholy understanding of "the doubtful doom of human kind" and his virtually Victorian insight into "Universal / Nature moved by Universal mind." The 1882 commemorations would seem to bear out Robert Graves's cynical thesis that "whenever a golden age of stable government, full churches, and expanding wealth dawns among the Western nations, Virgil always returns to supreme favour."[52] Precisely such imperial ages, based on order and stability, have little understanding for the irrational change implied by metamorphosis, little patience with the moral dubieties of a self-declared *tenerorum lusor amorum,* and no sympathy for the fate of exiled poets. It is symptomatic that the nineteenth centenary of Ovid's death in 1917, which occurred at the height of World War I, passed by wholly unremarked: no ceremonies, no celebratory articles in leading journals, no commemorations by European or American academies.

At the beginning of the twentieth century, in sum, although Ovid's works still provided an occasional source of stories for writers and artists, they had been reduced by the scholars to little more than texts suitable, if properly edited to eliminate the naughty bits, for school use and as models for Latin composition.[53] Within a decade, however, a few rebellious writers of the "high" or "classic" modernism that flourished about the time of World War I again turned to Ovid in a manner as bold as that of de Chirico and Hofmannsthal/Strauss—almost in fulfillment, it would seem, of Virginia Woolf's assertion that "in or about December, 1910, human character changed."[54]

PART I

▶

OVID AND THE
HIGH MODERNS

◢ 3 ◣

OVID *REDIVIVUS*

DAEDALUS IN DUBLIN

Ovid enters modern English literature in the person of Stephen Dedalus, the hero of James Joyce's *Portrait of the Artist as a Young Man* (1916). Daedalus, the legendary creator who invented the craft of carpentry, added masts to ships, and produced walking statues, was one of the most popular figures of classical antiquity, and his image was frequently depicted on vases and gems as well as in Greek sculptures and Roman wall paintings. While he is otherwise mentioned in Roman literature (e.g., in passing by Virgil at *Aeneid* 6.14–53), the principal source for our knowledge is Ovid, who recounts his story at length in both the *Metamorphoses* (8.159–68, 183–262) and *Ars amatoria* (2.21–98). Joyce has clearly indicated his source, for the epigraph to his novel is a line from the *Metamorphoses* (8.188): *et ignotas animum dimittit in artes* ("and he applies his mind to unknown arts"). (In the early draft of the novel, "Stephen Hero," while the hero is already named Stephen Daedalus [*sic*], the Ovidian epigraph and the principal Ovidian themes are not yet present.) Elsewhere Dedalus "recalled the shrewd northern face of the rector who had taught him to construe the Metamorphoses of Ovid in a courtly English, made whimsical by the mention of porkers and potsherds and chines of bacon" (179).[1] He is also keenly aware of his unusual name, to which his companions in any case often alert him. "You have a queer

name, Dedalus," remarks a schoolmate. "Your name is like Latin" (25). Years later
his classmates still refer to him as "The Dedalus" (167).

The line quoted (and incorrectly cited as *Met.* 8.18 rather than 8.188) in the
epigraph introduces, in the *Metamorphoses,* a long passage in which Daedalus,
having constructed the labyrinth to contain the Minotaur and been forbidden
by King Minos to leave Crete, "alters the laws of nature" (*naturamque novat*) by
inventing wings with which he and his ill-fated son Icarus flee the island. Clearly
it is Daedalus the creative artist, longing to escape his imprisonment on the island of Ireland, that Joyce has in mind as the model for the hero of his novel—
the artist whose only weapons are "silence, exile and cunning" (247). The parallel
is not precise because, for Ovid's Daedalus, Crete is the hated place of exile—
longumque perosus exilium (*Met.* 8.183–4) from which he longs to return to the
land of his birth.[2] Joyce's Dedalus, in contrast, wants to go into exile away from
his home in Ireland.

Beyond that, it is difficult to determine which other Daedalean associations
Joyce may have had in mind. One suggestion is that the frequent images of birds
and flight that occur to Stephen are triggered by his name and its association
with the inventor of human flight:[3]

> Now, at the name of the fabulous artificer, he seemed to hear the noise of dim
> waves and to see a winged form flying above the waves and slowly climbing
> the air. What did it mean? Was it a quaint device opening a page of some me-
> dieval book of prophecies and symbols, a hawklike man flying sunward above
> the sea, a prophecy of the end he had been born to serve and had been fol-
> lowing through the mists of childhood and boyhood, a symbol of the artist
> forging anew in his workshop out of the sluggish matter of the earth a new
> soaring impalpable imperishable being? (168–69)

(Was Stephen's image of the "hawklike" man stimulated by Joyce's confusion or
conflation of Daedalus with Daedalion, the son of Lucifer, whose transformation into a hawk [*accipiter*] is related at *Met.* 11.291–345?)[4]

The lovely young woman Stephen sees shortly after this moment of epiphany,
standing alone on the shore, "seemed like one whom magic had changed into
the likeness of a strange and beautiful seabird" (171) and who is described accordingly. Critics have also noted that images of mazes, snares, and nets permeate the text, symbolizing the stultifying atmosphere of family and society in
Ireland from which Dedalus strives to escape.[5] These images, as well as the long
aimless walks that Stephen Dedalus undertakes—his usual "devious course up
and down the streets" (102)—may well evoke the labyrinth that Daedalus constructed and in which King Minos imprisoned him to prevent his escape. It is

even conceivable that the old man from the west of Ireland with "redrimmed horny eyes," whom Dedalus describes in his diary entries at the end of the novel, is a kind of minotaur. "Ah, there must be terrible queer creatures at the latter end of the world," his interlocutor ruminates. Dedalus fears this creature. "It is with him I must struggle all through this night till day come, till he or I lie dead" (252).[6]

The novel, with its opening epigraph from the *Metamorphoses,* ends with an allusion to Ovid's figure, for the last line amounts to an apostrophe by the aspiring young artist to the Daedalus of antiquity: "Old father, old artificer, stand me now and ever in good stead." It has been suggested that Dedalus at this point is assuming the role of Daedalus's son[7]—an identification that is appropriate as long as we understand that Joyce means it only in the sense of being Daedalus's spiritual heir; there is no hint in the text that his hero is going to suffer any kind of Icarus-like fall.

The hero's full name, Stephen Dedalus, has further implications, for it points to the opposition between Christian and pagan that obsesses him throughout his boyhood and youth. St. Stephen, for whom Stephen's Green in Dublin was named, was the first Christian martyr, stoned to death after he enraged the Sanhedrin by accusing them of being "stiff-necked" and of murdering Jesus (Acts 6–7). Stephen's growing religious skepticism is similarly critical of the ruling church authorities. The polarity of Christian and pagan resounds throughout the novel, and notably in the great disquisition on aesthetics, which is stimulated respectively by Aristotle and St. Thomas Aquinas. Aristotle provides the starting point for Stephen's reflections on pity and terror and on "the tragic emotion," a static state that looks toward both (205). Aquinas, in turn, leads him to his understanding of "the necessary phases of artistic apprehension": wholeness, harmony, and radiance (211).

Before Stephen Dedalus can accept the pagan pole of his nature and set out on his Daedalean flight from the labyrinth of Ireland, he must first reject the call of St. Stephen: that is, the Catholic culture that surrounds and embraces him along with his own petit bourgeois family. This means that he must rebuff the impassioned exhortation of the school's director to accept a calling to the priesthood.

> He would never swing the thurible before the tabernacle as priest. His destiny was to be elusive of social or religious orders. The wisdom of the priest's appeal did not touch him to the quick. He was destined to learn his own wisdom apart from others or to learn the wisdom of others himself wandering among the snares of the world. (162)

Shortly before his departure he must even aggrieve his devout mother by refusing to attend, hypocritically, the Catholic Easter services in which he no longer believes. When Stephen leaves Ireland, then, Daedalus has won out over St. Stephen, pagan art over Christian faith.[8]

If Stephen Dedalus in his escape from the labyrinth of Ireland postfigures Ovid's legendary figure, Dedalus/Joyce also has a great deal in common with Ovid himself. His religious skepticism, in the first place, is close to that of the Roman poet who remarked: *expedit esse deos et, ut expedit, esse putemus* (*Ars amat.* 1.637: "It's useful for gods to exist, and since it's useful, let's believe that they exist") and whose works are filled with tongue-in-cheek disqualifications of the mythic tales he is recounting[9]—even in the *Fasti,* Ovid's exegesis of the Roman calendar and its festivals. Second, like Ovid himself (rather than Daedalus), Dedalus/Joyce went into a lifelong exile—not politically imposed, to be sure, but out of moral and intellectual necessity: a condition to which he dedicated his play *Exiles* (1918). Third, like Ovid, who is famed above all as the virtuoso of artistry among Roman poets, Dedalus/Joyce has the ambition to be a pure artist, who "like the God of the creation, remains within or behind or beyond or above his handiwork, invisible, refined out of existence, indifferent, paring his fingernails" (215). Like Ovid, finally, Dedalus/Joyce is the maestro of metamorphosis, a theme that occupies his imagination from beginning to end. In his boyhood daydreams of the girl Mercedes, for instance, he imagines that "he would fade into something impalpable under her eyes and then, in a moment, he would be transfigured. Weakness and timidity and inexperience would fall from him in that magic moment" (65). When he sees the girl on the seashore, "magic"—his imagination, that is—transforms her into a seabird, like Ovid's Alcyone (*Met.* 11.731–35). Later, when the awareness and acceptance of his poetic calling have alienated him from his fellow Irishmen, he is baffled that a young woman would "unveil her soul's shy nakedness" to a peasant priest "rather than to him, a priest of eternal imagination, transmuting the daily bread of experience into the radiant body of everliving life" (221). At this point St. Stephen has given way entirely to Daedalus; Joyce has found his spiritual forefather in Ovid, a kinship inherent in this novel since Ovid plays no such major role in either of Joyce's subsequent works. (In *Ulysses,* even though Stephen Dedalus reappears as one of the two principal figures, the authority of Ovid is replaced by that of Homer.)

The Sacralization of the *Metamorphoses*

Joyce, an Irishman sharing none of the nationalist-imperialist sentiments that endeared Virgil to most of his contemporaries, wrote the first of the modernist masterpieces featuring Ovid and themes from the *Metamorphoses.* However, the true herald of Ovid among English-language high modernists was not Joyce, but Ezra Pound. Unlike the other modernists, Pound was a trained scholar of classical literature. A good Latinist, he first studied Ovid no later than 1902–3, when he took a course at the University of Pennsylvania on Propertius and Ovid;[10] his reading in the Roman poets continued during his years of graduate work in Romance languages and literature. While his identification with Propertius resulted almost two decades later in his controversial and influential adaptations, *Homage to Sextus Propertius* (1919), the obsession with Ovid is evident throughout his lifetime. His early poem "The Tree" (in *A Lume Spento,* 1908) briefly recapitulates two of Ovid's stories of human beings transformed into trees: Daphne, and Baucis and Philemon. In *The Spirit of Romance* (1910), which the subtitle defines as "an attempt to define somewhat the charm of the pre-Renaissance literature of Latin Europe," Pound sought—decades before Ernst Robert Curtius or Edward Kennard Rand—to adumbrate for nonspecialist readers the role of Ovid and other classical poets in the literature of the Middle Ages. "I may have been an ensanguined fool to spend so much time on mediaeval literature," he wrote several years later, "or the time 'wasted' may help me to read Ovid with greater insight."[11] Pound sketches Ovid's character in a few lines that give evidence of his appreciation of the Roman poet's sophistication, skepticism, and literary style.

> Ovid—urbane, sceptical, a Roman of the city—writes, not in a florid prose, but in a verse which has the clarity of French scientific prose.
>   "Convenit esse deos et ergo esse credemus."
> "It is convenient to have Gods, and therefore we believe they exist," says the sophisticated Naso, and with all pretence of scientific accuracy he ushers in his gods, demigods, monsters and transformations. His mind, trained to the system of empire, demands the definite. The sceptical age hungers after the definite, after something it can pretend to believe. The marvellous thing is made plausible, the gods are humanized, their annals are written as if copied from a parish register; their heroes might have been acquaintances of the author's father.[12]

(Pound's misquotation of the well-known line from the *Ars amatoria* [1.637] suggests that he knows his Ovid well enough to quote from memory.) As a specialist in the literature of the late Middle Ages Pound emphasizes the centrality of Ovid as a source for medieval literature: "it was not from Apuleius, but from Ovid, that the mediaeval tale-tellers took so much of their ornament and inspiration" (10).

In 1917–18 Pound was studying Elizabethan translations of Ovid's *Heroides, Amores,* and *Metamorphoses* and continually urging his friends to read Ovid.[13] In his *ABC of Reading* (1934) he said that Ovid was "a store-house of vast matter that we cannot NOW get from the Greeks" and that Ovid, while uneven, was "clear" and "lucid."[14] "Ovid indubitably added and invented much which is not in greek [*sic*]."[15] His *Guide to Kulchur* (1938) lists, among the books that a man should read and second only to Homer, "Ovid, or Golding's and Marlowe's versions of the *Changes* and the *Amores*."[16] Golding, he never tires of reiterating, "made a new Ovid" (249). (Elsewhere he twice calls Golding's translation the most beautiful book in the English language.)[17] But gradually a new tone emerges: it is no longer Ovid the poet but Ovid the philosopher who occupies Pound's thoughts. In 1922 Pound stated that he considered Ovid's *Metamorphoses* "a sacred book"—sacred because it represents metamorphosis as a means of transcending death—and, along with the writings of Confucius, "the only safe guides in religion."[18] In his "Credo" of 1930 he responded to a query concerning his beliefs by claiming that "I have for a number of years answered such questions by telling the enquirer to read Confucius and Ovid."[19] In the *Guide to Kulchur* he stresses Ovid's interest in folklore (272)—this during the decade when Sir James Frazer, whose studies Pound knew and respected, had drawn attention in his five-volume edition of the *Fasti* (1931) to the anthropological value of Ovid's calendar poem. He asserts "that a great treasure of verity exists for mankind in Ovid and in the subject matter of Ovid's long poem, and that only in this form could it be registered" (299). He reminds his readers that "Ovid, I keep repeating from one decade to another, is one of the most interesting of all enigmas" (272)—a formulation that clearly distinguishes his view from the prevalent attitude of the scholars who regarded Ovid as felicitous but shallow and utterly unproblematic. Indeed, in his multipart essay "Cavalcanti" (dated 1910–31; published 1935 in *Make It New*) he asserts that "Ovid had in him more divine wisdom than all the Fathers of the Church put together."[20] So we can readily agree with the conclusion "that Pound accepted Ovid as a valuable predecessor; that Pound studied Ovid for content, for tone and for technique; and that Ovid had infused himself into Pound's critical and creative thinking."[21]

Pound was drawn to the Roman poets because, as he wrote in 1916, "they are the only ones we know of who had approximately the same problems as we have. The metropolis, the imperial posts to all corners of the known world. The enlightenments."[22] But the Roman poets responded as differently to their situation as did their modern counterparts. Pound's homage to Ovid was achieved at the expense of the two poets who constituted standard texts in the school and college curricula: Horace and especially Virgil, whom he considered, again in contrast to the scholarly and public consensus issuing from the recent commemorations of Virgil's death, "a second-rater, a Tennysonianized version of

Homer."[23] In Pound's mind Ovid along with Propertius represented voices in opposition to the ethos of such "public poets" as Virgil and Horace[24]—poets, that is, who put their art in the service of "the infinite and ineffable imbecility of the Roman Empire," an imperial imbecility no less dominant then than in the Great Britain of 1917.[25]

While Pound's advocacy of Ovid lasted throughout his career—e.g., he cites Ovid's line from the *Fasti* (6.5), *est deus in nobis,* almost as a leitmotif[26]—his use of Ovid's works in his own poetry was concentrated in the early years, notably in the *Cantos,* in roughly a dozen of which Ovid is quoted or mentioned (e.g., Canto 7 and Canto 20: "Qui son Properzio ed Ovidio") or in which stories from the *Metamorphoses* are used (e.g., the myth of Acoetes in Canto 2).[27] Ovid gradually disappears from the later Cantos as Pound's interest shifts to Chinese culture, American history, economic issues, and current politics.

The use of Ovidian themes is perhaps most prominent in Canto 4 (1919),[28] which amounts to a synopsis and conflation of several myths and legends.[29] The bloody tale of Philomela and Procne, who slaughter Procne's son Itys and serve his flesh to Procne's husband Tereus, who in turn has raped Philomela and cut out her tongue, is paired with another tale of punished adultery: the story of the Provençal troubadour Guillems de Cabestanh, who was allegedly killed by the husband of his lover, Seremonda; when the husband serves the lover's cooked heart to her, she commits suicide by leaping out the window of the castle.

> And she went toward the window and cast her down,
>   "All the while, the while, swallows crying:
> Ityn!
>   "It is Cabestan's heart in the dish."

The swallows refer to the birds into which Philomela and Procne (swallow and nightingale) were transformed, and the name "Ityn" not only suggests by its sound the boy Itys, but triggers alliteratively the phrase "it is," which completes the assimilation of the two tales.

The myth of Actaeon, one of Pound's favorite stories, occurs in several other poems.[30] Actaeon is transformed into a stag and killed by his own pack of hounds when he accidentally, while hunting, glimpses the nude Diana bathing in a pool. His myth is conflated with the story of the troubadour Peire Vidal, who dressed in wolfskins to court his lady (whose name "Loba" means she-wolf) and was then attacked by his own dogs. As Vidal flees stumbling through the woods, he recites lines from Ovid containing the names of three fateful pools of water: Gargaphia, the spring where Actaeon encountered Diana (*Met.* 3.156); Pergusa, which provides the setting in Ovid's account of the rape of Proserpina

(*Met.* 5.386); and Salmacis, whose nymph attempted to rape the youthful Her-maphroditus (*Met.* 4.287). Finally, the myth of Danaë, locked in a tower by her father Acrisius and seduced by Zeus in a shower of gold (*Met.* 4.608–11), is re-located to the ancient Near Eastern city of Ecbatana, where the marriage of heaven and earth was ritually reenacted by a virgin placed at the top of the zig-gurat to await the deity.

> It is Cabestan's heart in the dish,
> Vidal, or Ecbatan, upon the gilded tower in Ecbatan
> Lay the god's bride, lay ever, waiting the golden rain.

Through such conflations of myth and history, Pound reifies his conviction, as he stated in the preface to *The Spirit of Romance,* that "all ages are contempo-raneous"—that, especially in literature, "real time is independent of the appar-ent," and that literary scholarship should "weigh Theocritus and Mr Yeats with one balance."[31] All of the tales exemplify, furthermore, the profound belief in metamorphosis—Philomela and Procne into birds, Actaeon into a stag, Jupiter into a shower of gold—that underlies Pound's thought and poetry: his well-nigh religious belief in the endurance of the permanent within the transient and in the transmission and preservation of knowledge through the different cultures of the world. Appropriately, then, Ovid enters his poetic pantheon as the classic master of metamorphosis, both in its principle and its examples.

Metamorphosis not only accounts for specific themes, incidents, and confla-tions in the poems; it is the principle of organization underlying individual can-tos as well as the *Cantos* as a whole. Canto 4 is representative of the other cantos, revealing a flowing sequence from story to story that parallels Ovid's technique in the *Metamorphoses,* where tales are connected by a variety of means: meta-phoric or metonymic transformation, parallel analogy, variation and permuta-tion, intercalation, interlocking, or abbreviated allusion and listing (as in Ovid's ecphrastic description of the stories in the tapestries woven in their competi-tion by Athena and Arachne (*Met.* 6.70–128). At times the *Cantos* with their metamorphosis of themes and motifs looks almost like a zany poetic counter-part to Stith Thompson's six-volume *Motif-Index of Folk-Literature* (1955).

As for the organization of the *Cantos* as a whole, in 1928–29 Pound told Yeats, who visited him in Rapallo: "There will be no plot, no chronicle of events, no logic of discourse, but two themes, the descent into Hades from Homer, a meta-morphosis from Ovid, and mixed with those mediaeval or modern historical characters."[32] While Odysseus's *nekuia,* his compulsive descents into Hades, represent "the poet's conscious search for experience and knowledge,"[33] the metamorphoses enable him to impose order on history by determining eternal patterns underlying seemingly random events and isolated stories.

Pound's *Cantos* loom like a vast monument of high modernist poetry to the memory of Ovid, who is rescued by this skeptical and anti-imperialist American exile from the shadow of the "public poet"Virgil. When he was released from his own exile-like confinement in St. Elizabeth's Hospital in 1958, Pound remarked that he had not suffered as much as Ovid in Thrace.[34] But Pound's work of advocacy ended up being as important as his own poetic achievement.

THRACE IN THE MIDLANDS

D. H. Lawrence, himself no classics scholar, owed his enthusiasm for Ovid directly to his friendship with Pound during the years when Pound was writing and publishing *The Spirit of Romance* (1910).[35] (Pound was not introduced to Joyce's work until December 1914, when *A Portrait* with its Ovidian themes had already been written; impressed with it, Pound arranged for a serialization in *The Egoist*.) Arguments for the influence of Ovid on Lawrence's early poetry are not persuasive. To be sure, he called his second volume of poems *Amores* (1915), a title that may well be a tribute to Ovid, who liked to style himself the *magister* of love (*Ars amat.* 2.744, 3.812) and who, as Lawrence learned from Pound, was known to the Middle Ages as *doctor amoris*. But the poems, which have nothing in common thematically or stylistically with Ovid's elegies and in any case lost their Ovidian title in the later Collected Works, contain no direct allusions to Ovid of the sort characteristic of Pound's *Cantos*. Moreover, Lawrence's poems, which he called the "inner history of my life, from 20 to 26"[36]—that is, the story of a man who successfully courted an older married woman and then ran away with her—differ radically from the situation in Ovid's *Amores,* the fictionalized account in three books of the young married man's affair with a composite lover named Corinna.

Matters are quite different when we look at Lawrence's later life. In 1915 his novel *The Rainbow* was attacked by the National Purity League, confiscated, and ultimately destroyed.[37] Because of his antiwar statements Lawrence was placed under surveillance by the British authorities and, because his German wife Frieda was an enemy alien, forced to live in restricted areas. As a result, he felt a close personal identification with Ovid—no longer the *doctor amoris* but the exiled poet. There is no evidence that Lawrence knew Ovid's *Tristia* or the *Epistulae ex Ponto* at first hand or extensively. But the Ovidian refrain echoes through his writing during the period. "We are here, feeling very lost and quiet and exiled," he reported in May 1918 from the Midland village of Middleton-by-Wirksworth. "The place is beautiful, but one feels like Ovid in Thrace."[38] In another letter written that same day he complained: "I feel queer and desolate in my soul—like Ovid in Thrace."[39] Toward the end of his novel *The Lost Girl* (1921) he characterized his heroine Alvina as "a lost girl. She was cut off from everything she belonged to. Ovid isolated in Thrace might well lament."[40] And at the beginning of *Kangaroo* (1923) his hero Somers, thinking longingly in Australia about Europe, decides that he understands why the Romans preferred death to exile. "He could sympathise now with Ovid on the Danube, hungering for Rome and blind to the land around him, blind to the savages."[41] (Lawrence's comment suggests that he had not in fact carefully read Ovid's poems from his exile on the Black Sea.) But when the war ended, so too did the political reasons for Lawrence's rather superficial identification with Ovid, who now disappears from his works as Lawrence turns his attention to other interests and, in 1922, departs for his three-year sojourn in the United States.

If we summarize the reasons for Ovid's appeal to writers during the period of World War I, the most conspicuous is their sense of identification with the ur-exile. Indeed, it is more than chance that both Joyce and Pound were obsessed with the figure of that other exile, Odysseus/Ulysses. Closely related is the notion that Ovid was the victim of a ruthless imperial government not unlike Britain and other European governments of the early twentieth century. If Ovid rejected the Virgilian role of "public poet," moreover, he did so by placing his art above all else—a gesture of art for art's sake that amounted to a radical break with the Augustan poets who immediately preceded him and one that appealed to these high modernists. Similarly, the *Cantos* represented as sharp as break with the prevailing values as did Joyce's *Portrait* or Lawrence's early novels. Ovid's urbanity, his love of and longing for the sophistication of Rome, also captivated these essentially urban writers, who had little in common with the Old Roman ideals of *rusticitas* and *simplicitas* that appealed to Horace's generation, that made Virgil's *Georgics* so attractive to the Southern Agrarian poets in the United States, and that contributed to the popular success in England of Vita Sackville-West's georgic poem *The Land* (1926). Another corollary of the opposition to stable, powerful government was Ovid's notion of change, transformation, metamorphosis, which anticipated the sense of spiritual renewal that motivated so many writers and intellectuals as they looked about at postwar Europe. Is it an accident that the period under discussion was accompanied at the outset by Sigmund Freud's seminal "Introduction to Narcissism" ("Zur Einführung des Narcißmus," 1914) and ushered out by his essay "The Uncanny" ("Das Unheimliche," 1919)? While Freud mentions Ovid in neither essay, the one is concerned with a stage in the relationship of the individual to society that is clearly analogous to exile, and the other defines the uncanny in terms that precisely characterize metamorphosis—as the alienation of the familiar.[42] Meanwhile, other poets were on the point of turning toward Ovid in major landmarks of high modernist literature that distinguished the year 1922.

◄ 4 ►

ANNUS MIRABILIS OVIDIANUS

World War I, the years during which Joyce, Pound, and Lawrence were re-sponding in their alienation to the exiled Ovid and his artful tales of metamor-phosis, shattered the political stability and social foundations that had supported European culture since the Napoleonic era. In Russia, the Revolution of 1917 initiated a period of civil conflict that lasted until the establishment of the So-viet Union in 1922 and, in its wake, drove hundreds of thousands of citizens into an unsettled exile. The situation in Germany was dominated for years by that nation's calamitous defeat in the war. While the various revolutionary insurrec-tions of the immediate postwar winter months were put down, a major upheaval took place when the emperor, Wilhelm II, was forced to abdicate and a shaky German Republic was formed. But the early years of the so-called Weimar coali-tion were severely troubled: territorial disputes with France over the Ruhr and the Rhineland and with Poland over Silesia; disastrously escalating inflation, which culminated in 1923; disagreement with the Allies over Germany's heavy reparations; and, internally, steadily intensifying conflicts between left and right, and notably between the Communists and the upstart National Socialist party. In an effort to relieve their situation, the Germans in April 1922 met with the Russians in Rapallo and signed a treaty waiving reparation claims mutually and calling for increased trade between the two countries that perceived themselves as outsiders on the European political stage. Meanwhile, conflicting aspirations created an atmosphere of political terrorism in Germany that led to assassinations, such as that of the Jewish foreign minister, Walter Rathenau, in June 1922. Italy faced similar problems. The end of the war confronted the government with inflation and unemployment, a situation that exacerbated the threat of the Socialist party, which at its congress in 1919 voted to expropriate the capitalist industrialists and to institute a republic after the Soviet model. This threat produced its inevitable counterreaction when the Fascist party was founded that same year. The ensuing conflicts led by the end of 1922 to Mussolini's "march on Rome" and the establishment of a Fascist government.

While the war brought about no significant change in France's parliamentary republic, the government was deluged immediately after the war by a wave of strikes by workers whose wages had fallen significantly during the war years. This unrest provided fertile soil for the resurgence of the French Communist party, a development viewed nervously by men and women who had watched the Russian Revolution from afar and received many of its exiles. French foreign policy was dominated by the traditional hostility toward Germany: dissatisfaction with a League of Nations that could guarantee no military security; demands for reparations; claims to territories in the Saar, the Ruhr, and the Rhineland; and military alliances with Belgium and Poland in an effort to enclose the feared enemy. England was not so greatly obsessed with Germany as was France, but the new government that came into power with the December elections of 1918 had problems of its own. Many traditionalists and political conservatives in England had been appalled by the social and economic reforms enacted by the Liberal government following its rise to power shortly before the war (in the general elections of 1905) and dissatisfied with its conduct of the war. As a result, conservative candidates gained significantly in the elections and, accordingly, within the coalition government; by the end of 1922, they were strong enough to force out the Liberals and form a Conservative government. During these years of political struggle the government was confronted with strikes over rising prices and with drastic unemployment as millions of demobilized soldiers returned to civilian life. Meanwhile, the government found much to occupy it abroad. India's significant military contribution to the Allied war efforts had enhanced that country's expectation of greater independence within the British empire and required London's urgent attention. In Ireland the new home rule bill, which in 1919 established separate Irish parliaments for Ulster and for the rest of the country, generated unrest and street fighting, which was met by the violence of the notorious "Black and Tans."

These radical changes, which shattered many of the social, political, and economic assumptions of the nineteenth century, had inevitable cultural consequences. Regardless of their political stance, thoughtful writers and thinkers realized that a new age required new forms. It is by now a commonplace of intellectual history to speak of the breakdown of traditional values and views of reality produced by startling developments in science, and notably by Planck and Einstein when they challenged classical conceptions of matter, time, and space with non-Euclidean geometry and non-Newtonian physics. In psychology Freud and Jung were dismantling the comfortable concepts of human behavior and forging a vastly more complicated image of man. The budding fields of anthropology and sociology were preaching the relativity of standards of ethics and morality, thus undermining the already shaky foundations of Victorian and Wilhelmine society. The many readers who responded intuitively to the cultural pessimism of Oswald Spengler's *Decline of the West* (1922) were convinced that the old values had outlived their day. The apocalyptic visions of Expressionism were simply one symptom of a generation rebelling against the past and filled with a sense of change.

The dazzling formal developments of high modernism in music, art, and literature also necessitated a search for new models. While Picasso was looking to African art for inspiration, Stravinsky employed primitive rhythms to striking musical effect. As Virgil lost his appeal for a generation disenchanted with the stability of empire, Ovid's belief in the principle of change and metamorphosis as well as his personal experience of the injustice of political power made him attractive to those casting about in the ruins of tradition for a foundation upon which to build a new postwar culture.

OVID IN PROVENCE

One of the earliest and most representative expressions of the new zeitgeist is evident in Émile Ripert's delightful and eminently readable popularizing biography *Ovide: Poète de l'amour, des dieux et de l'exil* (1921). Ripert (1882–1948), called in 2000 "le poète disparu" in a regional Provençal newspaper because his name has virtually vanished from literary histories and even standard reference works,[1] was a leading poet of his native Provence and later held the chair for Provençal language and literature at the University of Aix-en-Provence. While he read Ovid and the other Roman classics as a schoolboy, he made no claim to be a classics scholar: his works prior to World War I consisted of several volumes of poetry, one of which received the Prix national de poésie in 1912, and several critical works, including the prize-winning *La renaissance provençale (1800–1860)* and a study of Frédéric Mistral. When he returned to Provence following five years of military service and internment in Germany as a prisoner of war, he spent several weeks in the spring of 1919 in spiritual retreat, where he dusted off the French, Greek, Latin, Italian, and Provençal works he had left behind.[2] As he picked up at random the familiar works of antiquity, he was dismayed to ascertain that his many hours of schoolboy study had left him incapable of deciphering the Greek and unable to handle the obscurities of Tacitus, the subtleties of Seneca, the abstractions of Lucretius. But when he opened the *Metamorphoses* he discovered, to his delight, that he could read Ovid with ease, that he had found an old friend who presented himself "comme un consolateur naturel" (viii).

In an imaginary conversation Ovid reminds Ripert that he had taught the young poet to see Phoebus in the sun, to hear Philomèle in the nightingale; and he promises to help him recover the secret of mythological vision. Looking around, Ripert suddenly recognizes Arachne in the spider whose web trembles in the open window; the reverberating shouts of children in the street remind him that Echo resides in the hills above; a white flower blossoming over the fountain in front of the villa is perhaps contemplating the image of Narcissus; and the lindens shading the terrace are surely Philemon and Baucis. The Latin countryside, he concludes, provides him with a perpetual commentary to Ovid worth at least as much as those of the scholars.

Encouraged and inspired by his discovery, Ripert reread the *Metamorphoses,* which had enchanted his early years, and then moved on to the *Heroides,* the *Amores,* the *Fasti,* and the elegies of exile. Having completed this review of the Greco-Latin past for his own benefit, he began to wonder if it would not be equally beneficial for France to do the same as the nation sought direction for the future. "Don't we need, in order to orient ourselves on the path of our true civilization, to take account of all our riches, to return for a moment to our origins?" (x). Others have rejuvenated Corneille and Virgil (Ripert is alluding here to recent popularizing biographies by his friends Auguste Dorchain and André Bellessort), but readers have been unjust to Ovid. "I would be happy if these few pages could mark for him too the moment of a greatly desired rehabilitation" (xi).

Does he dare, in the wake of so many learned tomes, to add his own modest pages on a much-studied poet? He wouldn't have been bold enough before 1914, he realizes. Why is it that he now can look without trembling upon the ever-lengthening list of German scholarly works? In the past the Germans had been able to impose their scholarship upon France because they had the power that victory always bestows. "If today I am able to read Ovid without feeling tyrannized by all that these Germans have written about him, it's because for five years I no longer had time to read it" (xiii). His humble desire to liberate Ovid and himself and all Frenchmen from the German expropriation ("l'emprise germanique") emboldens him to undertake his biography. He sees both himself and Ovid as captives who have escaped a fortress and returned from the prisons of Germany, where their spirit languished.

In this highly personalized style and with reference mainly to Ovid's own texts Ripert writes his biography in the hope of demonstrating Ovid's essential modernity or, conversely, the essential antiquity of the present. He achieves this effect in part by frequent extrapolations from the Roman past to more general human experience. "A banal story: the young provincial arriving in the capital to complete his education, to devote himself to literature and, if possible, to conquer glory. A story often painful in modern Paris, but a luminous adventure in ancient Rome" (14). He goes on to compare Ovid, witnessing the triumphant return of Octavian from the conquest of Anthony, to the young Victor Hugo, intoxicated by the glory of Napoleon's entries and clapping his hands at the passage of the imperial procession. He tactfully elucidates when necessary. Thus despite his own desires and because of his equestrian status Ovid is named triumvir: "that is, under the direction of the ædiles he's supposed to supervise order in the prisons, the fire brigade stations, the nightwatchmen—the latter function perhaps not altogether unpleasant" (34). Ripert allows implicit parallels to emerge between Ovid's day and his own. Ovid understood that, to write vivid poetry, he not only had to know his material but to experience it—to live in the intoxicating society of his day, both as a poet and as a man of the world. "A charming society, no doubt too much discredited today. After the civil wars people were finally enjoying 'la douceur de vivre'. No doubt there was no longer liberty, but also no more political struggles—in sum, less hatred, more social goodwill" (40). Elsewhere, as he closes his copy of the *Metamorphoses* one evening,

> I see that the first stars have appeared in the heavens and, as I remain in a pensive mood, that the entire celestial flowering is opening up gradually; and I dream, in the face of this starry evening, of the narrative by Mistral that Alphonse Daudet translated and in which we hear a shepherd of Provence tell stories of metamorphosis just as surprising as those of Ovid. . . . Metamorphoses, but they are still living on the lips of the herdsmen of Provence, different in form, but identical in spirit. (139)

Following a useful survey of Ovid's enduring reputation in France, he concludes that the Middle Ages "too easily made of him the moralizer that he scarcely is; the classical centuries made of him a salon poet and a court wit [poète de salon et d'alcôve], which he was only at certain moments. Let us see him with different eyes; let us rediscover in him a Rome that is familiar, colorful, charming, witty, as well as the Mediterranean décor of the mythological tales" (253). Having disencumbered Ovid from the moralizations of the Middle Ages, the preciosities of the seventeenth century, and the gallantries of the eighteenth century, and recognized him as a purveyor of scenes for opera and painting, "we can

love him, just as Ronsard loved him, in the plenitude of his Greco-Latin genius—as the Roman poet who, in certain respects, already Italian, is perhaps
closest to us" (254).

In his rejection of the prevailing scholarly disparagement, which he regards
as essentially German;[3] in his almost visceral Mediterranean identification with
Ovid; in his constant equation of the Roman past and the European present—
in all these respects Ripert's knowledgeable but unpretentious biography is
paradigmatic of the new view of Rome and of Ovid emerging during the troubled years following the war and reaching a high point in 1922.

In the concluding paragraph of *Ovid Recalled* L. P. Wilkinson observes with
acuity that "in the nineteen-twenties the time was ripe for a revaluation of
Ovid"; the narrow Victorian notions of poetry and morality were being rejected. But Wilkinson sees no signs that such a revaluation took place. This is
perhaps true if one looks only, as Wilkinson did, at "classical circles." The response elsewhere, however, was quite conspicuous.

TIRESIAS ON THE THAMES

T. S. Eliot (1888–1965) has been generally, and correctly, identified as a Virgilian
poet.[4] In the essay "What Is a Classic?" (1944) he presented Virgil as the ideal
illustration for his definition (maturity of mind, of matter, and of language); and
in his radio talk called "Virgil and the Christian World" (1951) he sought to define the "chief characteristics of Virgil which make him sympathetic to the
Christian mind": *labor, pietas,* and *fatum.*[5] In addition, Eliot made no secret of his
basically Augustan and "imperialist" attitudes, stating only a few years after World
War I that "I am all for empires."[6] However, Eliot's Virgilian phase is a phenomenon of his later years; apart from two allusive references—in "La Figlia che
Piange" (1916) and a single line in *The Waste Land* (1922)—his writing prior to
1930 betrays little more than a casual interest in Virgil, an interest limited essentially to the early books of the *Aeneid*.

Like Pound, Eliot had a sound classical education. At Smith Academy in St.
Louis he was awarded the Latin prize at age sixteen; and in the reading list prepared for his application to Harvard he cited, in addition to the entire *Aeneid*,
two thousand lines of Ovid (presumably a selection from the fifteen books of
the *Metamorphoses*).[7] No doubt Ovid constituted an appreciable segment of the
course in Latin poetry that he took at Harvard with Edward Kennard Rand,
whose book *Ovid and His Influence* (1925) was to be one of the earliest appeals
in English for the poet's scholarly and popular rehabilitation. When in 1920 his
mother moved from St. Louis to Cambridge and provided her son with a list of

the texts from school and college that he had left at home, his edition of *Metamorphoses* was one of the volumes that he marked for her to send.[8] His decision to leave the United States in order to make his career in England no doubt sharpened his interest in Ovid as an exile. That Ovid was very much on his mind in the early 1920s we may conclude from frequent passing references—for instance, in his essays on *Dryden* (1921) or *Andrew Marvell* (1921), where he cites Ovid as another poet with Marvell's "allegiance of levity and seriousness."[9]

Eliot's sharpened interest in Ovid about the time when he had begun to think seriously about the long poem that was to become *The Waste Land* was due in no small measure to the influence of Ezra Pound. Eliot met Pound in London in September 1914, and almost immediately the slightly older but more experienced *homme de lettres* took the promising young poet under his wing and tutelage. Pound urged Eliot to stay in England rather than return to the United States; he arranged for the publication of "The Love-Song of J. Alfred Prufrock" in *Poetry* magazine (1915); he helped Eliot make the selections for his first volume, *Prufrock and Other Poems* (1917); and in early January 1922, while Eliot spent several days with him in Paris, Pound assisted his protégé in reshaping the typescript of *The Waste Land*. During these same years, as we have seen, Pound was Europe's most energetic advocate for Ovid, whose works he constantly urged his friends to read and whose *Metamorphoses* he was touting, in 1922, as "a sacred book." It is no small wonder that John Rodker named his first and short-lived (1919–20) publishing enterprise, in which he published Pound's *Hugh Selwyn Mauberley* and Eliot's *Ara Vos Prec,* the Ovid Press.

In addition to Pound, an important stimulus also stemmed from Sir James Frazer's *Golden Bough* (1890), in which Ovid's *Metamorphoses* and *Fasti* are frequently cited as sources of information. (We have already noted that Frazer later produced an authoritative five-volume edition of the *Fasti*.) That Frazer was much on Eliot's mind at this time we may conclude from the casual reference in his 1921 review of the performance of *Le sacre du printemps* by Stravinsky, "the Lucifer of the season," where he observed that the vegetation rite underlying the ballet constituted a pageant of primitive culture.

> It was interesting to any one who had read The Golden Bough and similar works, but hardly more than interesting. In art there should be interpenetration and metamorphosis. Even The Golden Bough can be read in two ways: as a collection of entertaining myths, or as a revelation of that vanished mind of which our mind is a continuation.[10]

Two years later he hails *The Golden Bough* as "a work of no less importance for our time than the complementary work of Freud—throwing its light on the obscurities of the soul from a different angle; and it is a work of perhaps greater permanence, because it is a statement of fact which is not involved in the main-tenance or fall of any theory of the author's." No mere erudition or collection of data or theory, Frazer's work "has extended the consciousness of the human mind into as dark a backward and abysm of time [*sic*] as has yet been explored."[11]

The Waste Land is quite literally bookended by Pound and Frazer: on the ti-tle page is a dedication to Pound, "*il miglior fabbro*," and the notes immediately following the text begin with a statement that the poem is profoundly indebted to two works: Jessie L. Weston's *From Ritual to Romance* and Frazer's *Golden Bough* (in the twelve-volume edition of 1911–15 that Eliot consulted). Eliot's notes specify several dozen sources in seven different languages for the "frag-ments I have shored against my ruins" (431):[12] from the Old and New Testa-ments by way of Virgil, Petronius, and Augustine, Dante, Shakespeare, and Spenser, Baudelaire, Verlaine, and Wagner, to the Upanishads. Yet among these sources Ovid is at least in two senses central. First, the principal Ovidian bor-rowing, the tale of Tiresias, whom Eliot himself in his notes calls "the most im-portant personage in the poem," begins almost precisely in the middle of the text (verse 215 of 434). Second, the theme of transformation dominates *The Waste Land* at least as powerfully as it does Ovid's *Metamorphoses*.[13]

Eliot's relationship to Ovid can better be defined not as *influence* but as a *con-fluence* of minds: he did not discover metamorphosis through Ovid; rather, he came to recognize in Ovid a pagan analogy to the metamorphosis that he had already learned to see in the Christian idea of resurrection. He had read the *Metamorphoses* as a boy, and in his childhood he had been exposed to Chris-tianity in its Unitarian form. At Harvard he continued his reading of Ovid and intensified his study of comparative religion. But it was his encounter with Frazer's *Golden Bough,* along with a deepening religious sense culminating in 1927 in his conversion to the Church of England, that enabled him to view primitive myth as a variant and precursor of Christian belief.[14] His desire to en-compass within his own consciousness both of these polarities, pagan and Chris-tian, ancient and modern—indeed, *all* the "broken images" (22) of world culture that he assembles and cites—led him to Tiresias as the figure embodying that totality.

Tiresias occurs in a specific context. In "The Fire Sermon" it is his legendary bisexuality that enables him to understand both the male and female aspects of the tryst that he witnesses between the typist and the clerk: "I Tiresias, though blind, throbbing between two lives, / Old man with wrinkled female breasts" (218–19). (Eliot takes care to justify the anomaly that Tiresias can see despite his blindness by stressing, twice, that he enjoys vision only "at the violet hour" [215, 220] of twilight.) For our purposes the sordid details of the hasty coupling of the exhausted secretary and the coarse clerk are irrelevant. More to the point is that Eliot enlists Tiresias as the witness to the scene.

In the longest endnote attached to his poem he quotes, in the original Latin, the passage from the *Metamorphoses* (3.320–38) in which Ovid describes Tiresias's wondrous transformations. Once when Jove, joking with Juno, claimed that women got more pleasure from sex than men, Juno heatedly maintained the opposite. They agreed to submit to the judgment of Tiresias, "who knew both sides of love" (*Venus huic erat utraque nota; Met.* 3.323). Years before, strolling in the forest, he had come upon two huge serpents copulating and struck them with his staff. In punishment for this violation they changed him into a woman. Seven years later, chancing again upon the same two serpents and recalling the magical power of his earlier blow, he struck them again and was promptly transformed back into a man. Since he had enjoyed sex both as a man and as a woman, he was in a position to settle the quarrel and sided with Jove. Juno, enraged by his answer, struck him blind; but Jove, since gods are not permitted to undo the deeds of another deity, compensated him with the power of prophecy.

Making Tiresias into the witness of the scene enables Eliot to wrest from it the highest degree of irony—an irony, it goes without saying, based on a thoughtful acquaintance with Ovid's text. For in the *Metamorphoses* the blind prophet, called upon to judge who derives the greatest pleasure (*voluptas*) from sex, unhesitatingly identifies the woman. But in Eliot's version precisely the opposite is true: the woman is bored, listless, and indifferent to the crude caresses of her paramour; and when the hasty coupling is done, she is "hardly aware of her departed lover" and thinks: "'Well now that's done: and I'm glad it's over'" (252). The young man, in turn, having bestowed "one final patronising kiss, / . . . gropes his way, finding the stairs unlit" (247–48). Tiresias, thanks to his own experiences, can project himself into both of them.

> (And I Tiresias have foresuffered all
> Enacted on this same divan or bed . . .)
>
> (243–44)

It would of course be a trivialization to understand the role of Tiresias as limited to that of an aged bisexual voyeur. In his note Eliot explains that "Tiresias, although a mere spectator and not indeed a 'character,' is yet the most important personage in the poem, uniting all the rest; . . . and the two sexes meet in Tiresias. What Tiresias *sees*, in fact, is the substance of the poem." We have already mentioned the sublime irony implicit in the situation: the shift from the heights of the Olympian gods to the tawdry teatime rendezvous of two repre-

sentatives of the present-day working classes; and the inversion of the chief ben-
eficiary of sexual pleasure from woman to man.

But Eliot imposes a much more significant function on Tiresias. We do not
need to understand Eliot's statement in the most literal sense: that the Tiresias
depicted within the poem is also its implicit author. Eliot is simply making the
point that the poem is controlled by a unifying consciousness that assimilates
the various figures of the poem, that ties together its often seemingly disparate
parts, and that is capable of establishing connections between isolated cultural
and historical events: between the inhabitants of Dante's first circle of Hell and
the crowd flowing across London Bridge (62–63), between a soldier in the
Punic Wars and a passer-by in the financial district of London (69–75), between
Wagner's Rhine maidens and the daughters of a filthy Thames (273–78). Ultimately only such a Tiresian consciousness can contain and unify through
metamorphic association the "broken images" and "fragments" that otherwise
characterize a culture that, like its "falling towers" (374), has crumbled before
the "hooded hordes swarming / Over endless plains" (369–70) and, according
to Eliot's note, engulfing Europe. It is the all-embracing consciousness of Tiresias that brings order to this chaos. It is true, of course, that even Tiresias's point
of view is limited by his alienation: he observes but is not humanly affected by
what he sees.[15] Yet only within his consciousness does any ordering of the images take place. This re-visioning of Tiresias, and even Eliot's identification with
the prophet's impotence, constitutes Eliot's highest tribute to Ovid. Hence Ezra
Pound, in his annotations to the typescript of the poem, addressed Eliot as "you
Tiresias."[16]

I regard Eliot's concluding line about the "great anthropological interest" of
the passage as a throwaway tribute to Frazer, to Pound's allusion in his *Guide to
Kulchur* to Ovid's "folklore," and to the anthropological vogue of the 1920s.[17]
(For my purposes I take the poem along with notes as first published by Eliot in
book form to be the authentic text that represents the poet's intentions. The questions of genesis and unity, as fascinating as they may be for specialists, are not relevant for readers who first encounter the poem as a whole or for Eliot, who
regularly spoke of *The Waste Land* as one poem and not a collection of sections.)[18]

Eliot's interest in metamorphosis did not begin with *The Waste Land*. He initially intended to include the early poem "The Death of Saint Narcissus" (1915)
in his longer work, for it involves a sequence of Ovidian metamorphoses. Narcissus (a character based, like Joyce's Stephen Dedalus, on a conflation of the saint
and the mythological figure), before his flesh becomes enamored of the arrows
that puncture him, first imagines that he had once been a tree with twisted
branches and tangled roots; then, in a masturbatory image, a fish "with slippery
white belly held tight in his own fingers"; and finally a young girl raped in the

woods by a drunken old man.[19] In *The Waste Land* Eliot uses other images taken from the *Metamorphoses:*[20] e.g., the "handful of dust" (30), which has been attributed to Ovid's description of the Sibyl (*Met.* 14.129–53).[21] She tells Apollo that it is her wish, in exchange for her sexual favors, to have as many years of life as "grains of dust in the heap to which she points" (*pulveris hausti / ostendens cumulum; Met.* 14.136–37). Apollo grants her wish, but when she refuses to honor their agreement he withholds the eternal youth that would have made her agelessness tolerable. This interpretation enables us to tie that line to the poem's epitaph from Petronius, which quotes the Sibyl as desiring nothing but to die.

The most striking borrowing, however, is the tale of Philomela—a story central, as we saw, to Pound's Canto 4 (1919), but also generally popular among modern poets from the American John Crowe Ransom to the Russian Mikhail Kreps, the Greek Yannis Ritsos, and the Austrian Erich Fried.[22] In "A Game of Chess" the tale is depicted in the painting or tapestry hanging above the mantel in the home of a London lady, who has just been compared metaphorically to Cleopatra. In his notes Eliot attributes the scene specifically to Ovid's *Metamorphoses:*

> The change of Philomel, by the barbarous king
> So rudely forced; yet there the nightingale
> Filled all the desert with inviolable voice
> And still she cried, and still the world pursues,
> "Jug Jug" to dirty ears.
>
> (99–103)

Basically Eliot uses the image as it has been employed by many other poets: to exemplify the classic theme of poetry resulting from suffering. But Eliot teases out further dimensions of meaning. Many scholars have pointed out that "Jug Jug" is a conventional rendition by Renaissance poets for the nightingale's song (e.g., in Lyly's *Alexander and Campaspe*), but it was also in sixteenth-century vernacular a disparaging term for a homely woman or mistress. So the last two lines have the further implication that lovely innocence *qua* poetry is still today pursued and violated by an uncomprehending world. This "sylvan scene," as well as the "other withered stumps of time"[23] gazing down from the walls, seems to provide a setting less appropriate for the unfulfilled (through impotence? through indifference?) act of seduction portrayed in the lady's chamber than for the tawdry scene in "The Fire Sermon" between the typist and her "lover." Accordingly, it is echoed by the strophe in "The Fire Sermon" (205–8) that introduces the two crude erotic scenes from the present: the homosexual propositioning of the narrator by Mr. Eugenides and the violation of the typist:

> Twit twit twit
> Jug jug jug jug jug jug
> So rudely forc'd
> Tereu
>
> (203–6)

("Tereu" is the Latin vocative form of the name Tereus, but its truncated form might also suggest the moral fragmentation of modern man). At the end of the poem, when the poet is longing for fecundity to awaken the Waste Land and the power to sublimate his own sterile emotions and scattered bits of knowledge into the unity of poetry, the story is mentioned again indirectly. The line "*Quando fiam uti chelidon*—O swallow swallow" (429; "When shall I become like the swallow") is borrowed, as Eliot's note informs us, from the *Pervigilium Veneris*, a 93-line post-Ovidian Latin poem of unknown authorship and date, where it refers to Philomela's sister Procne, who is transformed into a swallow and represents the coming of spring and regeneration.[24]

The principal theme informing the poem is the myth of regeneration and the accompanying fertility rituals underlying, according to Weston's *From Ritual to Romance,* the religious theme of death and resurrection.[25] This theme provided the title—from the Waste Land ravaged through sympathetic suffering by the wounding of the Fisher King—as well as the many images of aridity, impotence, and sterility, both physical and spiritual. But it is the Ovidian conception of metamorphosis that provides the binding link between the many "broken images" and the figure of Tiresias that embodies the consciousness capable of comprehending those acts of metamorphosis.

Orpheus in the Alps

Just in the days when Eliot was putting the final touches to *The Waste Land* in London, another poet in the heart of Europe was experiencing one of the most spectacular bursts of creative energy in the history of world literature. From the 2nd to the 5th of February, in his lonely tower above the town of Sierre in the Swiss Valais, Rilke wrote the first twenty-five of his *Sonnets to Orpheus* (*Sonette an Orpheus,* published 1923).[26] Following a ten-day interval during which he completed his ten *Duino Elegies,* and greatly to his own astonishment, he then turned out the twenty-nine sonnets of the second part of the *Sonnets to Orpheus* (Feb. 15–23). Leaving aside the achievement of the *Elegies,* one of the key works of twentieth-century literature,[27] Rilke produced during these three weeks, and at the rate of five or six per day, some of the most astonishing and varied sonnets of European high modernism.[28] (In fact he wrote eight further sonnets that, for various reasons, were not included in the final cycle.)

Several factors came together to make possible this literary phenomenon. Rilke (1875–1926) had come to the Valais half a year earlier in search of the tranquillity and inspiration that would enable him to complete the great project of his *Duino Elegies,* which he had begun almost ten years earlier at Castle Duino near Trieste on the Adriatic coast. But after writing the first two in a great rush (late January and early February 1912) and adding a third and fourth in 1913 and 1915, he had reached a poetic stalemate. Having produced little but fragmentary efforts during the war years and disenchanted with the political and social turmoil of postwar Germany, in the summer of 1919 Rilke went to Switzerland on a lecture tour, which stretched out into a year as he found both responsive audiences for his poetry and generous benefactors happy to support his poetic genius. In the summer of 1920 he met the painter Baladine Klossowska (mother of the artist Balthus), whom he nicknamed Merline, and decided to stay in Switzerland in order to be close to her—not in Geneva, where she lived with her two sons, but near Zurich in a château owned by wealthy patrons. That fall, traveling with Merline in southern Switzerland, he made his first trip to the Valais and was immediately captivated by its dramatic alpine landscape. Accordingly, when he was next looking once again for a more permanent residence, and above all for a place where his elegies would finally come to fruition, the work that he regarded as his magnum opus, he thought of the Valais and enlisted Merline's assistance in locating appropriate quarters.

At Muzot, in the foothills above Sierre, they found one of the thirteenth-century towers, called "castles" locally, that seemed perfectly to suit his needs.[29] Thanks to patrons who bought and furnished the squat tower and arranged for a housekeeper, at the end of July Rilke moved into his new abode, to which he formed a well-nigh mystical attachment. So content was he in the almost total isolation of his tower that he decided, contrary to his own initial expectations, to spend the winter in the rather primitive accommodations: no electricity, no running water, and crude sanitary arrangements. There, following years of vacillation and anxiety, Rilke experienced the wondrous surge of creative activity. After many letters filled with complaints and petulant demands he was able to report on the 8th of February that "Something very lovely was given to me, from the 2nd to the 5th of February, for the world: a cycle of *twenty-five* sonnets."[30] The next day he confided to his publisher that he had gone outside in the cold moonlight and caressed the tower "like a large animal" because it was these old walls that had offered him this new inspiration.[31]

Rilke was able to respond so readily to the *genius loci* in part because—in his *New Poems* of 1907–8 and in his subsequent translations of the sonnets of Elizabeth Barrett Browning, Louise Labé, and Michelangelo—he had already brought the German sonnet to new heights of virtuosity.[32] Formally, in other words, he was prepared for the challenge, and the dazzling variety of line, rhyme, and rhythm exemplifies the ease with which he handled the genre. But why Orpheus?

In part his focus on Orpheus stemmed from the widespread generational interest in Orphism and primitive mystery cults.[33] Rilke was introduced to Orphism in Munich, where in 1915 and again in 1917 he attended two series of lectures by Alfred Schuler (1865–1923), a protégé of Johann Jakob Bachofen.[34] In such works as his *Versuch über die Gräbersymbolik der Alten* (1859; Essay on ancient grave symbolism) and *Das Mutterrecht* (1861; Mother right) Bachofen (1815–87) had refamiliarized modern readers with the ancient mystery cults, and in particular with the Orphic notion that human development takes place in a progression leading from the *tellurian* through the *lunar* to the *solar* level of pure *noûs* or spirit.[35] Rilke was enormously excited by his encounter with these heady ideas in Schuler's lectures, and by the notion, fed by the earliest myths, that "the dead are the ones who *are,* the Kingdom of the Dead a single incredible existence, while our little slice of life represents a kind of exception to it."[36] Schuler argues that human existence can be divided into two periods: a prehistoric age ("Urzeit"), characterized by luminousness (the Heroic Age, Paradise), and a historical age, characterized by a steady evacuation of luminosity. He contends that periods of light alternate with periods of darkness and that humankind, driven by its memories of the past, moves steadily toward transfiguration through evolution. Rilke borrowed from Schuler a book about Bachofen and later purchased a copy of *Das Mutterrecht;* and in his 1919 lectures in Basel he paid tribute to the memory of that great citizen of the city.[37] The Orphic attempt to overcome through a grand *coincidentia oppositorum* the modern rational separation of inner and outer, past and present, time and space, life and death, appealed greatly to Rilke and confirmed instincts that had informed his poetry for at least a decade. But the specific focus on Orpheus as a figure and as the embodiment of Orphism enabled him to give poetic form to his thoughts and feelings.

One of the two principal classical sources for the full story of Orpheus—the death of Eurydice and Orpheus's descent to Hades (*Met.* 10.1–85), the magical effect of his song on all natural beings (*Met.* 10.86–153), and the *sparagmos* (his dismemberment by the raging Maenads; *Met.* 11.1–66)—is Ovid. (At *Georgics* 4.453–558 Virgil tells essentially the same story.) For all the inadequacies of Rilke's classical education, we have evidence that Ovid was one of the few poets whose works he knew at least rudimentarily in the original—indeed, the only Roman poet to whose works he formed a lasting relationship.

Following his early training in two different military academies in Austria, where Latin and Greek played no part in the curriculum, Rilke was sent for a year (1891–92) to a business school in Linz. At that point, thanks to the support of a generous uncle, he was permitted to study as a "Privatist"—that is, privately with the teachers but not in the regular classes—at a gymnasium in Prague, where he was prepped for three years to take the entrance exams for university study. So at age sixteen he finally began the study of the required Latin. At least some of the reading was in Ovid—a favorite school author of the period—, with whose works he became acquainted presumably in the edition of *P. Ovidi Nasonis Carmina selecta scholarum in usum* by Heinrich Stephan Sedlmayer (Leipzig, 1887; 5th ed., 1894).[38] By 1895 he was able to translate thirty-six lines of the story of Arion from Ovid's *Fasti* (2.83–118) into elegiac distichs. In sum, even though Rilke was never at ease with Latin and certainly never came close to the competence of Joyce, Pound, or Eliot, he knew Ovid from his school days and was exposed to at least some of his work in the original. Another factor was no doubt the early influence of Burckhardt, whose "profound, erudite, and yet so human understanding," he wrote in 1902, "exceeds the observations of most scholars of our day like a tower from whose height one can survey for the first time the breadth of that age [the Renaissance] like a landscape."[39] Years later, in the 1919 lectures in Basel, he again paid tribute to Burckhardt.

Paradoxically, the immediate inspiration for his early poem "Orpheus. Eurydice. Hermes" (written in Rome, 1904; published in *New Poems*) was not Ovid's *Metamorphoses,* in whose account the figure of Hermes plays no role, but the representation of the scene in the Greek relief that Rilke had studied in 1902–4 on several occasions at the Louvre, in the Villa Albani in Rome, and in the Museo Nationale in Naples.[40] But just as Eliot had Pound, Rilke also had two intellectual provocateurs who reignited his interest in the Roman poet. Rilke met the aging Rodin in September 1902, and from the fall of 1905 until May 1906 served as his private secretary, living on the grounds of his estate at Meudon, where the poet was daily in the presence of the sculptor's works. Rodin was a great admirer of the *Metamorphoses* and created a number of sculptures based on Ovidian themes. In his 1902 essay "Auguste Rodin" Rilke had singled out the *Danaïde* for particular comment.[41] In the lecture on Rodin that he composed in the fall of 1905 for a lecture tour to Dresden and Prague, he depicted his sensations before Rodin's sculpture of *Orpheus and Eurydice* (1894) and the more recent *Orpheus and the Maenads* (1905).

And I already feel how his name disintegrates in my mouth, how it is now only the poet, the same poet who is named Orpheus when his arm makes a wide detour over all things to the strings of his lyre, the same one who in a desperate agony grasps at the feet of the fleeing muse who pulls away, *the same one* who finally dies, his face upright in the shadow of his still ever singing voices—and dies in such a way that the same small group is sometimes also called Resurrection.[42]

We are hardly surprised that mythological references based on Ovid now begin to occur more frequently in Rilke's writings.[43] A poetic fragment from 1909 concerns Danaë's son "Perseus," whom Rilke calls "son of the fallen gold."[44] In *The Notebooks of Malte Laurids Brigge* (1910) Rilke uses "the legend of Byblis" (*Met.* 9.450–665),[45] the story of the young woman so overpowered by incestuous love for her twin brother that she dissolved into a fountain of water, to exemplify his theme of absolute all-excluding love. In his essays "On the Young Poet" (1913) and "Dolls" (1914) he ruminates about the figure of Danaë, who received the "poured Zeus" much as the startled minds of certain young poets accept the world.[46] And in 1913 he wrote two poems entitled "Narziss," who "reincorporated by loving what went forth from him" ("Er liebte, was ihm ausging, wieder ein").[47] But during the war years the allusions disappear almost entirely. It was his lover Merline who rekindled Rilke's interest in Ovid for a second time. At Christmas 1920, she presented him with a Latin-French edition of the *Metamorphoses* bound in a cover that she had herself decorated with watercolors. Rilke thanked her in a letter written in his effusive French.

My tender friend, may I say it without appearing weak and partial: I adore the cover of the *Métamorphoses*—, and how happy I am to own henceforth this inexhaustible book! This tale of Myrrha, in the very center, how tenderly and sadly it is treated—, and the flight of Daphne with the red scarf, what violence, what passion, which nature, also impassioned, exploits with a single saving gesture. And yet the whole, while containing so much agitation, withdraws within itself and becomes tranquil; it does not overflow; the multiple clamor turns into the murmur of a brook. I admire the temperament that you have put into it, every touch of the paintbrush is like a little wave that hurls itself toward its own transformation—; I am completely delighted, Merline, with this lovely gift.[48]

Merline provided yet a second impulse. When she moved to Berlin with her sons in the autumn of 1921, she left behind in Rilke's study a small reproduction of an early sixteenth-century drawing by Cima da Conegliano, depicting Orpheus in repose beneath a tree and singing to two deer standing nearby.[49] This drawing, which hung directly opposite one of the two standing desks at which Rilke worked, was one of the immediate catalysts for the *Sonnets to Orpheus* and the direct source for at least two of them.

The second catalyst, as the dedication indicates, was the death from leukemia at age nineteen of Wera Ouckama Knoop, a childhood friend of Rilke's daughter. In 1919 Rilke was too deeply preoccupied with his own anxieties to react to the report of her death. But when he wrote to her mother in late 1921 to notify her of his daughter's engagement, Gertrud Knoop responded with a copy of Wera's firsthand account of her approaching death. How profoundly Rilke was moved by the report is evident from his reply early in January 1922. "For me, dearest, it is like a huge commitment to my own innermost and most serious and (if I attain it only remotely) most blessed being—that I have been permitted to take possession of these leaves of paper on the first evening of a new year."[50] Rilke's sense of commitment resulted only days later in the *Sonnets to Orpheus,* in which the deceased Wera assumed the role of Eurydice to his own Orpheus. (Rilke was stimulated by the death of friends to some of his finest poetic cycles: notably the 1908 "requiems" to Paula Modersohn-Becker and to Wolf Graf von Kalckreuth.)

The sonnets are *to* Orpheus, not about him. Only about a dozen of the fifty-five sonnets deal explicitly with the figure of the ur-poet. Only one poem (2:13) goes back to the ascent from Hades, which was the central theme of "Orpheus. Eurydike. Hermes." Here, rather than focusing as in the earlier poem on Eurydice, so wholly absorbed by her own death that she even forgets Orpheus, Rilke is concerned with the poet, empowered by his visit to the underworld to bring new dimensions of understanding to the world of mortals.

> Sei immer tot in Eurydike—, singender steige,
> preisender steige zurück in den reinen Bezug.
> Hier, unter Schwindenden, sei, im Reiche der Neige,
> sei ein klingendes Glas, das sich im Klang schon zerschlug.[51]

> (Be ever dead in Eurydice—, climb more singingly, climb
> more praisingly back into pure relatedness. Here, in the
> midst of vanishing things, *be;* in the realm of decline be a
> sounding glass that shattered from its own sound.)

Only one sonnet (1:26) alludes to the dismemberment, with an implicit allusion to the legend that Orpheus's decapitated head continued to sing as it floated down the river. Note also the Ovidian motif concerning Orpheus's singing, which continues to resound in all of nature: in the birds, animals, trees, and stones.[52] Above all, the sonnet concludes with the powerful assertion that all poets are the heirs of Orpheus, the ur-poet.

Du aber, Göttlicher, du, bis zuletzt noch Ertöner,
da ihn der Schwarm der verschmähten Mänaden befiel,
hast ihr Geschrei übertönt mit Ordnung, du Schöner,
aus den Zerstörenden stieg dein erbauendes Spiel.

Keine war da, daß sie Haupt dir und Leier zerstör.
Wie sie auch rangen und rasten, und alle die scharfen
Steine, die sie nach deinem Herzen warfen,
wurden zu Sanftem an dir und begabt mit Gehör.

Schließlich zerschlugen sie dich, von der Rache gehetzt,
während dein Klang noch in Löwen und Felsen verweilte
und in den Bäumen und Vögeln. Dort singst du noch jetzt.

O du verlorener Gott! Du unendliche Spur!
Nur weil dich reißend zuletzt die Feinschaft verteilte,
sind wir die Hörenden jetzt und ein Mund der Natur.

(But you, divine one, you, resounding to the end, when
the swarm of rejected Maenads overfell him, you sounded
over their screams with order; o beautiful one, out of the
destroyers arose your uplifting play. / None was there that
could destroy your head and lyre. No matter how they
struggled and raged, all the sharp stones they hurled at
your heart became gentle on you and gifted with
hearing. / Finally they crushed you, harried by revenge,
while your sound still dwelt in the lions and cliffs and in
the trees and birds. There you sing still now. / O you lost
god! You endless trace! Only because a ripping hostility
ultimately scattered you are we now the hearing ones and
a mouth of nature.)

Otherwise the poems revolve almost entirely around the middle stage of Orpheus's life—as the poet with the power to transform nature with his song, to sing of death in life, and to capture the essential permanence of all being in its various transformations. Here the theme of metamorphosis emerges as a central force in the sonnets.

The tone is established in the first poem, which as a description of the drawing hanging over his desk hints at the immediate inspiration for the poems. In Rilke's sonnet the tree against which Orpheus is leaning in the drawing is described as though it were growing from the poet's ear as reified song.

Da stieg ein Baum. O reine Übersteigung!
O Orpheus singt! O hoher Baum im Ohr!
Und alles schwieg. Doch selbst in der Verschweigung
ging neuer Anfang, Wink und Wandlung vor.

(There rose a tree. O pure transcendence! O
Orpheus sings! O lofty tree in the ear! And all was
silent. But even in the silence there was a new
beginning, sign, and transformation.)

The sonnet goes on to tell how, in the drawing, "animals made of silence" ("Tiere aus Stille") emerge from the forest and listen intently to the singing—creatures for whom Orpheus creates "temples of hearing" ("Tempel im Gehör"). Absolute song of the sort that Orpheus sings expresses no desire but only pure being: "Gesang ist Dasein" (sonnet 1:3). The sole function of his singing is to praise ("Rühmen, das ists!" 1:7, 1:8). But Orpheus is not of this world, for his nature embraces both realms—life here above and the underworld that he experienced.

Ist er ein Hiesiger? Nein, aus beiden
Reichen erwuchs seine weite Natur.
(1:6)

(Is he of this world? No, his wide nature grew out of
both kingdoms.)

Nur wer die Leier schon hob
auch unter Schatten,
darf das unendliche Lob
ahnend erstatten.
(1:9)

(Only he who has already raised his lyre even
among the shades may tentatively report the
unending praise.)

He requires no monuments (1:5) because he comes into being anew with every rose that blooms: "His metamorphosis in this and that." So there is no need to look for other names: "Once and for all, it is Orpheus when there is song" ("Ein für alle Male / ists Orpheus, wenn es singt"). Even when the world is transformed like cloud shapes, the primal song of Orpheus endures, the "god with the lyre" ("Gott mit der Leier," 1:19).

Mere mortals can achieve that godlike purity only when they have attained a similar Orphic state of consciousness embracing both life and death. In many sonnets, accordingly, Rilke addresses Orpheus as "Herr," the lord and master whom he seeks to emulate and from whom he learns to detect what is constant in the midst of transformations. He hails Orpheus as "the spirit that can connect us" ("Heil dem Geist, der uns verbinden mag," 1.12) so that he can act "from true connectedness" ("aus wirklichem Bezug," 1.12). For mortal poets live without connections to totality.

> Wir sind die Treibenden.
> Aber den Schritt der Zeit,
> nehmt ihn als Kleinigkeit
> im immer Bleibenden.
>
> Alles das Eilende
> wird schon vorüber sein;
> denn das Verweilende
> erst weiht uns ein.
>
> (1:22)
>
> (We are the drifters. But
> the pace of time, regard it
> as a triviality in the ever
> constant. / All the
> hastening things will soon
> be gone; for only what is
> constant consecrates us.)

The sonnets, especially in the second part, increasingly represent Rilke's effort in emulation of Orpheus to capture what is permanent in objects (real or imagined) of the transient world: flowers, fragrances, fountains, unicorns, bird cries, dancing girls, and mirrors (including here the theme of Narcissus, who "penetrated, purely dissolved," into their space [2:3]). The poems recapitulate most of the themes that had occupied his mind for years: the pain of love, the ambiguities of the poetic calling, the mystery of death, the threat of modern technical civilization to the human soul, the anxiety concerning time and transitoriness[53]—and, ever more insistently, the Ovidian theme of metamorphosis and change. Above all, he longs for the Orphic power to project himself spiri-

tually into the consciousness of life beyond this world so that he can imagine
and conjure up the dead Wera. "Where is her death?" he asks. "O, will you still
invent this theme before your song consumed itself? Whither does she sink away
from me? . . . A girl almost. . . ."

> Wo ist ihr Tod? O, wirst du dies Motiv
> erfinden noch, eh sich dein Lied verzehrte?—
> Wo sinkt sie hin aus mir? . . . Ein Mädchen fast. . . .
> (1.2)

By the end of the first group of poems, he feels up to the challenge.

> *Dich* aber will ich nun, *Dich,* die ich kannte
> wie eine Blume, von der ich den Namen nicht weiß,
> noch *ein* Mal erinnern und ihnen zeigen, Entwandte,
> schöne Gespielin des unüberwindlichen Schrei's.
> (1.25)

(*You* I now want to internalize, *you,* whom I knew like a flower
whose name I don't know—to remember you *one* time more and
show you to them, stolen from us, lovely playmate of the invincible
cry.)

If the first group of sonnets glorifies pure song in the person of Orpheus, the
second cluster is primarily concerned with the possibility of pure song in the
modern world: the regeneration of Orpheus in the person of modern poets who
represent various metamorphoses of the ur-poet.[54]

> Wolle die Wandlung. O sei für die Flamme begeistert,
> drin sich ein Ding dir entzieht, das mit Verwandlungen prunkt;
> jener entwerfende Geist, welcher das Irdische meistert,
> liebt in dem Schwung der Figur nichts wie den wendenden Punkt.
> (2:12)

(Desire transformation. O be inspired for the flame into which a
thing withdraws from you and flaunts its metamorphoses; that
projecting spirit that masters what is earthly, loves in the
momentum of the figure nothing but the turning point.)

The sonnet illustrates this theme with allusions to the Ovidian metamorphoses of Byblis, "who pours herself as a spring," and of "the transformed Daphne," who now feels "laurel-like" ("lorbeern").

At several points, and notably toward the end of each part, Rilke addresses the dead girl, Wera, in the hope of capturing her in song through a projection of his imagination, and thus of making her eternal.

> O komm und geh. Du, fast noch Kind, ergänze
> für einen Augenblick die Tanzfigur
> zum reinen Sternbild einer jener Tänze,
> darin wir die dumpf ordnende Natur
>
> vergänglich übertreffen. Denn sie regte
> sich völlig hörend nur, da Orpheus sang.
>
> (2:28)

> (O come and go. You, still almost a child,
> complete for a moment the dance figure into
> the pure constellation of one of those dances
> in which we transiently surpass the dull
> ordering of nature. / For it bestirred itself to
> listen only when Orpheus sang.)

In his modern Orphism, which through mystical visions seeks to encompass both life and death, Rilke has totally internalized Ovid's Orpheus and made of him an achievable ideal quite distinct and different from the Angel of the *Duino Elegies*.[55] The Angel is by definition a being apart—one to whose status the poet cannot aspire, but for whom he seeks in the inner space of his own being ("Weltinnenraum") to re-create the things of reality in a manner accessible to the Angel. Orpheus is quite different. As the ur-poet he represents a human achievement of metamorphosis and a familiarity with the realms of life and death. His modern disciple may not be able literally to make the descent to the underworld; but through the power of Orphic imagination he can go beyond the reality of the present to embrace the beyond. "Go in and out of transformation," Rilke writes in the final sonnet. "What is your most painful experience? If you find drinking bitter, turn into wine."

Geh in der Verwandlung aus und ein.
Was ist deine leidendste Erfahrung?
Ist dir Trinken bitter, werde Wein.
(2.29)

Narcissus in Paris?

Another poet who composed an early sonnet to Orpheus ("Orphée," 1891)—
a poet whom Rilke venerated and translated (1925)—does not quite belong
here. Paul Valéry also published a memorable volume of poems in 1922,
Charmes, whose title ("charme" is derived from the Latin *carmen*) is indebted indirectly to Ovid. The etymology and source were clarified when Valéry added
to a later (1933) edition, without attribution, the epigraph: *deducere carmen* ("to
spin out the song"), a phrase most familiar from the opening lines of the *Metamorphoses* (1.3−4): *primaque ab origine mundi / ad mea perpetuum deducite tempora
carmen* ("bring down my song uninterruptedly from the world's origin to my
own time"). One of the most illuminating of the volume's twenty-one poems,
"Fragments du Narcisse," bears a motto from Ovid: *Cur aliquid vidi* ("why did I
see anything?"), introducing the passage in *Tristia* (2.103) in which the poet
laments the *error* that caused his relegation. Ovid relates the passage to Actaeon
and his tragic fate; Valéry, in contrast, uses it to epitomize his imaginative re-vision of the story of Narcissus, whose consciousness is awakened when he sees
his reflection and whose most familiar source again is Ovid (*Met.* 3.339−510).
In another poem, "Au platane," the plane tree of the title is described as being
"white as a young Scythian" ("Blanc comme un jeune Scythe"), an image that
suggests Ovid's experiences in Tomis.

The Ovidian association is more than speculation. In 1917, following the publication of *La jeune Parque*, Valéry's stunning poetic meditation on the development of a young female consciousness, he was casting about in his notebooks for
a topic that would enable him to come to grips with "the experience of my sensibility."[56] On the same page "a lovely topic" occurred to him ("voici un beau
'sujet'"), which he tentatively called "O. chez les Barbares" or "Ovide chez les
Thraces"—a poem in which Ovid would represent the intellectual ("générale-
ment l'homme de l'esprit") cast into an environment of mediocrity where no
one understands him whenever he exposes even slightly the true profundity of
his nature. Almost immediately Valéry began a twenty-page folio of notes for a
poem that was now to be called "Ovide chez les Scythes."[57] And elsewhere in
his notebooks, Valéry occasionally quotes from the *Metamorphoses* and *Tristia*,
from memory (hence the occasional errors) and without attribution.[58]

These Ovidian allusions, in turn, encourage us to look more carefully at *La jeune Parque* (1917), which employs for the development of consciousness what Valéry once defined as "the depiction of a series of psychological substitutions."[59] In a remarkable passage immediately after the Young Fate (again, one of a triad of figures often cited by Ovid) has become conscious of her own maturity (lines 397–444), we hear—as examples of such "psychological substitutions" leading to emotional growth—unmistakable echoes of several characters from the *Metamorphoses:* Daphne transformed into a "misty tree" ("je m'apparus cet arbre vaporeux"); Ariadne, whose thread led Theseus out of the labyrinth ("Ce fil dont la finesse aveuglément suivie / Jusque sur cette rive a ramené ta vie"); Leda ravished by the swan god ("Ni, par le Cygne-Dieu, de plumes offensée / Sa brûlante blancheur n'effleura ma pensée"); and perhaps even Pygmalion's beloved statue ("le souci d'un sein d'argile parfumée"). The poem begins, moreover, when the Young Fate, like Eurydice, is first awakened by a serpent's sting to consciousness and the awareness of death.[60] And the form of the long dramatic monologue, which Valéry in his comments on the poem sometimes called a récitatif in the manner of Gluck's operas, goes back ultimately to Ovid's *Heroides.*

Yet neither the notebooks nor the poetic oeuvre contain any evidence of Valéry's interest in Ovid as compelling as, say, his later essay on Virgil and his translation of Virgil's *Bucoliques* (1942–44; published 1953).[61] The projected poem "Ovide chez les Scythes" was never written, and Valéry's notes on the subject have almost nothing to say about Ovid and, instead, much about the psychology of the poet. Neither *La jeune Parque* nor *Charmes* can be called Ovidian in the thematic sense of the other works thus far considered. In the mysteriously beautiful long poem, the mythological figures provide suggestive but fleeting images; and the quotations in *Charmes* are not further elaborated. So we must reluctantly but finally resist the temptation to include Valéry among the poets of the *annus mirabilis Ovidianus.*

TRISTIA IN THE CRIMEA

Osip Mandelstam deserves his place in this special year principally because his second volume of poetry was titled *Tristia,* after one of the longest and finest poems in the collection. His friend Mikhail Kuzmin supplied the name when he arranged for its publication that year (1922) in a Russian émigré press in Berlin. Although Mandelstam called the volume in its second edition simply *The Second Book* (1923), he subsequently reverted to the original title, which for a variety of reasons seems appropriate. Like his Anglo-American counterparts,

Mandelstam (1891–1938) had the benefit of a thorough training in Latin at St. Petersburg's Tenishev School (where he was followed a few years later by Vladimir Nabokov). His study of Romance philology at universities in Paris, Heidelberg, and St. Petersburg profoundly deepened his knowledge of the Roman tradition in literature. As a result, the Latin classics were familiar to him from his youth (he knew Greek much less well), and his works abound in allusions to, and quotations from, classical antiquity. "The old world is 'not of this world,'" he wrote in 1921 in an essay titled "The Word and Culture," "yet it is more alive than it ever was."[62] Along with Anna Akhmatova and her husband Nikolai Gumilev, Mandelstam was a central figure in the "acmeist" movement, which in reaction against romanticism and symbolism placed its emphasis on precision of language. In defiance first of the Slavophilic and later the Soviet rejection of foreign influences, he once defined acmeism as "a nostalgia for world culture."[63] Mandelstam's poetry is typical of acmeism in its assumption that the reader, knowledgeable in the classics of Western literature, will recognize explicit and implicit quotations from extraneous texts—an assumption, as we shall see, that was often borne out in his allusions to Ovid's works. The acmeist stress on precision of language and the use of quotations from the classical literary canon precisely parallels the convictions and practices developed independently during these same years by Ezra Pound and T. S. Eliot.

The circumstances of his life bound Mandelstam more closely to Ovid than to most other writers of antiquity, for Mandelstam was on many counts an outsider in his own culture. First, as a Jew in anti-Semitic imperial Russia he was made throughout his life to feel alienated from his society (and had to convert to Christianity in order to be admitted to the University of St. Petersburg). Second, as a Russian Jew born in Warsaw and growing up in St. Petersburg in a family with close ties to the intelligentsia, then as a foreign student abroad in Paris and Heidelberg, and later more at home in the border areas of Finland and the Crimea than in St. Petersburg and Moscow, he seemed always to be isolated from the centers of Russian culture. Third, as a nonreligious Jew who despite his great talent for languages refused to learn Hebrew, as a youthful socialist who soon rejected Marxism, and as a writer constantly and even ebulliently at odds with his literary colleagues, Mandelstam was the archetypal outsider—a situation highlighted by the erratic social behavior noted by many of his friends and later by his reckless and seemingly self-destructive provocations of the Soviet authorities.[64] These actions led to the official censure that sent him, toward the end of his life, into a three-year exile and then to his death in Siberia.

Mandelstam's first two volumes, *Stone* (1913; enlarged edition 1916) and *Tristia* (1922), contain several conspicuously Ovidian poems. These poems, products of a time of war and revolution, reflect the years of wandering that led Mandelstam—often in flight from the threats of the new Soviet regime as well as the vindictive vengeance of the White Guard—back and forth between Moscow, the Ukraine, and the Crimea. In the Crimean town of Feodosia, Mandelstam could gaze out across the Black Sea and imagine Ovid in his own exile on the western shore almost exactly nineteen hundred years earlier. Accordingly, his sense of identification with Ovid is strong in the poems written during these years and published in the various editions of *Stone* and in *Tristia,* which takes its title from a poem based explicitly on the Roman poet's elegies of exile.[65]

Ovid is mentioned explicitly or implicitly several times in the earlier volume, which contains a further half-dozen poems about Rome.[66] A poem written when he was only nineteen (no. 12; 1910) and still had little experience outside of the world of books, deals generally with the vagaries of life and fate, but ends with a dramatic allusion to savages who "raise javelins / Tipped with poison, poised to throw"—an image borrowed directly from Ovid's *Epistulae ex Ponto* (3.1.25–26). In 1914 (no. 60) his recollection of a scene in St. Petersburg, in which a horse-drawn carriage pulls up to an iron gate guarded by a lazy doorman who looks like a Scythian, reminds the poet of the epistles in which Ovid complained to his Roman friends about the bitter winters at Tomis, threatened by "the marching barbarian throng."[67] A year later, when Mandelstam had first visited the Crimea, the images of one of his most famous poems (no. 80) appear less bookish and much more vivid (even though the poet mistakenly identifies Ovid's birthplace as Rome rather than Sulmo), and the images of fall succeed in suggesting not only the autumn of Ovid's life but also the decline of empire.[68]

> Grazing horse herds joyfully neigh,
> The valley has gone red with Roman rust;
> Time's clear torrents are bearing away
> A classical spring's gold dust.

As the poet strolls through the autumn landscape, with its ripened apples that remind him of the orb of empire, he thinks of Augustus. But in this poem the poet is reconciled with his destiny.

> Here, amid the quiet fading of nature
> Far from the Forum and the Capitol
> I hear Augustus, and on the earth's rim I hear
> The years rolling, like the sovereign apple.

The last strophe combines associations of Romulus and Remus, nurtured according to legend by a wolf, with the last month of summer (that is, the month that Augustus named after himself but also the summer or most brilliant period of Ovid's career in Rome before his exile) and ends on a note of harmonious acceptance.

> When I am old, then let my sorrows shine:
> I was born in Rome and Rome has come back to me;
> The autumn was my she-wolf and was kind
> And August—the month of Caesar—smiled on me.

It is an easy step from the modern poet writing in the Crimea at the time of the World War I and Ovid in Tomis hearing from afar news of the Roman wars in Germany. "I want Ovid, Pushkin, and Catullus to live once more," Mandelstam wrote in his essay "The Word and Culture," "and I am not satisfied with the historical Ovid, Pushkin, and Catullus." Here, in a poem widely regarded as an attempt to compose for Ovid a final letter of reconciliation from Tomis, we see his effort to make the Roman poet live again.[69] It goes without saying that this identification implies a certain thematic belief in transformation.

The volume *Tristia* is unified by its focus on *Endzeiten*—final periods in the history of various pasts, from Troy before its destruction and postexilic Judea to St. Petersburg during the last years of Imperial Russia.[70] In this sequence, the period leading up to the decline of the Roman empire takes its natural place. The fact of his own exile enables Mandelstam to establish parallels between his time and Ovid's—a metamorphosis, as it were, leading from the Roman poet to himself.

The principal example is the title poem (no. 104).[71] Written in 1918 during yet another stay in the Crimea—this time to avoid the reign of terror following the revolution a few months earlier—the poem plays explicitly on lines from Ovid's elegy of leave-taking from Rome (*Tr.* 1.3). Mandelstam's familiarity with the poem, which was read widely in Russian high schools at the turn of the century,[72] is not a matter of mere speculation. In his essay "The Word and Culture," written three years later, he quotes the first four lines of the elegy in Latin:

> Cum subit illius tristissima noctis imago,
> Quae mihi supremum tempus in urbe fuit,
> Cum repeto noctem, qua tot mihi cara reliqui,
> Labitur ex oculis nunc quoque gutta meis.

> (When I am overcome by the gloomy image of that
> night which was my last hour in Rome; when I recall
> the night when I left behind so many dear things,
> even now a tear flows from my eyes.)

The first strophe of Mandelstam's "Tristia" amounts almost to a pastiche of allusions to lines where Ovid describes the weeping of his wife, household, and friends as he delays his departure to the last minute in the early morning hours, until Caesar's command finally forces him to depart. Some critics have even seen, in the phrase "a science of farewells," a play on Ovid's "science" of love, as though Ovid's Black Sea elegies constituted an *ars valedicendi* that the modern poet studied for his own purposes.[73]

> In night's bare-headed laments
> I've learned the science of farewells.
> Oxen chew, you wait, you wait,
> the city's last hour of watching, waiting,
> and I honor the ritual of a rooster night
> when tear-red eyes stared at the distance
> and took up a load of portable sorrow,
> and a woman's weeping mixed with the Muses' songs.

The following strophe, true to Mandelstam's acmeist theory of world culture, rings variations on the basic theme of leave-taking introduced by the Ovidian title and allusions, and begins to realign Ovid's paradigm of departure and exile onto a positive path.

> Who can know, when farewells are spoken,
> what separation will bring us,
> what cock-crows promise,
> when fires burn in the city,
> or why, at the dawn of some new life,
> an ox chews lazily in the hall
> and a rooster, herald of new lives,
> flaps his wings on the city wall.

In "The Word and Culture" Mandelstam speaks of "the rooster crowing outside the window" in Ovid's *Tristia,* but in fact no cocks appear in the farewell elegy. The mistaken association with Ovid, however, allows the poet, by the threefold reference to cock-crows, to make a transition to Peter's betrayal of Jesus;[74] but that biblical leave-taking is also a "herald of new lives" in a postclassical Christian future.

The image of spinning that governs the third strophe exemplifies the theme of Nietzschean eternal recurrence and also, by allusion, introduces Pushkin, the author of early poems to Delia.[75] The example of Pushkin, whose exile a century earlier produced his poem "To Ovid," underscores the analogy between the exiles and their Roman predecessor, quite in the spirit of Rilke's theory that all poets are later metamorphoses of an ur-poet, while the motif of spinning suggests Ovid's Arachne image in which weaving is a metaphor for the art of poetry.

> I like this routine of spinning:
> shuttle scurries, spindle hums,
> look, like swansdown, coming to meet you
> a barefooted Delia, running.
> Oh the thin, thin foundation of existence,
> the poverty-struck language of joy!
> Everything's been told before, everything will happen again,
> and all that's sweet is the instant of recognition.

The introduction of female figures adds a new dimension to the poem, which concludes with another image borrowed from Pushkin (*Eugene Onegin*)—an image of divination by means of wax drippings in water. The theme of soothsaying, coupled with a line concerning the stretched squirrel skin taken from Anna Akhmatova (to whom Mandelstam addressed his poem "Cassandra" [No. 95]),[76] brings the poem around from the weeping women of the opening strophe to women who foretell the future. The poet, implying that women have a connection to the beyond that men lack, juxtaposes the *vita activa* of ancient warriors and modern soldiers to the *vita contemplativa* of women (which presumably the poet also shares).[77]

> So be it: a tiny transparent figure
> lies in a clean clay dish,
> stretched like a squirrel skin,
> and a girl stares, bending over the wax.
> Telling fortunes about Greek Erebus: not for us.
> Wax is to women as bronze to a man.
> Battles work out our fate, only battles,
> but they can die, if they want to, while casting fortunes.

When Mandelstam was arrested in May 1934 for political slander and a ruthless satire about Stalin—a striking analogy, as has often been pointed out, to Ovid's crime of *carmen et error*—he was first sent to the remote northern town of Cherdyn and later, thanks to the intervention of powerful friends, to a less-severe exile in Voronezh. Having completed his term of exile in May 1937, he was arrested for a second time a year later and sentenced to hard labor in eastern Siberia, where he died in December 1938. The last four years of his life not only appear to reify the exile theme of his earlier poetry; they also reenact in an uncanny parallel the paradigm of Ovid's life, which ended in a remote and difficult exile for having offended his ruler.

Despite their brilliance, these various efforts in the year 1922 in France, England, Switzerland, and Russia to rehabilitate Ovid were not widely successful. Robert Graves's bitter poem "Ovid in Defeat" (1925), for instance, betrays an almost personal animosity toward Ovid, whom Graves finds "grotesque in Pontic snows / And bearskin breeches," and toward the love code of his *Ars amatoria*.[78] When Edward Kennard Rand wrote his pathbreaking introduction to *Ovid and His Influence* in 1925 he concluded sadly: "Ovid was too modern for the Dark Age; perhaps he is too modern for ours" (173). Yet Rand saw at least a ray of hope. "The Dark Age had the disadvantage of not possessing Ovid's works. We who have erred can easily make amends. It is a comfortable penance; open his books and read" (174). Apparently many writers did so.

◢ 5 ◤

THE MODERNIZATION OF METAMORPHOSIS

THE REDISCOVERY OF METAMORPHOSIS

The idea of metamorphosis was centrally prevalent in the minds of many high modernists immediately before and after World War I—metamorphosis as a reflection of the rapidly changing world that they saw around them as the social, political, and cultural foundations of the nineteenth century crumbled and the twentieth century began to emerge from the ruins. But for the writers considered up to this point, metamorphosis remained essentially a metaphor. Hofmannsthal's Ariadne and Bacchus are transformed by love, but only inwardly—to a consciousness of divinity and to the transformation of grief into joy. Stephen Dedalus dreams of the "hawklike" man as he prepares to leave Ireland, but retains his own physical form. For Ezra Pound, the mythological images of metamorphosis exemplify his belief in the cultural endurance of the permanent within the transient. T. S. Eliot introduces the bisexual Tiresias as the implied and unseen narrator of *The Waste Land,* but the figures upon whose behavior he comments belong very much to a nonmythic early twentieth-century Europe. The "transformation" that Rilke desires and recommends ("Wolle die Wandlung") is the power of imagination to reach past the reality of the present to embrace the beyond. Mandelstam's idea of transformation refers principally to his keen sense of identification with Ovid as exile, in whose spirit he writes his own elegies of departure and loss. But several of their contemporaries carried the idea of metamorphosis, and to striking effect, far beyond the metaphorical.

A familiar but curious fact of literary history is that Ovid never used the word that subsequently achieved renown as the title of his magnum opus. The Latin language of his time had no precise equivalent for the Greek vocable *metamorphosis,* and the noun *transformatio* was apparently first used in the fourth century.[1] But Ovid had recourse in rich abundance to variations on words such as those in his opening sentence: *In nova fert animus mutatas dicere formas / corpora* ("My mind inspires me to speak of forms changed into new bodies").[2] It was later critics of the first century who began to refer to his poem as *Metamorphoses:* notably the elder Seneca in his *Controversiae* (3.7), and Quintilian in his *Institutio oratoria* (4.1.77). Even in the absence of the word, Ovid provided a philosophical basis for the scores of metamorphoses that he related in his poem. Roughly half of the last book (15.60–478) is devoted to the extensive discourse of the "man born in Samos" and living in voluntary exile in Croton: the philosopher Pythagoras (who is never mentioned by name). Pythagoras's entire philosophy, including his aggressive vegetarianism, is based on the theory of metamorphosis: that "all things change, nothing perishes" (*omnia mutantur, nihil interit,* 15.165). "I teach that the spirit is always the same but migrates into constantly changing bodies" (*animam sic semper eandem / esse, sed in varias doceo migrare figuras,* 15.171–72). This is the central idea that he reiterates with examples ranging from the four shifting elements of nature (fire, air, earth, and water) by way of the changing seasons and geographical-geological formations to human development.

> Nec species sua cuique manet, rerumque novatrix
> ex aliis alias reparat natura figuras;
> nec perit in toto quicquam, mihi credite, mundo,
> sed variat faciemque novat, nascique vocatur
> incipere esse aliud quam quod fuit ante, morique,
> desinere illud idem. cum sint huc forsitan illa,
> haec translata illuc, summa tamen omnia constant.
>
> (15.252–58)

> (No shape retains its own form, and nature, the
> renewer of things, creates new figures from other
> ones: nothing perishes, believe me, in the entire
> universe; it simply varies and renews its
> appearance. Being born is nothing but a term for
> beginning to be something other than what it
> was before, and dying means ceasing to be that
> same thing. Although things are shifted about—
> those things to here and these things to there—
> the total sum remains constant.)

This theory of constant change had little appeal for ages whose entire justification depended on a belief in order and stability—the Christian Middle Ages
and the great empires of the seventeenth, eighteenth, and nineteenth centuries.[3]
The importance and meaning of the ancient theory of transformation was rediscovered and emphasized on the eve of the twentieth century by Jacob Burckhardt (1818–97) in his posthumously published *Cultural History of Greece*
(*Griechische Kulturgeschichte*, 1898–1902).[4] The third section of the work, which
deals with "Religion and Cults," opens with a chapter devoted entirely to "Metamorphoses."[5] Burckhardt begins with a reminder that the theory of metempsychosis sought throughout the 7th and 6th centuries BCE to penetrate the Greek
mind—an idea that, despite the efforts of Plato, was rejected by the people, who
preferred to retain their belief in a permanent beyond of some sort. Parallel to
the idea of metempsychosis, but unrelated to it, was the ancient notion of metamorphosis: the belief among many peoples that the souls of the dead pass over
into certain animals. Burckhardt concludes that this belief must at one time have
been widespread among the Greeks; otherwise the stories would not have fascinated and provided so much material for later poets and collectors. (While
most of the texts have been lost, various classical writers allude to the titles of
collections prior to Ovid and the second-century compiler Antoninus Liber-
alis.)[6] Burckhardt assumes that, in its original form, the idea must have run something like this.

> All of nature—not simply human beings and animals but also plants, min-
> erals, and waters—are imagined as alive and even conscious, as has been
> shown to be the case here and there among primitive peoples; man became
> acquainted with "his brothers in the quiet brush, in air and water," and rul-
> ing over them one imagined the gods, who perhaps destroy nothing and
> scarcely create anything, but are capable of transforming the individual liv-
> ing being magically from one shape into the other. What was human and in-
> dividual is then (be it out of revenge or pity and favor) given back to the
> fullness of nature, to what is constant and non-individual; and now people
> sense related beings everywhere in animals, trees, springs, and strangely
> shaped rock formations. (7–8)

The prevalence of legends about the gods themselves, and their identification
with specific animals, suggests what currency the idea of transformation enjoyed
among the Greeks. Burckhardt goes on, here and in the appended notes (396–
406), to analyze various categories of metamorphosis, whether as punishment
or favor: transformations into landscape objects, into animals, plants, other human beings, waters, birds, constellations, and so forth. He then turns his atten-

tion to other matters and has nothing further to say about metamorphosis, which ceases to play a role in Greek religions and cults.

However, metamorphosis appears to be an idea whose time had arrived by the early twentieth century. We have already observed its manifestations in the poetry of the period. And in the works of other thinkers, transformation begins to occupy a prominent position. Rilke, as we saw, was attracted to the ideas of Bachofen as promulgated by his disciple Alfred Schuler. (Schuler was a leader in the Bachofen Renaissance that began around 1900 in Munich in the so-called Cosmic Circle with Schuler, Karl Wolfskehl, and Ludwig Klages and later included such scholars as Benedetto Croce and Carl Albrecht Bernoulli.)[7]

Equally important for our purposes are the writings of yet another Swiss thinker after Bachofen and Burckhardt, Carl Gustav Jung (1875–1961). Transformation plays a significant role in Jung's first major and independent work, the one that precipitated the break with his mentor Freud: *Transformations and Symbols of the Libido (Wandlungen und Symbole der Libido,* (1912).[8] Jung, who had the benefit of a sound classical education and throughout his career ransacked Greek and Latin texts for his research, does not mention (or quote) Ovid's *Metamorphoses* often in his book: notably in connection with Bacchus and the Eleusinian cult (*Met.* 4.18–20), and with reference to Attis's transformation into a pine tree (*Met.* 10.104).[9] But as his title clearly indicates, transformation is a central theme in the work. One of the underlying tenets of Jung's system is that our dreams and imagination are filled with archetypal images preserved in the collective unconscious. Although we like to believe that civilization has refined primitive human traits out of our character, that is a severe misconception. Christianity sought to transform the immorality and brutality that it confronted. Yet, writing in 1912, just before the outbreak of the war, Jung ascertained that "never before has our civilization been so swamped with evil."[10] Even when individuals succeed in transforming themselves, they are simply substituting one archetype for another while the old form loses none of its appeal (236). In his psychology, Jung explains elsewhere, the self is an *imago Dei* and Christ a manifestation of the self. Seen in this light, the hero of typical hero myths is "the protagonist of God's transformation in man" (392). By analogy, the widespread fantasies of an apocalyptic end to human civilization, the world conflagration, is for Jung "the projected primordial image of the great transformation" of life into death (438). Nietzsche's radical "transvaluation of values" becomes, for Jung, a "transformation and conservation" rather than the destruction of what we hold sacred (357). Clearly, Jung as a psychologist is concerned chiefly with the inner transformation of the individual. But to achieve that end he makes extensive use of myths of metamorphosis borrowed from cultures all over the world, to which his encyclopedic reading and learning led him. Accordingly, the theme of metamorphosis and transformation continues to show up in such later works as *Archetypes and the Collective Unconscious, Civilization in Transition,* or the Eranos lectures on metempsychosis (*Über Wiedergeburt,* 1939).

Through such thinkers as Bachofen, Burckhardt, Jung, and Schuler, theories of transformation and metamorphosis, quite independently of Ovid, made their way into the consciousness of the early twentieth century. Transformation, as we have just seen, became thanks to Jung a central concept in modern psychology. But it also assumed a significant function in other fields of thought.[11] Metamorphosis is essential, for instance, to modern biogenetic theory, which posits development and change not simply in the organism but, through evolution, in the entire species. In religion the term is used to designate both the psychic transformation of the individual and, in Christian thought, the physical transubstantiation of the Eucharist. In anthropology metamorphosis is used in the aetiological explanation of ritual practices and myths.[12] At this point Ovid's *Metamorphoses* imposed themselves on the modern mind as the richest poetic source for tales of transformation.

Ovidian metamorphosis can take place either spiritually or physically, and it can be characterized as "degradation" (as Hegel viewed the transformation of human beings into lower forms of nature) or "ascension" (the Virgin Mary, but also Callisto). It can be reversible (Tiresias) or irreversible (Daphne). Finally, it can be either metaphoric or metonymic.[13] Metaphoric metamorphosis means, in narrative, the transformation of an individual into the object designated semiotically by his or her name: either positively (Daphne into a laurel) or negatively (Lycaon into a wolf).[14] Metonymic metamorphosis, in contrast, designates the process by which an individual is abruptly transformed into something with no semiotic connection to his or her character. Examples of the latter are unusual in Ovid, but he provides a classic example in the tale of Actaeon, who is transformed into a stag and then torn apart by his own hounds, simply because he accidentally glimpses Diana bathing in the nude. Neither his name nor his character anticipates or suggests in any way the terrible fate that awaits him. His case is unusual, moreover, in that he is transformed into something unique that is destroyed and not enduring or renewed (like the plant and animal species in the *Metamorphoses* or the stone formations, waters, or constellations in which most of the transformations result). These terms help us to categorize and distinguish among various literary forms of metamorphosis.

METAMORPHOSIS IN PRAGUE

Gregor Samsa's sudden transformation into a great insect constitutes a textbook case of metonymic metamorphosis:[15] as in the case of Actaeon, his metamor-

phosis is not foretold by his name; as there—a point emphasized by Ovid in order to heighten the horror of this fate—his mind remains constant during his
ordeal (*mens tantum pristina mansit; Met.* 3.203);[16] and as there his story ends with
his death, not with any redemptive or generic eternalization. Ovid narrates another case of metonymic metamorphosis: the story of Callisto (*Met.* 2.401–530),
who is transformed into a bear and still retains her consciousness (*mens antiqua
tamen facta quoque mansit in ursa; Met.* 2.485): unlike Actaeon, she is subsequently
eternalized along with her son in the constellations Ursa Major and Ursa Minor, but in her case, as in Gregor Samsa's, we are told about the fifteen years she
spends as a bear before her son Arcas grows old enough to confront her as a
huntsman and almost to kill her. By these Ovidian analogies, Kafka's *Metamorphosis* can be clearly distinguished from Gogol's story *The Nose,* to which it is
sometimes compared.[17] First, in *The Nose* there is no transformation as such;
Kovalyev simply loses a part of his body, his nose, which briefly leads a life of its
own—a fantastic occurrence of a type with no parallel in Ovid. Second, and
more significant, the process is reversible: at the end his nose is restored.

The point is worth making because it is not generally reported that Franz
Kafka (1883–1924) had a sound knowledge of Latin and the Latin classics. In the
Altstädter Gymnasium, the strictest secondary school in Prague, Kafka benefited
from unusually good instruction in Latin by the Piarist monk Emil Gschwind.[18]
In addition to seven or eight classroom hours per week, Gschwind required his
better students—and the records indicate that Kafka was one of the top three
students in his class—to do a considerable amount of outside reading and to
collect and memorize exemplary passages in notebooks, which they had to submit or declaim to Gschwind at regular intervals on Sundays in his monas-
tery. With this exceptional Latinist and fine humanist, then, over a period of
several years Kafka studied major sections of the *Metamorphoses* and, for his
supplementary reading, chose further passages from the same poem (from books
12 and 14) as well as from the *Epistulae ex Ponto* (4.3). In addition, the class read
not only an extensive passage from the *Fasti* but also the acclaimed departure
from Rome from the *Tristia* (1.3) as well as the autobiography (*Tr.* 4.10). In sum,
Kafka was acquainted at first hand with all of Ovid's works and, notably, with
the *Metamorphoses.*

Kafka's *Metamorphosis* (*Die Verwandlung,* written 1912) is not only technically
a metonymic transformation but is also by autobiographical transference a metaphoric metamorphosis. We know from several sources that Kafka's father had
the unpleasant habit of referring to his son and his son's friends contemptuously
as insects: "bedbugs" ("Wanzen"), "fleas" ("Flöhe"), and "vermin" ("Ungezie-
fer").[19] Kafka's story amounts in one sense to a microscopically detailed reification of that metaphor. There can be absolutely no question about Gregor
Samsa's transformation. It is neither a dream nor a projection of his imagina-

tion: he has, fantastically and inexplicably, become a huge bug. Kafka himself, in a letter to his publisher, refers to his hero as an "insect," even though he insists that the designer should not attempt to portray the insect on the book cover.[20] "When Gregor Samsa woke up one morning from restless dreams, he found himself transformed in his bed into a huge bug," the story begins.[21] And from that moment on, no one in the story questions his transformation.

In the first of the three sections, which covers the first day of his transformation from morning to evening, we see Gregor (like Actaeon and Callisto) becoming gradually aware of the details of his new body—its many tiny legs tipped with a sticky substance, its antennae, its toothless mouth, its diminished vision, its taste for spoiled vegetables and stale cheese, its new ability to crawl on the walls and ceiling—as he thinks about the train he missed, the ensuing visit of the general manager of the textile firm in which he is employed, and his dissatisfactions with his job. The second part, which covers the next two months, shifts the focus to Gregor's family—father, mother, sister—and the effect that his transformation has upon them. In the third and final section, which lasts for several more months down to the spring day on which Gregor dies, Gregor is preoccupied primarily with himself.[22]

What is open to interpretation, of course, is the meaning of this transformation, which has obsessed half a century of Kafka critics with exegeses and deconstructions ranging from the symbolic to the allegorical, from the religious to the existential, from the psychoanalytical to the metaphysical.[23] Kafka himself has provided one clue that cannot reasonably be omitted from any consideration. In a conversation with his friend Gustav Janouch some ten years after writing the story, Kafka talked about the current popularity of animal tales. "Each one of us lives behind a fence that he carries around with himself. For that reason people write so much nowadays about animals. It is an expression of our longing for a free, natural life. . . . Human existence is too arduous, and for that reason one wishes to shake it off at least in the imagination."[24] In fact it can be easily demonstrated that, in Kafka's metaphorical scale of values before World War I, animal imagery is used specifically to characterize men—like Josef K., the protagonist of *The Trial,* who dies "like a dog"—who renounce their freedom and responsibility.[25]

Kafka's story revolves in a very important sense around the dynamics of the family. As the story begins, Gregor is the sole support of his family: his father, whose business failed five years earlier, is unemployed and, in addition, heavily in debt to Gregor's employer; his mother is frail and suffers from asthma; his seventeen-year-old sister is a gifted violinist, and Gregor hopes to be able to send her to the music conservatory. In other words, they are wholly dependent upon Gregor, who hates his job as a traveling salesman for a textile firm: his haughty and paternalistic boss, the need to get up early, the worry about train connections, the bad food in second-rate hotels, the human contacts from day to day that never have a chance to develop and become genuine. "The devil take it all," he thinks as he lies in bed on that first morning. If it were not for his parents he would have given notice long ago and told his boss his true opinion. It is his fervent hope to save within five or six years enough money to pay off his parents' debt and then to resign from a detested position. Feeling trapped in his own existence, however, Gregor implicitly acknowledges the reluctance to accept responsibility suggested by the animal image that he reifies.

Consequently, he can only remain in his room and eavesdrop on the conversations taking place among his family in the adjoining room. Although his sister puts food in his room, she cannot bear to look at him; so he hides under the couch when she approaches. His parents refuse even to enter the room for the first two weeks. But as the family comes to grips with necessity they gradually become more independent. His father takes a lowly position as attendant at a bank, and in his blue uniform with its gold buttons he begins to feel important once again and moves around the apartment with authority. On one occasion he throws an apple at Gregor to drive him back into his room—an apple that embeds itself in Gregor's back and causes the infection that ultimately leads to his death. Soon the others begin to do their part. His sister takes a position as a salesgirl in a lingerie shop and studies stenography and French in the evenings— that is, she forsakes her artistic ambitions for a practical career. The live-in maid is replaced by a woman who comes in to do the heaviest chores. Meanwhile, his mother takes in sewing and prepares occasional meals for the three tenants to whom the family has rented a room.

When, after many months, Gregor ventures forth one evening to listen to his sister's violin, he is spotted by the tenants, who indignantly give notice and even threaten to demand compensation. At this point the family realizes that they must somehow dispose of "this beast," which his sister refuses any longer to call her brother. "We've got to try to get rid of it," she exclaims. "We have done what's humanly possible to care for it and to tolerate it; I don't believe that anybody can reproach us in the slightest." Gregor, who contrary to his family's belief understands the entire conversation, retreats to his room; and early the following morning, "in a state of empty and peaceful contemplation," he finally succumbs to the infection that has plagued him for months. The next morning the servant woman, the only person who still looks in on Gregor from time to time, announces to the family that "it has croaked" ("krepiert"—a coarse term for the dying of an animal) and discreetly gets rid of the scrawny remains. "Well, now we can give thanks to God," is Herr Samsa's only comment, and the three of them make the sign of the cross.

At this point and for the last two pages both the narrative point of view and the mood of the story change dramatically, for the entire family seems rejuvenated, hopeful, and optimistic on this lovely spring day. It is not irrelevant that Gregor's death has restored the family to the triadic unity that Kafka seems to regard as symbolically complete and whole: in many of his stories and novels figures appear in constellations of three. In any case, it is with a new sense of assurance that Herr Samsa kicks the three tenants out of his house. With a sense of relief, the family, now once again an integral triad, decides to take the day off for rest and relaxation. Leaving the apartment together—something they have not done for months, since Gregor's metamorphosis—they take the streetcar out into the countryside. There, in the freedom of nature and in the warm spring sun, they review their circumstances and conclude that things are not so bad after all. They decide to give up the old apartment with its bad associations and to take a smaller one, better situated and more reasonable. Gazing at their daughter, father and mother notice how greatly she has blossomed in recent months and realize that it is time to look around for a decent husband for her. The story ends with the confirmation of their new dreams and good intentions.[26] Kafka, anticipating some of his commentators, was dissatisfied with this epilogue, in which the sister's happy metamorphosis—the emergence of the nymph from the chrysalis of the home, as it were—seems to be an ironic and even cruel comment on Gregor's degradation.[27] Moreover, the epilogue demanded a radical shift in viewpoint, from Gregor to his family—a narrative strategy that may well have displeased Kafka's aesthetic sense.

The formal analysis of Kafka's *Metamorphosis* as an example of Ovidian metonymic metamorphosis raises several interesting questions. On the one hand, the choice of the insect image pushes any interpretation in a specific direction, for we know from his other works of this period (notably *The Trial*) that Kafka used animal images to suggest what Hegel would call degradation: that is, the choice of image in itself indicates Gregor's decision to renounce his human freedom and responsibility.[28] On the other hand, his transformation does not result from the curse of a goddess, as in the cases of Actaeon and Callisto; Kafka leaves unspecified the reasons for his metamorphosis, which has already taken place at the time we read the first sentence. The reasons must be sought in Gregor's relationship to his family, his job, and ultimately himself. Finally, the focus on metamorphosis, whether Ovidian or more generally Jungian, enables us to define the form of Kafka's story and also to put it in perspective through comparison with other works of the period.

TRANSFORMATIONS IN THE TICINO

While Kafka's *Metamorphosis* was written in the year of Jung's *Transformations and Symbols of the Libido,* the Strauss/Hofmannsthal *Ariadne auf Naxos,* and de

Chirico's Ariadne paintings—none of which he presumably knew—Hermann Hesse's story *Pictor's Metamorphoses* (*Piktors Verwandlungen*) appeared in the *annus mirabilis Ovidianus* of 1922.

Like Kafka and many other contemporaries, Hesse (1877–1962) was a solid Latinist. During his first semester at the distinguished Swabian boarding school at Maulbronn, to which he was admitted on the basis of country-wide competitive examinations, Hesse in his letters frequently mentions Ovid, whose *Metamorphoses* belong to his favorite subjects. In the first week (mid-September 1891) he reports to his parents that he needs three notebooks for Ovid alone.[29] A month and a half later he confides that he does not especially enjoy Latin prosody but that "it is a delight to read Ovid" (133). Within a few days Ovid makes his way into an early poem by the schoolboy:

> Solon, Lykurg und all die Alten
> In Lederbänden dick und schwer,
> Ovids verliebte Kerngestalten
> Erleichtern jedes Lernen sehr.
>
> (136)

> (Solon, Lycurgus, and all the
> ancients, thick and heavy in their
> leather volumes; Ovid's infatuated
> figures make all learning much
> easier.)

In the same letter (to his grandfather) he apologizes for stopping, but "leatherbound Ovid is waiting impatiently at my desk" (137). At the end of November, listing his favorite subjects, he calls Ovid "fine!" (142); and a week later he reports that he is reading the passage on "envy" from the *Metamorphoses:* "Splendid reading. I enjoy translating Ovid into German hexameters" (145).

Hesse's formal education ended a few months later when he ran away from Maulbronn. For the next year and a half his parents tried to place him in various schools but eventually gave up, and for several years he worked at a succession of jobs until he was able to establish himself as a self-supporting writer. But he retained his interest, and ability, in the classics for the remainder of his life. The volumes that he later edited, for instance, included "Tales from the Middle Ages" (*Geschichten aus dem Mittelalter*, 1925), to which he contributed his own translation from the *Dialogus miraculorum* of Caesarius of Heisterbach. And Ovid takes his place among the many works cited in Hesse's essay "A Library of World Literature" ("Eine Bibliothek der Weltliteratur," 1929).

It was not only Ovid who shaped Hesse's notions of metamorphosis. Hesse came to maturity in Basel, where he moved in 1899 to work in a bookshop. In an account of his early years in Basel (1899–1903) Hesse wrote: "Here everything was saturated by the spirit, the influence, and the example of the man who for several decades had served intellectual Basel as a teacher and, in cultural affairs, as *arbiter elegantiarum*. His name was Jacob Burckhardt, and he had died only a few years earlier."[30] Hesse goes on to say that he was too deeply enchanted at the time by Nietzsche to be completely susceptible to Burckhardt's influence. But he had already read *The Culture of the Renaissance,* and in Basel he continued to peruse Burckhardt's works—just during the years when his *Cultural History of Greece* was appearing. "I lived, a receptive young man eager to learn, in the midst of a circle of people whose knowledge and interest, whose reading and travels, whose way of thinking, conception of history and conversation were influenced and shaped by no one so much as Jacob Burckhardt." Three decades later the influence of Burckhardt made itself most directly felt when Hesse turned to his works and his person as the model for Pater Jacobus in *The Glass Bead Game (Das Glasperlenspiel,* 1943). It is unlikely that the young Hesse in Basel, the admirer of Ovid, was not exposed to Burckhardt's ideas on metamorphosis.

In 1916 Hesse suffered a nervous breakdown precipitated by various factors: the disintegration of his marriage; the death of his father; the serious illness of a son; the disparagement he had to suffer from one-time fans in Germany for the pacifism that he publicly advocated from his home in Switzerland. In 1916 and 1917 he undertook a series of consultations with Dr. Josef B. Lang, a disciple of Jung, in a sanatorium near Lucerne. In 1916 with Lang's encouragement Hesse read Jung's *Transformations and Symbols of the Libido,* a work that impressed him enormously and contributed to the shaping of the symbols in his novel *Demian* (1919). That same year, through Dr. Lang, Hesse met Jung. Later he read selections from his works to Jung's psychoanalytic association in Zürich, and around 1921 Hesse had a few analytic sessions with the master himself.[31]

The impact of psychoanalysis, despite Hesse's critical reservations, showed up in his works of these years, which can be read in one sense as a continuous act of self-analysis. Hesse accepted the need for a drastic inner transformation if he was to come to terms with the various conflicts that had driven him into an emotional breakdown. Hesse's own solution to this dilemma was what, in his essay on Dostoevsky's *Idiot* (1919), he defined as "magical thinking."[32] By "magical thinking" he meant the capacity of the individual to see beyond the apparent disharmony of polar opposites and to perceive the essential unity and totality of all things, within the individual as within the world.[33] Such novels as *Demian* (1919) and *Siddhartha* (1922) reflect these ideas, along with the essays on Dostoevsky published as *Blick ins Chaos* (1920; In sight of chaos), which captivated T. S.

Eliot so profoundly that he traveled to Switzerland to visit Hesse and then added a quotation from the volume to his notes for *The Waste Land*.

Jungian ideas are pronounced in *Demian:* the idea, for instance, that every individual bears within his soul all the cultural baggage of earlier souls or that Christ is not a person but a mythic hero; and the talk of mysteries and early religions. Above all the idea of "awakening"—that is, transformation into a new and higher level of consciousness—parallels the principles of Jungian analysis. But in *Demian* and most of the other works the transformation is a purely spiritual one. Occasionally the narrative goes a step further, as at the end of *Siddhartha,* where Govinda peers into the face of the dying Siddhartha and "no longer saw the face of his friend Siddhartha. Instead he saw other faces, many, a long series, a streaming river of faces, hundreds, thousands, all of which came and went, and yet all seemed to be there simultaneously, constantly changing and renewing themselves, and yet all were Siddhartha." Yet it is never suggested, in the long paragraph describing the many existences reflected in Siddhartha's face, that an actual physical transformation takes place. This situation changes in the fairy tale *Pictor's Metamorphoses.*[34]

The tale was written in 1922 for Ruth Wenger, to whom Hesse was later briefly married, after he moved to Montagnola, a village in the mountains above Lugano in the Swiss Ticino, only about a hundred kilometers east of Rilke's retreat in the Valais. Until its facsimile publication in 1954 it was available only in a small bibliophile edition (Chemnitz, 1925) and in manuscript copies that Hesse produced for sale and for which he painted accompanying watercolors reflecting the lush southern Swiss landscape).

The story is simple. As soon as Pictor (an obvious pseudonym for Hesse himself as "the painter") arrives in Paradise, he sees a tree that is simultaneously man and woman; but when a serpent emerges from it, he moves on and soon sees another tree—the Tree of Life—that is both sun and moon. (The accompanying watercolor shows a tree with two trunks, each bearing respectively smiling sun and moon faces—much like the Smiley Faces we have all seen.) Going on, he sees flowers that sing and laugh, that have large blue eyes and stick out their tongues flirtatiously. Captivated by these sights, he comes upon a bird sitting in the grass, variegated in multiple colors. When he asks the bird where to find happiness, the bird laughs and changes into a flower, a butterfly, and finally a glittering crystal. (Hesse's watercolors depict these various metamorphoses.) As Pictor seizes the stone, the serpent appears and tells him that it will change him into anything he wishes, but that he must wish quickly. Overjoyed, Pictor says the word and is immediately transformed into a tree because trees seem to enjoy so much tranquillity and dignity. For years Pictor enjoys his arboreal existence, plunging his roots into the earth and harboring beetles in his bark and birds in his branches. But eventually he notices that, while all the other beings in Paradise undergo constant transformations, he alone is not part of this magical stream of metamorphoses. "If creatures do not possess the gift of metamorphosis, they succumb in time to sadness and withering, and their beauty is lost." One day a girl wanders into his part of Paradise, singing and dancing. As he watches her, it dawns on Pictor that the serpent long ago gave him bad advice. Drawn by the rustling in his branches, the girl approaches and sits down under his tree. Leaning against the trunk, she feels his trembling and is overcome by a responsive melancholy. At that moment the multicolored bird comes flying up, attracted by the girl, and drops a colorful crystal at her feet. As soon as the girl takes the magical stone in her hand, Pictor's wish is fulfilled: she sinks down and becomes one with the tree, growing out of his trunk as a strong young branch. Now at last, Pictor has found true Paradise, for together with his Victoria his half has become whole, and they are able to enter the unending stream of transformations. "He became a deer, he became a fish, he became man and serpent, cloud and bird. But in every form he was whole, was a pair, contained moon and sun, man and woman within himself, flowed as a twin stream through the lands and stood as a double star in the heavens."

In this illustrated fairy tale Hesse is giving vivid narrative and pictorial expression to his theory of magical thinking and Jungian transformation. To achieve this goal, he has produced his own version of Ovid's tale of Hermaphroditus, the handsome son of Hermes, of whom the nymph Salmacis became overpoweringly enamored (*Met.*4.285 – 388). When he unsuspectingly bathes in her pool, she dives in and clings to him so fast that, with the aid of the gods, they are merged into one. Indeed, Hesse's image is so close to Ovid's that he might well have borrowed it or at least had it in mind:

> velut, si quis conducat cortice ramos,
> crescendo iungi pariterque adolescere cernit,
> sic, ubi conplexu coierunt membra enaci, . . .
> (*Met.* 4.375 – 77)

> (As when someone grafts branches on the
> bark of a tree and sees them growing
> together and maturing simultaneously, so
> were their members joined in a tenacious
> embrace.)

This association can be no more than speculation. But we know from other writings of this period that Hesse regarded hermaphroditism as an apt image for the attraction of certain great figures in their old age: Goethe, Lao-tse, and "from Leonardo da Vinci a similar mystery radiates, dangerously enticing like the charm of a hermaphrodite."[35] In any case, Hesse's tale represents as clearly as Kafka's *Metamorphosis* a metonymic transformation with clear analogies in Ovid's work. Here, however, the metamorphosis depicts an ascension rather than a degradation because Hesse regards transformation in the Jungian sense, and "magical thinking" in his own terminology, as a necessary stage in human development. And it reflects Burckhardt's portrayal of early Greek thought as permeated by the idea of a nature undergoing constant transformation and interaction with humankind.

DEGRADATION IN OXFORDSHIRE

Sometime around 1922 Kafka's friend Gustav Janouch handed him a copy of David Garnett's short novel, *Lady into Fox* (1922), with the comment that the author had copied the method of Kafka's *Metamorphosis*. "Oh, no," Kafka replied, "he didn't get that from me. It's in the times. We both copied from there. Animals are closer to us than people. . . . Relationships with animals are easier than with human beings."[36]

It is unlikely that Garnett (1892–1981) knew Kafka's story. *The Metamorphosis* was not translated into English until 1937, and Garnett, despite his fluency in French and competence in Russian, commanded the barest tourist's rudiments of German.[37] He came, to be sure, from an almost implausibly bookish family. His grandfather, a poet and biographer, had been keeper of printed books in the British Museum. His father was a writer and publisher's reader who sponsored Joseph Conrad and D. H. Lawrence among others. His mother, Constance, was the well-known translator of Tolstoy, Dostoevsky, Chekhov, and other Russian authors. Garnett himself, at the time he wrote his novel, owned a bookstore in London that was frequented by the literati. But there is nothing in his memoirs of his family and their wide circle of intellectuals and writers to suggest even the slightest interest in German literature, and certainly no mention of Kafka, at that time still unknown outside literary circles in German-speaking countries.

More important, however, is Kafka's comment that such stories were "in the times," a comment we have already seen substantiated by Hesse's fairy tale. Moreover, Garnett knew his Ovid. French and Latin, we read in his autobiography, were the two subjects in which he took pleasure and excelled in the course of his irregular schooling, and Ovid belonged to the standard curriculum of the time. His mother, before she turned her attention to Russian, had studied classics at Cambridge and taught Greek and Latin. Later we learn that an edition of the *Metamorphoses* from 1530 was "one of the treasures of my library."[38]

Garnett tells us precisely why he wrote his little novel. In the spring of 1922 and shortly after his marriage, he and his wife Ray were walking in the woods when Garnett, suspecting that there were fox cubs in the vicinity, insisted that they wait quietly for half an hour in the hope of seeing one. Finally realizing that their wait was futile, he quipped to his wife: "'There's no hope of seeing a fox—unless you were suddenly to turn into one. You might. I should not really be much surprised if you did.'"[39] Ray, amused by the conceit, immediately told him he should write it as a story. Spinning out the notion as they chatted, he imagined "how easily my intense love for her would overcome the trifling difficulties that would arise if she actually were transformed into one." The next day he began to write. Initially he had in mind a title with clear Ovidian resonances: "The Metamorphosis of Mrs Tebrick." But since it appealed to neither of them, his wife reminded him of a woodcut in his 1530 edition of the *Metamorphoses: Daphne mouée en laurier*. As they lamented the fact that English had no good word for the old French *mouée* ("turned into" or "transformed into"), it occurred to Garnett that he could shorten it simply to "into": *Lady into Fox*. Soon even the Ovidian subtitle was dropped. So there is no need to turn to Kafka as a source or stimulus for Garnett's novel—his second after an earlier potboiler about a heroin addict—, which was not only a surprise bestseller but also hailed as "a little masterpiece of perfect art" and as "a brilliant *tour de force*."[40]

Unlike Kafka's *Metamorphosis*, which is a typical metonymic transformation, *Lady into Fox* is at least partly metaphoric like Ovid's accounts of Daphne and Lycaon. The maiden name of Mrs. Tebrick, the woman who is transformed into a fox, is Fox; we learn from an old nurse that "Miss Silvia"—a given name that hints at a forest habitat—"was always a little wild at heart" (5).[41] Her family kept a half-tame fox chained up in the courtyard of their estate; and when as a child of ten she was "blooded" during a hunt, she was so disgusted that she vomited and never again rode to hounds in pursuit of the "poor foxes" (3). In sum, the opening pages anticipate metaphorically her transformation into the animal for which she is named. But this transformation is not ascendant, like Daphne's; more like Lycaon, she lives up, or down, to her animal nature. In addition, she resembles Actaeon and Gregor Samsa inasmuch as her transformation is not generic but specific and she dies at the end—killed, like Actaeon, by pursuing hounds. However, Garnett's story differs from both Ovid's and Kafka's to the extent that the sudden physical metamorphosis is followed by a gradual and continuous mental transformation.

Like Kafka, Garnett treats the seemingly supernatural events of his narrative in a straightforward manner. "The sudden changing of Mrs. Tebrick into a vixen is an established fact which we may attempt to account for as we will" (1)—a fact confirmed by dozens of respectable witnesses. Once we accept the absurd premise, the narrative proceeds strictly according to logic and is recounted in a rigorously realistic style. As in *The Metamorphosis,* Mrs. Tebrick's transformation takes place suddenly and almost on the first page of the story. "What adds to the difficulty to my mind," the narrator reflects, "is that the metamorphosis occurred when Mrs. Tebrick was a full-grown woman, and that it happened suddenly in so short a space of time" (2). The anatomical change would have been monstrous even had it occurred slowly as part of a child's development. But in this case "a grown lady is changed straightway into a fox. There is no explaining that away by any natural philosophy. The materialism of our age will not help us here" (2).

Here the similarities to Kafka end because Garnett's emphasis is completely different. Even as his insect body deteriorates with illness, Gregor Samsa's mind remains human and alert. Garnett, in contrast, is interested in the process of degradation—the meticulously recounted process during which Mrs. Tebrick gradually loses her human qualities and even Mr. Tebrick—wholly unlike the Samsa family—takes on animal characteristics from his wife. The metamorphosis or transformation—Garnett uses both terms several times—takes place in 1880 during the first year of Silvia's marriage, when she is twenty-three or twenty-four years old. One morning, as the affectionate couple are walking near their estate in Oxfordshire, they hear the sound of hounds and the huntsman's horn. Mr. Tebrick, himself an eager hunter, quickly moves forward to a position where he might get a good view of the hounds, but his wife hangs back reluctantly.

> Before they gained the edge of the copse she suddenly snatched her hand away from his very violently and cried out, so that he instantly turned his head.
> *Where his wife had been the moment before was a small fox, of a very bright red.*
> It looked at him very beseechingly, advanced towards him a pace or two, and he saw at once that his wife was looking at him from the animal's eyes. (5)

Although the vixen cannot speak, she appears to appeal to him with her eyes, imploring his pity and cuddling in his arms. For the first days and weeks he treats the animal as though it were still his wife, hoping all the time that she will revert to her normal shape. Indeed, "the womanliness in her never failed to delight him, for it showed she was still his wife, buried as it were in the carcase of a beast but with a woman's soul" (16). He sends away the servants, lest the neighbors gossip, and kills his own hounds so that they will not howl at or chase the fox. The vixen, in turn, retains for a time very human habits, wearing her former dressing gowns, allowing herself to be perfumed, drinking tea from a saucer, eating delicately at table, playing cards with her husband, enjoying music, looking into the stereoscope, making the sign of the cross with her paw, sleeping in the matrimonial bed, and nuzzling her husband. "Then anyone seeing them would have sworn that they were lovers, so passionately did each look on the other" (15).

Gradually, however, the process of degradation begins, albeit innocently at first. Mr. Tebrick first becomes aware of it when the vixen begins to take pleasure in startling the ducks in the pond. Next he catches her staring hungrily at her pet dove in its cage; and so he frees the bird. Soon she begins to crunch the bones of the chicken wings that he feeds her. Then she kills and devours a rabbit that he brings home as a test of her nature, smearing its blood over the furniture and rugs, her face sprinkled with blood and her claws full of fur and skin. To rid herself of the last trace of humanity she tears off the ribbons of the dressing gown in which her husband still tries to clothe her.

At this point Mr. Tebrick's own degradation begins subtly. Playing with the vixen one evening after several glasses of wine, he finds himself unsteady on his feet and goes down on all fours to chase her. "To what lengths he went then in that drunken humour I shall not offend my readers by relating" (38). Then Mrs. Tebrick's former nanny, Mrs. Cork, shows up and expresses her dismay at the disorder in which the two of them are living. To avoid the inquisitiveness of the neighborhood, Mr. Tebrick decides to move with his vixen to Mrs. Cork's cottage some miles away. But matters go from bad to worse. Tricking her husband one day, the vixen tries to escape into the wild and bares her teeth at him when he recaptures her. After she makes further desperate attempts to dig under the wall, he finally lets her go free. Meanwhile his own behavior deteriorates, and the rumor spreads that Mr. Tebrick is mad and that his wife has run away from him.

Months pass as Mr. Tebrick neglects his appearance and begins drinking heavily. It becomes clear that he is no longer grieving for his lost wife but for the vixen, whose "foxey ways" have become so precious to him (66). When he sees a fox trotting across the field with a hare in its mouth, he first thinks that he recognizes his Silvia. The sudden awareness of his madness, his degradation into beastliness, shocks him into the resolution to recover. But several days later he sees a vixen in whom he recognizes in fact his wife. She leads him for some distance to a foxhole from which she emerges proudly bearing a litter of five puppies. Despite his best resolve, Mr. Tebrick becomes over the summer almost an animal himself, experiencing insane jealousy of the fox who fathered his vixen's pups, bringing delicacies for the litter, and affectionately naming each of them. One day, having spent the previous night with the cubs, he has the sudden insight that "all human customs and institutions seemed to him nothing but folly. . . . The beasts are happier and I will deserve that happiness as best I can" (89). Soon he is able to adapt to animal ways, following the cubs anywhere, moving silently through the woods, concealing himself from passing human beings, creeping almost on all fours, and hunting with them.

At the end of the summer the cubs have grown and gone their own way with their mother. Mr. Tebrick returns to his cottage, and the hunting season again approaches. One day, hearing the clamor of the hounds, he goes out and sees the vixen Silvia running toward him, almost in the teeth of the pursuing hounds. The vixen runs through the open gate and leaps into Mr. Tebrick's arms, "and before he could turn back the hounds were upon them and had pulled them down" (96). Those standing nearby hear "a scream of despair" more like a woman's voice than a man's (96). When the hunters manage to get the dogs off, Mr. Tebrick is mauled and bleeding, and the vixen is dead. The story ends with a short epilogue that is as blissfully optimistic as Kafka's. "For a long while his life was despaired of, but at last he rallied, and in the end he recovered his reason and lived to be a great age, for that matter he is still alive" (97).

SEX AND GENDER IN BLOOMSBURY

Virginia Woolf's *Orlando: A Biography* (1928) is first and foremost the symbolic biography of Woolf's friend and "Sapphic" lover, Vita Sackville-West, to whom the book is dedicated.[42] Many of the personal details of the novel—from the repeated praise of Orlando's fine legs and sexual proclivities to the description of his/her ancestral home, which is based on the Sackville's estate, Knole—are taken directly from Vita's life and circumstances. Orlando's poem *The Oak Tree,* which he begins as a boy in 1586 (236) and for which she wins a literary prize in 1928 (312),[43] is clearly an analogue for Vita Sackville-West's prize-winning and popularly successful georgic poem *The Land* (1927). Vita's son called *Orlando* "the most charming love letter in literature."[44]

But the often dazzling novel, which Woolf began as "a joke" and regarded as little more than a jeu d'esprit,[45] is a complex work of many facets. It is among other things a cultural history of England from the late sixteenth to the early twentieth century—a history of the metamorphosing "spirit of the age," which is frequently cited by the author in the course of her narrative (236, 244, 264–66). It also constitutes an account of sensual perception and responsiveness (to colors, tastes, sounds), a feminist re-vision of English literary history, and a vigorous pamphlet against social stereotyping, especially of sex and gender.[46] All in all, the figure of Orlando, by the time she reaches the twentieth century, represents a reification and embodiment of English cultural memory.

In addition, the novel contains a good deal of playful intertextuality. Apart from the frequent hidden allusions to Vita's poem *The Land,* the author's sly suggestion (268) that Orlando might take a gamekeeper as her lover seems to nod in the direction of D. H. Lawrence's *Lady Chatterley's Lover,* which appeared that same year (1928). Orlando's conversation with herself on June 16 (albeit in the year 1712), might well be a hidden tribute to Molly Bloom's monologue on that same date in Joyce's *Ulysses,* which Woolf came increasingly to admire in the course of the 1920s. Orlando's repeated allusions to his lover, the Russian princess Sasha, as "foxlike" surely acknowledges her friend David Garnett's *Lady into Fox:* Orlando calls her Sasha "because it was the name of a white Russian fox he had had as a boy" (44); she hangs over him "sinuously, like the fox that had bit him" (51); when he comes upon her gnawing a discarded candle, it occurs to him that there is "something rank in her" (52); and to describe the howling across the Russian steppes, "she barked like a wolf" (54). The figure of Orlando, who experiences life first as a man and then as a woman, must have struck many sophisticated readers of the 1920s as Eliot's unseen Tiresias come to life. Finally, the arras hanging in the great gallery of Orlando's ancestral home, depicting Daphne fleeing before mounted huntsmen, sways in the drafts in such a manner as to make it seem that Daphne is flying (111, 171, 317); the use of a tapestry with a mythological theme as a leitmotif reminds us of the tapestry in *The Waste Land* depicting Philomela. Woolf knew Eliot well; she and her husband had published his first volume of *Poems* (1919) in their Hogarth Press.

The mention of Daphne brings us to the author's knowledge of Ovid. Virginia Woolf (1882–1941) was the daughter of Sir Leslie Stephen, the distinguished essayist, biographer, and intellectual historian. While her formal education was sketchy, she had the benefit of her father's great library, in which she read voraciously; his circle of eminent friends; and tutors in Latin and Greek, including G. C. W. Warr and Walter Pater's sister Clara.[47] Greek was the language in which she acquired the greater competence and for which she developed enormous enthusiasm, as documented in her essay "On Not Knowing Greek."[48] In her novel *Jacob's Room* (1922), for instance, Jacob Flanders reads classics at Cambridge, studies Plato's *Phaedrus* in the British Museum, quotes Sophocles in conversations with his friends, and finally visits Greece, which he regards as "the height of civilization" (164).[49] But although he feels that Roman civilization was "a very inferior affair" (136), he attends lectures at Cambridge on Virgil by an idiosyncratic professor of Latin poetry, to whom the author devotes a lengthy paragraph. Virgil occupies a special place in Woolf's imagination, owing no doubt to the explicit and frequently noted analogy between *The Land* and Virgil's *Georgics,* which provided both the organizational principle and the motto for Sackville-West's poem.[50] In *To the Lighthouse* (1927), written while

Vita was completing her poem, Augustus Carmichael, who bears the same fore-name as the emperor lauded in Virgil's *Georgics,* likes "to lie awake a little read-ing Virgil," and his own work is described in terms characteristic of Virgil's poetry.[51] In general, Woolf's diaries and letters refer often to the Greeks and have almost nothing to say about the Romans. Even so, it is unlikely that a stu-dent who learned her Latin around the turn of the century would not be ac-quainted with Ovid's *Metamorphoses* in the original.

As an owner of the Hogarth Press, which during the 1920s published Freud's *Collected Works,* Woolf must have been aware of Jung's work, if only as that of the disloyal disciple; as a central figure in the Bloomsbury Circle, she was ex-posed to the swirling intellectual currents of the day. And as a person with par-ticularly close connections to Cambridge, the focal point of twentieth-century myth study, and as an appreciative reader of *The Waste Land,* she was hardly un-familiar with Frazer's *Golden Bough* and the lively debate surrounding meta-morphosis. In any case, it is not implausible to conclude that Woolf had a firsthand, if only casual and general, acquaintance with Ovid rather than to as-sume that her use of Ovidian themes came only indirectly through some such source as Shakespeare's *Taming of the Shrew.*[52]

Sarah Annes Brown has persuasively identified striking parallels between Woolf's description of the Great Frost of 1604 and Ovid's account of the del-uge in the *Metamorphoses* (1.293–303), "set pieces describing a profound up-heaval in the natural world."[53] And the mythological aura of the novel is suggested by the representative titles of the fifty-odd poems dealing with "some mythological personage at a crisis of his career" written by the young Orlando (76). But the only specific reference to an Ovidian theme is the Daphne arras, which recurs like a leitmotif throughout the novel. The most detailed descrip-tion is the first, given as Orlando's ancestral home is being prepared for a great feast: "All now was ready; and when it was evening and the innumerable silver sconces were lit and the light airs which for ever moved about the galleries stirred the blue and green arras, so that it looked as if the huntsmen were rid-ing and Daphne were flying" (111). Noteworthy here is the absence of Apollo; Daphne is pursued by mounted huntsmen. This scene elicits several associations. We are reminded, first, that the handsome/beautiful Orlando is constantly pur-sued by men and women of the same or opposite sex. The motif of flight, in turn, is appropriate for Orlando's movement down through the centuries, in which she lands along the way now in one century and now in the next. A third association is even more conspicuous; for in the next paragraph we are told that Orlando often left his guests when the feasting was at its height and locked him-self in his room. "There when the door was shut, and he was certain of privacy, he would have out an old writing book, stitched together with silk stolen from his mother's workbox, and labelled in a round schoolboy hand, 'The Oak Tree, A Poem.'" In this he would write till midnight chimed and long after" (112–13). The passage goes on to describe the changing style of the poem that reflects the changing times, but the essential point is established by the simple contiguity of the two passages: the oak tree is to Orlando as the laurel to Daphne. Orlando, at the end of his/her flight through the centuries, leaves a signed copy of the poem "unburied and dishevelled" beneath the oak tree (325), signaling her identity with the tree just as clearly as Daphne's eternalization in the laurel tree signals hers.[54]

Ovid provides two further striking though unstated parallels. The more obvious one is the story of Iphis (*Met.* 9.666–797), the girl brought up by her mother as a boy because her father threatened to kill any female child at birth; on the eve of the marriage that would have exposed her deceit, Iphis is transformed by the goddess Isis into a youth, and the young couple are able to consummate their marriage happily. Like Orlando, who is portrayed as having the lovely androgyne features of Vita Sackville-West, Iphis, "even when dressed as a boy, had a face that would have been regarded as beautiful in either a girl or a boy":

> cultus erat pueri; facies, quam sive puellae,
> sive dares puero, fieret formosus uterque.
> (*Met.* 9.712–13)

Iphis, to be sure, is transformed from girl to boy and not, like Orlando, from man to woman; but both find their ultimate persona and sexual happiness in the altered rather than in the original sexual condition.

The second Ovidian tale of sex change is perhaps even closer to *Orlando* because it provides more than an analogy to the plot: it anticipates many of Orlando's thoughts and feelings. Woolf had recently been reacquainted with Ovid's account of Tiresias, including its Latin text, in the notes to Eliot's *Waste Land.* Tiresias offers initially a precise analogy to Orlando: beginning as a man, he is transformed for seven years into a woman; at the end, unlike Orlando, he is changed back into his original masculine form. As a result of his transformations he experiences sex in both forms and is thus able to adjudicate the dispute between Jupiter and Juno on the relative pleasures of male and female love. The question as formulated by Jupiter—whether "your pleasure is greater than that of men" (*maior vestra profecto est / quam quae contingit maribus . . . voluptas; Met.* 3.320–21)—and answered by Tiresias is strikingly similar to Orlando's reflections when, having recently been transformed into a woman, she discovers the delights and power of womanly wiles. "Which is the greater ecstasy? The man's or the woman's? And are they not perhaps the same? No, she thought, this is the most delicious" (155). At first Orlando is equivocal in her response to her new situation: "here it would seem from some ambiguity in her terms that she was censuring both sexes equally, as if she belonged to neither; and indeed, for the time being she seemed to vacillate; she was man, she was woman; she knew the secrets, shared the weaknesses of each" (158). By the time she has reached the late eighteenth century and learned the advantages of cross-dressing "she had, it seems, no difficulty in sustaining the different parts, for her sex changed far more frequently than those who have worn only one set of clothing can conceive. . . . From the probity of breeches she turned to the seductiveness of petticoats and enjoyed the love of both sexes equally" (220–21). When in the nineteenth century she encounters and marries her true love, Marmaduke Bonthrop Shelmerdine, Esq., the relationship is in Woolf's terms a perfect one, almost Platonically whole, because both evince such an intuitive understanding of the male and female mind alike that she suspects he is a woman and he that she is a man (252).

But Orlando shares more than Tiresias's bisexual experience. Tiresias is also wise: when Ovid's infuriated Juno strikes him blind for his response, Jupiter in compensation gives him the gift of prophecy.

> at pater omnipotens (neque enim licet inrita cuiquam
> facta dei fecisse deo) pro lumine adempto
> scire futura dedit poenamque levavit honore.
> (*Met.* 3.336–38)

> (But the all-powerful father [since no god has the
> right to invalidate the deeds of another god] in
> exchange for the deprivation of his sight enabled
> him to know the future and lightened the
> punishment by the honor.)

Precisely this capacity for wisdom—in Orlando's case not the ability to foretell the future but to experience the future and to assimilate the past into her eternal present— gives meaning and structure to the novel as a whole. Woolf's Tiresias analogue journeys through time, yet even as Orlando exemplifies from century to century "the spirit of the age"—in her garb, in her response to the world of the senses surrounding her at any given moment, even in her literary style—, "she had remained, she reflected, fundamentally the same" (237), like Ovid's figures (notably Actaeon and Callisto) who retain their *mens antiqua* even in transformation. She recalls her various pasts: or, more precisely, she keeps the past constantly alive in her memory. When she encounters Nicholas Greene again in the twentieth century, the former second-rate Elizabethan poet has become a portly, prosperous, and powerful literary critic. Yet as Greene speaks, lamenting the loss of past glory and denouncing the degeneracy of the present, "she could have sworn that she had heard him say the very same things three hundred years ago" (278), as indeed she had (88–89). To put it in modern terms, Iphis anticipates in sex and Tiresias in gender the experiences of Woolf's Orlando.[55]

The biographer engages us throughout with comments on the problematics of her undertaking. "The biographer is now faced with a difficulty which it is better perhaps to confess than to gloss over," she concedes on the point of describing Orlando's first psychic, not yet physical, transformation following the disastrous affair with the Russian princess (65). "Our simple duty is to state the facts as far as they are known, and so let the reader make of them what he may." Later she confronts Orlando's sex change with the same forthrightness as Garnett in discussing Mrs. Tebrick's transformation into a fox. "Orlando has become a woman—there is no denying it. But in every other respect, Orlando remained precisely as he had been. The change of sex, though it altered their future, did nothing whatsoever to alter their identity" (138). After recapitulating the public theories about Orlando's transformation, she concludes: "It is enough for us to state the simple fact; Orlando was a man till the age of thirty; when he became a woman and has remained so ever since" (139).

At the end, recapitulating Orlando's adventures through more than three centuries, the biographer reminds us that she has had time to account for only six or seven of Orlando's various hypostases through time, although any individual may have a thousand times as many (309). This concludes a rumination on human consciousness that might have come straight out of Jung, albeit with a more homely image.

> For if there are (at a venture) seventy-six different times all ticking in the mind at once, how many different people are there not—Heaven help us—all having lodgment at one time or another in the human spirit? Some say two thousand and fifty-two. . . . these selves of which we are built up, one on top of another, as plates are piled on a waiter's hand, have attachments elsewhere, sympathies, little constitutions and rights of their own, call them what you will. (308)

Like Ovid's *Metamorphoses, Orlando* begins with a natural disaster and traces the history of the world from that moment down to the writer's own present. Woolf's novel, to be sure, covers a shorter historical period and has a different kind of unity: rather than scores of stories linked in various ways, it focuses on one individual transformed not only in his/her sexual nature but also through time. Whereas the consciousness of change and continuity through time in the *Metamorphoses* is symbolized by the timelessness of the species or substances or constellations into which the individual figures are subsumed, in Woolf's novel it is embedded in the consciousness of a single figure who himself/herself experiences change and continuity through time. This figure, as I have argued, is based on three Ovidian myths: explicitly on Daphne and implicitly on Iphis and Tiresias. In the final analysis this entire Jungian or Cambridge-anthropological experiment in metamorphosis is undertaken as an exemplification of Woolf's passionate belief in the liberation of the psyche from what she perceived as the bonds of gender stereotyping.

The rehabilitation of Ovid, which was begun by European and American poets in the years surrounding World War I, undergirt theoretically by the early twentieth-century scholars of myth and metamorphosis, and paralleled by a group of writers who, aware of Ovid's model, found in metamorphosis a useful device for their various fictions, came to an abrupt end in the 1930s, at least in Western Europe. Only a few artists, attracted by the theme of metamorphosis, turned from time to time to Ovid's work for inspiration. Picasso issued a folio containing a cycle of thirty vivid etchings based on the *Metamorphoses* (Lausanne, 1931): a half-page illustration for the beginning of each book and a full-page depiction of a scene within each book.[56] Other artists were attracted by specific episodes: e.g., Salvador Dali's striking *Métamorphose de Narcisse* (1937) and André Masson's *Pygmalion* (1939).[57]

Meanwhile a new historical situation, the rise of fascism in Europe and a fresh national consciousness in the United States and elsewhere, called for different literary and historical models. The break about 1930 in Germany is characterized by a political and ideological "usurpation" or even "disfigurement" ("Verhunzung") of the classics, as the humanistically educated middle class or *haute bourgeoisie* (*Bildungsbürgertum*) that we have been discussing up to this point retreated in the face of party propagandists.[58] Whereas the nineteenth anniversary of Ovid's death in 1917 passed unnoticed in the midst of war, the bimillennial of Virgil's birth in 1930 was celebrated all over the world—most elaborately in Italy, but also in France and Germany as well as in North and South America; at the same time the Roman analogy was enjoying enormous popularity.[59] While Oswald Spengler and Arnold Toynbee detected alarming parallels to the modern world in the decline of the Roman empire, Hitler and Mussolini appropriated Augustus as their model for the dictator who restores order to a chaotic society. After Virgil had been celebrated in 1930 as the poet of empire, the bimillennial of Augustus's birth in 1937 provided an occasion, especially in

Fascist Italy, for a large-scale experiment in politico-cultural and militaristic propaganda. Virgil's praise of Augustus, who thundered across Asia imposing Roman law on "willing" peoples (*Caesar dum magnus ad altum / fulminat Euphraten bello victorque volentis / per populos dat iura; Geo.* 4. 560–62), seemed to provide the perfect justification for wars of aggression in Ethiopia and the invasion of Czechoslovakia and Poland. In the face of cries for order and stability—both by the Fascists and National Socialists and by their democratic opponents in Europe and the United States—there was little interest in a poet like Ovid, who seemed to represent a pure poetry untouched by politics, who spoke for the rights of the individual rather than the nation, and who proclaimed a world of change and metamorphosis. The high modernist *aetas Ovidiana,* after a short but brilliant flourishing, had suddenly ended. For these reasons a British scholar lamented in 1934, following the worldwide celebrations in honor of the bimillennium of Virgil's birth, that "Ovid died, for at least the third time, in the nineteenth century, and was buried deep under mountains of disparaging argument to make a throne for Virgil."[60]

Part II

▶

Ovid and the Exiles

◢ 6 ◣

THE UR-EXILE

Shortly after the publication of his novel *The Death of Vergil* (*Tod des Vergil*, 1945) Hermann Broch admitted that he was initially attracted to the subject as the result of a confusion. Invited in 1935 by Radio Vienna to give a reading from his works, Broch proposed instead a talk called "Literature at the End of a Cultural Era." Because of programming considerations that topic was deemed inappropriate, and so Broch decided to incorporate his views on cultural decline into a short story. It did not require much deliberation, he reports (given the publicity surrounding the current bimillennial celebrations of Virgil, Horace, and Augustus), to think of parallels between the first pre-Christian century and our own age:

> civil war, dictatorship, and a dying off of the old ancient religious forms; yes, there was even a striking parallel to the phenomenon of emigration—that is, in Tomi, the fishing village on the Black Sea. Furthermore, I knew of the legend according to which Virgil had wanted to burn the *Aeneid* and might therefore assume—accepting that legend—that a mind like Virgil's was not driven to an act of such desperation for trivial reasons, but that the entire historical and metaphysical meaning of the epoch played a role.[1]

Broch, who was not trained in the classics, soon realized—or had it brought to his attention—that it was not Virgil who died in Tomis, but Ovid, and he altered the plot of his novel accordingly. But his confusion points to the easy co-optation of Ovid by many writers in the 1930s as an analogy to their own political destinies. In the very year of Hitler's accession to power a volume appeared in Vienna devoted to "exiles from Ovid to the present."[2]

In volume 2 of his impressive three-volume autobiographical fiction of the Nazi years in Germany and Europe, *The Aesthetics of Resistance* (*Die Ästhetik des Widerstands,* 1975–81), Peter Weiss recalls his acquaintance with Bertolt Brecht during the émigré years. When Brecht left Sweden in 1940 for Finland and the United States, Weiss was asked to make a selection of books from Brecht's large library to go into the seaman's chest that accompanied him. Among the works that made the journey was a Teubner school edition of the poems of Ovid and Catullus as well as a 1791 edition of the *Metamorphoses.* That these works, which he first read as a schoolboy, were familiar to Brecht, and not simply decorative, is demonstrated by his well-known poem (from his *Svendborger Gedichte* of 1939), "Visit with the Exiled Poets" ("Besuch bei den verbannten Dichtern"). When the poet in a dream enters the hut of the exiled poets (next to that of the exiled teachers) Ovid greets him at the entrance and whispers: "It would be better if you didn't sit down. You haven't yet died. Who knows whether or not you might want to return? Even if nothing else changes besides you yourself."[3] The poem ends, after Brecht has been welcomed by a group of other exiled poets, when they ask if he left anyone behind who knows his poems by heart. And will those persons escape persecution? Here the welcoming laughter breaks off because "The new arrival had turned pale." Again, as in Broch's case, the first exiled poet who comes to Brecht's mind is Ovid.[4] Brecht also introduces a sub-theme that emerges frequently among modern exile writers: their fate is worse than Ovid's because their fame and immortality are not assured.

A third writer of that generation, Lion Feuchtwanger, reacted in much the same way in his talk at a 1943 writers' congress in Los Angeles. Feuchtwanger recalled a seminar called Experience and Fiction at the University of Munich, in which the professor declared that the years of exile "might have influenced the authors' choice of material but not their inner landscape." Even as a student Feuchtwanger was suspicious of that thesis. "I could not bring myself to believe that the exile of Ovid, Li-Tai-Po, Dante, Heinrich Heine, and Victor Hugo had influenced only the subject materials of these poets. It seemed to me that the innermost character of the works which these authors wrote in the period of their exile was conditioned by their external circumstances, by their exile."[5] Again it is striking that the first name that occurs to Feuchtwanger is that of Ovid, who is acknowledged as the exile par excellence, the "ur-exile" whose works, in the happy phrase of one classicist, created a veritable "typology of exile literature"[6] and, for another, the "metaphor of exile."[7] When the poet Karl Wolfskehl died in New Zealand in 1948, he had simply the Ovidian phrase EXUL POETA engraved on his tombstone.

In 1980, to take a final example, the seventy-five-year old Polish-Galician writer Manès Sperber, who fled from Germany in 1933 and established his career as a novelist and essayist in France, published an article on writers in exile, in which he first acknowledged Ovid as the archetypal exile and then immediately went on to maintain that modern exiles have a worse time of it:[8]

> Tristia was Ovid's name for the laments that he directed to the Romans from a land that he considered barbaric. He hoped until the end to be pardoned and summoned back. He died inconsolate in the remote "gloomy" Danube province on the Black Sea. In comparison to the exiled writers of our time, to be sure, Ovid was quite privileged since he could hope that he would continue to be read in his mother tongue, which after all was understood as a *lingua franca* far beyond its original home. He did not have to fall silent, as in a nightmare; he was not under any total prohibition to write; it was not regarded as a state crime to read him and to publicize his works.

It is beside the point here that Sperber is mistaken about Ovid's circumstances. In fact, Ovid was sent away in part so that he could not continue to corrupt Roman society by his writing; he could hardly be more assured about his fame among his contemporaries than could the modern exiles; his works were removed from the public libraries; and he sent his poems of exile to his friends anonymously so that they would not be endangered by receiving and reading them. What matters in the present context is simply that Ovid is again adduced as the paradigmatic poet of exile.

While most urgent in Germany, the identification of Ovid with exile was also evident in other countries in the 1930s. We have already considered the case of Osip Mandelstam, whose early identification with Ovid seemed eerily to foreshadow his actual exile in the mid-1930s. John Masefield (1878–1967) witnessed the first wave of political exiles fleeing to England, and his "Letter from Pontus" (1936) reflects the resignation that beset many of them. Masefield's extended poem in blank verse is allegedly a letter from the elderly Ovid, incapsulated within the report of a young officer who, in the first year of Tiberius's reign, is dispatched to Tomis to inspect at first hand the conditions on the Danube frontier.[9] There he encounters Ovid, "an old, bleak, broken-hearted man" living in dire poverty, who nevertheless entertains the junior legate throughout the winter and even writes his report for him. When the younger man departs, Ovid gives him a letter, the "Letter from Pontus" of the title, asking him to read it on the Pincian Hill when he gets back to Rome. The letter, it turns out, explains the reasons for Ovid's exile. In the course of preparations to mount his drama *Medea,* not only did he witness the love affair between Julia and Silanus but he also unintentionally overheard plans by conspirators headed by the two lovers to kill Livia and Tiberius and to install Agrippa Postumus on the throne. The conspirators allow Ovid to live, but an informer within the group denounces him to Augustus. Augustus arrests the conspirators and sends Julia and Ovid into exile. "It may be that the miseries of men / Fulfil some purpose of the deities / For each man's spirit on its pilgrimage," Ovid's letter ends. "But I / Now ask for nothing, save perhaps to help / What misery I can, with what I have, / Before an everlasting peace of death." Years later, the young Roman concludes his report, a distinguished old lady sent for him and asked much about Ovid,

> And wept to hear, and blessed me for my caring.
> She said "I was the one he called Corinna,
> When Life was April and between us two."

The interest in Ovid as exile did not begin in the twentieth century. Scholars since the early Renaissance, and quite independently of their interest in Ovid's poetry, have been fascinated by Ovid's exile, and particularly by the reasons that might have caused it. Ovid, as we noted earlier, attributed his relegation to *carmen et error.* By "poem" he is clearly referring to his *Ars amatoria;* but he kept silent until death about the nature of his "mistake." He tells us a great deal about the circumstances—it was something that, owing to his own stupidity or gullibility or rashness, he unwittingly witnessed (like Actaeon); a secret known to others in high places but not to the general public; something that personally offended and possibly threatened Augustus; and something whose disastrous consequences he might have precluded by prompt action. But his silence on the precise nature of his mistake has invited speculation through the ages.[10] From the fifteenth century until the late eighteenth, the reason was sought primarily in some sort of sexual adventure of Ovid's or in the ruling house: Ovid's affair with Corinna or adultery with Livia; Augustus's pederasty or incest with his daughter; the notorious adulteries of Augustus's granddaughter Julia. The political climate of the revolutionary era in Europe prompted writers to consider some sort of political crime: possibly Ovid's knowledge of a conspiracy against the ruling house. Scholars of the late twentieth century, finally, tended to look for the *error* in Ovid's individualism in an age of absolutism, his refusal to take on political offices appropriate to his rank, or his free-thinking disregard of religious practices and beliefs. Classicists and historians have also interested themselves in the actual circumstances of Ovid's exile—the town, the climate, the inhabitants and Ovid's relationship with them.[11] If today, for instance, Constanța (the ancient Tomis) is designated by the *Great Soviet Encyclopedia* (13:92) as the internationally famous "center of Black Sea health resorts," then how much truth and accuracy can we attribute to Ovid's constant complaints about the weather and how much is rhetorical exaggeration designed to win sympathy from his readers in Rome?

In contrast to the scholars, poets through the ages have tended to be less concerned with the reasons for the relegation and, taking Ovid at his word, have focused on their own sense of identification with a predecessor's paradigmatic exile.[12] The earliest identifications occurred among ninth-century poets of the Carolingian Renaissance: Modoinus of Autun, known as "Naso" at the court of Charlemagne; the Allemanic poet Wahahfrid Strabo; and the Aquitanian Ermoldus Nigellus. All three wrote elegies of consolation or personal lament in which they cited Ovid as their companion in exile. Two centuries later Hildebert of Lavardin, archbishop of Le Mans, journeyed to Rome to have his politically endangered position confirmed by the pope and, in the process, wrote a ninety-line elegy (*De casu huius mundi*) that uses allusions to Ovid's *Tristia* and *Epistulae ex Ponto* to establish parallels between his own destiny and Ovid's, both threatened by unjust rulers. "Until recently I was prosperous," the poem begins, "blessed with many friends, and favorable fates long smiled upon me."

> Nuper eram locuples, multisque beatus amicis,
> et risere diu fata secunda mihi.[13]

But he learned to his dismay that there is "no reliance, no steadfastness in the affairs of life" (*ei mihi. nulla fides, nulla est constantia rebus;* 19). Fortune plays with all men, masters and servants alike. But his troubles, Hildebert continues, were intensified by "a new and terrible tyrant, under whose rule all law perished among the Gauls" (*accessit damnis novus ille gravisque tirannus, / quo Cenomannorum consule ius periit;* 39–40). It was "shame for his country," as he sought "not without peril to himself to protect the laws of justice, that finally drove him into exile" (*ille pudor patrie me, non impune tuentem / iustitie leges, expulit a patria;* 43–44). Embarking (like Ovid) for his place of exile, he was saved from shipwreck by God; and the final third of the poem amounts to wholly un-Ovidian protestations of his Christian faith. Baudri de Bourgueil, another poet from the Loire circle, composed a fictitious correspondence between the exiled Ovid and a friend remaining in Rome, referring to the need for caution in view of the omnipresence of the ruler's spies.[14]

By the thirteenth century Christian exegetes began to exploit the theme of exile to suggest that Ovid was converted and baptized by the evangelist John on Patmos and that Ovid, in turn, worked as a missionary among the Getae, who called him Sanctus Naso.[15] Perhaps the best-known, and certainly the oddest, appearance of Ovidius Christianus is the 2400-line late-thirteenth-century pseudo-Ovidian poem known as *De vetula* ("The Hag").[16] The poem, according to the preface of the fictitious editor Leo, is allegedly Ovid's autobiographical account, when he realized that he would never be allowed to return to Rome, of his life and spiritual conversion. Buried with him, the manuscript was not discovered until the thirteenth century near Dioskurias, the capital of the Colchians, and sent to Constantinople for editing and publication. The first of its three books (none of which has the slightest basis in Ovid's actual biography) is an account of Ovid's life in Rome during his happy days—his love affairs, his activities (swimming, bird catching, hunting, and fishing), social amusements, including an attack on the evils of gambling, and satirical remarks about lawyers and political office. "O how dear to me and how desirable was the female sex," the poem begins, "without which I believed it was impossible for any man to live."

> O quam carus erat michi quamque optabilis ille
> femineus sexus, sine quo nec vivere posse
> credebam quemcumque virum, . . .
>
> (1–3)

Book 2 amounts to a comic novella on a popular medieval theme: Ovid, attracted to a young noblewoman, bribes her chaperone to get him into her bed; but the cunning and ugly hag (the *vetula* of the title) takes the young woman's place, whereupon the disgusted poet curses her. The young woman is soon married away, but she returns twenty years later after the death of her husband and is united with Ovid. In the meantime Ovid has realized that the long delay has moderated his passion. "Those are the reasons," the third book begins, "why I no longer wish to live as I was formerly accustomed, nor do I intend to submit my neck any longer to the yoke of all-consuming love"

> Iste sunt cause, propter quas amodo nolo
> vivere sicut eram solitus nec subdere collum
> plus intendo iugo nervos carpentis amoris.

But how is he to spend his time if he forsakes all the pastimes of his youth? He dedicates himself to study: mathematics, music, and astronomy (including a cosmogony and cosmology of creation). He reflects on such religious themes as the immortality of the soul and resurrection, and his belief in an almighty God shields him from the fear of death. "Death will be welcome," he feels, "to the extent that it will end his exile, which involves living beneath northern skies, among the Getae, and—since nothing is worse than having the Getae as neighbors—a life that he regards as tantamount to death itself."

> Porro non penitus caret utilitate, quod ipsa
> terminat exilium, quale est habitare sub arcto,
> quale Getas inter, quia proximitate Getarum
> deterius nichil esse potest, ubi vivere certe
> non aliud reputo quam mortem continuare.
>
> (439–43)

Drawing on his astrological knowledge he foretells the birth of a child named Jesus—and specifically, according to ancient Indian, Chaldean, and Babylonian prophecies, by a virgin. But he is incapable of understanding how that will happen.

> Sed via possibilis non est, hec clausa videtur
> porta meis oculis, quis non intelligo plane.
>
> (668–69)

> (But there is no possible way; this gate appears
> closed to my eyes since I simply don't understand.)

He does know one thing for sure: that a man would never be able to become a god (*Hoc unum novi, quod homo fieri deus unquam / non posset*). Unable to comprehend other revealed truths, such as the nature of the Trinity, he can only have faith and hope that the savior will show him the right way.

> Docturus tamen est, qua nos veniamus ad ipsum,
> monstrabitque viam, quia, per quam venerit ad nos,
> illa tenenda via est; illac nos ire necesse.
>
> (765–67)

> (But he will teach us how we may come to him
> and will show us the way through which he came
> to us since that is the way we must follow; that's
> the direction we must go.)

In the Renaissance the identification of writers with the exiled Ovid becomes virtually a commonplace: at the turn of the seventeenth century, the

Neo-Latin poet Dominique Baudier (Dominicus Baudius) exclaims at the end of his elegy *Manibus P. Ovidii Nasonis* that, "should he have the honor of sharing fate in such company [as Ovid's], he would gladly forsake the fertile fields of Italy and the city of Rome for Scythia and the snows of Sarmatia."

> o mihi si tantos adispisci detur honores,
>   et liceat tali cum grege fata sequi:
> fertilibus campis Italae telluris, et urbi
>   praetulerim Scythiam Sarmaticasque nives.[17]

The editors of Ovid's works in the age of critical rationalism, Nikolaus Heinsius (1661) and Pieter Burman (1714), adduce the fact of the poet's exile as an opportunity to attack the character and rule of the tyrannical Augustus—a hidden critique of the prevailing absolutism. In the course of the eighteenth century, however, the exiled Ovid was reduced in status, along with the author of the *Metamorphoses*, as the spokesmen of rising empires began to look askance at writers who lost favor with their governments and favored, instead, such poets as Virgil and Horace, who were seen as propagandists for the state and its imperialism. At the same time, Dryden and other influential critics began to deny Ovid's poetic originality and to decry his lax morals, contrasting him with Virgil and even Chaucer.[18]

For historical reasons, and despite scholarly neglect of the author of the *Amores*, writers of the early nineteenth century began once again to be attracted to Ovid as the poet of exile[19]—not so much for political reasons as for more subjective ones. Among the early poems of the Austrian dramatist Franz Grillparzer, who drew on the *Heroides* for his plays *Des Meeres und der Liebe Wellen* (Hero and Leander) and *Sappho*, we encounter one that apostrophizes the exiled Ovid ("An Ovid," 1812–13); and at the time Grillparzer was already planning the cycle of seventeen poems to which he gave the Ovidian title *Tristia ex Ponto* (1833).[20] Grillparzer (1791–1872) was not an exile in the usual sense of the word; at the time he wrote his poem "To Ovid" he was a sickly twenty-one-year-old, acting as household tutor to a haughty noble family in Moravia and far from his native Vienna. He was well acquainted with Ovid's works, and the first four strophes of his poem echo many details from the *Tristia*. Grillparzer addresses the poet, "whom the anger of Rome's crafty ruler forced into wild and inhospit-able wastes where no happy person was to be seen, to the sea-beaten coasts of Pontus."

> Dir, den in wilde, unwirtbare Wüsten,
> wo nie ein Glücklicher sich schauen ließ,

auf Pontus ferne meerumtobte Küsten
der Grimm von Romas tückschem Herrscher stieß.

Ovid was "punished by the emperor's harsh judgment because he had seen too
much and said too much."

> Weil du zu viel gesehn, zu viel gesprochen,
> traf dich des Kaisers harter Richterspruch.

But "the torment of his punishment is softened by the memory of sins that were
sweet as they were committed."

> Für Sünden, lieblich im Begehn, zu büßen,
> das stumpft der grausenvollsten Strafe Qual.

In contrast, the young Austrian poet feels sorry for himself because he has been
punished by an even crueler henchman, "the mighty iron hand of fate" ("des
Schicksals allgewaltge Eisenhand") and for no transgression: "my heart is pure;
I know nothing of crimes!" Speaking of the storm that has driven his ship of
life off course and toward the abyss (in the shipwreck image we hear echoes of
the frequent references to *naufragium* in the *Tristia*),[21] he can see nothing before
him but destruction. Yet even should the next hour crush him under foot, "I
shall live eternally in the mouth of posterity"—a clear echo of the sphragis with
which Ovid concludes his *Metamorphoses*. In other words, the inexperienced
young poet, still without accomplishments, internalizes Ovid's tragic experience
into little more than the alienation of genius.

In contrast, Alexander Pushkin's elegy *To Ovid* (1821) is based on his own experience of exile on the Black Sea not far from Ovid's Tomis and on his identification with Ovid as a poet of freedom punished by a harsh ruler.[22] When
Pushkin (1799–1837) reaches the Black Sea, which he knew principally from
Ovid's descriptions in his poems from exile and which he had often visualized
in his imagination—the first fifty lines recapitulate many motifs from the *Tristia*—he is surprised to find a much gentler landscape and milder climate than
he had expected. "My sight does not discover what the dream promised. How
quietly your exile captivated my eyes, which knew only the snow of the gloomy
north. Here the blue of the sky glitters long, and the harshness of the winter
storms prevails only for a short time." While December strews snow across
Russia, the warmth of spring breathes on the Black Sea and the orb of the sun
rolls above. But unlike Grillparzer, who takes consolation from the conviction of
his future fame, Pushkin (like the later exiles from Hitler's Germany) is despon-

dent. While Ovid's wreathe is as green as ever, he fears that he will die unknown. He dedicates his voice to Ovid, "united with you not in fame, but in fate."

In France, Lamartine addressed his ode "La gloire" (1818) "à un poète exilé," the Portuguese poet and translator Francisco-Manoel Nascimento (1734–1819), who was arrested for heresy and escaped to France in 1792, where he lived until his death. In the last strophes Lamartine consoles the poet with the thought of other famous exiles:

> Aux rivages des morts avant que de descendre,
> Ovide lève au ciel ses suppliantes mains:
> Aux Sarmates grossières il a légué sa cendre,
>   Et sa gloire aux Romains.[23]

> (Before descending to the shores of the dead,
> Ovid raises his suppliant hands to heaven: he has
> bequeathed his ashes to the uncouth Sarmatians
> and his glory to the Romans.)

Baudelaire, in his report on the Salon of 1859 and apropos Delacroix's *Ovide chez les Scythes,* observed that "all the delicacy and bounty that one finds in Ovid has entered Delacroix's painting; and just as exile gave to the brilliant poet the sadness that was lacking, melancholy has adorned with its enchanting glaze the abundant landscape of the artist."[24] In 1887, perhaps inspired by the scene depicted in Delacroix's painting, Paul Verlaine wrote his melancholy "Pensée du soir" (in *Amours,* 1888), in which he portrayed Ovid, "resting in the pale cold grass of exile, beneath the yews and pines silvered by sleet, or perhaps wandering, like forms stirred up by dreams, through the horror of the Scythian countryside, while all around, shepherds of fabulous flocks, white barbarians with blue eyes, are startled: the poet of The Art of Loving, tender Ovid, embraces the horizon with a long avid regard and sadly contemplates the vast sea."

> Couché dans l'herbe pâle et froide de l'exil,
> Sous les ifs et les pins qu'argente le grésil,
> Ou bien errant, semblable aux formes que suscite
> Le rêve, par l'horreur du paysage scythe,
> Tandis qu'autour, pasteurs de troupeaux fabuleux,
> S'effarouchent les blancs Barbares aux yeux bleus,
> Le poète de l'Art d'Aimer, le tendre Ovide,
> Embrasse l'horizon d'un long regard avide
> Et contemple la mer immense tristement.[25]

The exile's thinning hair is graying, his clothing neglected, his eyes wan, his beard thick—signs of grief that suggest a lamentable story of excessive love and of the anger and responsibility of the emperor. "A morose Ovid thinks of Rome, a Rome adorned by its illusory glory."

> Ovide morne pense à Rome, et puis encore
> À Rome que sa gloire illusoire décore.

Jesus has "justly punished him," concludes the recently converted and repentant sinner Verlaine; but "at least, since he is not Ovid [that is, a pagan], that is left to him [the consolation of being Christian]."

> Or, Jésus! vous m'avez justement obscurci:
> Mais, n'étant pas Ovide, au moins je suis ceci.

This, then, was the status of the exiled Ovid at the beginning of the twentieth century when, as we have seen, suddenly the high modernists rediscovered and rehabilitated the man and his works. But among the modernists, exile, while often present, remained a spiritual theme: Joyce, Pound, and Eliot—even Mandelstam prior to 1934—were voluntary expatriates. It took the 1930s and the reality of exile in the face of fascism, nazism, and communism to elevate that theme once again from minor to major. As Joseph Brodsky, an exile from the Soviet Union, remarked in 1987: "Displacement and misplacement are this century's commonplace."[26] But the transposition had already begun to take place, appropriately, in the land where Ovid spent the last decade of his life and died.

◢ 7 ◤

THE ROMANIAN CONNECTION

THE PROTO-ROMANIAN OVID

Because he died in the Roman province of Moesia Inferior or Scythia Minor (present-day Dobrudja) Ovid has long occupied a special place in the folklore, culture, and literature of Romania.[1] As Edward Gibbon observed, "the tender Ovid," exiled among these "monsters of the desert," had the unique opportunity of collecting in his writings from the Black Sea "many curious observations, which no Roman, except Ovid, could have an opportunity of making"— observations that are invaluable for the history and culture of the Getae and Sarmatians.[2] Under Roman control until the seventh century, the territory then became Greek and was later incorporated into the Ottoman Empire. During these centuries the memory of the exiled Roman poet was forgotten along with the place of his exile, whose name was changed by the emperor Constantine in the fourth century to Constantiniana. The situation was exacerbated by the successive invasions of various peoples, which made of the western coast of the Black Sea a veritable patchwork of cultures and languages. As a result, Romanian literature emerged with a strong national consciousness and linguistic integrity much later than the literatures of the other Romance languages. Yet local folklore retained memories of a "Roman ruler," "a saint who suffered martyrdom for his faith," "an old fisherman," "a man from afar," "a stranger from the other end of the world," and a man so eloquent that "honey flowed from his

lips" (a tradition echoed by the Old Man in Pushkin's poem "The Gypsies")—
memories attached locally to a so-called Tower of Ovid, an Isle of Ovid, a Lake
of Ovid, and Ovid's Tomb. But any specific knowledge of the poet, his works,
and even his place of exile was long forgotten.

The earliest signs of cultural rehabilitation occurred during the humanistic
Renaissance of the seventeenth century. In 1679 a few lines by Ovid, apparently
the first translation of any Latin text into Romanian, appeared in an anthology
published at Sibiu by Valentin von Franckenstein. A few years later Miron
Costin (1633–91), a Polish-educated Moldavian diplomat, included the translation of four verses from the ninth of Ovid's *Epistulae ex Ponto* in his chronicle *On the Origins of the Moldavians,* specifying Ovid's "indecent verses" as the
reason for his relegation and locating the site of the poet's exile in the Moldavian citadel town of Cetatea Albă (near the present-day Russian border). When
Costin was decapitated for allegedly plotting against the reigning monarch, his
son Nicolae completed his chronicle, adding among other things the myth of
Deucalion and Pyrrha from Ovid's *Metamorphoses.* Two decades later the famed
polymath and polyglot Dimitrie Cantemir (1673–1723), son of the ruler who
had executed Costin, extended his broad interests to Ovid, dealing in his *De-
scriptio Moldaviae* and *The History of the Ottoman Empire* with the causes of Ovid's
exile (his erotic poems) and discussing the various theories concerning the place
of exile. Cantemir was the first in a series of writers who concerned themselves
with the works written in exile as a source of Romanian history. And he concluded, like the unfortunate Costin, that Ovid's place of exile must have been
Cetatea Albă, mainly because local tradition called the nearby body of water
"Ovid's Lake" ("Lacul Ovidului").

There followed another period of silence until, at the beginning of the nineteenth century, the prolific poet and translator Vasile Aaron, himself a Romanian living in Transylvania, wrote the first complete biography of Ovid (1807; first
published in 1898–99), addressing the poet directly and claiming his own descent not from the wild Getae or Sarmatians but, like Ovid, from the Romans.
Conceding the difficulty of determining the precise reasons for Ovid's exile, he
used textual evidence to place ancient Tomis at the location of modern Ti-
mişoara (in western Romania close to the border with Hungary). In 1807 Aaron
also published poetic adaptations of Ovidian tales: Pyramus and Thisbe, and Narcissus and Echo.

Aaron's work seems to have acted as a catalyst because the first half of the
nineteenth century produced at least three further translations of the *Metamorphoses* into Romanian. During the same period the poet and painter Gheorghe
Asachi (1788–1859) published his elegy *The Lake of Ovid near Cetatea Albă on the
Dniester River.* Following a rehearsal of the poet's exile and sufferings, far from

his beloved Rome and in the midst of a barbaric people, and drawing extensively on the *Tristia* and *Epistulae ex Ponto,* the poem goes on to portray Ovid's
consolation through poetry as he composes harmonious verses in the local language and sings them to the fierce Scythians, who crown his melancholic fore-
head with flowers. The elegy ends with a translation of the famous epitaph that
Ovid wrote for himself at the end of book 3 of *Tristia.* In 1840, Asachi planned
the publication of a series of prints based on Ovid's life in exile, one of which
was entitled "Ovid amidst the Dacians." While it was never completed, the project anticipates by two decades the theme treated by Delacroix in his painting
Ovide chez les Scythes.

The next turning point in the Romanian response to Ovid resulted from three
factors: the establishment of modern Romania in 1859; the liberation of Dobrudja from Ottoman domination and its incorporation into Romania in 1878;
and the determination shortly thereafter by archeologists that the ancient seaport town of Tomis, Ovid's place of exile, was actually present-day Constanţa,
directly on the Black Sea some hundred kilometers south of the Danube delta.
No sooner had that fact been ascertained than, in 1887, the citizens of Constanţa inaugurated a monument to their poet with a large public ceremony. A
decade later a new literary review, *Ovidiu* (1898), was founded at Constanţa,
and its first number contained a poem by Petre Vulcan "Ovidiu in exiliu,"
which recapitulated the principal stages in the poet's life from the time he left
Rome until his death. By all standards, the major creative contribution to the
late-nineteenth-century Ovid Renaissance was the drama *Ovidiu* (1885) by
Vasile Alecsandri, who had already written a play revolving around Horace
(*Fântâna Blandusiei,* 1883) and was projecting a verse drama about Virgil (it
was never written). Alecsandri's story begins in Rome at the peak of the poet's
popularity and success. Ovid, involved in an affair with Augustus's granddaughter Julia, is betrayed to the emperor by a jealous Corinna and Ibis (the
target of Ovid's fierce satire from exile), and both lovers are sent into exile.
Ovid establishes good relations with the people in Tomis and contributes to
the defense of the town when barbarians attack. In the last act (and utterly un-
historically) Julia arrives in Tomis with a repentant Ibis, bearing news of Ovid's
pardon, but it is too late for the poet, who is already on his deathbed. In his
dying vision Ovid foretells the fall of the empire and the rebirth in Dacia of a
new Rome. In this manner he is linked to the origins of the Romanian people, becoming the herald of its future Latinization. Alecsandri's drama, first performed in the National Theater at Bucharest, was an immediate success and is
still performed regularly as part of the classic repertory in Romania. (It provided the libretto for an opera composed in 1941–48 by Constantin Nottara.)

By the turn of the century, Romanian literature and culture had recovered the exiled Ovid as its tutelary genius and the symbol of its cultural continuity since classical antiquity. Indeed, because he also wrote poems in Getic—a threnody on the death of Augustus—he is regarded by many as the first known Romanian poet.[3] (Today the university located in Constanţa is officially named the Ovidian University.)

From that point forward Ovid is steadily present as a major force in Romanian literature. In 1915 Victor Eftimiu published his poem "Statuia lui Ovidiu" (The statue of Ovid). The year 1924 saw two further Ovidian poems: Adrian Maniu published an elegy ("Elegie") recapitulating in a succession of scenes the circumstances depicted in Ovid's own poems from exile; and Corneliu Moldovanu's "Ovid at Tomis" ("Ovidiu la Tomis") contrasts Ovid's one-time glory in Rome with his isolation and resignation in his Pontic exile. In 1931 Nicolae Iorga wrote a five-act dramatic poem, *Ovidiu,* which takes place at Tomis and ends with a prophetic vision positing Ovid as the precursor of a resurgence of Roman culture at the mouth of the Danube. Constantin Salcia's poem "Pont Euxin" ("The Black Sea," 1939) portrays Ovid walking along the shores and observing the flight of migratory birds returning from the south, harbingers of a hoped for but never achieved reprieve. During these same decades many translations of Ovid's works, and particularly of the poems from exile, were published in Romania.[4] Despite all this literary and cultural activity, however, the Romanian connection remained without impact in western Europe because it was celebrated almost entirely in the national language, which was not widely known outside Romania.

This situation began to change in 1957–58 when the bimillennial of Ovid's birth was celebrated in Europe—and nowhere more enthusiastically than in Romania, where the festivities continued for several months. A bust of Ovid was dedicated in a public garden in Bucharest, and Constanţa mounted a spectacular festival entitled "Two Thousand Years from the Birth of Ovid." Of course most of the activity still took place in the national language. A substantial memorial volume of scholarly studies was published—*Publius Ovidius Naso* (Bucharest, 1957)—as well as numerous articles and poems in various literary journals, not to mention two poems in Latin (St. Bezdechi's *Ad bis millesimos P. Ovidi Nasonis natales* and Tr. Lăzărescu's *Ad Ovidium*).[5] The State Theater in Constanţa produced a five-act tragedy, *Ovidius* (1958) by Grigore Sălceanu, in which Ovid, involved in a plot to bring Agrippa Postumus out of exile and put him on the throne, also serves as a confidant in the affair between Julia and her lover Silanus. Exiled to Tomis, Ovid is mortally wounded by a barbarian arrow as he defends the walls of the town. In Petre Manoliu's drama *Ovidiu la Tomis* (1957), the poet heads a republican movement opposing Tiberius's succession to the throne. That

same year a symphony entitled *Ovidiu* by the Romanian composer Sigismund
Toduţa was premiered, recalling first the splendor of Rome, then the sadness of
exile in Tomis, and finally Ovid's apotheosis in future centuries. Ten years later,
Sulmona, the town of Ovid's birth, and Tomis, the place of his death, were formally linked as sister cities.

The same occasion for the first time brought leading Romanian scholars to
the attention of the West, notably at two conferences in Italy in 1958: an international conference held at Ovid's birthplace of Sulmona (*Atti del Convegno internazionale Ovidiano* [Rome: Istituto di Studi Romani, 1959]); and a series of
conferences in Rome with contributions subsequently published under the title *Studi Ovidiani* (Rome: Istituto di Studi Romani, 1959). Meanwhile in France
the volume *Ovidiana: Recherches sur Ovide* (Paris: Les Belles Lettres, 1958) presented an anthology of studies in different languages by international scholars
and edited by N. I. Herescu, former professor at the University of Bucharest. All
three volumes contained papers by prominent Romanian scholars, notably on
Ovid's life among the Getae and on the town of Tomis. In the Roman volume,
Nicolae Lascu, the doyen of Ovidian studies in Romania, dealt with "La for-
tuna di Ovidio dal rinascimento ai tempi nostri," which at the end contains several pages providing Western readers with its first authoritative look at the
Romanian connection. Now, finally, not just a few specialists but all interested
readers could tap into the rich tradition of Ovidiana in Romania—a situation
considerably simplified in 1971 when Ovidiu Drimba published in Italian his
gracefully written and readable life of Ovid, which is informed by details most
easily accessible to the native Romanian and including an epilogue recapitulating most of the relevant information about the Romanian reception of Ovid.[6]
Now, too, at least three Romanian writers sought to reach an international public by writing novels about Ovid in world languages.

The first effort, to be sure, can hardly be called a success. Written by Georg
Scherg, a Transylvanian German, it was published in Bucharest and failed to
reach a broader audience outside Romania. At the same time, because it was
written in German it hardly contributed to the national revival of Ovid, except
perhaps within the community of Transylvanian Germans. Above all, since it
makes no use whatsoever of the strong Romanian tradition regarding Ovid, it
is hardly representative of the national literature. Scherg (born 1917), who in
1942 founded the newsletter of the Protestant Society in Romania (*Blatt der
Evangelischen Gesellschaft*), later held the chair for German literature at the University of Sibiu and was the author of many novels, poems, and translations, beginning with a tragedy *Giordano Bruno* (1954). A year later, in anticipation of the

bimillennial celebrations, he wrote *Ovid,* a tragedy in eleven scenes and in a rhythmic though not metric language.[7]

The play takes place in a scheming, threatening atmosphere in which everyone is endangered. (1) Ovid presents Augustus with his tragedy *Medea;* but Livia berates them both—Ovid for scheming to alienate Augustus's affection and Augustus for ignoring her for a mere flattering poet. Ovid throws the text of his play at her feet and leaves. (2) The rash and violent Tiberius presses Corinna (Augustus's granddaughter) to marry him, but she scornfully refuses and threatens him with a dagger. (3) When Tiberius accuses Ovid of alienating Corinna, Ovid tries in vain to persuade him to respect poets as does Augustus. (4) When Corinna tells Livia what has happened, the scheming mother pretends to be glad that she has refused Tiberius. Later Livia tells Tiberius that it is her plan for him to become Augustus's successor; if successful she will help him to win Corinna. Tiberius plots with Sejanus to entrap Ovid at the upcoming Lupercalian festivals. (5) Julia and Corinna warn Augustus against Livia's schemes, suggesting that Livia and Tiberius are responsible for the murder of Augustus's sons. Augustus cannot understand why Corinna refuses to marry Tiberius. (6) Corinna complains to Ovid, who advises her to marry Tiberius and to achieve greatness through him. Livia overhears only that part of the conversation in which Ovid appears to be confessing his love for Corinna. (7) At the Lupercalian Feast, Tiberius feigns a reconciliation with Ovid. Julia publicly accuses Livia and Tiberius of killing her brothers and of scheming to marry Tiberius to Corinna in order to gain the throne, and to get rid of the troublesome Ovid. Camillus is killed by Tiberius's people before he can confess to murdering Caius and Lucius at their behest, and Livia accuses Ovid of making love to Corinna. Augustus, arguing that his responsibilities as ruler override his feelings as an individual, sends both Julia and Ovid into exile. (8) Augustus tell Tiberius and Corinna that they must make sacrifices for the good of the state. Tiberius must become his son and assume the principate; and Corinna must marry Tiberius. Both agree reluctantly. (9) When Ovid hears the news from Rome, he can scarcely believe that Corinna is marrying Tiberius. A Greek merchant offers him a way to freedom; but Ovid still respects the will of his ruler. (10) When Augustus, hearing of Ovid's noble words, determines to recall him from Tomis, he is poisoned by Livia. Corinna contemptuously rejects Tiberius, who sends her into exile. (11) Corinna arrives in Tomis just in time to see Ovid before he dies. Everyone is now unhappy—except perhaps Livia. While the political scheming and deathbed reconciliation are reminiscent of Alecsandri's *Ovidiu,* Scherg's play adds little to the internationalization of Romanian Ovidianism. But the fact of its publication confirms the renewed popular interest in Ovid among Romanians.

The Proto-Christian Ovid

The case is entirely different when we turn to the novel *Dieu est né en exil* (1960) by the Romanian exile Vintila Horia (1915–92). In 1940 Horia became a press attaché in the Romanian embassy in Rome, was transferred in 1942 to Vienna, where he was interned in 1944 by the Nazis, and liberated in 1945 by the British.[8] Tried in absentia on political grounds by the Romanian Communist government and condemned to lifelong imprisonment, Horia emigrated to Argentina. In 1953 he returned to Europe and worked in Madrid as a hotel clerk and reporter while he wrote his first novel (in French). In the remainder of his thirty-year literary career, Horia wrote many more works, including philosophical-historical novels about El Greco and Plato.

That early novel, *God Was Born in Exile,* created a scandal.[9] Certified by a preface by Henry Daniel-Rops of the Académie française, it was awarded the Prix Goncourt. Almost immediately, however, the author was attacked by the French Communist Party newspaper, *Humanité,* on the grounds that he had been a member of the Fascist Iron Guard and had in the 1930s written anti-Semitic articles supporting Hitler and Mussolini. Horia, while declining the prize and admitting that he wrote some of the cited articles, denied any political affiliation with the Iron Guard or otherwise. The political ambivalence surrounding its publication also characterized the literary reception of the novel, which was greeted with reactions ranging from contempt[10] to enthusiasm.[11]

The political and literary responses of the early 1960s missed several central points. It seems inevitable, in retrospect and in light of the national literary tradition, that the first novel about Ovid's exile should have been written by a Romanian, and notably by an exiled writer obliged, like Ovid, to express himself in an acquired language. "I know from personal experience that exile is not only a prolonged cry of pain, but also a subtle technique of understanding."[12] We learn from Daniel-Rops's preface that Horia was prompted by the international celebrations in 1958 to return to the works of Ovid, which he had first read in school.[13] It now came as an epiphany to him that Ovid had also been an exile—an exile, moreover, in Horia's own homeland (11).[14] This circumstance released in Horia the love of Romania, to which for fifteen years he had been unable to return. The "fervent hommage" in his postscript tells us that Horia was already familiar with the magisterial work by the Romanian archeologist Vasile Pârvan, *Getica* (1926), from which he informed himself about the history, religion, and daily life of the ancient Dacians.[15] The bimillennial celebrations had produced further contributions by Romanian scholars, stressing Ovid's Dacian (Getic) connections.[16] In a very significant sense, Horia's novel is as much a paean to his native land as it is an homage to the Roman poet—an aspect missed by early readers, such as the *TLS* reviewer who was put off by its "un-likely disquisitions which read as though copied from a textbook."[17] It is symptomatic of the seriousness of Horia's project that the eminent French classicist Jérôme Carcopino was inspired by it to update and reissue his earlier monograph on Ovid's spiritual conversion during the exile in Tomis.[18]

Although Horia had literary sources, the novel also relies heavily upon personal memories:"As a child I heard the same wind of unhappiness and the howling of the wolves that accompanied [Ovid] and the crackling of the icy snow at the windowpanes."[19] In a journal published a few years later Horia noted that the portrait of one of the main characters, Ovid's friend Comozous, is based on a peasant whom he knew as "Mos Toma" ("Uncle Thomas") when he was a boy of ten and whom, with his long hair *à la dacienne,* he regarded as "l'image des ancêtres anonymes."[20] Other figures are based on similar recollections of peasants among whom Horia spent several years of his childhood. Accordingly, the Romanian writer devours Ovid's *Tristia* and *Epistulae ex Ponto*—even the *Halieutica* (which is adduced in connection with the fish [*ichthys*] symbol of Christ)—with more fascinated eyes than other readers. For the Roman poet is describing Horia's ancestors, their countryside, and their manners.

Horia's novel is presented as Ovid's secret journal covering his eight years at Tomis—not the public epistles that he addressed to his wife and friends in Rome—and exposing "le vrai visage d'Ovide" (20) rather than the public image of the exile soliciting the favor of the emperor. (Horia's Ovid names the stray dog he adopts "Augustus" and derives a political satisfaction whenever he kicks him; the dog's death in the claws of an eagle later foretells the emperor's death.) The Rome from which this Ovid has been exiled is described in terms that evoke modern totalitarian states with their secret police and informers, their conspiracies and assassinations, their atmosphere of terror and imperialistic policies. Some of the incidents—for instance, Ovid's departure and his voyage to his Euxine exile, for instance, or the siege of Tomis in Ovid's second year among the Getae, at which the aging poet must take up arms to guard the walls—are based on incidents mentioned in Ovid's exilic epistles. And the book teems with quotations and allusions that make clear Horia's familiarity with Ovid's works.[21] These quotations as well as material from Pârvan's *Getica,* from Tacitus (on the wars in Germany), from Suetonius (on the scandals at Augustus's court), and from other classical sources, lend texture and depth to the work. But most of the plot is invented: Ovid's affair with the courtesan Artemis; a visit to Dacian friends at Histria; an expedition up the Danube to Troesmis and beyond to the sacred mountain Kogaionon (in the Transylvanian mountains; in the French edition Horia conveniently provides a map), where Ovid meets a priest of the Dacian god Zamolxis;[22] Ovid's acquaintance with a Greek physician named

Theodore, who tells him about the birth of a miraculous child-savior which he witnessed in Bethlehem;[23] Ovid's involvement in the ultimately fatal love triangle embracing the innkeeper Herimon, his wife, and his mistress Lydia; the secret marriage of the centurion Honorius and Ovid's Getic servant Dokia; the hostility of the new centurion, Valerius, who replaces Honorius when he flees with Dokia to the northern wilderness to join other Roman soldiers who have sought the freedom of the Scythian steppes; and the hallucinations preceding Ovid's death, when he is left alone in Tomis.

Some of the early reviewers (perhaps unaware of the medieval tradition of Ovidius Christianus) were put off by Horia's suggestion that Ovid was a proto-Christian.[24] It is true that his Ovid ruminates repeatedly about religion: about his own Pythagoreanism in the last book of the *Metamorphoses;* about the gradual displacement among Roman women of the Olympian gods by the cult of Isis, Osiris, and Horus, in which Horia hints at a prefiguration of the Christian trinity; about Virgil's presentiments in the Fourth Eclogue of a messianic child; about the Dacian monotheism revolving around Zamolxis and his teaching of eternal life; and about the messianic rumors circulating around the Mediterranean and Ovid's familiarity with "une secte de Palestine appelée des Esséniens."[25] Yet is it after all improbable that the author of the *Metamorphoses* should be interested in questions of religion? And if Ovid as early as the *Ars amatoria* had come to the conclusion that the old gods are false, then why should he not in his loneliness seek for the consolation of a new one—especially if, as Ovid learns from Theodore, the new god was also born in exile? When he first hears of the monotheistic deity of the Getae, he reflects that their god, "tout petit et tout seul au milieu d'un silence et d'une solitude insupportables" (21), is in that respect like him. By the end, he has come to the conclusion, not unlike that of the dying poet in Hermann Broch's *Death of Virgil,* that he is living in a transitional age, "le temps de l'attente et de la certitude" (244).[26]

The religious speculation, which enables Horia to mount an indirect attack against the atheistic-communist government of Romania, is related to what might be called Horia's national and ethnic allegiance, the exile's love of Romania and its history—what one scholar has accurately called his "Romanian nationalism."[27] Here Horia aligns himself with the tradition of Romanian Ovidianism going back to Dimitrie Cantemir. In passage after passage of his journal Horia talks about the character of his ancestors, the Dacians, who, in a vast realm extending from the Dniester to Bohemia, seem to be "comme les ancêtres de l'Occident et comme les précurseurs européens du Dieu unique" (252). When their history is better known, he speculates, the West will find in it a new foundation, an appropriate complement to that of Rome and Athens. The Romanians—whose wars have always been defensive and who have always been "le peuple de la Résistance" (38), preferring to assimilate their invaders and to incorporate the incoming knowledge into their own wisdom—have been preserved by history to accomplish a vast cultural synthesis of East and West (as exemplified in the novel by the daughter born to the Dacian Dokia and her Roman husband Honorius). It is this profoundly felt belief in his people's destiny that Horia sets out to render in his novel: not simply or primarily to make up fictional episodes about Ovid's life in his Euxine exile but to expose through his eyes the character of a nation—a people whose freedom prompts Roman soldiers to desert, whose monotheism paves the way for Christianity, and whose humanity appeals to an exiled Roman disenchanted by the corruption of Rome and its imperialism.[28]

In the *Tristia* and *Epistulae ex Ponto* Ovid alludes repeatedly to the *carmen* and the mysterious *error* that were responsible for his exile. In Horia's novel the *error* plays no role whatsoever: his Ovid refers exclusively to his love poetry—that is, a moral rather than a political crime—as the cause. "Ces vers qui exprimaient mon bonheur d'alors furent, hélas, la cause de mon exil" (30). And he goes on to explain that, while Augustus himself is pure, prudent, austere and patriotic, the same is not true of his family or court, who wallow in vice and corruption. Ovid, who had often attended those debauches, was simply describing what he himself had witnessed. "Mes *Amores* ne sont pas la cause de ce mal, mais le seul reflet." In general, however, Ovid's life in Rome prior to his exile takes second place to his growing appreciation of the Getae, their culture, and their religion that prepares him for the doctrines of Christianity.

THE CONVERT TO ZALMOXIS

Leaving aside the works written in Romanian, we must leap ahead almost forty years to find the next prominent novel about Ovid written in an international language by a Romanian. Unlike the exiled Horia, Marin Mincu (born in 1944), who taught for several years at universities in Turin and Florence, is a professor of literature and theory at the University of Constanța. A prolific writer, he has published novels, essays, and poetry, including *Il diario di Dracula* (1992), a study of Italian literary semiotics, and a volume of Romanian fables of magic. His novel, *Il diario di Ovidio* (1997), is a consistently fascinating modern metamorphosis of Ovid, surprising in its imaginative modifications. Not really a diary-novel, it is rather a collection of aphoristic reflections on life, death, religion, morality, metamorphosis, and reincarnation, allegedly penned by the dying Ovid in the last days of his exile. Not divided into chapters as such, it is organized simply as a sequence of more than five hundred brief sections with such sub-

headings as "The Void," "Immortality," "Punishment," "Horror Vacui," and returning obsessively to the themes of "Metamorphosis" and "Medea." It is left to
the reader to reconstruct the story from these bits and pieces.

Focusing on Ovid's years at Tomis, the novel includes flashbacks to the poet's
childhood in Sulmona and his life in Rome, with frequent quotations in Latin
from both *Tristia* and the *Epistulae ex Ponto*. But the work introduces several surprising twists. In the first place, we are told, Ovid was not forced into exile; instead, he arranged for his own voluntary relegation from Rome because he was
thoroughly disillusioned by life in the capital, where he witnessed among other
things various incestuous relationships within the imperial family: Livia with
Tiberius, Augustus with Julia, Julia with Tiberius. Moreover, he had become disenchanted with his own writings: "My books seem to me merely ridiculous:
they have perfect verses but lack all significance" (16).[29] His emotional and physical state has deteriorated to the point that he is even impotent with his mistress
Corinna. "I had fallen into a state of utter apathy and indifference in the con-
frontations of life that transpired" (67). So he designs "strategies" to justify his
departure from Rome, suggesting that he is a subversive and an enemy of Augustus. Even the title of the *Metamorphoses* is calculated to play a role in this deception, because the emperor cannot tolerate any kind of transformation or
change: he wants everything to remain exactly as he has ordained it. Ovid's *error*,
in other words, was an invention to conceal the truth and to provide a reasonable motive for his departure. He repeatedly stresses that he left Rome by choice,
to find a new life where he could change and develop: "I left Rome because in
that city I could no longer continue to live; I had even considered the idea of
suicide: perhaps my own cowardice prompted me to go away" (29). He chose
Tomis as his place of residence in order to change his mode of existence as radically as possible. "I left Rome because it was now nothing but a locus of luxury, of degradation, and of depravity. To be a Roman citizen no longer signified
anything, even if the empire stretched across the whole known world. I chose
Tomis, a sacred place: the place where Medea, transgressing all the rules of family, of countryland, of religion, cut to pieces the body of her little brother" (244).

A second surprise (and here we hear the voice of the proud Romanian and
inhabitant of modern Constanța): in Tomis he finds a thriving seaport, a pleasant climate, and a region with the best grain on the Black Sea coast. Moreover,
it can boast a cosmopolitan Getic culture that is the product—shades of Nietzsche!—of a union of Greek Apollonian and Getic Orphic strains (176). (He reminds us that Orpheus came from the mountains of Thracia.) The reports about
hardships in his *Tristia* and *Epistulae ex Ponto* are nothing but an elaborate fiction to dissuade acquaintances from visiting him and interrupting the serenity
of his last days in this "paradiso terrestre" (49), where he has been embraced by

the native peoples and where he can live life more fully than ever before. "In a few years I have lived more intensively than during my entire previous existence" (199). Back in Rome, meanwhile, and as a confirmation of his gloomy assessment of the city's moral tone, he is denied by his wife Fabia, by his former friends (all but Cotta), and by Corinna, who takes his worst enemy as her new lover.

At Tomis Ovid finds a hut on an island in a small lake adjacent to the sea. (Mincu is clearly playing here with local legends concerning an "island" or "lake" of Ovid.) He has a dog that he names "Imperatore" (a tribute to Horia's Ovid with his dog "Augustus"?). Ill with swollen legs, bleeding gums, and digestive problems, the poet is cared for by Aia, a sorceress as well as a priestess of Zalmoxis, the Getic deity about whom Herodotus (bk. 4.94–96) reports in a passage reproduced here in the original Greek (94–95). For years they live together in a Platonic *amor intellectualis* (217) until, finally, Aia is forced by her family to enter into a marriage with a member of the royal family—a forced marriage that results in her suicide two pages from the end. But during their time together she teaches Ovid about the religion of Zalmoxis, which amounts to an acceptance of death and the belief in reincarnation: the body is restored to the earth through burial (not Roman cremation), but the spirit survives and returns in higher, purer forms. Indeed, the frequent passages on Zalmoxis amount virtually to a seminar on the subject of Getic religion. In a talk delivered while he was still at work on his novel, Mincu reviewed the obsession with Ovid among Romanian writers for whom "exile is taken for granted as an ontological given."[30] He goes on to explain that his own primary motivation was to expose the sense of spiritual tranquillity that Ovid experienced following his initiation into the teachings of Zalmoxis.

On the basis of what he learns at Tomis—notably also a closer relationship to nature, through which he recaptures the happiness of his youth at Sulmona—Ovid revises his *Metamorphoses* and substitutes Pythagoras (book 15) for the figure of Zalmoxis (reported by Herodotus to have been a protégé of Pythagoras), who was initially quoted there. Ovid also comes to understand that Medea's actions, about which he had written an earlier drama and on which he reflects continually here in the land that generated her legend, were essentially an act of liberation from the constraining past, not unlike his own sharp break with Rome.

The final twist comes at the end. Ovid has reached a point of such liberation from his past and such a desire for ultimate freedom through death, metamorphosis, and reincarnation, that he offers himself as a sacrificial victim in the quadrennial ceremony for Zalmoxis on the sacred mountain of Kogaionon, where (in accordance with the ceremony as reported by Herodotus) he is tossed into the air and impaled on three spears—a theme anticipated by the novel's epigraph (*et desunt fatis sola sepulchra meis; Ex Ponto* 3.4.76). Given the combination of an ingenious plot with philosophical speculation in the form of a historical novel, it is hardly surprising that Umberto Eco hailed the work in a dust-jacket blurb: "Even if Ovid had never existed, this book would have fascinated me just as much."

The question of the extent to which these novels written in French and Italian can be regarded as belonging to Romanian literature per se, an issue for scholars of that national literature, is irrelevant here.[31] Regardless of their language, both works are rooted deeply in a characteristically Romanian cultural tradition and succeed in communicating that tradition to a Western audience. Vintila Horia and Marin Mincu, while shaped by wholly different generational experiences, share at least two traits that many would regard as typically Romanian. First, like their countryman Mircea Eliade, they are profoundly interested in questions of comparative religion. Horia, continuing a certain medieval tradition, sees in Ovid a proto-Christian, for whom the monotheistic religion of "Zamolxis" is simply an intermediate stage; the younger writer ties him more directly to the ancient Dacian religion of Zalmoxis and its belief in reincarnation. Second, both are driven by their traditional national pride to locate Ovid within Getic-Dacian culture: as its admirer and as the forerunner of modern Romanian *Latinitas.* Accordingly, we can ascertain a line of continuity in the Romanian connection with Ovid extending from the late sixteenth-century Dimitrie Cantemir by way of Vasile Aaron and Vasile Alecsandri to the present—a tradition, as we shall see, that clearly distinguishes the Romanian view of Ovid's exile from that of other writers in the twentieth century.

◄ 8 ►

INTERIORIZED EXILE IN THE WEST

EXILE IN ENGLISH

Unlike the Romanians with their explicitly national view of Ovid, Western writers since the late 1970s have increasingly tended to view him in a more personal and subjective manner. Because the state of exile in which most of them find themselves is voluntary or purely intellectual, they are not greatly concerned with the reasons for Ovid's exile. Their attention is focused almost wholly on his response to the situation of exile, a focus echoing W. H. Auden's sentiment in 1947 that, "should circumstances ever drive me, like Ovid, into exile, I shall retire, if I am allowed, to a little fishing town in Iceland at the bottom of a grim fjord where the sun is not seen for five months in the year."[1] A similar personal view is mirrored by the historian Ronald Syme, who states in his preface that the essays in his *History in Ovid* (1978) go back to "an ancient predilection for the *Epistulae ex Ponto,* reinforced by that fruitful companion, portable on long peregrinations."

David Malouf (born 1934) is the son of Lebanese refugees who emigrated to Australia. His remarkable poetic novella *An Imaginary Life* (1978), which focuses on personal metamorphosis, only hints at the reasons for the poet's exile. Ovid, punning on his name "Naso," tells us that unlike other poets, who have an ear for language, he has a nose: "And noses are political, even when you are putting them into the most private places" (25).[2] But Malouf's interest is focused on other matters altogether. As he observes in his afterword, it was the very absence of facts regarding Ovid's life and exile that made him attractive. Malouf knows much less about Dacia than did Horia and the Romanian writers supported by an authority going back to Pârvan. Even though he uses the poems of exile for his image of Tomis, his depiction of that place—"a hundred huts made of woven branches and mud" (16)—shows a settlement much more primitive than Ovid describes it. At the same time, like Horia he was drawn to Ovid because the latter lived in "an age, the dawn of the Christian era, in which mysterious forces were felt to be at work and thinking had not yet settled into a rational mode" (154).[3] Unlike Horia, however, the author is concerned not with the religious atmosphere of the period but with its psychic mood.

It is this era of prerational thought that Malouf sets out to render in his narrative, which, though presented as a letter to readers in the future (18), amounts to a sustained interior monologue ending with the poet's death. His Tomis is a primitive community where matriarchal power still asserts itself along with shamanic magic and where the earth is still "in its original bleakness" (28), lacking the order imposed by industry and cultivation. During his first year in these surroundings Ovid—understanding nothing of the language, unfamiliar with the herbs used in the cooking, and utterly despondent in his exile—is reduced to a primal helplessness, "discovering the world as a small child does, through the senses, but with all things deprived of the special magic of their names in my own tongue" (22).

In the autumn of his second year Ovid accompanies the villagers on a deer hunt, where he witnesses shamanic rituals and sees Scythian funerary mounds. There, in the birch forests, he catches his first glimpse of the wild child whose relationship with him becomes the central theme of the narrative. As a prepubescent child, he reports in his introductory note, Ovid regularly saw, or imagined that he saw, a wild boy, whom he identified in his imagination with the lycanthropes of whom the shepherds spoke (in terms borrowed from Ovid's own account of Lycaon in book 1 of the *Metamorphoses*). So when he first glimpses the wild boy in the Dacian wilderness, he is not sure whether the latter is real or a reappearance of the feral child of his own boyhood visions.

Ovid becomes obsessed with the forest child and thinks of little else, as he gradually adjusts to his primitive surroundings. On the deer hunt the following year he is disappointed to find no trace of the boy. But on the third hunt—by now he has learned Getic—he again sees the child and manages to lure him to the edge of the encampment with food. On the fourth hunt, finally—by now Ovid has fully adjusted to life in Tomis, where he weaves nets and plants a flower garden as a symbol of civilized play and freedom within the constraints of barbarian Getic life—the deer hunters succeed in capturing the wild boy, whom they take back to Tomis.

The remainder of the novella focuses on the complex relationship between Ovid and the child—an account based extensively on Jean-Marc-Gaspard Itard's observations of Victor, the eighteenth-century "wild boy of Aveyron" (154).[4] (Both boys are the same age, about eleven or twelve years old.) As he patiently observes and instructs the child, teaching him human sounds and then a few words of Getic, Ovid is simultaneously reacquainted with repressed memories from his own childhood and youth—of his brother, his father, his experiences at Sulmo. Although the feral child is viewed with suspicion by the villagers, especially the old women and the shaman, who take him to be a lycanthrope, Ovid's activities are tolerated until the winter of the fifth year, when the boy and the headman's son are seized by a terrible fever and almost die. When the feverish wild boy utters his first word in Getic, the terrified family, convinced that the wolfboy has seized the soul of the other boy, summons the shaman.[5] Both boys recover and these fears are temporarily allayed. But the headman himself becomes ill with the same fever and dies in terrible agonies, which suggest to the villagers that his body has been occupied by the spirit of the wolf.

Knowing that they are no longer safe in the village, Ovid flees with the child, crossing the Ister (Danube) and heading north into the wilderness. In the visionary conclusion Ovid believes that he has now passed beyond dreams into "the last reality" (141), "the Child's world" (143), a place without time and a space without dimensions, like that which the shaman experiences when in his trance he departs from his own body. In these final days of his life, as he learns from the feral child to make bird sounds, Ovid experiences the unity of being from which he had been alienated by civilization. "We are continuous with earth in all the particles of our physical being, as in our breathing we are continuous with sky. Between our bodies and the world there is unity and commerce" (147). With the boy as psychagogue—the closest parallels in modern literature are the conclusions of Thomas Mann's *Death in Venice* (*Der Tod in Venedig*) and Hermann Broch's *Death of Virgil*—Ovid achieves the sense of plenitude and immeasurable happiness that foreshadows the "new era that will come to its crisis at some far point in the future" when "the millennium of the old gods . . . shudders to its end" (19).

Malouf uses Ovid's exile for his own purposes. His Ovid is not so much a political or even a literary exile, but a refugee from his time—a poet in the state of ecstasy that enables him to achieve shamanic visions inaccessible to the writer caught up in the trivial realities of his day, political or religious or other. Like the Romanians, he views the Dacian realm beyond the Ister as a place of freedom; but unlike the Ovids of Horia and Mincu, who die in or near Tomis, Malouf's Ovid makes the break into that place beyond earthly time.

Derek Mahon (born 1941) presents an Ovid displaying all the characteristics of the outsiders and victims prominent in other works of this Northern Irish poet, who has also published translations from Ovid's *Amores*.[6] His "Ovid in Tomis" (1980)[7] pendulates between ancient Rome and a modern world in which the old gods have been transformed into a "gear-box in the rain beside the road" and nereids into "the unsinkable / Hair conditioner / Knocking the icy rocks." Ovid, himself now metamorphosed into a stone, has almost forgotten the time before his name was "A dirty word in Rome." Six years after his relegation to Tomis, while his wife and friends do for him what they can, he fastens his sheepskin "By greasy waters / In a Scythian wind." This Ovid has no wish to die here

> Among these morose
> Dice-throwing Getes
> And the dust of Thrace

even though he can imagine that the huddle of mud huts (like those described by Malouf) will one day become a handsome city and an important port with an oil pipeline, a popular resort with a statue of himself gazing out to sea. As in Malouf's novel the birds, an image of enduring nature, are again singled out.

> I often sit in the dunes
> Listening hard
> To the uninhibited
>
> Virtuosity of a lark
> Serenading the sun. . . .

But unlike the Ovids of Horia and Malouf, Mahon's urbane Ovid has no wish to return to nature.

> I know the simple life
> Would be right for me
> If I were a simple man.

He understands the spirit of rock and tree and the sigh of syrinx. But in the modern world, she and her kind are "bulk-destined / For the pulping machines."

> Pan is dead, and already
> I feel an ancient
> Unity leave the earth. . . .

Ovid himself has "exchanged belief / For documentation." The Muse has departed—or else he is himself "Not poet enough / To make the connection."
Alone with our physics and myths, we would do better to ignore "the silence
of infinite space" and focus on "the infinity / Under our very noses." The texture of paper, "woven of wood-nymphs," is more articulate than any words the
poet can write, so alienated has he become from reality and nature.

> I incline my head
> To its candour
> And weep for our exile.

Like the Ovids of Horia and Malouf, this one too has become alienated by urbanity and civilization from any unity with nature.[8] But unlike them he finds
no consolation in a return to the people or to nature; Mahon leaves him alone
to "weep for our exile"—exile as the condition not only of the poet but of
modern man altogether.

C. H. Sisson (born 1914) is well known for poems on classical, including
Ovidian, themes:"Metamorphoses," "Daphne," and "Narcissus," as well as adaptations from the *Metamorphoses* and *Tristia*.[9] So it is hardly surprising to find
among his poems a bleak eleven-line "Ovid in Pontus" (from *In the Trojan Ditch,*
1974).[10] His Ovid who speaks to us in the first person is "an old man whose
death is foreseen," both respected for his wisdom and pitied for the infirmity of
his age. Still troubled by the religious doubts of his youth, he wonders "if the
air / Is empty enough to receive prayer" or whether it is simply the frailty of
old age in the harsh Pontic winter that tempts him to pray.

> A suitable place to die, or to make amends;
> Failure makes enemies as success friends.

Seamus Heaney (born 1939), writing his poem "Exposure" from County
Wicklow and therefore in no sense an exile from his native Ireland, nevertheless finds cause to identify with Ovid as he weighs his "responsible *tristia*." A
dedicated classicist, whose oeuvre sparkles with Greco-Roman themes and images, Heaney confesses that "I am neither internee nor informer; / An inner
émigré, grown long-haired and thoughtful; . . ."[11]

It is hardly surprising, finally, to find an Ovidian piece in the works of Anne

Carson (born 1950), a Canadian poet who teaches classics at McGill University in Montreal and who, in addition to translations of Sophocles' *Elektra* (1997) and Sappho's poetry (2002), has published a book on love in early Greek poetry (*Eros the Bittersweet,* 1986). A hallmark of Carson's poetry is the interpenetration of past and present, as in the scintillating counterpoint between Thucydides and Virginia Woolf on the nature of war (*Men in the Off Hours,* 2000). Such an interpenetration of Ovid's classical world and the poet's own century is conspicuous in the "short talk" entitled "On Ovid" (1995), in which Carson imagines him on a moonlit night, walking after supper back to his room, where a radio plays softly as he writes: "people in exile write so many letters."[12] "Each night about this time he puts on sadness like a garment and goes on writing." But Ovid is also in ancient Tomis where, the brief *poème en prose* concludes, he is learning Getic in order to compose an epic poem that no one will ever read. For Carson, apparently, every poet is a spiritual exile writing in a language that will be understood by few, if any.

In sum, all five Commonwealth writers transcend the narrow political reading of Ovid-in-exile to see in him, by means of poetic vision, an existential model for contemporary humanity. The situation changes dramatically when we turn to writers of Communist East Germany.

EAST GERMAN RE-VISIONS OF EXILE

Ernst Fischer (1899–1972), while not an East German, was the leading Communist intellectual in Austria during the Second Republic following World War II, and published many of his works in the German Democratic Republic. The son of a general, Fischer served as a soldier in World War I and then participated in the military mutiny at war's end. In 1920, while still a student in Graz, he published his first essay of cultural criticism in a Social Democratic newspaper, and from 1927 to 1934 edited the official party newspaper in Vienna, the *Arbeiterzeitung.* Having joined the Communist Party in 1934, he emigrated first to Prague and then spent the war years as an exile in the Soviet Republic. Following his return to Austria in 1945, he served in the national parliament as a representative of his party and edited the Communist newspaper *Neues Österreich.* Expelled from the Party in 1968 for his criticism of the Russian invasion of Czechoslovakia, Fischer wrote his memoirs of the years 1945–55 under the title *Das Ende einer Illusion* (1973; The end of an illusion).

When Fischer composed his *Elegien aus dem Nachlaß des Ovid* (1963; Elegies from Ovid's unpublished works), he was still a Communist, but the elegies suggest hidden doubts in his hitherto stalwart Stalinism, despite an afterword that makes quite explicit their Marxist basis.[13] He interprets Roman history as a class struggle between aristocrats and plebeians in a Rome corrupted by the gold of Egypt, the riches of the Orient, and a slave economy, where trade and industry prospered at the expense of the peasants and workers. Caesarism and the *pax Augusta* simply gilded the decadence of a society in which a ruthless dictator only superficially shared his power with the bureaucracy taken over from the republic. Augustus so successfully depoliticized Rome that it was difficult to attract young people to the service of the state. In this corrupt society the lives of the two Julias, mother and daughter, were an "individualistic revolt" against the cynical exploitation of sex for politics. Citing Karl Marx's doctoral dissertation on the retreat from the social to the private realm in antiquity, Fischer designates the two Julias and Ovid as the "incarnation of a new age," in which erotics replaced politics and the *Ars amatoria* became a "manifesto of opposition." When Ovid was relegated to Tomis, he found there a state of "ur-communism." Imagining that Ovid must have written other elegies more personal than the official appeals of the *Tristia* and *Epistulae ex Ponto,* Fischer offers his poems as those elegies from Ovid's unpublished works.

The poems, written in vigorous and graceful elegiac distichs, are divided into three sections. "Rome" amounts to a hard-hitting social critique along the lines of the afterword.

> Sklaven ackern sein Feld, er preist auf dem Forum die Freiheit.
> Fett vom gestohlenen Gut, lobt er das römische Recht.
>
> (8)

> (Slaves work his fields, while in the forum he praises
> freedom. / Fat from his stolen goods, he extols Roman law.)

The poet is grateful for his relegation, which has removed him far from the lies, outrage, decline, and betrayals of Rome. In distant Scythia he can still cultivate Rome at its finest in a verse by Virgil, in a woman's fragrance. (This is a frequent refrain of such German exiles as Thomas Mann, who proclaimed: "Where I am, is German culture.")

Fischer tells a different version of Leda and the swan, in which Leda—"Arm und nackt lag sie dort, die bleiche Leda des Elends" ("Poor and naked she lay there, the pale Leda of misery")—is the victim of a violent and vicious bird, "a bastard of vulture and raven" (i.e., the Roman eagle). Augustus for his part has become so inhuman that "he began to resemble his own image" ("Also dem Standbild zu gleichen begann er"). Ovid urges his daughter, in a phrase modified from Karl Marx, to dare to imagine the world differently; that's how the future begins. Meanwhile he, "the exiled, forgotten, powerless poet, on the boundary between the world and nothingness, praises the power of poetry."

> Ich, der Verbannte, Verschollne, Ohnmächtige, hart an der Grenze
>   zwischen der Welt und dem Nichts, preise der Dichtung Gewalt.
>
> (18)

The men of power, the steersmen of state, need poetry: without Homer's song there would be no Achilles. Ovid regrets that he was for too long a servant of power ("Trauer vor allem, wie lang ich Diener der Macht war!") and asks people to report to Caesar that Ovid, exiled to the edge of the civilized world, is freezing, yet cheerful and free (19).

The second section, "The Scythian Woman," comprises love elegies (with a seemingly autobiographical intensity) to the woman who has made his exile happy.

> Alles erneut sich, seit wir uns trafen.
>   Mit weißen Schläfen
>   kehrt dem gereiften Gefühl traumhaft die Jugend zurück.
>
> (26)

> (All is renewed since we met. With whitened temples Youth
> returns, dreamlike, to ripened feeling.)

Their love has restored his longing for permanence and he dreams "that we, ever transformed, shall never pass away" ("daß wir, Verwandelte stets, niemals Vergehende sind"; 31).

The concluding section ("Der Traum") presents Ovid's/Fischer's dreams for the future. He introduces the image of a lighthouse ("Der Leuchtturm," 38) that gives direction. Initially everyone sailing past saw Caesar's name painted in large letters on its walls; but gradually the sea erased the painted letters, and there reemerged, graven in eternal stone, the names of the artisans who built the tower (another Marxist commonplace). He remembers the "pain of metamorphosis" ("Schmerz der Metamorphose"; 39), the pain of being part of a transitional generation between tyranny and freedom, between the past and a better future yet to come: "to be no longer the being of once-upon-a-time and not yet the new one" ("Nicht mehr das Wesen von einst, noch nicht das neue zu sein"). He urges humanity to seek its golden age ("Goldenes Zeitalter," 40) in the future and not in the past. "I know the ruins of a desperate world. And the graying man knows that living means—to live despite everything."

> Ich kenne die Trümmer
> einer verzweifelten Welt. Und der Ergrauende weiß:
> Leben heißt—trotzdem leben.

A lengthy dialogue with the overthrown statue of Augustus (43–46) turns into an exercise in dialectics between power and freedom, between a Caesar who craved stability and order and a poet who desired change and liberty—and who created a rubble heap in the process.

> Stets nach dem Chaos zurück strebt die gestaltete Welt.
> Wir aber halten, was ist, in festen Händen. Und bergen
> unsre geordnete Welt hinter den Mauern der Macht.

> (The shaped world always strives back toward chaos. But we hold whatever is in strong hands. And protect our ordered world behind the walls of power.)

"A world must always disintegrate," Ovid replies, "if something new is to be created." Augustus confesses that he has always feared the seducer more than the conqueror, the man who conquers hearts. "May there always be an Ovid," the poet replies, to seduce the children and peoples away from you rulers of the world. Augustus maintains that Ovid's dream arose out of eternal Rome itself. But Ovid hopes that the day will come that will cleanse him from the poison of his overly Roman blood. The cycle of elegies concludes with "Daybreak" ("Anbruch des Tags," 47) proclaimed by the Scythian woman who announces harmony and peace in the world as once implicit in Homer's poetry.

> Herb noch vom Winter, bestürzt dem Hauche des Frühlings sich öffnend,
> bildet dein skythischer Mund neu das Gedicht des Homer.

> (Still harsh from winter, opening itself surprised to the breath of spring,
> your Scythian mouth forms anew the poem of Homer.)

Paradoxically, Fischer's elegies are more explicitly Marxist than the three East German Ovids. Hartmut Lange's drama *Staschek, oder Das Leben des Ovid* (1972; Staschek, or The life of Ovid) specifically incorporates the author's "experiences with the first socialist revolution on German soil,"[14] where he witnessed the "expropriation of the expropriators," the land reform and collectivization of agriculture, the cultural revolution, and the violent overthrow of all forms of social intercourse. But Lange (born 1937), an East German writer who moved to West Germany in 1965, sees himself as a twofold exile. Stalinism, regarding literature as private property, punished those who seek to make free use of it. Meanwhile the late-capitalist market economy regards all social work, including literature, as private production and its products as nothing more than goods made to be sold, forgotten, and discarded.[15] In both cases the writer is disenfranchised and exiled.

Lange adopts a more Brechtian approach to his material than does Fischer.[16] The Staschek of the title—a character carried over from *Marski,* an earlier play by Lange—is a proletarian from "east of the Elbe," who has left his former home because of a quarrel with the manager of the cooperative farm where he worked. In the twelve scenes of the play he wanders through time and space to discover that political reality has always and everywhere been the same. In the first scene, a bleak place where he encounters Vladimir and Estragon, who are still waiting for Godot (and who turn up from time to time as observers in other scenes), he witnesses Cicero's murder. When he then tries to extinguish the fire in a barn (by urinating on it), he is beaten by Roman soldiers who accuse him of being Quintus Horatius Flaccus, a lackey of Julius Caesar's assassins. After their departure the real Horace appears and apologizes for the confusion. Staschek accompanies Horace to Rome, where Horace takes a job copying business accounts in a bank, but spends his time writing odes in praise of Maecenas and Octavian. Staschek, who has seen corpses flung into the Tiber by Octavian's men, wonders why Horace praises such a ruler. Horace explains the political realities: that Virgil received his villa in return for his poetic offerings to the ruler. (Horace puts it more graphically: "Vergil kriecht Oktavian in den Hintern, das weiß hier in Rom jedes Kind," 313). Staschek delivers the odes to the avantgarde publisher Mucius, who finds them "not bad," but thinks he should choose other themes. "He is so talented that he doesn't need to lick spittle. I know a young man who has just started writing: Publius Ovidius Naso. He has written a treatise on the art of love, a genuine piece of resistance literature in this prudish atmosphere. Yes, we would have people if Virgil hadn't brought literature into disrepute through his officious style" (316). In the following scene Horace, his odes having found favor with Maecenas and Octavian, has become a celebrated poet with a Sabine villa. He declares his intention to write satires and no more odes. Spoiled by success, however, he also exploits Staschek and his slaves, even though he is himself of proletarian origins. When Staschek tries to incite the slaves to rebel, he is again beaten—this time by the slaves.

Back in Rome, Mucius complains that literature is in terrible shape: "Horace has written his I-don't-know-how-manyeth ode to Maecenas. Virgil is composing away at a national epic in which Octavian's rule is praised as the dawning of the golden age. The only person who gives me any joy is Ovid, [who is writing] an encyclopedia about the creation and transformation of the world in 800 cantos" (323). Ovid was bold enough to refuse Maecenas's demand that he undertake a national epic in the manner of Virgil. His friend Piso warns that Ovid is openly ridiculing the matrimonial laws of the new regime and making fun of Maecenas. At this point Staschek shows up in the garden, filthy and hungry, and explains that he has left Horace. "To be perfectly honest, I find a life that consists only of whoring, wine drinking, and song making rather shallow. Men have to have an ideal" (324). When Mucius objects that Horace is a Stoic with the reputation of incorruptible ethics, Staschek counters that he sleeps with the wives of his servants and beats anyone who tries to object.

Mucius takes Staschek, who needs a new employer, to Ovid. But the poet is rushing off to Elba because Maecenas is now demanding from him a propagandistic ode for the Secular Games: Ovid, taking on Staschek as a copyist, orders him to tell the spies who may seek him out that he has been on Elba for the past eight weeks and therefore has not responded to Maecenas's demand. Later at the Ludi saeculares (which bear a striking resemblance to Communist May Day celebrations), as Horace recites his new ode (not the *carmen saeculare*, but a pastiche of verses from *Odes* 4.14 and 4.15), Ovid learns that he has been ordered into exile and that a group of praetorians are waiting at his house to arrest him.

Following Ovid's departure, Staschek cleans out his house. Mucius has no further interest in Ovid's manuscripts "because literature by émigrés can't be sold" (336). Staschek, astonished at the change in Mucius's character, decides to follow Ovid to Tomis. When he finally arrives at a frontier town, however, he learns that it is Bordeaux, not Tomis; that the date is now 485; and that Ovid has been dead since the year 17. He meets the Gallo-Roman poet Sidonius Apollinaris, who is surrounded by a horde of Visigoths (Lange's comment on Western society). When the barbarians become unruly as Sidonius attempts to recite his poetry, Staschek advises him to smear his hair with rancid butter, as do the Visigoths. Now the barbarians applaud the poetry (which they still cannot understand), while the poet, nauseated by the rancid butter, constantly interrupts himself to vomit. To escape this "ancient problem," Staschek crosses the nearby river and finds himself again—at the Elbe. The final scene repeats the first almost literally; but as Staschek wipes off the butter, he discovers in his pockets a manuscript of Ovid's poetry. At first he tears it up and throws it away as useless; then he picks up the scraps again on the chance that they might someday be useful or valuable.

Lange's powerful tragicomedy uses the past to make a cynical comment on the role of the poet in history: the only ones who enjoy popular success either sell out ideologically (like Virgil and Horace) or debase themselves before their public (like Sidonius Apollinaris); writers with principles (like Ovid) must go into exile while publishers (like Mucius) sway with the political winds. Having interiorized the past, the modern writer can play freely with history, unconstrained by annalistic sequence.[17] Lange's mid-twentieth-century refugee from Central European Communism ranges through antiquity to encounter everywhere the same conditions, as symbolized most dramatically by the repetition of action in the first and last scenes of the play. In the process, Lange has produced the most interesting of the Middle European receptions of Ovid as a prototype of the poet who refuses to subjugate his art to the demands of either an Eastern totalitarian regime or a rebarbarized Western public.[18]

In comparison with Fischer's tumultuous and provocative elegies or Lange's cynical drama, Volker Ebersbach's *Der Verbannte von Tomi* (1984; The exile of Tomis) is an unpoetic fiction about political intrigue during Ovid's first two years at Tomis, making extensive use of details from *Tristia* and *Epistulae ex Ponto*.[19] Ebersbach (born 1942) studied classics and modern German literature at the University of Jena and wrote his dissertation on Petronius. A prolific author living in Leipzig, he has published—along with essays on Nietzsche and a history of his hometown Bernburg an der Saale—several historical novels, of which *Der Verbannte von Tomi* was one of the earliest. In his novel we expect, and find, reflections of the social situation in the German Democratic Republic in which Ebersbach was educated and lived.

Ovid has been exiled because he was tricked by Augustus's granddaughter Julia into watching her engage in adulterous sex and then betrayed by an opportunistic librarian jealous of Ovid's success as a poet. (The scene is depicted in vivid detail as Julia couples with her lover in a mirror-walled room, at one point turning and grinning lasciviously at the astonished poet. Julia and her friends scoff at Ovid because he has written about sex that he himself has never experienced.) Initially, still hoping to be pardoned and summoned back to Rome, Ovid resists all efforts at acclimatization: he establishes no relations with the Greek mayor of Tomis, Polymachos; he rents his fisherman's hut instead of buying it; and he seeks no friendship with the other exile in the city, a nameless hundred-year-old Greek philosopher, exiled decades earlier for his anarchic refusal to acknowledge the validity of any government. (Toward the end the Greek leaves Tomis and wanders off, like the Roman deserters in Horia's novel, to join the barbarians in the north.) Ovid escapes his depression by writing versified appeals to Augustus and letters to his wife and daughter. He also begins to have doubts about his wife's all too eager decision not to accompany him into exile.

The wholly fictitious plot revolving around intrigues at Tomis concerns the family of the city prefect, Sextus Quillius Postumus. An opportunistic and arrogant Roman, he has been married for many years to a woman of the Getae, with whom he has two children: a son Lucius, who has a weakness for Greek poetry, and a daughter Lilla, who has been brought up half "barbarian" by her mother. Postumus, who withholds letters from Ovid and apparently also neglects to forward some of Ovid's letters to Rome, is contemptuous from the start of the exiled Roman poet and eager not to affect his own chances of advancement by consorting with the man accused of treason. They disagree about politics: the prefect believes in Roman might while the poet is convinced that "no one has true and lasting power if he doesn't educate to freedom those he rules" (81). His son Lucius tries to cultivate the Roman poet, but Ovid is attracted more by his sister, who gradually falls in love with him and the sound of his poetry. When Lucius goes to Rome for his education, he coolly betrays Ovid for his own advantage.

Meanwhile, the Getae are becoming restless. One of their princes offers to keep the peace if he can marry the prefect's daughter. When Lilla rejects the offer, saying she loves someone else (meaning Ovid), war breaks out. The prefect's wife is captured and strangled by the Getae; the Romans finally outmaneuver and defeat the Getae; Lucius returns from Rome with the message announcing the futility of Ovid's hopes; and the prefect, thanks to his success in the war with the Getae, is given a new position and property in Italy.

Shortly before his departure he sends Lucius on a mission, but his son is captured by the Getae and held for ransom. Lilla takes the ransom money to the Getae, but tells them that she has merely come to bargain. When she asks Lucius what he reported about Ovid in Rome, he confesses his betrayal of the poet. Outraged, Lilla tells the Getae that their offer has been rejected; they kill Lucius by throwing him into the air and impaling him on their spears (*nota bene*: the traditional sacrifice in the rites of Zalmoxis); she then casts the money before them and offers herself as bride; refused because she is no longer a virgin, she disappears into the steppes and is never seen again.

The prefect, who has now lost his Getic wife and half-barbarian son and daughter, is not perturbed; he will marry a Roman woman when he gets back home. But in his haste to get away, he urges the ship's captain to depart with the overladen boat just before a storm, in which he perishes. (Ovid finds his corpse the next day.) At this point Ovid makes his own peace with Tomis. He buys his hut and has it improved. He establishes friendly relations with the Greek inhabitants of the town, who make him an honorary citizen and consult him on various matters. He speaks Greek and learns Getic. And when the report of Augustus's death reaches him, he makes no effort to change his life.

Ebersbach's interests, though his Ovid is finally reconciled to his life in Tomis, are clearly more political than religious. The Getae do not represent, as they do for the Romanians, the origins of a national culture but a kind of Noble Savage, whose virtues stand out in sharp contrast to the degeneracy of a Rome on the point of decline—a contrast that Ebersbach exploits for the implicit GDR critique of contemporary West German society.

A third East German writer, Waldtraut Lewin, was born 1937 in Wernigerode and studied German literature, theater, and Latin philology at Humboldt University in Berlin. Originally active as musical director of GDR theaters and opera companies, she is the prolific (book-per-year) author of popular historical novels, fairy tales, children's stories, radio plays, and libretti for two rock-operas, for which she received various prizes. Since the unification of Germany she has written several successful detective novels.

Her feminist fantasy, *Die Frauen von Kolchis* (1996; The women of Colchis),[20] revolves around a mild-mannered Roman weaver, Pamphilus, and his wife Tabea, a former prostitute, who go to Colchis in order to take advantage of land provided by Augustus as an attraction for the Roman urban proletariat. The native Getae are divided into two camps: the matriarchal women with their magical cultic practices and warlike demeanor, and the weaker men, who seek to overthrow the women and enforce their own rule.

Pamphilus, known in the local language as Fillo, is abducted by a tribe of Scythian warrior-maidens—to teach them the art of weaving and to impregnate them without the aid of their own men, with whom they are in constant conflict. Much of the story involves the fantastic magical and cultic practices of this matriarchal society with its contempt for their men and for the Romans. Meanwhile Tabea, now known as Tawa, succumbs to the male Evil Spirit, by whom she becomes pregnant. (A subplot involves sowing her field with seed that will produce a race of warriors and a Golden Fleece.) At the end, and through Fillo's mediation, the Scythian women and the Romans come to an agreement: the Romans sell their iron weapons to the Scythians in return for gold that the Scythians don't value; and the "Golden Fleece" is set up in a special temple at which the two races can henceforth meet in peace for trade.

Ovid—called only "Publius" or "the Poet"—enters the story as the neighbor of Fillo and Tawa, a clown-like figure of ridicule for all: "this braggart and pauper, this cocky guy who hides beneath his slouch hat and looks down at people—and can suddenly say something that makes your heart burn for joy and sadness," is Tabea's reaction when she hears his poetry for the first time (138). He is regarded by the Romans as a ludicrous nuisance, "a former Augustan court

poet" with patriotic zeal, whose wish is father of the thought, regardless of reality, says the Roman banker Plotius. "In the course of this winter his visions almost seem to have been realized" (266). When Pamphilus is kidnapped by the
Scythians, in an effort to enhance his own importance the poet persuades Tabea
to accompany him on a "propaganda tour" of the neighboring farms and villages and to work up enthusiasm for a civilian guard to protect the Roman set-
tlers against the (actually entirely peaceful) Scythians.

Lewin's novel stands clearly in the tradition of such recent German feminist
re-visions of classical antiquity as Christa Wolf's *Kassandra* (1983) and *Medea*
(1996). Unlike the Romanian novels, this fantasy has little basis in the historical
reality of ancient Dacia. But the feminist re-vision almost by definition involves
a satirization of the principal male figures, who are reduced to the roles of stud
(Pamphilus) and naive fool (Ovid).

POSTFIGURATIONS OF EXILE

At least since Joyce's "parallel use of the Odyssey" in *Ulysses* and its "continuous
parallel between contemporaneity and antiquity," to which T. S. Eliot attributed
the importance of a scientific discovery,[21] writers have frequently used familiar
mythic patterns—Jesus, Parzival, Hamlet, Faust, Don Quixote, and others—to
provide structure and meaning to their modern postfigurations.[22] The technique is doubly striking when the prefiguring model—like Virgil in Dante's
Divine Comedy or in Thornton Wilder's *Cabala* (1926)—makes a visionary appearance within the more recent work. Both devices are evident in Derek Walcott's poem "The Hotel Normandie Pool" (1980).[23] The first of its three parts
sets the scene. It is New Year's morning, and the fifty-year-old poet, noted for
his poems based on ancient models, is sitting at a table beside the pool of "a
small, suburban tropical hotel" in Trinidad, smoking, writing, and undergoing a
midlife crisis. Reminiscing about his ex-wife and three children, he contemplates "the disfiguring exile of divorce" and appeals to Aquarius to "Change me,
my sign, to someone I can bear." At this point, and as though conjured up by
these reflections on exile and metamorphosis, a man—seemingly a "petty businessman" in sandals, robe, and sunglasses—emerges. As the newcomer stands
"with Roman graveness" at the edge of the pool, his white towel "toga-slung,"

> a phrase was forming in that distant tongue
> of which the mind keeps just a mineral glint,
> the lovely Latin lost to all our schools:
> "*Quis te misit, Magister?*" And its whisper went
> through my cold body, veining it in stone.

In the imagination of the poet, himself now transformed into a piece of statuary, the pool is magnified into "that Ovidian / thunder of surf between the Baltic pines." (Walcott apparently confuses the Baltic with Ovid's Black Sea.) Recalling the squares and palaces of Ovid's Rome, he longs for an epiphany: "Turn to us, Ovid." The poet recalls that his own ancestors "were slave and Roman."

> My own face
> held negro Neros, chalk Caligulas;
> my own reflection slid along the glass
> of faces foaming past triumphal cars.

This analogy prompts thoughts on the similarities between the totalitarian state of Augustan Rome and the dictatorships of Caribbean islands.

> Master, each idea has become suspicious
> of its shadow. A lifelong friend whispers
> in his own house as if it might arrest him;
> markets no more applaud, as was their custom,
> our camouflaged, booted militias
> roaring past on camions, the sugar-apples
> of grenades growing on their belts; ideas
> with guns divide the islands; in dark squares
> the poets gather like conspirators.

At this point Ovid speaks,[24] saying that in his exile he first missed his language and his own daughter. In a strophe replete with images reminiscent of Malouf—notably the clod fires, the allusions to wolves, and the songs of birds—he recalls:

> "Tiled villas anchored in their foaming orchards,
> parched terraces in a dust cloud of words,
> among clod-fires, wolfskins, starving herds,
> Tibullus' flute faded, sweetest of shepherds.
> Through shaggy pines the beaks of needling birds
> pricked me at Tomis to learn their tribal tongue,
> so, since desire is stronger than its disease,
> my pen's beak parted till we chirped on song
> in the unequal shade of equal trees."

Ovid suggests that he sought out his exile in order to find freedom to write and to escape the political tyranny of Rome. He consoles the poet against detractors who will criticize him for his adherence to traditional forms.

"Romans"—he smiled—"will mock your slavish rhyme,
the slaves your love of Roman structures, when,
from Metamorphoses to Tristia,
art obeys its own order. . . ."

(44)

With those words the figure, once again the small-time businessman, ties his robe and goes back into the hotel. As the poet wonders why this epiphany came to him here of all places, in a small hotel, he hears a final ironic echo: "Because to make my image flatters you." The modern poet finds comfort, in other words, in the ancient prefiguration, which has of course been suggested to him, and dreamily imposed on the figure of the other hotel guest, by his own recollection of, and immersion in, the life and works of Ovid.

In the two concluding strophes, as dusk falls over the hotel, the poet gazes at the water and understands a truth that had eluded him in his Narcissistic obsession with his own image:

what this pool recites is not a phrase
from an invisible, exiled laureate,

but the ultimate truth that, in time and space, nature alone endures and supersedes all petty human concerns, whether personal, political, or literary: "Suspension of every image and its voice."

Ovid makes no walk-on appearance in *The Old Man and the Wolves* (*Le vieil homme et les loups,* 1991) by Julia Kristeva, but his exile prefigures symbolically the life of the contemporary thinker in intellectual exile. Kristeva was born in 1941 in eastern Bulgaria, not far from Ovid's place of exile. Emigrating to France in 1965, she received her doctorate in French literature and later completed her training in psychoanalysis. Her allegorical work is located in a country named Santa Barbara—a locale, the narrator tells us, that might be a New England forest near the Canadian border, a savage corner of the Carpathians, or the northern mountains of Greece (27)[25] but which sounds very much like the Bulgaria where the semiotician and feminist theoretician was born and educated, with its culture of icons, Gregorian chants, and late modernization.[26] The country has been invaded by wolves that have killed thousands of inhabitants. The wolves are clearly metaphorical: a political image for the Soviets who invaded Bulgaria and other East bloc countries; and a philosophical metaphor for a civilization gone lupine and "barbarian" (Santa Barbara!)—a reading confirmed by the statement on the last page, "Santa Barbara is everywhere" (268). When it is discovered that ten thousand officers, "the elite of the army, of the aristocracy, of the nation" (19), have been slaughtered—by Scythians? by wolves? by the Russians and their collaborators?—a French journalist arrives to investigate the story: Stéphanie Delacour, the daughter of the former French ambassador to Santa Barbara. When she arrives, she discovers other mysteries: Are her former schoolmates Alba and Vespasien, now married, trying to poison each other? Who is the dead girl found in the lake, and were the marks on her throat made by a knife or by wolves? Above all, who killed the Old Man by unplugging his life-support system in the hospital? Having arrived with the intention of writing a political commentary, Stéphanie tells us, she ends up with a detective story (259). Ultimately she returns to Paris, leaving all these questions unresolved.

What makes this curious novel relevant in an Ovidian context is the Old Man of the title, a former classics master with whom Stéphanie and her friends all studied. Known simply as "le Vieil Homme" or Septicius Clarus (a name borrowed from the friend to whom Suetonius dedicated the first books of his *Caesars*) or Scholasticus or the Professor, he is writing a collection of erudite observations and epiphanies entitled *Près* or *Prata* (44)—another (unspecified) allusion to the lost Suetonian miscellany *Prata*. Through him and his protegée Alba many classical allusions enter the works. Virgil is never cited, but there are frequent references to Suetonius, to Tibullus's love elegies, and above all to Ovid. The book opens with a motto from Ovid: "I have conceived the plan to tell about the metamorphoses of beings into new forms," which is cited again almost on the last page (267) in Ovid's Latin (*Met.* 1.1–2). The characters frequently quote Ovid. And the theme of metamorphosis governs the entire work—the metamorphosis of modern men into wolves, which the Old Man is able to understand through and by means of Ovid. "Between the two of them, Ovid and Septicius, throbbed the undecidable, the pernicious human condition" (32). This theme also accounts for the frequent allusions to Lycaon, who "became a wolf and kept traces of his old form": *Fit lupus et veteris servat vestigia formae* (171–72; *Met.* 1.237). By the end of the book Stéphanie has come to believe that the Old Man has been reincarnated in her—"A metamorphosis that would perhaps have amused the persistent reader of Ovid" (249).

The Balkan setting is appropriate because the Old Man is also Ovid in exile. "In which century are we? In the first, in exile on the shores of the Black Sea, dreaming of metamorphoses of human beings who are engaged in a new era, no less burdened with all the animality of the world? Or in the present, in Santa Barbara, where a Big Booby is soon going to disconnect the artificial lung that still keeps alive the Old Man haunted by the memory of Ovid?" (172). His death, she continues, has introduced her to the realm of myth. The Old Man had dreamed of a world without wolves. He finally died, or was eliminated, she concludes, because he realized that the wolves have invaded even those closest to him, that there is no longer a "Berlin Wall" between his people and the wolves, and that there is no place in this country for anyone who believes in Western culture and a civilized society. "This interpretation of the two worlds that his consciousness, inevitably moral, took to be incompatible, seems to me logically as the true cause of his end" (260).

Although he never appears, Ovid is the dominating presence in this philosophical novel on the power of evil to corrupt: as the author of the *Metamorphoses,* a poem that symbolizes the transformations reshaping the modern world; and as the exiled author, whose destiny prefigures that of the mysterious Old Man, who indeed might even be Ovid reincarnate in this novel of transformations. Kristeva, widely known from her teaching at universities in France and the United States, is presumably a better psychoanalyst and theoretician than a writer of fiction. Her attempt to combine the philosophical novel with the thriller is ultimately satisfactory in neither genre: the philosophical issues are only fuzzily adumbrated, and the plot lacks the clear solutions of the detective story.

The exiled Ovid again makes an appearance in a much finer postfigurative novel by Luca Desiato, who was born in 1941 in the Rome that plays a prominent role in all his fiction.[27] In his early twenties Desiato spent four years in Buenos Aires, where he studied philosophy and theology and became acquainted with Jorge Luis Borges. The influence of such thinkers as Jacques Maritain and Henri-Louis Bergson as well as contemporary Latin American fiction are both apparent in the work of this prolific writer, who is known especially for historical novels about such figures as Galileo (*Galileo mio padre,* 1983), Caravaggio (*La notte dell'angelo,* 1994), and Julian the Apostate (*Giuliano l'Apostate,* 1997).

Desiato's *Sulle Rive del Mar Nero* (1992; On the shores of the Black Sea) deals with a few months in the life of the elderly Italian writer Saverio—"In fifty years of creative activity: ten novels and a dozen other works" (198)[28]—who lives in Rome, widowed and plagued by high blood pressure, weak bladder control, and constipation. In the kitchen, his dead wife Dora appears to him in visions; his daughter Giulia died years earlier. He is visited daily by his grandniece Lena and attended by an elderly housekeeper, Zaira. Now, three months before his eightieth birthday, which is to be celebrated with public acclaim and a prize, he recalls the bronze monument to Ovid that he saw in Sulmona (his wife's birthplace) years before and begins to write a novel about Ovid's exile. "The moment had come when his suffering settled into ancient grief" (17). Perhaps modernity means nothing more than to be ancient, he thinks, "to repeat a mysterious assent, like the leaves of trees that its branches put forth every year" (24). Drawing a parallel between Ovid's exile and his own spiritual isolation, he comes to the melancholy conclusion that the human condition is perhaps nothing other than "a point of grief in the circularity of lives" (153).

During the next three months the third-person account of Saverio's daily life alternates with chapters from the first-person account he writes about Ovid, and the parallels between the two lives emerge more and more vividly in a work that Desiato has termed "the double exile of Ovid."[29] Saverio dreams (stimulated by the account of a friend) of Mauthausen concentration camp, where he must push stones like Sisyphus; the rector of the seminary where he studied as a boy is compared to Ovid's enemy "Ibis"; Lena, returning from trip to Greece, becomes Iris, the messenger of Juno (175).

Saverio's account begins in ancient Rome at the time when Ovid learns that he is being sent into exile "for a serious mistake, which was not named" (19). Saverio has studied the records and finds no clear motives for the exile: the most plausible being that he acted as an intermediary for Augustus's granddaughter Giulia in her love affair with a man from the hated party of Anthony. In Tomis, Ovid is initially sustained by letters from his wife Fabia and his friend Cotta, accounts based directly on the *Tristia* and *Ex Ponto* (e.g., the attempts of "friends" in Rome to swindle him, as at *Tr.* 1.6). Ovid acquires—through the mediation of his friend, the cheese-merchant Eaco—an Ethiopian slave whom he names Julia (for his daughter? for Augustus's granddaughter?). When after many years Augustus dies, Ovid still gets no reprieve. And he learns that his wife wants to divorce him. He ultimately dies: "Now you can finally open the door—thief, benefactress, smuggler of oblivion—that will carry me back to my city, to my proper place, to my projects, a creature like me, entanglement of my reason [intricaio della mia ragione], my other self. Sweet death" (196).

While he is writing his account, Saverio himself suffers fits of senile paranoia. When his housekeeper goes away for a vacation and his niece departs for Greece with her boyfriend, Saverio entertains himself increasingly with thoughts of the past and memories and visions of his wife and daughter—just as Ovid does in his exile. At the end he prepares for his birthday celebrations. As he stands shaving, he sees an apparition in the bathroom mirror: Publius Ovidius. For a short time, he tells the Roman poet, we were companions. "You were my daemon, I was your explanation" (201). Now, he says, he is liberating himself from Ovid, each having had his own life and punishment. When Ovid shakes his head, Saverio tries to explain: "I was supposed to write about you, about impatience, about resignation. A protest," he begins. But ultimately, for Ovid, "to live in solitude, under inclement skies but far from the foulness of a world where knowing how to live means to corrupt or be corrupted, was a kind of unexplored liberty" (202). Ovid continues to shake his head. "How to make you understand that life, love, art itself are exile? Not from a preceding blissful existence, but from itself.

Exile and life itself are a failure to recognize oneself." Saverio now understands that the Latin poet has "infected" him. Exile is more than physical relegation to a remote place. Life itself, the absurdity of human existence, amounts to a state of exile—a constant struggle to reconcile happiness with despair, life with death. It is the goal of life, whether ancient or modern, to accept that never-ending cycle with courage.

The exiled Ovid has been adapted to a variety of ends. From the proto-Christian and ur-ancestor of the Romanians to the spiritual exile of the Commonwealth writers, from the political foil and feminist dupe of the Germans to the existential mirror of the French and Italian writers, Ovid and Tomis have undergone a series of metamorphoses that strikingly transform the poet's life and works. Unlike any other figure from classical antiquity, the person of Ovid has entered and established for himself a conspicuous place in modern European literature.

PART III

OVID AND THE
LATE MODERNS

◢ 9 ◣

Ovid in the Sixties and Seventies

The Bimillennial Celebrations

It seems singularly appropriate that the major scholarly work initiating the post-war reception of Ovid in the West should have been written in exile. The eminent classicist Hermann Fränkel (1888–1977) left Germany in the 1930s and spent the remainder of his academic career in the United States at Stanford University. Fränkel established his reputation in Germany as a scholar of classical Greek literature and philosophy. So it is striking that, invited to deliver the Sather Classical Lectures at the University of California at Berkeley, he chose a Roman topic—a topic on which, as he confides in his preface, he had never previously published a line: *Ovid: A Poet between Two Worlds* (1945).[1] If, as he goes on, he "enjoyed writing this study more than anything before," that enjoyment and his choice of topic can surely be attributed at least in part, though he never says so, to a sense of personal identification with the poet who had himself experienced exile almost two thousand years earlier.

Fränkel undertakes his project explicitly as the rehabilitation of a Roman poet whose reputation has been "under a cloud for more than a hundred years" (1). To be sure, to the extent that Fränkel points to Ovid's shortcomings, finds him "more frank than we should wish in matters of sex," and ranks him lower in stature than Virgil, he is bound by standards of the past: he fails to acknowledge that the aspect of the Roman character represented by Ovid, though wholly different from the *pietas* and *rusticitas* exemplified by Virgil and Horace, is equally indigenous and legitimate. At the same time, while maintaining that Ovid's writings "mark the beginning decline of Antiquity," he also detects in them "elements indicating the emergence of a new world" and sees Ovid as "a true child of an age of transition" (3)—a view unwittingly akin to the spirit of the Romanian scholars and poets (with whose works he gives no evidence of being acquainted). Fränkel's *Ovid* is a "life and works" based on an exhaustive familiarity with Ovid's texts, from which he quotes liberally in English for the nonspecialist American audience of his lectures. (The scholarly apparatus, as well as all the Latin, is relegated to the extensive endnotes.) In eighteen chapters he deals with all the works, including the *Remedia amoris* and the *Ibis,* as well as Ovid's life: his youth, his banishment (which Fränkel attributes to Ovid's knowledge of the younger Julia's adultery), and his years of exile.

Fränkel's work, though praised by reviewers as being "friendly, unassuming, and direct," was nevertheless criticized as being confused about its target audience and hence thought incapable of reaching "the general public."[2] The real turning point in the postwar reception did not arrive for another decade. The intervening years saw occasional works on mythological themes such as André Gide's poetic novella *Thésée* (1946), William Carlos Williams's poem "Narcissus in the Desert" (1953), Leopold Ahlsen's postfiguring radio play *Philemon und Baukis* (1956), or Zbigniew Herbert's poem "Apollo and Marsyas" (1961),[3] but in most cases of mythological poetry, it is difficult to specify Ovid as the source.[4] Lalla Romano's work *Le metamorfosi* (1951), a collection of seventy-four brief dreams, owes nothing but its title to Ovid, as the author conceded in a later edition.[5]

One conspicuous exception is Gottfried Benn's poem "The Death of Orpheus" ("Orpheus' Tod" in his *Statische Gedichte,* 1948). Benn (1886–1956) composed his poem (1946) in conscious counterpoint to Ovid's *Metamorphoses,* which he read in the classic German translation by Johann Heinrich Voss (1798).[6] "Do you have Ovid's *Metamorphoses* at hand?" he inquired of a close friend on 31 August 1946. "In 'Orpheus and Eurydice' I always found the second part more striking than the familiar first part."[7] (In Voss's translation the two separate episodes are given different titles: "Orpheus und Eurydice" at the beginning of book 10 and "Orpheus Tod" at the beginning of book 11.) In the same letter Benn reports that he has just returned from a visit to his wife's grave and confesses that it is his fervent wish to be buried beside her. In his mind, Ovid's account of Orpheus and Eurydice is clearly linked with his own life. The poem constitutes an attempt to come to grips with his own grief through poetic objectification.

While Benn does not say so, his poem can also be regarded as a response to

Rilke's *Sonette an Orpheus*. In his influential lecture and essay "Problems of Lyric Poetry" (1951) Benn posits Rilke as the key example of everything a modern poem should *not* be: it should not apostrophize; it should not use genitive metaphors; it should avoid colors; and it should eschew the "seraphic tone."[8] Benn's 54-line poem closely follows Ovid's account of Orpheus's death—and thereby differs sharply from Rilke's sonnets. It begins at the moment when Orpheus has been left by Eurydice and rejected by the underworld—left alone with the power of his lyre to cover the mountains with forests.[9]

> Wie du mich zurückläßt, Liebste—
> von Erebos gestoßen,
> dem unwirtlichen Rhodope
> Wald herziehend, . . .

> (As you leave me behind, dearest,
> rejected by Erebos, moving from the
> forests of inhospitable Rhodope. . . .)

Now, three years after Eurydice's death (Benn's own wife had died a year earlier), Orpheus believes that he can hear her voice more purely, though she is with the shades below. He is pursued by the nymphs, who first urge him to forget his dead wife and then threaten him;

> "fort die Töne—
> Vergessen—!"
> —drohen—!

> ("Away with the sounds
> —forget!"—they threaten)

Another entices him, vainly, with hints at unrestrained passion and then again with threats. But Orpheus keeps thinking of Eurydice, willing her image not to be transformed into some form of nature like the metamorphoses of Ovid's poem and willing himself not to seek consolation in the arms of a courtesan while thinking of her.

> Nein, du sollst nicht
> verrinnen,
> du sollst nicht übergehn in
> Iole, Dryope, Prokne,

> die Züge nicht vermischen mit Atalanta,
> daß ich womöglich Eurydike
> stammle bei Lais.

> (No, you must not ebb away, must not
> turn into Iole, Dryope, Procne, must not
> mingle your features with Atalanta, so
> that I might possibly stammer
> "Eurydice" when I'm with Lais.)

Still they threaten him. As he loses his power over nature, stones no longer follow his song: they strike the singer as the women hack at him with primitive tools. Exposed to the blows of the furious maenads, with wet eyes and bleeding mouth, his body, now wholly dehumanized and lacking even a name, floats down the river as the shores resound.

> nun wehrlos dem Wurf der Hündinnen,
> der wüsten—
> nun schon die Wimper naß,
> der Gaumen blutet—
> und nun die Leier—
> hinab den Fluß—

> die Ufer tönen—

> (now defenseless against the throwing
> of the bitches, the wild ones—now
> already the eyelids damp, the mouth
> bleeds—and now the lyre—down the
> river— / the banks resonate—.)

Benn's utterly un-Rilkean poem amounts to a violent lyrical concentration of Ovid's epic lines and images (the hound-like women; the lifeless bleeding mouth; the resounding shores) with occasional archaic words borrowed from Voss's translation.[10] But with few exceptions Ovid played at best a peripheral role in Western culture of the immediate postwar years: musically, for instance, in Richard Strauss's "study for twenty-three solo strings" *Metamorphosen* (1946); in Benjamin Britten's composition *Six Metamorphoses after Ovid* (1951), in which Britten creates (through the use of various musical forms) tonal portraits of Ovidian figures, ranging from an exuberant Bacchus ("Allegro paesante") to an introspective Narcissus ("Lento piacevole") and including Pan, Phaethon, Niobe, and Arethusa;[11] or George Balanchine's ballet adaptation of *Metamorphoses* (1952). The postwar period was still an *aetas Virgiliana,* as evidenced by Broch's magnificent *Death of Virgil.*

This situation began to change in 1957–58, when the bimillennial of Ovid's birth—in sharp contrast to the neglect of the anniversary of his death in 1917—was widely commemorated in Europe. We have already noted the international conferences in Sulmona and Rome, where the Romanian scholars first came to Western attention. At an official ceremony in Rome on May 10, 1958, the laurels were restored to Ovid that Augustus had stripped from him centuries earlier. An important volume of papers—*Ovidiana: Recherches sur Ovide*—appeared in France. A corresponding German volume—*Ovid,* edited by Michael von Albrecht and Ernst Zinn (Darmstadt: Wissenschaftliche Buchgesellschaft, 1968)—was not published for ten more years, but the occasion was variously observed in Germany.

In 1957 Ulrich Fleischer published an article titled "On the Bimillennial of Ovid," which was devoted mainly to a scholarly study of "epic tradition and personal statement in the proemium of Ovid's *Metamorphoses.*"[12] But the specific analysis is preceded by a five-page general introduction, in which the author calls for a revaluation of Ovid and points out the relativism of value judgments. "Every value judgment, if it is not foolish or lunatic, always grasps 'something' about its object and at the same time characterizes the person making the judgment." Virgil, Horace, and Augustus were celebrated during the 1930s by readers who paid more attention to their "political" dimension than to their human or aesthetic aspects. Ovid was rejected precisely because of his refusal to be aligned with the Augustan chorus of literary propaganda. Scholars of Latin culture, focusing on the Augustan age and realizing that Ovid somehow did not fit that model, tended to neglect him, just as he was often cut out of the school curriculum. Fleischer proposes a new approach. "If, in contrast to a tradition of centuries, we no longer regard Ovid as a classic of the Augustan Age but as the most significant poet of the incipient Age of the Caesars, if we no longer see him directly beside Virgil and Horace and, mostly to his disadvantage, compare him to them, then his bimillennial celebration can inspire us to a new and livelier sympathy and compensate for long neglect."

The next year, in a lecture delivered at his university to commemorate the bimillennial, the Tübingen classicist Ernst Zinn took this suggestion a step further.[13] With reference to Freud's essay *Civilization and Its Discontents* (*Das Unbehagen in der Kultur,* 1930) Zinn maintained that Ovid's poetry is characterized precisely by the blissful "contentment" he experiences in the sophisticated urbanity and culture of Rome. This contentment can be sharply differentiated from the cultural pessimism of the preceding generation—notably Sallust, Horace, and Virgil—and their fondness of *rusticitas* and *simplicitas*. More vigorously than Fleischer, Zinn insists that Ovid incorporates an aspect of Latinity that since Plautus and Terence had lost its literary representatives, an aspect of elegance and urbanity that Germans of the past five decades, as a result of their own historical situation and overseriousness, had ignored. Zinn's essay, thanks to its position as the first piece in the widely distributed essay-collection *Ovid* (1968)—and no doubt also to his appeal to Sigmund Freud, which at that time in Germany was still unusual enough to be startling—received considerable attention and contributed to the general revaluation of Ovid.

In 1959 the Artemis Press in Zurich circulated as a gift to friends of the publishing house a charming little book by the Swabian poet Josef Eberle (1901–86), a book dealer and journalist, a socialist and pacifist who had to publish during the war under a pseudonym. A doctor of philosophy honoris causa of Tübingen University and poet laureate of his hometown Rottenburg, he was the author of several volumes of poems in Latin (*Horae,* 1955; *Laudes,* 1959; *Amores* 1961; *Cave canem,* 1962). Eberle's *Stunden mit Ovid* (1959; Hours with Ovid) opens with a sketch of the poet's life, reliably narrated on the basis of Ovid's elegies, which he gracefully translated into German distichs. The second chapter depicts Ovid's birthplace of Sulmo as Eberle experienced it in 1958 when he attended the international Ovid conference—with its *Corso Ovidio,* its *Ristorante Ovidio,* and its monument to Ovid (a copy of the 1887 statue in Constanţa). It goes on (chap. 3) to survey the reception of Ovid over the centuries and his rejection, toward the end of the eighteenth century, because of the Rococo spirit in his *Amores*. Eberle then analyses the tale of Pygmalion as exemplary for the themes and techniques of the *Metamorphoses*. The penultimate chapter recapitulates the image of Rome that emerges from Ovid's poems and the inevitable grief that its loss caused him. The little book ends with reflections on Ovid's view, and that of Roman literature, of immortality—an immortality that in fact the poet achieved long after the grandeur of ancient Rome had receded into the past. Eberle's prose is graced by striking aperçus: "It is typical that the two powers that penetrate so profoundly into his own life, 'love' and 'art,' are fused into a well-nigh programmatic unity in the title of his masterpiece, 'The Art of Love,' and that they also emerge inextricably bound together in the figure of his Pygmalion, determining his destiny and his happiness" (51). Thanks to such different works, which reached different audiences, the bimillennial penetrated the literary consciousness in Germany as profoundly as in France and Italy.

In England L. P. Wilkinson anticipated the bimillennial celebrations with his widely praised introduction to the poet's life, works, and influence: *Ovid Recalled* (1955).[14] Wilkinson acknowledges the contribution of his predecessors: notably

Ripert, Rand, Fränkel, and Edgar Martini's short *Einleitung zu Ovid* (1933). But of the two earlier works in English, he finds Rand's "all too brief," while Fränkel's "suffers from what most critics seem to agree to be fanciful interpretation" (ix). Wilkinson intends his own book not as a contribution to scholarship but as an introduction for "the Latinate reading public" in the nature of "an anthology with running commentary" (xi). Accordingly, the work contains extensive passages in Latin accompanied by Wilkinson's own skillful translations into rhyming couplets. In ten chapters he covers Ovid's life and works with knowledgeable contextualization of such topics as the Latin erotic elegy, Roman didactic poetry, and classical aetiological works. The longest chapter is devoted to the *Metamorphoses*. Wilkinson takes a critical stance, arguing that Ovid's feelings become suspect to the modern mind "when he solicits our sympathy for one woman after another" in the *Heroides* (89) and that the first eleven books of the *Metamorphoses* are more successful than the "epic seriousness" of the last four, where Ovid is competing with "poets who surpass him in this vein" (237–38). The last two chapters are devoted to useful surveys of Ovid's reception in the Middle Ages and the Renaissance. The book concludes, following an analysis of reasons for the decline of his reputation in the nineteenth century, with the suggestion that "perhaps even now it is not too late" for a revaluation of Ovid in classical circles. Wilkinson's work was heralded as "erudite and generally humane," as a "scholarly and sprightly defense of Ovid," and as "a mine of information and a feast of criticism" from which Ovid emerges as "a delicate, bookish, witty intellectual who realized early in life that nothing but a total devotion to poetry would satisfy him."[15]

THE SKEPTICAL GENERATION

It is symptomatic that the bimillennial year, with its international chorus of scholars, also saw the publication of a major study by a distinguished German sociologist, Helmut Schelsky, on the postwar youth of Western industrial society—those who came to intellectual maturity between 1945 and 1955—who labeled its German manifestation as "the skeptical generation."[16] This generation, whose counterparts in England were known as the "cautious" young men and in the United States as the Eisenhower conservatives, was characterized by a radical depoliticization and de-ideologization of consciousness, in contradistinction to a preceding generation that was both open to political loyalties (in fascism and communism alike) and ideologically active.[17] The skepticism of this new postwar generation involved, first, a rejection of the vague idealism and romantic freedom raptures of the preceding generation and, second, the will to find its security in personal existence. It amounted to a turning away from any form of collectivization and a search for refuge and security in the private realm.

Schelsky's analysis of the "skeptical" generation applies with surprising precision to Ovid's attitudes in contrast to the preceding generation of Horace and Virgil. And it helps to explain why, after an interlude of some four decades, Ovid again attained a certain popularity. The bimillennial celebrations of 1957 and 1958, which produced an appreciable renewal of scholarly activity concerning Ovid, were accompanied by a conspicuous revival of literary interest. We have already spoken of the novels and poems that responded to Ovid as the archetypal exile. Other writers of the skeptical generation were addressing his earlier life and the reasons for the exile.

While Eckart von Naso (1899–1972) does not belong by date of birth to the skeptical generation, this conservative and legally trained dramatist and novelist, who became well known in the Weimar Republic as artistic director on West German stages, shares and projects the values of his younger contemporaries. Unlike Horia's *God Was Born in Exile* (1960), Naso's virtually contemporaneous *Liebe war sein Schicksal* (1958; Love was his destiny) devotes only a few concluding pages (25 of 380) to the period of exile.[18] The novel, in which Ovid's life is embedded in a well-informed political and cultural context, is much better than its kitschy title suggests. To be sure, love—that is, the private rather than the political sphere—constitutes the unifying theme, but several other themes are introduced: notably the reasons for Ovid's exile and the tantalizing suggestion that Ovid through two of his lovers (a Jewish hetaera and a Roman actress) learned about Hebrew prophecies of the Messiah, their religion of monotheism ("the Unknown God"), and the birth of Jesus in Bethlehem, and that he was tempted to write about it. But the theme of proto-Christianity, which parallels the contemporaneous Romanian ideas, is not carried through.

Naso's literary device is the constant back-and-forth between present and past, indicated by chapters alternating between the modern narrator and various first-person voices from the past: mainly Ovid's, but also official protocols, dialogues between others (Messalla and Pollio; Ovid's first wife Cornelia and her friend Lalage; Ovid's supervisor in government and a friend), a letter from Horace to Virgil, and so forth. Other techniques of alienation are also introduced. For instance, the narrator relates the poignancy of Ovid's exile poems to Shakespeare's sonnets (378), compares Ovid's elegy on sexual impotence (*Amores* 3.7) to Goethe's treatment of the same topic in his poem "Das Tagebuch" (197), discusses the similarities of Augustus and Frederick the Great (228), and reports on Catherine the Great's visit to the Black Sea to visit Ovid's place of death. On occasion, history (e.g., the relationship of Augustus and Livia) is recounted in the form of contemporary gossip, and elsewhere a Greek doctor analyzes Julia's sex-craze in modern terms as "a product of her genetics and her environment" (242). In one chapter the ancient Ovidius Naso is interviewed by the modern author Naso, who informs him that "you belong to the bestsellers of the 20th century even if you don't understand the American phrase" (237).

The story of Ovid's life is told in four parts. In the first part, based extensively on details from the *Amores,* we learn about his early marriage to Cornelia (the wife who was neither *digna* nor *utilis; Tr.* 4.10.69), who deceives him with men and women alike. To rid herself of an unwanted child she secretly undergoes an abortion, an action that precipitates their separation and subsequent divorce. To distance himself from his wife, Ovid makes a trip to Greece, where he has a sudden epiphany on the Acropolis—"Transformation is the essence of poetry and of our world" (87)—and decides that he ought to write book about it. At a symposium with friends in Athens he meets the Jewish beauty Judith, who tells him tales of Hebrew religious lore.

His infatuation with Judith, who does not reappear in the novel, and his fascination with her tales leads him to the Near East. There he is visited by a Jewish scholar who presents him with a copy of the biblical Song of Solomon, which astonishes Ovid by its parallels to his own *Amores.* On his way back to Rome, to take up reluctantly the office obtained for him by his father, he stops in Sicily, where he encounters a traveling theater troupe who reenact scenes from his *Amores.* He falls in love with the actress playing the role of Corinna and in whom he recognizes "a piece of eternally active nature," just as Judith was "a piece of the mystery of prophecies" (165). (They make love in a pool in a scene that the narrator compares to the watery mingling of Alpheius and Arethusa at *Met.* 5.572–641.) Following a festive dinner to celebrate the premiere of his *Medea,* he tries to sleep with his wife's (bisexual) friend Lalage but turns out to be impotent. Lalage (whose name in Greek means "babbler") reports their encounter to Corinna in the hope of undermining her love (just as she had undermined Cornelia's love).

At the beginning of part three, Ovid meets Augustus's daughter Julia in a disreputable inn. After publication of the *Ars amatoria* he is summoned by an angry Augustus, but is saved from the emperor's wrath by Julia's intervention. Following a sexual encounter with the voracious Julia, Ovid is introduced into her literary cénacle, where he admires a gifted young poet, Perilla, who turns out to be the daughter of the elegant patrician, Fabia Marcella. When Corinna pursues her career to the East, Ovid marries Marcella. Augustus, catching his daughter at one of her notorious orgies, sends her into exile, but Ovid, now married to a member of the respected Fabian family, is spared. When Corinna dies in the Near East, her account of the miraculous birth at Bethlehem of a

Jewish Messiah is sent to Ovid. Meanwhile, at a *naumachia* sponsored by Augustus, Ovid arranges for Silanus to meet the emperor's granddaughter Julia.

Now at the peak of his life and career, Ovid is teeming with literary plans, including the story of Jesus as he has learned it from Corinna's account. Julia (the granddaughter) pays him a visit and arranges to meet Silanus in Ovid's garden house. When the secret police catch the two lovers, Augustus orders both Julia and Ovid into exile, whereupon Ovid burns the manuscript of his *Metamorphoses* in anger. The account of his last days in Rome and the months-long trip to Tomis closely follows the *Tristia*. At Tomis, where he has reached the "nadir of human existence" (358), he is attended by a small Getic girl he calls "Parva" and her brother. He soon learns to wear Getic garb for warmth, and by the third year speaks Getic and has friends among the natives. But after Augustus's death his hopes for a reprieve are dashed. Old and sick, Ovid hopes that his books will bring him lasting fame. Then he walks out into the Black Sea and drowns himself.

In its focus on the private sphere and its explanation of Ovid's exile on wholly nonpolitical grounds Naso's novel exemplifies the attitudes of the new "skeptical" generation of postwar Germans—a view also characteristic, if we look back at the preceding chapter, of Hartmut Lange (born 1937), whose Ovid is a wholly nonideological writer and, as a result, suffers the consequence of exile in a society driven by ideological commitments.

The English poet Geoffrey Hill (born 1932) wrote his short poem "Ovid in the Third Reich" (1964)[19] as a full-fledged member of the skeptical generation. Hill, at the time he wrote his poem a lecturer in English at Leeds University, believed in the responsibility of poetry to resist the temporal forces of politics and history by creating visions of beauty and order—a perennial struggle between aesthetics and power in which innocence does not always clearly prevail. This tension is clearly evident in the two quatrains of Hill's poem, which are introduced by a quotation from the *Amores* (3.14)—*non peccat, quaecumque potest peccasse negare, / solaque famosam culpa professa facit* ("she who is able to deny having sinned does not sin; only confessed guilt makes a woman renowned")—suggesting that guilt depends upon its acknowledgment. The poem is a monologue implying that Ovid's apolitical stance, transposed into Nazi Germany, would be no defense against evil.

> I love my work and my children. God
> Is distant, difficult. Things happen.
> Too near the ancient troughs of blood
> Innocence is no earthly weapon.

> I have learned one thing: not to look down
> So much upon the damned. They, in their sphere,
> Harmonize strangely with the divine
> Love. I, in mine, celebrate the love-choir.

While the poet, whether in Augustan Rome or Nazi Germany, celebrates love and innocence, the reader realizes that his skeptical stance amounts to complicity.

A SKEPTICAL TOUR DE FORCE

Perhaps the most dazzling metamorphosis of the poet Ovid is the novel *Nazo poeta* (1969; Naso the poet) by Jacek Bocheński, a recent president of the Polish PEN organization. Born 1926 in Lemberg and thus a bona fide member of the skeptical generation, Bocheński is the author of short stories, journalistic essays, and several highly successful historical novels based on extended study trips to Greece and Rome—notably *The Divine Julius* (1961), focusing on the role of ideology and deification in the career of Julius Caesar. *Nazo poeta*—the title is an allusion to a phrase from Ovid's epitaph (*Tr.* 3.3.74)—makes knowledgeable use of the familiar facts of Ovid's life, the standard facts that we have encountered in other works dealing with Ovid's life up to the time of his exile.[20] While Bocheński comes up with a few ingenious plot twists, the novel is a stunning entertainment for other reasons: the role of the narrator as well as an original and varied form.

The narrator, who introduces himself as our master of ceremonies ("conférencier") in the program of Ovid's life and constantly intrudes into his own account, is a Shandyean figure closely resembling the whimsical *skaz* who relates many of Gogol's tales.

> I, the conférencier, have no scholarly ambitions; I am here solely in order to announce the individual numbers and to spice the program with jokes; and if by way of exception I allow a little information to creep in, then only so that you, ladies and gentlemen, do not have to rack your brains and desperately try to remember the school teachings that may occasionally be useful for the full understanding of the program. (54)

He calls on any professors and Ovid scholars who may be in the audience to verify his statement that poets make use of not only literary conventions but also their own experience and that Ovid in his *Amores* was not always simply copying other love elegists (66). He adds explanatory footnotes that, like Gogol's, lead nowhere; he inserts parenthetical digressions; and on one occasion he even refers to his own previous work. "As you will perhaps still remember, ladies and gentlemen, the antiquary in *The Divine Julius* has already reported on this historical fact" (162). He repeatedly reminds us that he is nothing but a

> a simple conférencier, but a conférencier is after all a kind of artist. In agreement with the nature of every form of art I have let myself now and then be carried away by general visions at the expense of the authenticity of one detail or another. Perhaps, therefore, my parentheses have occasionally gotten a bit confused and have permitted my own suggestions to slip in, mixed with the presentations of the illusionist. But believe me, please, ladies and gentlemen, the truth on the whole has not suffered in the least thereby. (104)

This capricious narrator portrays Ovid's pre-exilic life in three stylistically quite different sections. Part 1, "The Pulse Beat," deals with Ovid's early life and career, notably the love affair with Corinna and other women along with the erotic poems. "A new program, just as you wish," the novel begins,

> a little rhythm perhaps? Something simple, to mark time with one's foot, tam-ta-ta, tam-ta-ta, tam-ta-ta, I propose something of this sort, a little rhythm, verse scanning, doesn't that appeal to you, ladies and gentlemen? (9)

This establishment of the dactylic rhythm that dominates Ovid's poetry, both the elegiac distichs and the hexameters of the *Metamorphoses,* sets the mood for the theme of the section.

> I'll tell you in advance that all this pulsating and leaping expresses sex. And I don't need to add that the presence of sex in our program results from the spirit of the times. In these blossoming years of peace, when wars take place at most on the periphery and affect us only indirectly, in these splendid years of relaxation and progress, I say, sex has taken charge of human imagination and everything has become soaked with sex: morals, art, business, even politics. (10)

This passage leads inevitably to speculation on the time and place being portrayed. It could be any city and any age, he opines, but conspicuously ancient Rome. In this stylistically overheated atmosphere and with constant reference to the *Amores* and the *Ars amatoria,* the conférencier relates the familiar facts about Ovid's affair with Corinna, including their encounter at the races, their passionate noontime trysts, her abortion, and other episodes. We hear of his friendship with his patron Messalla, of his happy marriage, and of his family life in his villa in the hills outside Rome. Like Messalla, an aristocrat by birth and a radical by disposition, Ovid loves urban civilization, intellectual independence, and worldly manners. "But with time he ascertained that this urban civilization despite its youthful age had developed something that he could tolerate less well, namely, the profit mentality, the tendency toward a mercenary way of life, calculating, despising everything that couldn't be exchanged for money or objects" (95).

The second part begins with a stroke of the gong. "Cigarette pause. Refreshments are at hand, relax, grab a little fresh air, this is the intermission. A brief pause for reflection, a blue cloud of smoke in the air, how did it please you? You, sir? You, madame?" (121). This part assumes a different form, into which the narrator intrudes less obtrusively. Passages providing a historical account of the early years of the new era in Rome alternate with recapitulations of the *Metamorphoses*. We learn how Ovid came up with the universal principle governing and unifying his poem: the capacity for transformation, which allowed him to say everything in the context of an epic work with a grand theme (126–27). We hear about the orgies of Augustus's daughter Julia and her exile. In a grand monologue Augustus expresses an incipient distrust of Ovid and his influence. And at the end, with the apotheosis of Julius Caesar, the history and myth of the *Metamorphoses* are brought skillfully together.

The third part is called simply "The Investigation" ("Die Ermittlung"), and here, in a grand retrospective consideration of Ovid's guilt, our narrator takes over the role of a grand jury or committee of inquiry. "I would now like to look through the chronicle of events of the year 8. I shall read them in reverse order. Do you find that absurd, ladies and gentlemen? Perhaps this method will turn out to be naive. I have never in my life conducted an investigation and possess no experience whatsoever. I am a conférencier" (178). In the course of his investigation the narrator interviews the accused. When Ovid's defense attorney declares categorically at one point that the questions are directly contradicted by the absolute judgment of the Divine Emperor, the narrator loses his temper. "I don't give a damn about the judgments of the Divine! Do you hear, accused? The Divine can kiss my. . . . I'm living two thousand years later. That's all I need: for somebody to try to intimidate me with the Divine!" (200). Elsewhere he complains about the absence of certain documents, conceding that "the dossier of this case is unclear" (182). Ovid's *apologia* in *Tristia* 2 is staged as a dialogue between the poet and Augustus. By these and other means the narrator reviews the various scenarios proposed for Ovid's guilt. For, as we were told at the very beginning, this is no ordinary detective story, in which the crime is concrete and the doer unknown. "In our day the public has a right to interesting novelties," he maintains and proposes an almost Kafkaesque reversal: "Let the doer be concrete and the deed unknown. Let's look for the guilt, not the guilty party! For the guilty one is a given, like the style and the times" (12).

Among the various scenarios, including Ovid's possible participation in a conspiracy to liberate Agrippa, the conférencier gives preference to his own unique reading and combination of certain historical events as portrayed by Tacitus, Pliny, Plutarch, and Suetonius—what he calls "our new working hypothesis" (240). He conjectures that Ovid's friend Paullus Fabius was involved, along with the emperor, in a plot to harden the accusations that sent Augustus's grandson Agrippa into exile: by hiring a copyist recommended by Ovid, Junius Novatus, to forge a crude invective against Augustus, allegedly written by the psychically disturbed Agrippa. When Ovid goes to the copyist's house to recover the manuscript of the *Metamorphoses,* he accidentally catches a glimpse of the forged document and realizes what is going on. Although Ovid decides for his own security and because of his thoroughly unpolitical nature to keep the secret, Augustus worries about the poet's confidentiality. Taking his annoyance about the *Ars amatoria* as an excuse, he sends Ovid away to Tomis, where the secret can do no harm, and dispatches a murderer to do away with Agrippa. "But I must warn you, ladies and gentlemen," the narrator frankly concludes his argument, "our hypothesis, while supported by many facts, is still not complete. A certain simple detail remains doubtful. In our investigation up to this point we were not successful in producing proof that Junius Novatus was a professional copyist and that Ovid made use of his services" (248).

At this point the conférencier introduces yet another possibility. He imagines a scene in which Ovid is summoned to the palace of the emperor's granddaughter Julia, where he arouses the listeners with a reading of the *Ars amatoria*—and here at the end the sexual "pulse beat" of tam-ta-ta is introduced again—while Julia does an erotically charged striptease. "Total nakedness, divine nakedness of Julia reveals itself to cries of enthusiasm" (263). Augustus, informed by the same man whom Ovid later assails in his poem as "Ibis," sends Julia into exile; and this time Ovid does not escape his wrath. "In this way, ladies and gentlemen, the whole thing could have taken place," the conférencier concludes his program.

The narrative continues for several more pages in which a few further hypotheses are rejected for lack of evidence. The conférencier reviews his evidence and its sources down to Sidonius Apollinaris (the same Gallo-Roman poet whom Staschek encounters at the end of Hartmut Lange's play), speculates further on the identity of "Ibis," and suggests that "Corinna" may actually have been the older Julia. "The investigation, which by its nature is not a court, yet at the same time partially constitutes a modest kind of court of posterity, accordingly keeps to the fundamental principle of Roman law: *in dubio pro reo.* Inasmuch as

we have advanced all doubts in favor of the accused, the investigation in the absence of proof acquits the poet Publius Ovidius Naso of guilt" (272).

But since there was no crime, why did Ovid admit that he was guilty? Here
we hear the voice of the politically skeptical generation. Although Ovid lived
happily in the Augustan Age and believed in the greatness of Augustus and the
divine constitution of the Augustan world, the very act of writing forced him
to perceive and communicate the truth, and that truth involved impieties. "For
this tale of being, of the gods and mortals, which according to its original intention was edifying and religious, surprised its author by its freethinking con-
tents, which it brought together. But this conscientious look at the divine was
anything but devout" (274). Ovid's guilt, therefore, consisted in his realization
that, as a poet, he had an obligation to a truth higher than that of his own age—
a truth that would live above and beyond the epochs. Ovid was horrified and
tormented by the knowledge that, "thanks to the genuine and sinful qualities of
poetry, the true evil of the world exposed itself and that he had to see it, even
against his own will" (278). With that final insight the conférencier begs our permission to leave the stage of life's comedy along with his hero, Ovid.

It would be difficult to find a more brilliant fictional treatment of Ovid's life
than this hilariously serious entertainment. In its focus on Ovid's life prior to
his exile and on the nonideological reasons for his exile Bocheński presents himself and his straight-faced conférencier as leading spokesmen for the skeptical
generation. Above all, in his investigation of the deeper reasons for Ovid's sense
of guilt, which he locates ultimately in the poet's vocation to a truth higher than
ideology, he becomes an advocate for the power of poetry.

OVID IN THE SEVENTIES

Events of the 1960s combined to produce a mood in its young that differed
sharply from that of the exiles or the skeptical generation. The skepticism and
political detachment of their parents was now being undermined by such political experiences as the building of the Berlin Wall and the war in Vietnam, by
the assassinations of John F. Kennedy and Robert Kennedy, by the civil rights
movement and the murder of Martin Luther King, by such social upheavals as
the youth movement ushered in by the Beatles and the counterculture, and
by the religious experience of non-traditional forms of worship. The literature
of the period reflected this mood, even when the authors did not belong to the
generation of the sixties, who were born mainly after World War II.

Ovid and the traditional literary canon were part of the cultural baggage discarded by the *soixante-huitards,* who forced universities to abandon requirements

in foreign languages and Western literature along with history. Among the literary works that emerged from that turmoil, we find few direct literary representations of Ovid. However, the countercultural mood is reflected at least indirectly in the isolated Ovidian works that appeared during the seventies, as in David Malouf's *An Imaginary Life* (1978), in which—as we saw—the exiled Ovid flees with the feral child into a kind of spiritual Woodstock in the uncivilized realm beyond the Danube.

One of the most successful novels of the decade was *Ragtime* (1975) by E. L. Doctorow (born 1931), an exuberant parable of three families, exemplifying in their parallel structure—husband, wife, child—representative aspects of the American experience in the early decades of the twentieth century and the intermingling of their destinies: a WASP family from New Rochelle; a black family from Harlem; and a family of Jewish immigrants from the Lower East Side. The astonishing cast of characters constituting Doctorow's dazzling fictional tapestry goes far beyond these three groups to embrace figures representing the main social, intellectual, political, and economic forces of the times, ranging from Harry Houdini and Sigmund Freud (on his trip to the United States) to the anarchist agitator Emma Goldman and the multimillionaire capitalist J. P. Morgan. By the end of the novel, a rich and anthropologically "thick" description of American culture from about 1900 to the end of World War I has been woven. Indeed, the historical forces are depicted with considerably more energy than the rather flat characters who people the novel.

The main plot is a postfiguration of Heinrich von Kleist's novella of revenge and retribution, *Michael Kohlhaas,* from which the black jazz musician "Coalhouse" Walker gets his name. Most important, by the end of the action several major sociological changes have taken place. The widowed "Mother" of the New Rochelle WASPs has married the now prosperous Jewish film producer Tateh, whose wife has died. With their combined families, including the adopted orphan of Coalhouse Walker, they move to California. One morning Tateh looks out the window of his study and sees the three children sitting on the lawn: "his daughter, with dark hair, his tow-headed stepson and his legal responsibility, the schwartze child" (369).[21] He has an idea for a movie resembling the popular serial from the 1920s and 1930s, *Our Gang*—and not incidentally exemplifying the multicultural ideal of the countercultural 1960s.

A bunch of children who were pals, white black, fat thin, rich poor, all kinds, mischievous little urchins who would have funny adventures in their own neighborhood, a society of ragamuffins, like all of us, a gang, getting into trouble and getting out again. Actually not one movie but several were made of this vision.

While Doctorow's novel revolves around—or rather, repeatedly alludes to—the striking and profound industrial, political, social, intellectual and cultural transformations taking place in the early twentieth-century United States, the author presents a counterpoint in the worried ruminations of the aging J. P. Morgan, who hires scholars to teach him about ancient civilizations that were based on the same "lust for order" (158) motivating him. "His desperate studies settled, inevitably, on the civilizations of ancient Egypt, wherein it was taught that the universe is changeless and that death is followed by the resumption of life. He was fascinated. His life took a new turn" (162). Later he tries to prove to Henry Ford that "there are universal patterns of order and repetition that give meaning to the activity of this planet" (169).

In this novel depicting the nineteenth-century world of empire and permanence giving way, according to the familiar Marxist pattern, to a twentieth-century world of change and democracy, it is hardly surprising that Ovid shows up in an important passage almost precisely in the middle of the story as the spokesman of metamorphosis. The ninety-year-old grandfather of the WASP family is a retired professor of Greek and Latin from an Episcopal seminary in central Ohio. Now he sits in the parlor and tells his grandson stories from Ovid.

> They were stories of people who became animals or trees or statues. They were stories of transformation. Women turned into sunflowers, spiders, bats, birds; men turned into snakes, pigs, stones and even thin air. The boy did not know he was hearing Ovid, and it would not have mattered if he had known. Grandfather's stories proposed to him that the forms of life were volatile and that everything in the world could as easily be something else. The old man's narrative would often drift from English to Latin without his being aware of it, as if he were reading to one of his classes of forty years before, so that it appeared nothing was immune to the principle of volatility, not even language. (132–33)

Although the boy is unaware of its source, he is instinctively convinced by the Ovidian principle of change. "He found proof in his own experience of the instability of both things and people" (133)—a hairbrush sliding off the bureau, a window falling shut, the moving pictures at the theater downtown. With an obsession that his mother mistakenly takes for vanity, he studies himself in the mirror to detect changes in his own appearance. He notes the changing appearance and manner of his father and observes his uncle "shedding his hair and his lassitude" (134). He regards the statues in the city parks as a way of transforming humans, while the statues themselves undergo changes in color. "It was evident to him that the world composed and recomposed itself constantly in an endless process of dissatisfaction" (135). With his Ovidian sense of transformation, the boy embodies the antithesis of J. P. Morgan's lust for order and permanence and exemplifies the principle of metamorphosis that characterizes the world of Doctorow's *Ragtime*. What he lacks is the sense of irony that characterizes the author's narrative.[22] Indeed, Doctorow's postfigurative use of Kleist's novella— the story of a sixteenth-century German horse trader as the plot on which to hang the adventures of a black ragtime piano player—is in itself a major structural example of metamorphosis.

In sum, while the interest in Ovid generated by the bimillennial celebrations had fallen off considerably by the 1970s, Doctorow's novel invoked the principle of change and transformation so dear to the countercultural generation of the sixties and, in a central passage, pointed to its most conspicuous canonical source in Ovid's *Metamorphoses*.

◢ 10 ◣

OVID IN THE EIGHTIES

The eighties saw the rise and revival of two forces that pervaded much of the intellectual life of the decade: postmodernism and metamorphosis. There is little agreement on the precise meaning of "postmodernity," a catch-all term that emerged in the early 1960s to define a negative response: the rejection of earlier generations of high-modern thinkers, writers, and artists including Pound, Joyce, Eliot, Yeats, Kafka, Rilke, Woolf, Benn, and others. As early as 1960 Harry Levin was asking elegiacally "What Was Modernism?"[1] A decade that tended to designate itself mainly by its posteriority—posthistorical, postindustrial, postcapitalist, but also postcommunist—soon enough attached the prefix to "modernism." In 1971 a special issue of the journal *New Literary History* opened with a piece by Ihab Hassan provocatively titled POSTmodernISM." In 1983 Hans Robert Jauß began a talk with a wordplay on the opening sentence of the *Communist Manifesto:* "A specter is haunting Europe—the specter of postmodernism."[2] Indeed, the decade was haunted by a seemingly endless stream of books and articles trying to define postmodernism or postmodernity.

There is no need, and certainly I have no desire, to recapitulate the weary theoretical and definitional debates of the eighties, which today seem dated and antiquated.[3] The participants rarely agreed even on basic questions. Was postmodernism a radical break with the past or a continuation of modernism (like

Clausewitz's war as an extension of politics by other means)? Were there entirely different postmodernisms in the United States, France, and Germany? Did it have a new aesthetic theory or was it utterly anti-aesthetic? Did it reject modernism altogether or only "high" modernism in favor of mass culture? It will be useful to recall a few of the phrases and leading ideas that dominated the discussion.

Postmodernism was essentially a climate of opinion that permeated much of the thought as well as many of the arts of the period: from the playful deconstructions of French theorists to the ponderous profundities of German social philosophers, from the pop art of Andy Warhol to the sculptural constructs of Joseph Beuys, from Susan Sontag's naive antihermeneutics to Leslie Fiedler's critical populism, from serial music to the neo-Palladian ornamentation of Philip Johnson. It co-opted indiscriminately, and often without understanding, whatever terms and concepts from the natural sciences seemed relevant to its project, from entropy to chaos theory.

Although no single thinker or system incorporated all the notions, the thinkers and systems shared certain premises. They posited a philosophy of antirationalism because rationalism and its logocentrism, according to the argument of Theodor Adorno and Max Horkheimer in their influential *Dialectics of Enlightenment* (*Dialektik der Aufklärung,* 1947), were felt to be tools of intellectual and social oppression. They renounced the legitimation of the past—its thought as well as its literature. The great Hegelian/Marxian ideological constructs of the nineteenth century, which Jean-François Lyotard in *La condition postmoderne* (1979) termed *métarécits* or "master narratives," were discarded as no longer having any claim to validity. Literary texts, liberated by Jacques Derrida's belief in the priority of language from any responsibility to an external reality, were set free for playful and often irresponsible appropriation and interpretation. The self as an independent entity, the autonomy of the thinking subject, was rejected in favor of a shifting consciousness constantly redefined by the social discourses in which it participates and which therefore require constant "deconstruction." Myth was no longer held to reflect patterns of meaning, since there is no meaning, but simply an intertextual play according to Hans Blumenberg's notion of "work on myth" (*Arbeit am Mythos,* 1979). Since literature is not constrained by rational rules of logic, it may freely intermingle times and places.

The belief in a constantly shifting world no longer governed by rationality, logocentricism, and oppressive master narratives and in which myth was open to ceaseless reinterpretation cleared the way for a new appreciation of metamorphosis. We have already noted the modern turn to metamorphosis in the period immediately preceding and following World War I. The scholarly interest in metamorphosis after World War II can be dated from 1953, when Clemens

Heselhaus published his influential article on metamorphosis poems and meta-morphosis ideas.[4] Heselhaus begins with a brief glance at the role of metamor-phosis in Hellenistic mystery cults and Judeo-Christian thought before turning to Ovid, Dante, and other medieval and Renaissance views. Surveying the role of metamorphosis in early modern scientific thought, he concludes his brief but provocative article with Goethe's principle of *Steigerung* (heightening, intensifi-cation, escalation) in organic life. Interest initially developed sporadically: repre-sentative examples include Mary Bernetta Quinn's *The Metamorphic Tradition in Modern Poetry* (1966), which deals with a small group of modern poets in En-glish; Pierre Brunel's *Le mythe de la métamorphose* (1974), which includes one hundred pages of quoted examples from intellectual history and literature; and such works, already cited in earlier chapters, as Irving Massey's *Gaping Pig: Lit-erature and Metamorphosis* (1976), Harold Skulsky's *Metamorphosis: The Mind in Ex-ile* (1981), and Charles Tomlinson's *Poetry and Metamorphosis* (1983). In the last two decades of the twentieth century the topic reached well-nigh unsurveyable proportions, extending from Leonard Barkan's *The Gods Made Flesh: Metamor-phosis and the Pursuit of Paganism* (1986), which defines metamorphosis almost mystically as "the moment when the divine enters the familiar"[5] and treats prin-cipally Ovid, Augustine, Dante, and Shakespeare, to Friedmann Harzer's "poet-ics of epic metamorphoses" in Ovid, Kafka, and Christoph Ransmayr, *Erzählte Verwandlung* (2000). Philip Terry has observed shrewdly that "two landmark studies of postmodern aesthetics take their titles from Ovid: Ihab Hassan's *The Dismemberment of Orpheus* and Linda Hutcheon's *Narcissistic Narrative*."[6]

Any trend so pronounced inevitably carries over into the popular media fa-vored by postmodernism. The Japanese feature film *Winds of Change* (1978), nar-rated by Peter Ustinov, in which the hero undergoes a series of adventures featuring episodes based on Actaeon, Orpheus, Phaethon, and Perseus is only one of several films that have adapted Ovid: the Spanish film *Actaeon* (1964), by Jordi Grau, credits Ovid as a screenwriter; and the Czech film *Metamorfeus* (1969) retells the story of Orpheus and Eurydice.[7]

The literary reappropriation of metamorphosis began sporadically.[8] (Many poems bearing the title "Metamorphoses"—e.g., by Wallace Stevens or Sylvia Plath—have nothing to do with Ovid or his *Metamorphoses*.) In 1968 C. H. Sis-son published a volume of poems entitled *Metamorphoses* (London: Methuen, 1968), which included as its lengthy title poem a sequence of nine "Metamor-phoses" retelling in Sisson's skeptical, laconic style several of the most popular stories.[9] His Actaeon is incriminated by a malicious Diana, who sets his hounds upon him "to show her bitter virgin spite" (I). Or, by a weird inversion (II), he was originally a rutting stag transformed into a man because he is captivated by the sight of the naked Diana. Sisson's Pygmalion (III) is a misogynist who finds women troublesome, even though he admires their beauty. When his prayers and "slobbering" kisses bring his shapely statue to life, he often has reason to wish her returned to her silent state of marble; but "The bitch retained her human heart, / The conquest of a stone by art." Sisson recounts Jupiter's conquests of Europa and Leda (IV) and Danae (V). Phaethon falls from the heavens, burning the world in his course; but, in a surprising metamorphosis, it turns out to be Christ who visits the underworld and is the person whom the poet asks if he saw Eurydice among the shades. In the conflation of pagan myth and Christianity it is uncertain whether "The naked figure in the grove [is] / Diana's or the risen Christ's." The last three "metamorphoses" are dominated by a similar syncretism as Eurydice walks in the grove where the biblical Tree of Knowledge stood (VIII), and Noah's ark introduces a new Ovidian golden age to a world that had declined to an age of iron (IX). In this subtle manner Sisson introduces the Ovidian principle of metamorphosis into the postmodern world, relativizing ancient myth together with Christian faith and exposing new aspects of both.

POSTMODERN APPROPRIATIONS OF OVID

The writer who first inscribed Ovid's *Metamorphoses* in the postmodern canon of literary archetypes was undoubtedly Italo Calvino (1923–85). In his poetic testament, the Charles Eliot Norton lectures at Harvard titled *Six Memos for the Next Millennium* which he was scheduled to deliver in 1985–86 before his death, Calvino intended to talk about what he considered six indispensable literary values: lightness, quickness, exactitude, visibility, multiplicity, and consistency.[10] To illustrate the first of these values—the intellectual lightness (*leggerezza*) required to offset the heaviness of being—Calvino evokes Ovid and various of his mythological figures. "I felt that the entire world was turning into stone: a slow petrification, more or less advanced depending on people and places but one that spared no aspect of life. It was as if no one could escape the inexorable stare of Medusa" (4). Perseus, Medusa's destroyer, avoids her deadly gaze by supporting himself "on the very lightest of things, the winds and the clouds," and disarms her weightiness by looking at her only indirectly, as an image caught in a mirror. Calvino goes on to single out other images of lightness associated with Perseus—e.g., the winged horse Pegasus, or Perseus's own delicacy of spirit when he places Medusa's head on a bed of leaves. Above all: Perseus becomes for Calvino the perfect image for the writer. "Perseus's strength always lies in a refusal to look directly, but not in a refusal of the reality in which he is fated to live; he carries the reality with him and accepts it as his particular burden" (5).

Calvino adduces Lucretius's *De rerum natura* as the first encyclopedic poem in which the solidity of the world is dissolved by knowledge and understanding. "For Ovid, too, everything can be transformed into something else, and knowledge of the world means dissolving the solidity of the world" (9). In the eyes of Lucretius as well as Ovid, "lightness is a way of looking at the world based on philosophy and science: the doctrines of Epicurus for Lucretius and those of Pythagoras for Ovid" (10). But the quality of lightness is not simply an intellectual attitude; it is also an aesthetic one. For both Lucretius and Ovid, "the lightness is also something arising from the writing itself."

Calvino illustrates the second quality, quickness (*rapidità*), with classic short stories from Boccaccio to Borges and, oddly, does not mention Ovid. In his earlier preface to an edition of Ovid's *Metamorphoses* (1979), Calvino had stressed his view that "The *Metamorphoses* are above all the poem of rapidity" (155).[11] The poem, in which everything happens at high speed, is dominated by "a law of the greatest internal economy" (157). In the preface, however, Calvino is concerned principally with another aspect of Ovid's poem, an aspect mentioned only glancingly in the Harvard lectures, where he speaks of "an essential parity between everything that exists, as opposed to any sort of hierarchy of powers or values" (9). Here Calvino focuses on the contiguity between gods and human beings, notably in their love affairs, as "a particular instance of the contiguity between all the figures and forms of existing things" (147)—what he defined as "parity" in the later lectures. The interpenetration of gods, men, and nature in Ovid's poem implies "an intricate system of interrelations in which each level can influence the others" (150). This analysis is a precise description of the postmodern texts that Calvino composed after his early phase of socialist neorealism—texts in which everything turned out to be connected to everything else. Calvino makes an important distinction, however: "The passion that dominates [Ovid's] compositional talents is not arrangement but accumulation" (154). For arrangement is the principle that governs Calvino's later texts.

The centrality of Ovid in Calvino's own texts is most strikingly exemplified in the postmodern classic that first brought him international acclaim. In *Invisible Cities* (*Le città invisibili,* 1972) the young Marco Polo describes for the aging Kublai Khan the (imaginary) cities that he has visited in the course of his travels. The work consists of nine chapters, of which the first and last contain descriptions of ten cities, while the other seven describe five each. The principle of contiguity emerges not only in the organization within each chapter but also from the eleven overlapping categories to which Calvino assigns each of the fifty-five cities: cities of memory, desire, signs, eyes, names, the dead, the sky, and trade along with continuous, slender, and hidden cities—each one named for a woman and each one a metaphor for a spiritual state of mind. The configuration of chapters and categories constitutes an amazing pattern of organization, which Calvino (and his critics) have represented visually as a diamond shape or parallelogram and which exemplifies the high degree to which this text has been carefully arranged and not simply accumulated.[12] Each of the nine chapters, in turn, is framed by dialogues between Marco Polo and the Khan.

Invisible Cities, then, is a rapidly moving text whose fifty-five short parts are architectonically contiguous and whose governing theme is the tension between lightness and heaviness—the hallmarks of Ovid's *Metamorphoses,* as Calvino later characterized them in his preface and in his lectures. But Ovid's work enters the narrative directly in the third section of chapter 5: that is, the precise center of the nine chapters. Through its placement in this numerologically organized work, in short, Calvino draws attention to Ovid's *Metamorphoses.*

In the dialogue introducing this section, the Grand Khan confesses his fear that his vast empire, which has expanded to the outermost limits of viability, is in danger of collapsing under its own weight. He relates a recurrent dream in which he sees "cities as light as the north wind, perforated like lace, as transparent as mosquito nets," with delicate spires on which the moon could rest in its course—a city privileged to grow in lightness (*leggerezza*).[13] Marco Polo tells him that the name of the city of which he dreams is Lalage (the name of one of Horace's favorite lovers),[14] and these remarks introduce a section in which each of the five cities is named for a figure from classical antiquity: Octavia, Hersilia, Bauci, Leandra, and Melania. Two of these have specifically Ovidian associations. The inhabitants of the city of Hersilia (the wife of Romulus; *Met.* 14.829–51) stretch threads of various colors between their houses to indicate various family and social relationships; when the threads become so numerous that they are no longer able to pass between them, the inhabitants dismantle their houses and rebuild them elsewhere, leaving behind on the plain the symbolic tangle of threads and poles. Any traveler in the territory of Hersilia encounters the ruins of the abandoned cities: "webs of intricate relationships seeking a form" (2:422). The allusion to Arachne's web, and possibly also to Ariadne's thread, is evident.

The city of Bauci ("cities and eyes"), in contrast, is supported on slender stilts that rise from the ground and disappear beyond the clouds (2:423). It is reached by ladders, but its inhabitants only rarely descend to the ground: they have all necessities of life up above and prefer not to come down. Marco Polo presents three hypotheses to explain their behavior: they hate the earth; they respect it so greatly that they avoid touching it; or they love it as it was before and observe it untiringly with field glasses and telescopes, "contemplating in fascination their own absence." Again, the text contains a clear but unspecified allusion to the Ovidian tale of Philemon and Baucis (*Met.* 8.618–724), whose town and its inhabitants were destroyed by a flood because of their inhospitality to the gods as the aged couple look down from a mountaintop.

Although Calvino does not spell out the meaning of his symbolical allusions, the implications of Ovidian lightness are abundantly clear in the webs of Hersilia and the stilt-borne city of Bauci. And the placement of the Ovidian Bauci in the precise architectonic center of the complex organization of *Invisible Cities* exemplifies clearly why Calvino, twelve years later, asserted that "the *Metamorphoses,* in sum, continue their metaphorical life in the literature of today. Ovid's book will be the principal source of Italian literature for many centuries."[15] The notion of changeability, of contiguity, of the "visibility" of representation, and the effort to project through poetry a model of the entire world—these are the main points of similarity that tie Ovid to Calvino's conception of a postmodern literature.[16]

These same criteria are strikingly evident in *The Satanic Verses* (1988) by Salman Rushdie (born 1947). The novel concerns neither Ovid nor his *Metamorphoses.* But since it deals conspicuously with change and transformation—key words that occur throughout the text—Ovid makes his appearance at an important juncture as its symbolic spokesman.[17] The long novel begins as two Anglo-Indians, Gibreel Farishta and Saladin Chamcha, are plummeting toward the earth from an Air India flight that has been blown up by terrorists high above the English Channel. By the laws of magical realism governing this work, the two men survive their fall, but the experience produces in them certain temporary metamorphoses that transform them into religiously symbolic beings. Gibreel acquires a halo and, under the illusion that he is the archangel Gabriel, has a series of dreams about a prophet named Mahound and his forged prophecies (the notorious and allegedly blasphemous passages that outraged the Muslim world and prompted Ayatollah Khomeini to issue a *fatwa* against the author). Meanwhile Chamcha turns into "a figure out of a nightmare," hairy, with the hoofs of a goat, and horns on his head (194).

These symbolic transformations into angel and devil lead to complications of plot and inevitable conflicts between the two principal figures. By the time the work ends, the differences between the two men, between their apparent manifestations of good and evil, have been effaced. Gibreel commits suicide while Chamcha, who has lost his goatish shape, returns to India, where he is reconciled with his father and changes his name to Salahuddin.

During the months of their metamorphoses, however, they experience and witness transformations at every level of being. Thus in nature "An iceberg is water striving to be land; a mountain, especially a Himalaya, especially Everest, is land's attempt to metamorphose into sky" (313). In urban ecology:

Gibreel enumerated the benefits of the proposed metamorphosis of London into a tropical city: increased moral definition, institution of a national siesta, development of vivid and expansive patterns of behaviour among the populace, higher-quality popular music, new birds in the trees (macaws, peacocks, cockatoos), new trees under the birds (coco-palms, tamarind, banyans with hanging beards). (365)

And in culture generally:

It seemed to him, as he idled across the channels, that the box was full of freaks: there were mutants—'Mutts'—on *Dr Who,* bizarre creatures who appeared to have been crossbred with different types of industrial machinery: forage harvesters, grabbers, donkeys, jackhammers, saws, and whose cruel priest-chieftains were called *Mutilasians;* children's television appeared to be extremely populated by humanoid robots and creatures with metamorphic bodies, while the adult programmes offered a continual parade of the misshapen human by-products of the newest notions in modern medicine, and its accomplices, modern disease and war. (419)

Most conspicuously, metamorphosis is adduced as an image to explain the construction of the Anglo-Indian self through the discourse (racial prejudice) of the British. When Chamcha after his fall is taken to the hospital of a detention center for immigrants, he wakes up to find himself surrounded by other weirdly metamorphosed shapes: a male model from Bombay transformed into a manticore with a human body and the head of a tiger; Nigerian businessmen who have sprouted tails; holiday makers from Senegal who have turned into snakes. Chamcha asks the manticore how these transformations come about, and the other responds with a statement straight out of postmodern identity theory. "'They describe us,' the other whispered solemnly. 'That's all. They have the power of description, and we succumb to the pictures they construct'" (174). As Duncan Kennedy observes, "Metamorphosis is here appropriated as an anti-racist discourse."[18]

The theme of metamorphosis is announced in the opening sentence: "'To be born again,' sang Gibreel Farishta tumbling from the heavens, 'first you have to die. Ho ji! Ho ji! To land upon the bosomy earth, first one needs to fly" (3).[19] The same thought is echoed on the last page, as Saladin Chamcha, now calling himself Salahuddin, gazes out at the Arabian Sea from his childhood home. "Childhood was over, and the view from this window was no more than an old and sentimental echo. To the devil with it! Let the bulldozers come. If the old refused to die, the new could not be born" (561).

Ovid first enters this remarkable text indirectly when the narrator anticipates a possible confusion on the reader's part regarding the miraculous transformations taking place in the two men falling through the sky. "Notice anything unusual? Just two brown men, falling hard, nothing so new about that, you may think; climbed too high, got above themselves, flew too close to the sun, is that it?" (6). Here the allusion to the Ovidian Phaethon is used in a twofold sense: first, in the literal sense that in their Boeing 747 they actually flew too close to the sun; but, second, in the imputation that English readers would react to the incident with an unconscious prejudice—that the two Indians got what they deserved for attempting to transcend their proper social status. As they fall further, they encounter "a succession of cloudforms, ceaselessly metamorphosing," that are clearly Ovidian: "gods into bulls, women into spiders, men into wolves" (7).

Soon the hints become more specific. As we learn about Gibreel's acting career before he became the most famous movie idol of India, for instance, we hear clear allusions to Narcissus, Arachne, and other Ovidian metamorphoses: "To get his mind off the subject of love and desire, he studied, becoming an omnivorous autodidact, devouring the metamorphic myths of Greece and Rome, the avatars of Jupiter, the boy who became a flower, the spider-woman, Circe, everything" (24). Finally, close to the middle of the book, Ovid is introduced by name in a conversation between Chamcha and a friend, a kindly old man who suggests that perhaps Chamcha's transformation resulted from his possession by a spirit that could be exorcised by religious intercession. Mutability of the self, the former schoolmaster informs him, has long been the subject of debate. He quotes Lucretius in Latin, who argues in *De rerum natura* (1.670–71) that metamorphosis necessarily involves the destruction of the earlier self: "for whenever something is transformed and passes beyond its natural limits, that [transformation] is straightway the death of that which existed before" (*quodcumque suis mutatum finibus exit, continuo hoc mors est illius quod fuit ante*). Then as a counterexample he cites Ovid, who takes the opposite view.

> He avers thus: "As yielding wax"—heated, you see, possibly for the sealing of documents or such, —"is stamped with new designs And changes shape and seems not still the same, Yet is indeed the same, even so our souls,"—you hear, good sir? Our spirits! Our immortal essences!—"Are still the same forever, but adopt In their migrations every-varying forms." (285)

> (He is paraphrasing Met. 15.169–71: *utque novis facilis signatur cera figuris, / nec manet ut fuerat nec formas servat easdem, / sed tamen ipsa eadem est, animam sic semper eandem / esse sed in varias doceo migrare figuras.*)

The old man seeks to console Chamcha, assuring him that his soul is still the same although in its migration it has taken on a new form. "For me it is always Ovid over Lucretius." Chamcha is not reassured: "'either I accept Lucretius and conclude that some demonic and irreversible mutation is taking place in my inmost depths, or I go with Ovid and concede that everything now emerging is no more than a manifestation of what was already there" (285–86). In his bitterness he initially chooses Lucretius over Ovid. "The inconstant soul, the mutability of everything, das Ich, every last speck. A being going through life can become so other to himself as to *be another,* discrete, severed from history" (297). But by the end, as we have seen, his bitterness gives way to resignation. "If the old refused to die, the new could not be born." Ovid has won out over Lucretius: enduring essence prevails over temporal existence.[20]

   In the final analysis, Ovid is only one source for the theories of transformation in this postmodern novel where reincarnation summons up a host of mythic associations: "phoenix-from-ashes, the resurrection of Christ, the transmigration, at the instant of death, of the soul of the Dalai Lama into the body of a new-born child . . . such matters got mixed up with the avatars of Vishnu, the metamorphoses of Jupiter, who had imitated Vishnu by adopting the form of a bull; and so on . . ." (85–86). In addition to Ovid and Lucretius, Rushdie refers to Apuleius's *Metamorphoses* (*The Golden Ass*) and to the biological theories of Lamarck and Darwin. While his presence demonstrates the new centrality of Ovid for the postmodern consciousness, Rushdie's use of the principles and practices of postmodern fiction—deconstruction of the self, construction of the self through discourses, intertextual use of myth, intermingling of times and places—prevent *The Satanic Verses* from moving beyond the kind of playfulness that we observed in *Invisible Cities,* by the author whom Rushdie in a glowing evaluation (1981) called "an indispensable writer."[21]

Postmodern Metamorphoses

It is ironic that in 1996 Salman Rushdie shared the prestigious Prix Aristeion of the European Union with Christoph Ransmayr. When the Austrian writer's highly acclaimed Ovidian novel *Die letzte Welt* (1988) was published in English translation as *The Last World,* Rushdie ranked it rather disparagingly as "a brilliantly clever artifice," whose borrowed power suffers by comparison with its Ovidian source.[22] He downplays Ransmayr's "excessively tricksy time-jumbling" as a fictional version of the theatrical practice of presenting the classics in modern dress. (Classics scholars have pointed out that Ovid himself, by mixing Greek myth with contemporary Rome—e.g., in the opening portrayal of the assembly of the gods as a counterpart to Roman senators attending upon Augustus on the Palatine Hill—provided a model for the conflation of ages.)[23] He is skeptical about Ransmayr's "vision of art conquering defeat by remaking the world" because, while art may endure, the artist is all too easily destroyed. Although he acknowledges the lyricism through which Ransmayr explores the world's ugliness, he does not like it that the reader understands the events long before the novel's protagonist, Cotta. Behind Ransmayr's novel, he concludes, "there stands a far greater work of literature" and behind Ransmayr, "one of the most important figures in the whole of literature."

In *The Last World* Ovid occupies the spiritual center but never appears in person. Indeed, the image of the poet that emerges has little connection with the known facts of his life. Nine years after Ovid's relegation his young admirer Cotta (in history, the adopted son of Ovid's patron Messalla Corvinus, known to posterity as the addressee of six of the *Epistulae ex Ponto*),[24] having heard reports of the poet's death, sets out to track down the manuscript of the *Metamorphoses* that Ovid is rumored to have left behind in remote Tomi (the alternate form that Ransmayr uses consistently throughout). Cotta's expedition is at least in part a flight from compulsory military and civil service. We learn through flashbacks that Cotta first encountered Ovid when the poet came to his school to give a reading, and that Cotta was also present on the occasion that led to Ovid's downfall: a performance at the dedication of a stadium when the poet, having failed to make the proper obeisances before the emperor and assembled nobles, recited an utterly inappropriate poem: a version of the plague of Aegina and the legend of the Myrmidons (*Met.* 7.614–60) according to which the industrious ant-people are not loyal warriors but the mindless proletariat in a bureaucratic state. A cabal of Ovid's enemies exploited that opportunity to discredit the poet, already in disfavor for his political satires, and then willfully interpreted a casual gesture of the inattentive emperor as a command to send Ovid into exile. There is no reference in this wholly unpolitical novel to *carmen* or *error*: the poet, preoccupied with his visions, is manipulated by enemies jealous of his success and popularity. Following his relegation, his works—e.g., his utopian vision of a land without the need for laws and soldiers—are exploited by various opposition groups for their own purposes. This appropriation was used by Ovid's enemies retrospectively as a further justification for his relegation, despite the protests of his wife, here named Cyane.[25]

Unlike earlier writers, Ransmayr is concerned neither with the reasons for Ovid's relegation nor with his life during his years of exile, although he does speculate on the poet's shifting reputation at home—from traitor to martyr to the Great Son of Rome. Indeed, to the extent that Ovid's exilic poems are used at all, they lend color to Cotta's experiences. Ransmayr's interest is focused entirely on the problematic relationship between fiction and reality and on the poet's visionary powers. According to Ransmayr's plot, the *Metamorphoses* were known in Rome only from various recitations that Ovid delivered before he was sent away; on the eve of his departure he burned the manuscript of his work, and (unlike Ovid's assumption in the *Tristia*) no other copies remained in circulation. Cotta hears, however, that Ovid left behind a copy at the time of his death in Tomi, and hopes to track it down. When he arrives in Tomi, Cotta enters to his increasing amazement a twilight world (*Zwischenwelt*, 220) or nightmare realm "where the rules of logic seemed have no validity"—a state of uncertainty (*Schwebezustand*, 231) between the reality of Rome and the incomprehensibilities of the Black Sea. "The ages brushed off their names, entered into one another, penetrated one another" (241)—in a postmodern interpenetration of times. At Tomi he finds a town of about ninety houses, but it bears no resemblance to the settlement familiar from the *Tristia*—a fact that led one reviewer to suggest plausibly that the setting is closer to the Alpine mining villages of Ransmayr's Austria.[26] This town lies at the edge of a mountainous mining region which has cast a pall of rust over the ironwork of the houses—an image that recalls the Age of Iron, the "last world," described by Ovid at the beginning of his poem (*Met.* 1.127–150: *de duro est ultima ferro*) and mentioned again at the end (*Met.* 15.260–61).[27] It also is situated in a timeless realm resembling a backward Balkan country of the early twentieth century with newspapers and billboards and firearms, where transportation is provided by dilapidated buses (112), where every Easter a missionary comes from Constantinople to rail against Rome, where for a few weeks each spring a traveling film projectionist arrives in his covered wagon to show the latest movies (featuring such mythologically morbid subjects as the violent deaths of Hector, Hercules, and Orpheus) on the whitewashed walls of the local slaughterhouse, and where from time to time the sea-trader Jason pilots his tramp steamer, the *Argo,* into the harbor to exchange his goods for the iron and amber accumulated by the citizens of Tomi (208).[28] Rome has become such a harsh dictatorship that more and more citizens are fleeing the metropolis "to escape the apparatus of power" (125) and—shades of Horia and the exile novelists—to find freedom at the wild borders of the empire. Cotta himself must travel with a false passport in order to make his escape from Rome.

Cotta never finds Ovid: it remains unclear whether the poet has died or simply moved elsewhere. But in the course of his ten months in Tomi—during which the earth itself goes through a series of cataclysmic events, beginning with a hurricane during Cotta's journey, a pestilentially humid summer, torrential rains and avalanches, and the volcanic birth of a new mountain (Olympus) im-

mediately behind the village—he encounters many residents who knew the
poet: the crazy Greek émigré Pythagoras, Ovid's servant at his house at Trachila
(a deserted hamlet in the mountains five hours north of Tomi—a place not
mentioned by Ovid);[29] the shop owner Fama, Cotta's source for local gossip;
the rope maker Lycaon, who rents Cotta a room in his attic; the deaf-mute
weaver Arachne, who has woven into her tapestries stories told to her by Ovid;
the discreet local prostitute Echo, who becomes Cotta's confidante; and others.

From various fragments of poetry that Pythagoras has copied onto scraps of
cloth and attached, pennant-like, to piles of stones, Cotta concludes that Ovid
must have written poetic episodes featuring all these inhabitants. But the relationship between life and art remains mysterious. For one thing, Ovid told different kinds of stories to each of his interlocutors: to Echo he had recounted
stories about people being changed into stones and to Arachne tales about transformations into birds. With Pythagoras, regarded as an idiot by the villagers for
claiming that he had at times occupied the body of a salamander, an artillery
man, and a swineherd girl (17), Ovid discussed metempsychosis. Other metamorphoses take place in dreams: e.g., Cyparis's dream that he is transformed into
a tree, or Cotta's nightmares about Io, Argus, and Mercury. But it is suggested
that Ovid did more than merely record stories or transmute into mythological
narrative the incidents and figures he witnessed. It is hinted that the poet,
through the power of language, actually brought about some of the metamorphoses he described. For instance, long after Ovid's disappearance, Cotta witnesses how his landlord Lycaon, who scampers through the mountains dressed
up in a wolf's pelt, is seemingly transformed into a wolf and killed by a rock-
slide. The most terrifying episode comes at the end, when the ancient tragedy
of rape and infanticide is reenacted by the butcher Tereus, his wife Procne, their
son Itys, and her sister Philomela. Cotta, cowering in the dark to hide from the
raging butcher with his axe, sees what appears to be "the fulfillment of what had
long been written on the scraps and pennants of Trachila" (284): when the enraged Tereus raises his axe, two birds—a swallow and a nightingale—flutter away,
pursued by the hoopoe into which the butcher was seemingly transformed.

Cotta concludes that Ovid "liberated the world from people and their systems by telling *every* tale to its ultimate end" (287)—that is, by following every
human history to its redeeming transformation back into some natural object.
(Ransmayr's sobering implication is that natural catastrophes are somehow related to mankind's ecological carelessness and that the earth can be preserved
from human depredations only when mankind has again been reduced to a part
of nature.) Once he had cleared the earth by his metamorphoses of all human
beings, Ovid simply entered his own narrative and rolled down the hillsides as

a tiny stone, floated over the tides as a cormorant, or clung triumphantly as a bit of moss to the last remnant of a town wall (287). The account ends as Cotta sets out into the mountains in hope of finding a scrap of cloth with two syllables inscribed upon it—Cotta? or Ovid? The answer is left open, for when he screams these syllables into the air, the echo returning his cry in the last words of the novel bears "his own name" (288).

Ransmayr was born in 1954 in Austria, where at a Benedictine school near Gmunden he read Ovid's *Metamorphoses* as a required text in the Latin curriculum.[30] This initial contact left little impression because it was encumbered, he felt, by too much "bourgeois rubbish" ("bildungsbürgerliches Gerümpel"). It was some years later, following his study of philosophy at the University of Vienna (where he was influenced by the writings of Adorno), that he again approached Ovid. Invited to contribute a translation from the *Metamorphoses* to an anthology in the series *Die andere Bibliothek,* Ransmayr did not believe that his Latin was up to a verse translation. Instead he provided a prose adaptation of a passage about Daedalus (*Met.* 8.155.70), which was published in 1985 under the title "Das Labyrinth."[31] The effort brought him back to the *Metamorphoses,* which he reread several times, gradually conceiving the idea of a novel in which he would "apply Ovid's own procedure, namely to take this tradition, the figures of Greco-Roman mythology, and use them as a kind of raw material for my own story, to make the attempt to transform these figures in a novelistic narrative context."[32] In fact, Ransmayr produced a brief outline for such a novel, which was published in the yearbook *Jahresringe 87–88.*

The theme of this project for a still untitled novel was to be "the disappearance and the reconstruction of literature, of poetry; its material are the *Metamorphoses* of Publius Ovidius Naso."[33] The presuppositions are already essentially the same: Ovid was banned to the Black Sea before the completion of his work, which he destroyed in despair and rage, and then died in Tomi without having written it down a second time, leaving behind nothing but memories in the minds of a few inhabitants of the desolate coast. In the original proposal it is not Cotta who goes in quest of the manuscript but an ambitious young man named Posides, who is commissioned by an academy in Rome to look for the vanished work. Generally speaking, the proposal continues, the fifteen books of the *Metamorphoses* lead the reader from mythos to enlightenment—from the description of the four ages in the first book to the great speech of Pythagoras in the last one. Posides reverses everything (and here we begin to sense the influence of Adorno and the postmodern rejection of logocentric reason): he begins with enlightenment gone mad in the person of the crazed Pythagoras and at the end is ensnared once again in the world of myth as witnesses tell him about the Golden and Iron Ages and of an earth drenched in blood. With the exception of the figure of the young researcher, who becomes Ovid's admirer Cotta, the proposal contains essentially the outline of the novel.

On publication in 1988 *Die letzte Welt* was widely hailed as the brilliant product of a fresh young talent, and it immediately won several prizes.[34] In recent years scholars have caught up with the early critical response, providing detailed analyses of the novel in the context of Ovid's *Metamorphoses*.[35] Ransmayr uses only thirty-three episodes from the *Metamorphoses* and provides in the lengthy appendix to his novel a comparison of the respective roles of the figures in Ovid's text and in his novel—an "Ovidian Repertoire" that in fact goes beyond the text and adds to our understanding as an integral component.[36] He omits many of the most familiar stories and gives great prominence to other figures, such as Echo, who play at most a peripheral role in Ovid's account. In addition, the novel contains over sixty allusions to passages from the *Tristia* and the *Epistulae ex Ponto* dealing with Ovid's exile in Tomis.[37] In contrast to Ovid's accumulative organization, however, Ransmayr introduces various devices that unify his novel. Several of the figures—e.g., Echo, Arachne, Pythagoras, Fama, Tereus, the Frisian undertaker Thies (Dis) and his wife Proserpina—appear throughout or in sustained passages of the novel, which is unified by place (almost all the action takes place in or around Tomi) and time (the action follows the course of a single annual cycle, from spring to spring)—an organizational principle closer to that of Ovid's *Fasti* than of the *Metamorphoses*.[38] In the wholly human novel, finally, there are no deities.

While Ransmayr's novel has gained the respect of classics scholars, it has at the same time been cited frequently as the model example of a postmodern text.[39] Among the more obvious characteristics are, in Blumenberg's phrase, the playful "Arbeit am Mythos" and the corresponding indeterminacy of the text, which is left open to question and doubt. The (literal) disappearance of the author contributes to the play of reality and fiction that pervades the novel; Arachne's concern only with her weaving and her total disregard of the finished tapestries, which she leaves rolled up in a corner, reflects the postmodern literary interest in process rather than product; and Cotta's fruitless search implies that it is difficult, if not impossible, to gain knowledge of the past. The inversion of Ovid's order, which leads us out of history and returns us to nature at the end, means that Ovid's humanization of nature gives way in Ransmayr to a more pessimistic dehumanization of man. In short, metamorphosis leads to a destabilization of social reality rather than to any ordering and explanation of nature. Ovid's exile, attributed to an almost random malice rather than to any reasoned punishment, reinforces Ransmayr's sense of cultural pessimism and socio-political criticism.

If Ransmayr's novel represents an exemplary document of postmodernism, it demonstrates equally well his generation's obsession with the idea of metamorphosis.[40] Since Ransmayr is not writing, like Rushdie, in the mode of magical realism, he cannot allow actual transformations of his characters, even reversible ones, to take place. The single case of apparent petrification, Fama's epileptic son Battus, is explained rationally by the cynical Lycaon as a medical anomaly, perhaps the result of an exotic disease brought to Tomi by Jason's tramp steamer and its cargo of unemployed riffraff. The challenge, therefore, is to account for metamorphosis in a reasonably plausible manner, and Ransmayr does so through various devices. In the first place, many of the stories of metamorphoses are recounted by informants who allegedly heard them from Ovid: Echo, for instance, relates stories ending in the petrification of human beings while Arachne weaves into her tapestries nothing but tales of birds and flying. Second, Cotta has visual experiences of transformation in his dreams (notably of Argus and Io), in the films shown by the dwarf Cyparis (Ceyx and Alcyone, and the series of violent deaths), and in the advertisement painted on the canvas cover of Cyparis's wagon (Actaeon). The transformations of actual human beings, finally, are always only apparent: Lycaon the rope maker, who in his (reversible psychic) state of lycanthropy runs barefoot across the hills clad in a wolf's pelt; or the citizens of Tomi who during their carnival—a conflation of Shrovetide and Saturnalia—dress up as mythological beings and deities (a ragged Medea and Orpheus and a Jupiter whose glory is produced by battery lights). Metamorphosis is successfully postmodernized.

It is useful to recall Calvino's *Invisible Cities* in connection with *The Last World* because transformation has an entirely different meaning for the two postmodern writers. Calvino's (and Kublai Khan's) urge for transformation into lightness stemmed, we learned, from a compulsion to offset the petrification overcoming reality. But according to Ransmayr's Echo, Ovid's tales of petrification had precisely the opposite function: as "a way out of the chaos of life" (156). How much more dignified, he felt, was petrification than "the disgusting stinking process of organic decay" (158)—a return of mankind to the stones from which it was awakened by Deucalion and Pyrrha. It was Ovid's hope, Cotta realizes in a startling epiphany, "to liberate the world from human beings and their order by telling every story to its end" (287)—and that end in Ransmayr's cultural pessimism was the restoration of civilization to nature: a process signaled in the opening description of Tomi, whose rows of empty houses "seemed gradually to be falling back into the coastal mountains" (10). At this point the theme of petrification coincides with the disappearance of the author, for in Cotta's final vision he imagines that Ovid "himself had also entered the picture empty of human beings and rolled down the slag heaps as an invulnerable pebble" (287). The novel leaves us with various provocative questions unanswered. Is Cotta simply mad? Is Cotta ultimately identical with Ovid? Are Ovid's *Metamorphoses* the fictionalization of real people and incidents that Cotta/Ovid observed? Is our world headed toward petrification?

We can conclude our review of postmodern metamorphoses with the eerily beautiful "Dream of Publius Ovidius Naso" by Antonio Tabucchi (born 1943). The brief "Sogno di Publio Ovidio Nasone" is one of Tabucchi's *Dreams of Dreams* (*Sogni di sogni,* 1992), twenty fictional dreams of figures from history and myth ranging from Daedalus and Apuleius by way of Villon and Rabelais to Chekhov and Freud.[41] In each case the dreamer is imagined to enter one of his own works: thus Daedalus goes into his labyrinth to encounter what turns out to be a gentle Minotaur, whom he enables to escape by means of the wings he has invented; Freud dreams on the last day of his life that he has returned to Vienna in the form of his famous patient Dora and experiences her sexual fantasies. In Ovid's dream, which is dated to the night of January 16 sometime after the birth of Jesus Christ, the exiled poet is brought back to Rome in triumph by the emperor.[42] In the dream, however, he is miraculously transformed by the news into a man-sized butterfly with handsome colored wings and large spherical eyes. (His transformation not only suggests the winged Cupid, whose powers Ovid celebrated in many of his poems; the butterfly also implied in antiquity hints of a morally reprehensible sexual passion.)[43] Because in his new condition with butterfly legs he can barely stand, he must recline on the cushions of the golden chariot sent to bear him to Rome. Arriving in Rome, Ovid manages to rise and place a laurel wreath on his head as the crowd prostrates itself, mistakenly taking him for an Asian deity. When Ovid tries to tell them that he is the poet Ovid, he is unable to speak and emits nothing but a shrill whistle that causes people to cover their ears and run away. At the imperial palace, Ovid forces himself to make his way clumsily up the stairs, where he finds the emperor drinking wine and awaiting his arrival. When the emperor asks to hear a new poem, Ovid, unable in his insect form to recite, decides to communicate his verses by gestures. But his huge wings cause the curtains to move and stir up a breeze in the palace. In his annoyance at the "effeminate ballet" of the indecent insect, Caesar orders his guards to cut off Ovid's wings, which fall to the ground like soft feathers. Understanding that his life is ending, Ovid sways out of the palace on his insect legs and encounters a mob now eager to tear him apart. "And then, tripplingly, Ovid danced down the palace stairs."[44]

The dream is clearly a wish-dream of the exiled poet, who repeatedly sought in his epistles from the Black Sea to obtain pardon and rehabilitation, and also an entry of the poet into the realm of his own *Metamorphoses*. The ambivalent figure of the butterfly suggests both the theme of love that dominates much of his poetry and, at the same time, the reasons for his exile. The emperor, depicted here as drunk, uncouth, and violent, is an unsubtle comment on political power, while the behavior of the crowd, whose initial adulation is quickly transformed into the bloodlust of a mob, hints at the irrationality of mass hysteria as well as the mutability of public opinion. But the poet's dancing descent to meet his fate is Tabucchi's acknowledgement of the Ovidian conviction that his poetry will survive—and the postmodern belief that the writer vanishes behind his own work.

◄ 11 ►

OVID IN THE NINETIES

OVID AND GENERATION X

The disengagement of the skeptical generation was a product of the postwar disenchantment with politics and the Cold War conviction that the individual was powerless in the face of great impersonal forces. Accordingly its Ovids turned to love or, in exile, sought escape—like the hippies who fled to Tibet and Nepal—in New Age religions and in realms beyond the imperium. (David Malouf's novel *An Imaginary Life* directly mirrors these sentiments.) The postmodern generation in its deconstruction of the self and rejection of the past had little use for the historical Ovid. But in its obsession with metamorphosis and its playful appropriation of myth it turned with renewed interest to his major poem. The generation of the 1990s, a product of the globalization that followed the collapse of the polarized world of the Cold War, had yet a different view. "Generation X," as it was identified and popularized in Douglas Coupland's "tales for an accelerated culture,"[1] was a "fun society" ("Spaßgesellschaft"), a cynical urban culture that in the United States projected itself, or at least its wish dreams, in such TV series as *Sex and the City,* snickered at the ironies of *Seinfeld,* worshiped at the altar of "Madonna," and adhered to a self-adulating *culte du moi.* "Becoming fluid and many-sided," the new persona of the 1990s that Robert Jay Lifton labeled—with an Ovidian image—"the Protean Self," evolved a mode of being "appropriate to the restlessness and flux of our time" and engaged in "continuous exploration and personal experiment."[2] Believing in its infinite capacity to reshape itself—through divorce, a new career, body building, a sex change—this Protean Self was attracted by the virtual reality made possible by the electronic media. Individuals disenchanted with a reality grown stale turned increasingly to violence and fantasy to fulfill their expectations.

The apt metaphor for this society, which existed in France as well as in Germany and the United States, was created by Marie Darrieussecq in her runaway bestseller *Truismes* (1996), which depicts in anatomically precise detail the gradual transformation of the heroine into a sow and which is sometimes mentioned in an Ovidian connection.[3] While the self-centered and voluptuous farm girl, who goes happily to work in an elegant Parisian bordello, is nothing like Mrs. Tebrick, in its plot the novel represents a surprisingly close parallel to Garnett's *Lady into Fox:* both women degenerate slowly into an animal state; both eventually desert their human consorts in favor of their new kind (here it's a "very virile wild boar"; 130); and both bear a litter of young in their new condition. But there is almost nothing Ovidian about Darrieussecq's work. Indeed, if there were any classical source, it would be Apuleius's *Golden Ass:* both are first-person narratives, and in both the hero/ine uses the condition of metamorphosis as an occasion for amusing social satire, which in the soft porn of the French novel, scrawled with a pen she can barely clutch in her hoof (like Ovid's Io? *Met.* 1.649), is mainly feminist and sexual in its object.

It seems inevitable, under these circumstances and as the flurry of Virgilian activity following the bimillennial of Virgil's death in 1981 subsided, that Ovid should again emerge as the classical writer of choice. Ovid, after all, celebrated love; he reported on the convergence and conflict of diverse cultures in Tomis; he gave priority to poetic reality over the reality of politics; his tone was ironic; and his works offered an abundance of sex, violence, and fantasy. Above all, he was the champion of change, the master of metamorphosis. At times Ovid's sensibility appears almost flagrantly contemporary:

> prisca iuvent alios, ego me nunc denique natum
>   gratulor; haec aetas moribus apta meis.
>   (*Ars am.* 3.121–22)

> (Let others delight in antiquity; I consider
> myself fortunate to have been born just now;
> this age suits my temperament.)

A second wave of scholarly reappraisal got underway some thirty years following the bimillennial celebrations of 1957 and introduced new angles of attention. In 1985 the journal *Helios* devoted its spring issue to "Contemporary Interpretations of Ovid." The occasion, as the editor (Mary-Kay Gamel) pointed out in her introduction, was not an anniversary, nor were the contributions meant as simple celebrations. "They are intended instead to question the way now dominant of reading Ovid's work among classical authors, and to offer alternatives" (3). Gamel noted that the number of publications dedicated to Ovid's work increased from twenty-four entries in the annual bibliography for 1966 to fifty-seven in 1982. Yet, she continued, many scholars continued to accept the disparaging opinion initiated in the first century by Seneca and Quintilian and reaffirmed by scholars of the nineteenth century. The problem stemmed from several causes: the critically unsophisticated conflation of Ovid with the views of his characters; the apparent frivolity of his themes; a prudish response to what many regarded as the excessive sexuality of his works; the anti-Augustan sentiments of his views; and, not least, the indifference of the countercultural generation of the sixties to "canonical" works. In any case, the lively contributions to the issue helped to initiate a scholarly revaluation of Ovid.

That same year the Women's Classical Caucus of the American Philological Association adopted the topic "Reappropriating the Text: The Case of Ovid" for its annual panel. In her paper, which was published as the theme piece for the 1990 issue of *Helios,* Phyllis Culham reviewed some of the issues that had recently emerged in feminist scholarship on Ovid: that he strikes readers as modern; that he had an extraordinary insight into female psychology; that as an early proponent of the "modern construct of heterosexual love" he believed in the equality of women or, conversely, that his texts contain "elements of actual misogyny"; and, finally, that he was a rebel out of tune with the ideals of Augustan Rome (163). Within a short time feminist re-visionists were analyzing Ovid's female figures, and notably Corinna, in terms of what they called his "womanufacture."[4]

These initiatives from the late 1980s were the prelude to a resounding chorus of scholarly expression during the next decade, which resulted in such collective efforts as *Ovid Renewed: Ovidian Influences on Literature and Art from the Middle Ages to the Twentieth Century* (1988), the proceedings of the 1994 Sulmona conference published under the title *Metamorfosi* (1997), *Ovidian Transformations: Essays on the Metamorphoses and Its Reception* (1999), and the two-volume festschrift for Michael von Albrecht, *Ovid: Werk und Wirkung* (1999). It also produced popular introductions[5] and such scholarly contributions as a study of the *Metamorphoses* in art, a thoughtful appraisal of Ovid's relationship to Augustus, a review of his reception in English literature, several life-and-works volumes, and a bio-bibliographical handbook,[6] in addition to numerous books on specific works as well as translations (or reprints) in various languages of Ovid's entire oeuvre. As was the case at the time of the bimillennial celebrations, the scholarly revaluation was accompanied by a pronounced literary response.

INTERNALIZATIONS OF THE *METAMORPHOSES*

The first two "Ovidian" works of the new decade, novels that departed distinctly from the postmodern efforts, are only indirectly Ovidian but clearly depend upon the *Metamorphoses* for their plots and effect. Cees Nooteboom (born 1933), the Dutch poet, playwright, and travel writer, is best known outside the Netherlands for his novels. In 1986–87 he delivered a series of Regents' lectures at the University of California at Berkeley, and his frequent stays in Germany have produced travel accounts and the successful novel *All Souls' Day* (English translation 2001).

His remarkable short novel, *The Following Story* (*Het volgende verhaal,* 1991), purports to be the deathbed account of his life by a fiftyish classicist from Amsterdam, Herman Mussert, who makes his living by writing travel books under the pseudonym "Dr. Strabo." These books, which he often compiles entirely from secondhand reports, are typical of the deceit that he has practiced all his life—a deceit foreshadowed for Dutch readers by his name. (Anton Adriaan Mussert was a notorious Dutch Fascist executed in 1946 for high treason against his country.)[7] Twenty years earlier, we learn, Mussert had taught Greek and Latin in a provincial Dutch gymnasium, where for his homeliness and love of philosophy he was known as Socrates. Mussert was fired from his position because he was involved in a liaison with a colleague, the biology teacher Maria Zeinstra. Zeinstra, married to the poetry-writing gym instructor Arend Herfst, takes up with the homely Mussert mainly out of a desire for revenge against her philandering husband, who is engaged in an affair with a beautiful student named Lisa d'India. When the two men get into a fight on the school grounds, they are both dismissed; Lisa is killed in a car wreck when she goes off with Herfst; Maria and Herfst emigrate to the United States; and Mussert stays in Amsterdam to pursue his new career as a travel writer.

The story consists essentially of two dreams or visions that Mussert has on the last night of his life in Lisbon. (To this extent the book resembles Hermann Broch's *Death of Virgil* more than the other modern fictions that have been proposed, e.g., Thomas Mann's *Death in Venice*.)[8] First he recalls an earlier trip to Lisbon that he undertook with Maria Zeinstra. Then he imagines a Charon-like boat trip from Lisbon to the Amazon in the company of five other men who happen to die at the same moment as he. Each tells his own story; and at the end, when he catches sight of Lisa d'India on the shore, Mussert prepares to tell his own story, "het volgende verhaal" (which turns out to be the story that we have just read). In the last sentence of this circular account he addresses Lisa as "my dearest Crito, the girl who was my pupil, so young that you could talk to her about immortality. And then I told her, then [with a switch in form of address] I told you THE FOLLOWING STORY."[9] (She is his Crito, from his favorite Platonic dialogue *Phaedo*, and the person he has actually always loved without realizing it.)

Ovid enters the narrative because, along with Plato, he is Mussert's favorite writer. Mussert is translating the *Metamorphoses* and at the time of his death has reached book 12, the burial of Achilles.[10] Ovid's work is frequently mentioned in the course of his account. For instance, when Mussert visits Maria's biology class, she is talking about the continuity of life, using the example of a dead rat in whose cadaver beetles lay their eggs, feed, and reproduce their young. Mussert invites her to visit his Ovid course where, he assures her, "transformation also takes place, albeit without rats in balls of rotting flesh" ("Daar wordt ook iets veranderd. Geen ratten in aaskogels, maar toch . . . ," 37). When she visits the class, he is discussing the death of Phaethon and tries afterward to tell her about the transformation of Phaethon's sisters into trees: "All the transformations I talk about are metaphors for the transformations that concern you," (41). But in nature, she objects, everything takes place without the assistance of deities. "Nobody does it for us; we do it ourselves." Mussert sounds almost like a postmodern theorist when he explains that the individual "I" changes and does not remain constant over the course of fifty years. The self is "a bundle composed of ever changing circumstances and functions that we call 'I'" (42). Modern man no longer thinks the same as did earlier ages: "We are descendants; we have no mythic lives, only psychological ones."

In the second part he rehearses the Platonic idea of a self that transcends the body, but ultimately concludes that Socrates is dead. And when he dies, Mussert reflects—in a passage that sounds like a recapitulation of Rushdie's Chamcha deliberating between Lucretius and Ovid—that it will not be his soul that goes away but his body, which will set out upon an endless wandering. "It can no longer be gotten out of the universe and will take part in the most fantastic metamorphoses" (91). (The journey motif is signaled at the very beginning when Mussert falls into his last sleep holding a photograph of the universe made from the spaceship *Voyager*.) While Ovid's role in the story is secondary rather than central, the narrative technique, which involves overlapping tales, resembles that of the *Metamorphoses*—notably at the end, where the last moments of the other passengers are related. Above all, the presence of Ovid clearly signals the new familiarity that emerged from the preceding decades.

That same year another remarkable novel appeared across the Channel, not the later work of an experienced writer but the first novel of a young author, Lawrence Norfolk's *Lemprière's Dictionary* (1991).[11] This brilliant, often fantastic fiction—part historical novel, part detective story—is based throughout on detailed knowledge of the cultural and political history of the late eighteenth century. It also is patterned precisely after the eighteenth-century Gothic thriller or the so-called League Novel (*Bundesroman*) of German Romantic literature— complete with a secret society headquartered in a mysterious location, a secret symbol, an emissary of the league, and an unsuspecting hero whose life it controls. That hero, John Lemprière (died 1824), is none other than the author of the well-known *Classical Dictionary* (1788), which into the twentieth century has remained a standard handbook of classical mythology.

The action takes place in 1787–88 in (mainly) the island of Jersey, London, Paris, and the French port of La Rochelle. An international conglomerate, which controls the East India Company from its headquarters in secret caverns below the city of London, is planning to help revolutionaries in France overthrow the government. The Cabbala, as they call themselves, originated in 1600 as a commercial venture of nine Huguenots in La Rochelle. Driven out by Richelieu's forces, their descendants now operate from London, where they have acquired fabulous wealth by subverting funds from the East India Company. They have converted this wealth into gold hidden in statues of classical mythological figures for shipment to France on July 14, 1788—one year before the Revolution. The Cabbala is destroyed at the end, but the gold is successfully delivered to the revolutionaries in France. The background in London involves mob riots and political rabble-rousers and various complicated subplots (involving an Indian assassin, a shipful of elderly pirates, and several historical figures).

John Lemprière's fictionalized life is introduced through the claim that he is a descendant of one of the nine original members of the financial consortium— a dissatisfied member whose descendants have for five generations sought to destroy the evil Cabbala. The Cabbala attempts to forestall the family vengeance by murdering its members. (They succeed in killing Lemprière père, and the novel involves their machinations to dispose of the younger Lemprière.) The Ovidian (though unattributed) motto of the novel—*Barbarus hic ego sum, qui non intellegor ulli* (*Tr.* 5.10.37: "Here I am a barbarian, understood by no one")—accurately characterizes his uncomprehending role as an outsider. The Cabbala undertakes its plot by inducing in the learned but impressionable young man various mythologically based visions that appear to foretell and even cause events to take place.

Attracted by the lovely Juliet Casterleigh, he agrees to help her father catalog his library. As a reward Casterleigh, a member of the Cabbala, sends him a handsome edition of the *Metamorphoses* featuring a notably spectacular full-page lithograph of Actaeon and Diana, which the young Lemprière studies, "half consciously looking for clues as to why it should fascinate him" (29). A short time later, in a murder staged by the Cabbala, he sees his father killed by a pack of hounds when the two of them, seemingly accidentally, come upon the naked Juliet bathing beneath a waterfall. This experience confirms his belief that he possesses mystical powers. "He never dreamed it could come true. And yet he *had* dreamed. The cloud above turned the waters gray and his father's blood turned them red. The dream was his and no one else's" (75). Juliet reports that "He reads things. He believes they come true—" (165).

When Lemprière goes from Jersey to London to settle his father's estate, he is given papers that put him on the elusive trail of the Cabbala, assisted by Septimus Praeceps, a young man in the service of the secret society. It is Septimus who suggests that he consult a physician, Ernst Kalkbrenner, about his troubling visions: for instance, he thinks that he has seen a local deity known by the classical name "the Vertumnus" in the fields outside his parents' house; and at a wild drinking party he witnesses "the transformation of a Covent Garden madam into Circe" (107) and her patrons into swine. They come up with the idea that he should exorcise his dreams by writing them down in a mythological lexicon. "'Lay the ghosts of antiquity to rest!' Ernst had exclaimed. 'Do it to them before they do it to you.'" (110).

Lemprière sets about his task and within a few months actually finishes the *Dictionary*. "Discharged of any therapeutic function, the entries were guided along no course but that of their author's passions" (261). Still he continues to witness apparitions: e.g., the murder of a young Juliet look-alike who is filled with molten gold (like Danaë). He goes to a warehouse peopled with statues and encounters a scene out of *Metamorphoses* 7 (Jason and the dragon's teeth): "Blind eyes stared at him as he held up the lamp. Hundreds of them, thousands, a petrified forest sewn from dragons' teeth" (246). Walking through London, he begins to make out signs on the stones. "A snake skin sloughed by the python sent by Juno to pursue the pregnant Latona told him that they had passed and gone" (317).

Septimus insists that he date all his entries as he writes them down. As it turns out, this is part of the Cabbala's plot: they want to put him out of action by convicting him of the various murders, which always take place shortly after he has read or written about them—mostly in Ovid's *Metamorphoses*. In his obsession, Lemprière constantly sees reality in terms of metamorphoses based on Ovid: "A transformation is taking place behind him. Most, if not all, of the spectating revelers are showing signs of piggish metamorphosis, noses thickening and flattening, bellies extending taut, rounded contours" (88). Gradually convinced of his own guilt, he tries to confess to the police, but is released as innocent. Eventually the villains are killed off, the mysteries are resolved, and Lemprière ends up with Juliet, who was initially led to believe that she is his half sister—another one of the Cabbala's lies. They go back to Jersey where they presumably live happily ever after.

Norfolk's novel is evidently not a life or postfiguration of Ovid but a skillful modernization of the Gothic thriller. But the plot depends extensively on stories related in the *Metamorphoses,* and Norfolk has fixed for his hero on the one historical figure whose obsession with classical mythology could plausibly be used as the justification for such mythological visions and incipient madness. In an interview, Norfolk explained that the real Lemprière had an unexciting life. "So I invented a life for him. But to give him a life, I had to invent a history."[12] The history he has invented is thoroughly plausible and located neither in a never-never land of magical realism like Rushdie's nor in a conflated past and future that never existed like Ransmayr's. He has modernized and psychologized Ovid's work more in the spirit of such modern classics as Joyce's *Ulysses* or Broch's *Death of Virgil* than of Calvino, Rushdie, or Ransmayr.

FANCIFUL FICTIONS

The attempt to uncover the reasons for Ovid's exile did not end with the writers of the skeptical generation, but efforts by writers born a generation later lack the underlying seriousness of the skeptical generation and depend on increasingly playful and improbable plots: e.g., Ron Burns's story "Murderer, Farewell" (1996).[13] Burns had previously written two mystery novels set in ancient Rome, *Roman Nights* (1991) and *Roman Shadows* (1992), revolving around Julius Caesar and Marcus Aurelius, respectively. "Murderer, Farewell" concerns the murder of Marcellus Gaius, a popular young general recently returned from a victory at the German front, who is found butchered in the royal palace. Augustus summons Ovid, who has once before given him astute advice (by suggesting he call himself Augustus and *princeps* rather than emperor), to solve the murder. Ovid is said to have been for many years a favorite of the emperor, who protects Ovid—"in the truest sense a ladies' man"—when he is threatened by friends of the lofty husbands he has cuckolded. Ovid quickly establishes that robbery was not the motive: Marcellus still has on his person a purse filled with gold sesterces, and the murder weapon is a distinctive bejeweled dagger. Ovid interviews various persons: Marcellus's widow, Camilla; his benefactor, the senator Gallius Novo; his friend Avitus Lollianus. Tracing Marcellus's last movements, he determines that the young general was summoned to the palace late on the night before the murder. When because of a recent argument suspicion is cast on Tiberius, the son of the emperor's wife by a previous marriage, Ovid searches his palace quarters in "platter and loincloth" (to ensure no planted evidence) and discovers hidden beneath the tiles of a mosaic a bloody tunic, sash, and sandals. Yet despite the evidence Ovid hesitates to arrest Tiberius. He withdraws into seclusion for three days and then goes secretly to see Augustus, where he reports the evidence but refuses the emperor's order to arrest Tiberius. Why? He informs Augustus that he happened to be in the adjoining room on the night of the murder and heard Marcellus reject Augustus's amorous advances. Enraged, Augustus then stabbed the general with his dagger. The homicide investigation is quietly quashed, but ten days later Ovid is sent into exile at desolate Tomis. The pornographic nature of his poems is cited as the official reason. Even after Augustus's death Tiberius refuses to bring him back because he discovers that Ovid had been his wife's lover and that Augustus had helped the poet to cover up the affair.

David Wishart (born 1952), who studied classics at Edinburgh and taught Latin and Greek for several years, is the author of an earlier novel *I, Virgil* (1995), which is allegedly the first-person account written by Virgil at the end of his life as he awaits death by poisoning from Augustus. The emperor has come to the realization that the *Aeneid* is actually an attack on his bloodthirsty ways veiled in pious platitudes. Wishart's *Ovid* (1995) takes place after Ovid's death but also, like Burns's story, involves a court intrigue surrounding Tiberius. The story features the nephew of Ovid's patron Messalla, Marcus Valerius Messalla Corvinus—not to be confused with Messalla's adopted son Cotta featured in Ransmayr's *Last World*—a rich, spoiled, twenty-one-year-old ne'er-do-well.

The bawdy tone of the first-person account, which differs markedly from the witty sophistication of Bocheński's sly conférencier, is established in the opening words:

> I'd been at a party on the Caelian the night before. My tongue tasted like a gladiator's jockstrap, my head was pounding like Vulcan's smithy, and if you'd held up a hand and asked me how many fingers you'd got I'd've been hard put to give a definite answer without using an abacus.[14]

It is Wishart's fiction that Corvinus is approached by Ovid's stepdaughter, Perilla, for help in recovering the poet's ashes from Tomis. The seemingly simple assignment leads to many false starts and thriller-adventures—threats from high places, beatings, and kidnappings—until Corvinus uncovers the reason for the bureaucratic reluctance to release Ovid's ashes: a plot stemming from Livia's dynastic ambitions for her son Tiberius and her scheme to discredit and manipulate Augustus by conspiring for the defeat of the Roman army in Germany by Arminius. Livia continues to hate Ovid because he nearly ruined her plans.

> Had he been a politician we could have dealt with each other, but he was not. He was a well-meaning bumbler who wouldn't have understood bargaining if it had hit him in the face. Yes, I hated Ovid so much. I still do. I would have had him killed, only Tomi was worse. (358)

By blackmailing the imperial mother with the disclosure of her plot, Corvinus obtains her permission to recover and bury the poet's ashes and to marry Perilla. Unlike most other novels previously discussed, this one includes mainly historical figures, as the author assures us in his concluding note and in the introductory table of "Dramatis Personae." Unlike them, too, Wishart has little interest in Ovid, either before or during his exile. He is fascinated, as he tells us in his note (368), by the corrupt palace bureaucracy and by Augustan political scheming, none of which adds to our understanding of Ovid or his times.[15]

Aunt Margaret's Lover (1994) by Mavis Cheek (born 1948) is an odd postfiguration, a fluffy bit of fashionable comedy, redeemed by its use of Ovid's love poetry—the *Amores,* the *Ars amatoria,* and the *Remedia*—as the leitmotif.[16] Margaret Percy is a picture framer and the foster parent of her niece Saskia. When Saskia goes off to Canada to visit her father, "Aunt" Margaret comes into an unexpected legacy that enables her to enjoy a year's leave from her responsibilities. Deciding to take a lover for the period, she first responds to ads in a weekly magazine and then places her own: "Woman, 39, seeks lover for one year. I offer good legs, bright mind, happy disposition, in return for well-adjusted, solvent male between 35 and 40. April to April. No Expectations." The story concerns her pleasant affair with an architect, Simon, whom she calls "Oxford" and who is scheduled to go off to Nicaragua at the end of their affair. Much of the story concerns the jealous or spiteful reactions of her various friends, who are unhappy or disappointed in love. Newsy postcards from Canada from her niece Saskia introduce each chapter.

Margaret reads and cites Ovid's love poetry constantly. About her boring companion Roger, whom she dumps: "Ovid says you should never tell a failing lover what their faults are unless you want to bind them closer, for they will try to improve them" (15). "Ovid says that rivers do this to the soul because they know all about love themselves, and since his definition of love is generally looser than most, I took it as a sign" (42). After first meeting "Oxford": "He *will* be my lover. I vowed to go home that night and read my Ovid *avidly.* He is a wonderful antidote to romantic love. With Ovid, as with life, it always ends in tears" (126). And again, sitting with an old lover and discussing her new one, she refers to *Amores* 3.6.24–26: "I reminded him that Ovid had used a river several times to illustrate just such a fantasy, and that he had been among the most pragmatic of poet/lover combinations going. 'Rivers know all about love themselves. / Inachus pined, we're told, for Melia the Bithynian / At her touch his icy shallows thawed'" (162). When they go for dinner at a country hotel, "Oxford" tells her "Don't forget the Ovidian code" (173); accordingly, in the following scene they write words in the wine and sip from the same glass. "No wonder Ovid and Corinna stayed so hot for each other. I did as the good book instructed, and licked the place his lips had touched with the tip of my tongue" (177). When they run up the stairs to their tapestried room, it is "Hardly the romantic discretion of Ovid's persuasion, but you have to come up to date sometimes" (179). Shakespeare is "the honey-voiced descendant of Ovid, past master of the rituals of love" (229). On their last night together Margaret tries to think of words to inscribe in the book she has given him: "Nor lines from Ovid's *Cures for Love*—too bitter" (263). The novel ends with quotations from Ovid and Picasso. "'*Si latet ars, prodest*,' says Ovid. 'Art is a lie that makes us see the truth,' says Picasso, two thousand years on" (275).

THE OVIDIAN BOOM

Accompanying the efflorescence of Ovidian studies and fanciful fictions, the nineties experienced a resurgence of often brilliant and ingenious translations and adaptations of the *Metamorphoses*. The poet Allen Mandelbaum is noted for his lively rendition of Virgil's *Aeneid* (1972), which received the National Book Award for Translation, as well as for his translations of Dante's *Divine Comedy* (1980–84), Homer's *Odyssey* (1990), and the modern Italian poets Ungaretti and Quasimodo. His version of the *Metamorphoses* appeared in 1993, a vigorous, reliable, and readable verse rendition of Ovid's text. Mandelbaum puts Ovid's hexameters (as he did with Virgil's) into a blank verse that carries the story forward rapidly and steadily without drawing attention to itself.

> Before the sea and lands began to be,
> before the sky had mantled every thing,
> then all of nature's face was featureless—
> what men call chaos: undigested mass.[17]

Mandelbaum (born 1926) came to Ovid after his other major translations, and his Afterword gives us the sense that he has little personal affinity for the man

Ovid. "L. P. Wilkinson was not alone," he says, "in finding 'the bulk of the poems from exile . . . abject.' And the exiled Ovid is surely no Dante, no Herzen, no Solzhenitsyn" (554). The attraction was, rather, indirect and slow to develop. Mandelbaum observes that he had long been "attached to Ortygia and other sites of Greek Sicily that Ovid catalogued in one of his verse letters written in exile," of which he translated a section (*Ex Ponto* 2.10) under the title "My Eyes." Later, on a trip through the Apennines in search of a friend's family hometown, he visited Sulmona. But only gradually did he come to appreciate Dante's use of Ovid as an "exemplar of 'narrative variety'" (555). Indeed, Mandelbaum characterizes Ovid's fictions as "a bacchanalian narrative revel" (558) and asserts that the otherwise irreverent Ovid is reverent in one area alone: "the domain of art" (557). It is therefore principally as an admirer of Ovid's artistry, and in its spirit, that Mandelbaum undertakes his translation of the *Metamorphoses*.

We find—at least I sense—a wholly different spirit when we turn to the *Metamorphoses* as "translated freely into verse" by David R. Slavitt (1994). The enormously prolific Slavitt (born 1935) has published a dozen volumes of poetry, over twenty novels, and a critical study of Virgil as well as earlier translations of Ovid's *Tristia* (1986) and *Poetry of Exile* (1990). Slavitt's attitude is expressed in the brief comment (in the bibliography of his *Virgil*) where he assesses Mandelbaum's translation of the *Aeneid*, which he places second among modern versions after that of Robert Fitzgerald. Both, he says, "manage to suggest the resonance of Virgil, offering a kind of grandiloquence that never sounds totally ridiculous, and this is no mean feat. The good parts they get right, too, but the way to judge translators and translations is sometimes to look at their improvisation at those places that are less than wonderful."[18]

Unlike Mandelbaum, Slavitt translates the *Metamorphoses* into hexameters, a form that has not often been employed successfully in English. Slavitt relaxes the metrics as well as the lines, achieving a loosely dactylic six-beat rhythm that moves along at a lively pace.

> Bodies, I have in mind, and how they can change to assume
> new shapes—I ask the help of the gods, who know the trick:
> inspire me now, change me, let me glimpse the secret
> and sing, better than I know how, of the world's birthing.[19]

If we apply Slavitt's own test and look at the places that are less than wonderful, we immediately see the difference between his translation and Mandelbaum's. For instance, he plays freely with the names in the catalog of Actaeon's hounds, providing witty equivalents rather than straight transpositions of Ovid's Greek names (which in other translations are often footnoted): we find Valley

Girl, Julius Seizer, Gnasher and Slasher, along with "Damned Spot (who always wants to go out)" (49–50). When his Salmacis refuses to join Diana's "sportsy" crowd for their hunt, she is teased: "'Get off your delicate butt, grab a spear or a quiver, / and see what you can bag'" (72). This is a style that calls attention to itself. Purists may object that it goes beyond the limits of Ovidian taste, but that very boldness has often made Slavitt's *Metamorphoses* into the translation of choice in "World Lit" courses of the nineties. When Salmacis has succeeded in her demasculinizing rape of Hermaphroditus, he cries out to the gods "in his new-found voice, a kind of a husky contralto" (73). When Medea persuades the daughters of Pelias to kill their own father, she plunges his remains into "that boiling cauldron that she had prepared with its potpourri" (135). When Caunus reads the letter from his incest-seeking sister, he turns his wrath on the delivering servant: "'Get out of here,' he warns. 'Pimp! Monster! I'd haul you / before a judge except that I'd only bring disgrace / on our house'" (188).

Slavitt is equally bold in his interpretive intrusions into the text, as when he tells us that Medea, like many women in love, never knew where to draw the line. "And this is precisely what / we are refusing to think of, as Ovid goes on with his elegant / patter" (135). When she departs following Pelias's slaughter, he wonders "What's going on here? Medea / is supposed to go back to Corinth, to Jason, where she will discover that he is engaged to Creusa" (135). But Ovid avoids the terrible story and gives us, instead, "a bizarre catalogue in the effete Alexandrian style / of references we're supposed to get and respond to." Later, as Themis intones her myths in which time stands still, "Our attention / wanes, as the voice—of Themis? Ovid?—falters and drones. / Tired perhaps?" (183). As we learn a few lines later,

> The question is one of trust, which Ovid invites or tests.
> Have we learned in these pages to yield to his moods and moves, to read
> with that mixture of love and awe we felt many years ago
> in the upstairs hall?
>
> (184)

Then, as Ovid goes on with the tale of Byblis and Caunus, Slavitt notes that "we're back on track now. This story, a somewhat mannered performance, / is one of those nice rhetorical set pieces Ovid loved / to dazzle with." Since even Ovid finds it daunting to try to imitate Orpheus's voice, Slavitt observes perceptively, "Ovid turns our attention / from cause to effects" (196).

Here we sense a more intimate affinity with Ovid, a sympathy expressed in Slavitt's preface, where he talks about the "anxiety of influence" weighing upon Ovid as he wrote in the shadow of Virgil. "It is not impossible for a poet my age to understand at least a little of what this must have been like" (ix). Slavitt recalls that the debuts in the fifties of such poets as James Merrill, Richard Wilbur, and Howard Nemerov were celebrated "not only because these were collections of impressive and accomplished poems from writers of great talent but also because, in a more general way, these successes demonstrated that it was possible to go on from the achievement of Eliot, Pound, Joyce, and the modernists." In order to accommodate epic to his own sensibility—"more intimate, livelier, funnier, and more self-mocking" (x)—Ovid had to transform epic itself. It is precisely such a transformation that Slavitt now undertakes in his own translation, which constantly surprises our expectations. "My enthusiasm for Ovid's work and my delusion that I have understood his poem, that I have seen it and seen through it to these new words, are brash but necessary, and no more implausible, after all, than that first impossibility of any reader's leap of sympathy, intuition, understanding, and, finally, collaboration" (xii).

One of the best-known translations of the *Metamorphoses* in the history of English literature is the collective enterprise organized by Samuel Garth (1717) and "translated by the most eminent hands," including Joseph Addison, John Dryden, John Gay, Alexander Pope, and several other neoclassical contemporaries. A similar enterprise was undertaken almost three centuries later by Michael Hofmann and James Lasdun in their anthology *After Ovid: New Metamorphoses* (1994). Unlike Garth's work, which constitutes a full translation of the entire poem into rhyming couplets, *After Ovid* includes only some sixty individual episodes spanning the entire scope of Ovid's poem from book 1 (the creation) to book 15 (Pythagoras). But it resembles Garth's undertaking to the extent that it involves forty-two different English-language poets, albeit from five different countries and writing in a variety of meters, ranging from loose hexameters (Michael Longley's "Ivory and Water") and rhymed fourteeners (Kenneth Koch's "Io") to free verse and strophes of different elaboration. The book consists of "occasional" poems in the most literal but also finest sense, for they were all written within a year and a half specially for this volume.[20]

The project arose from the editors' perception in the mid–nineties that "Ovid is once again enjoying a boom"—a renewed appeal that they attribute to various factors: his mischief and cleverness, his use of shock, and his affinity with contemporary reality. His stories, they continue, "offer a mythical key to most of the more extreme forms of human behaviour and suffering, especially ones we think of as peculiarly modern: holocaust, plague, sexual harassment, rape, incest, seduction, pollution, sex-change, suicide, hetero- and homosexual love, torture, war, child-battering, depression and intoxication form the bulk of the themes." (The characterization of these horrors as "peculiarly modern" betrays a peculiarly postmodern sense of history.) The result, they suggest, constitutes "a kind of anthology of contemporary poetic practice."

The majority of the treatments, while contemporary in form, are retellings of familiar tales in a fairly straightforward manner: Io, Perseus, Arethusa, Philomela, Medea, Philemon and Baucis, Orpheus, Pygmalion, among others. Other renditions, while staying close to the original story line, rework them in a conspicuously modern idiom. In Robin Robertson's wittily grotesque "The Flaying of Marsyas" the torturers ridicule the scrawny satyr who is "all skin and whipcord."

> So, think you can turn up with your stag-bones
> and outplay Lord Apollo?
> This'll learn you. Fleece the fucker.
> *Sternum to groin.*
> Tickle, does it? Fucking bastard,
> coming down here with your dirty ways . . .
> (154)[21]

James Lasdun's "Erisychthon," an "Ex-boxer, self-styled entrepreneur, ex-con" (198), is now a thriving, cheating building contractor who takes his chain saw to a grove of sacred trees. Reduced by hunger to rummaging for cold cuts at the fridge and "stopping off for Big Macs / And cheese-steaks" (208), he is finally savaged by wolves and left to die in a sewage ditch, where he is transformed appropriately into "a yard of concrete pipe."

In some cases the retelling is given a modern analysis. "In our age of scrutiny and dissection we know Deianira's mind better than she does herself," C. K. Williams states in the terrible vengeance tale "Hercules, Deianira, Nessus" (213). Frederick Seidel relates the story of Myrrha's incest "with the help of radical feminist therapy" (243). Thomas Gunn looks at "Arachne" and sees "a tangle of despair" (145). Several other poets locate their accounts in our own present. William Logan's "Niobe" (147–50) is the wife of a Wall Street banker who, dressed in "the latest fashions from Milan," drives her BMW to their remodeled farmhouse in the Berkshires, where she stirs up the very primitive revenge of a mysterious mountain woman. Alice Fulton's "Daphne and Apollo" (28–58) brings together two "profoundly superficial" pop musicians: a bullying "Swoon Pope" and a player in Phoebe's "all-girl band." In Glyn Maxwell's "Phaeton and the Chariot of the Sun: Fragments of an Investigative Documentary" (65–78) a cinematographer interviews various witnesses (the horses) and experts (Mulciber, and a scientist) to get to the truth about Phaethon's unfortunate ride:

What are the gates of the Palace of the Sun made of? Would Phaethon have suffered? Carol Ann Duffy's "Mrs Midas" (261–63) is a divorcee who, now fearing her husband's embrace—"the kiss that would turn my lips to a work of art"—and hating his "lack of thought for me," has left him, sold the house, and moved to the South, where she mourns for the early days of their marriage, when she still thrilled to the touch of his warm hands. *After Ovid,* then, celebrates retellings of some of the best-known tales from the *Metamorphoses* in an often Ovidian manner—with his irony, his wordplay, his social criticism, his use of different voices—and, at the same time, a representative sampling of poetic style in the nineties. In our specific context, it provides a striking example of Ovid's real boom in our day and of the revitalized interest that motivated forty poets enthusiastically to take up the editors' challenge.

The boom manifested itself in other ways. In *Ovid in English* (1998) Christopher Martin collected a rich selection of translations by writers extending from Chaucer, Gower, and Golding to Slavitt, Mandelbaum, and Ted Hughes, with texts covering the entirety of Ovid's oeuvre: the *Amores, Ars amatoria, Remedia amoris, Heroides, Metamorphoses, Fasti, Tristia,* and *Epistulae ex Ponto*—and including even *De medicamine faciei* and *Ibis.* It was the editor's dual intention "to represent the Ovidian canon broadly" and, "given the vast extent to which Ovid pervades English poetry," to expose the "peculiar virtue each of our literary ages brings to the task of initiating Ovid into an English context"—an enterprise in which the volume succeeds admirably.[22]

Perhaps the most enduring monument to Ovid from the 1990s will be Ted Hughes's dazzling *Tales from Ovid* (1997), which began with his four contributions to the anthology *After Ovid.* (Hughes [1930–98] had already produced earlier translations of Seneca and Aeschylus.) The volume contains twenty-four tales (of which several include other incapsulated tales) related in a variety of poetic forms, ranging from three-line strophes ("Venus and Adonis," "Pyramus and Thisbe") to unbroken narratives in various mainly short-line meters. "Different aspects of the poem continued to fascinate Western culture,"[23] Hughes observes in his introduction, and his own translation reflects these shifting aspects. But there are distinct points of emphasis. Hughes, like Ovid, is fascinated by passion. "Or rather, in what a passion feels like to the one possessed by it. Not just ordinary passion either, but human passion in extremis—passion where it combusts, or levitates, or mutates into an experience of the supernatural" (ix). Many of Hughes's selections in his *Tales* reflect this obsession: from Pluto's rape of Proserpina and Juno's disastrous jealousy of Semele and Venus's infatuation with Adonis to Myrrha's incestuous passion for her father, Salmacis's obsession with Hermaphroditus, and the shared love of Pyramus and Thisbe. Beyond this, we are constantly aware in Hughes's retellings of his feeling that the Augustan Age "was at sea in hysteria and despair, at one extreme wallowing in the bottomless appetites and sufferings of the gladiatorial arena, and at the other searching higher and higher for a spiritual transcendence—which eventually did take form, on the crucifix" (x). Leaving aside any reservations concerning this reading of Roman history, we see that Hughes feels an intense identification with Ovid as a man for our times, a poet whose work reflects thoughts, feelings, and tensions that are as endemic to the last decade of the twentieth century as to the years embracing the turn from BCE to our era.

Like Slavitt, Hughes uses conscious anachronisms to modernize Ovid's text. Jupiter's thunderbolt destroys Lycaon's palazzo along with its "household idols and jujus" (16), and later he tries vainly to tone down "the nuclear blast of his naked impact" (91) to protect Semele. Phoebus anoints Phaethon with "a medicinal blocker" to protect him against sunburn (29). On her way to her father's bedchamber Myrrha is warned three times by "a screech owl, death's *doppelgänger*" (114), and Midas criticizes Apollo's singing as

> nothing but interior decoration
> By artificial light, for the chic, the effete.
> Pan is the real thing—the true voice
> Of the subatomic.
>
> (195)

Hughes employs other devices familiar to his readers, such as alliteration: Myrrha's nurse's hair bushes out "in a halo of horror" (112), and Acoetes tells Pentheus that he inherited from his fisherman father nothing but "the wilderness of waters" (177). Metaphors enliven the remains of Itys as Procne and Philomela cook them, some "gasping in bronze pots, some weeping on spits" (226).

Most conspicuous are the rapidity and tempo that Hughes achieves by rendering Ovid's hexameters in much shorter lines: 111 dactylic verses for Pyramus and Thisbe stretch out to 205 briefer lines; 140 verses of Ovid's account of Arachne become 240 in Hughes's rendition.

> Post ea discedens sucis Hecateidos herbae
> Sparsit, et extemplo tristi medicamine tactae
> Defluxere comae, cum quis et naris et aures,
> Fitque caput minimum . . .
>
> (*Met.* 6.139–42)

> The goddess
> Squeezed onto the dangling Arachne
> Venom from Hecate's deadliest leaf.
> Under that styptic drop
> The poor girl's head shrank to a poppy seed
>
> And her hair fell out.
> Her eyes, her ears, her nostrils
> Diminished beyond being.
>
> (168)

As we have noted, Hughes provides vivid depictions of passion, horror, and violence. These emotions are intensified, if anything, by the ironic and often grim detachment with which Hughes characterizes the gods who contrive the metamorphoses of life "for your own amusement" (3; Hughes's reading of *nam vos mutastis et illas, Met.* 1.2: "for you have changed them too"); and who, listening to Salmacis struggling with Hermaphroditus, "heard her frenzy—and smiled" (213; *vota suos habuere deos; Met.* 4.373: "her prayers persuaded the gods"). In addition, Hughes is partial to the tales of artists, notably Pygmalion and Arachne.

While Hughes succeeds brilliantly in re-visioning Ovid's text for a new age, his shifts of emphasis are equally symptomatic. We have noted his preference for the extreme scenes focusing on the passion of love, horror, and violence. His selections are clearly set pieces, meant to be taken as complete within themselves. To this end he frequently omits Ovid's transitional beginnings and endings, which often soften the effect of the tales. The account of the disastrous flood that destroys humanity is not followed by any replenishment of the earth by Deucalion and Pyrrha. Rather it ends starkly as "Drowned mankind, imploring limbs outspread, / Floats like a plague of dead frogs" (21) and then continues immediately in the next section with the second ecological disaster involving Phaethon. Ovid's passage on Salmacis and Hermaphroditus (*Met.* 285–388) begins and ends with a discussion of the wondrous powers of Salmacis's pool, which weakens and unsexes any man who bathes in it; while Hughes's set piece begins with Salmacis's infatuation and ends with their embrace in "the giddy boil" of the water. The tale of Pyramus and Thisbe ends when the two lovers "were closed in a single urn" (237), without Ovid's opening and closing comments on the fruit of the mulberry tree, which turns dark when ripe. In sum, Hughes makes short stories out of aetiological myths.

The most radical changes, however, are reflected in the decision to reorganize the sequence of the tales, which Hughes presents in loosely thematic groupings. Some of the set pieces occur in the order Ovid gave: Callisto after Phaethon

(*Met.* 2), Arethusa after Proserpina and Echo/Narcissus after Tiresias (*Met.* 3).
But another cluster is inverted for no apparent reason when the tale of Pygmalion, the father of Cinyras, grandfather of Myrrha, and hence ancestor of
Adonis, is placed after their stories. The birth tales of two heroes from different
books of Ovid's account, Bacchus (*Met.* 3) and Achilles (*Met.* 11), are put to-
gether, as are four tales relating the dire punishments of presumptuous mortals:
Arachne (*Met.* 6), Pentheus (*Met.* 3), Midas (*Met.* 11), and Niobe (*Met.* 6). While
Hughes begins with the account of creation and the four ages of man, he ends
with the tale of Pyramus and Thisbe (from *Met.* 4), rather than with book 15.
The story of Pyramus and Thisbe is one of the most frequently reworked Ovidian tales in English literature, but ever since Shakespeare (*A Midsummer-Night's
Dream*) it has usually been given a distinctly comic twist. Here it adds a different dimension, enabling Hughes to round off his work, which opens with the
creation, with death, and thereby to bring quiet closure to a poem otherwise
dominated by violent passions.[24] Equally symptomatic is the absence of any allusion to the Pythagoras story of book 15, which contains Ovid's theoretical justification for his theory of metamorphosis. For Hughes, metamorphosis does
not imply any continuity of the spirit—Ovid's forms into bodies—but simply
a physical change: "Now I am ready to tell how bodies are changed / Into different bodies" (3). Metamorphosis, as we know from his introduction, simply
marks the moment when passion explodes into the supernatural (ix). He wants
and needs no Pythagorean or any other theory because, to the modern mind,
metamorphosis is unique—a singularity that epitomizes the emotions in moments of passion in extremis.[25]

Inevitably such a resonant boom made its vibrations felt on the stage, and the
vehicle was Mary Zimmerman's *Metamorphoses,* which had its world premiere
in Chicago in 1998. Hailed when it reached New York in the 2001–2002 season as "the theater event of the year" and as "the most moving, intriguing, and
ultimately entertaining evening of theatre in New York,"[26] the Tony Award–
winning play brought the *Metamorphoses* to life for thousands of theater-goers
who had probably never heard of Ovid. The idea of performing episodes from
his work on the stage would have appealed to Ovid, who routinely recited his
poems publicly and whose works provided material for Roman performers—
performances, he reminds Augustus in his *Tristia* (2.519–20), that the emperor
himself often attended. Mary Zimmerman, a much-acclaimed director and
recipient in 1998 of a MacArthur "genius" fellowship, is an experienced adapter
of epic narratives: among her earlier credits are the stagings of such classics as
the *Odyssey,* the *Arabian Nights,* and the Chinese *Journey to the West.* Her *Metamorphoses* is based, as the title page indicates, on Slavitt's translation, whose lan-

guage in some scenes is retained almost literally, while in others it has been consulted mainly for plot.[27]

The ten principal scenes, which vary appreciably in presentation and style, are performed in and around a rectangular pool of shallow water surrounded by a deck. In the introductory scene, Ovid's depiction of creation is narrated in a brief paraphrase of Slavitt's translation by two women, one looking at her reflection in the pool and another dressed as a scientist in a lab coat, while Zeus, smoking a cigarette, interjects occasional comments. Later Phaethon, wearing sunglasses, floats on a yellow raft as he complains to his therapist about his difficulties with his father. The story of Eros and Psyche, which of course is non-Ovidian,[28] is acted out in pantomime on a raft in the pool, and the action is commented on by two voices in a catechismic question and answer. The device of the pool and the surprising variations of style make for lively and entertaining theater.

The scenes, presented without transition and not in the Ovidian sequence, are organized in an alternating rhythm featuring the themes of destructive passion and the redeeming power of love. Midas, a rich businessman who has come up from poverty, makes his avaricious wish as three laundresses washing linens in the pool look on and kibitz—all in a slangy contemporary language. Ceyx leaves his loving wife Alcyone not for the serious reasons given by Ovid but because he is bored by his marriage and feels "domesticated, diminished, a kind of lap dog" (21; the phrase along with the entire interpretation is not Ovid's, but Slavitt's addition in his translation). In the next episode the greedy Erysichthon sells his mother rather than, as in Ovid, his daughter—a change made by the adapter, no doubt, as a comic reification of the cynical idiom "He would sell his own mother." The tragic story of Orpheus and Eurydice is followed by an interlude in which Narcissus acts out his self-obsession. The amusing courtship of Pomona and Vertumnus is interrupted by an account of the incestuous passion of Myrrha. The self-destructive wish of Phaethon is followed by the story of Eros and Psyche, which is carried through to its happy ending. The play closes with the moving love of the aging couple, Philemon and Baucis, and their wish to be transformed into neighboring trees.

Zimmerman's treatment of Orpheus and Eurydice is characteristic of her postmodern re-visioning of the story. The moment when Orpheus looks back and Eurydice slips back into the underworld is enacted three times (44): first the narrator asks: "Is this story a story of love and how it always goes away?" Then: "Is this a story of how time can move only in one direction?" Finally: "Is this story a story of an artist, and the loss that comes from sudden self-consciousness of impatience?" The scene changes the original by introducing the figure of Hermes, who comes not from Ovid but from Rilke's poem "Orpheus. Eurydice.

Hermes" (see chap. 4 above), which in the second part of the same scene is then recited and reenacted. If "Orpheus and Eurydice" shows Ovid as modified by a hermeneutical impulse—the post-Freudian desire to analyze everything—the psychological interpretation of myth is revealed most conspicuously in the "Phaeton" [sic] scene, which comes by way of Freudian psychoanalysis and Joseph Campbell, to whom Zimmerman has acknowledged her debt.[29] As Phaethon, a spoiled brat who has been sent to the most expensive schools, whines about his father, the therapist comments: "Where better might we find a more precise illustration of the danger of premature initiation than in this ancient tale of alternating parental indulgence and neglect?" (63). In jargon-laden language that contrasts comically with Phaethon's adolescent complaints, she informs us that the father's absence has undermined his "primitive role as initiating priest for the younger being." When his father promises to give his son the keys to the car, "the conventional exordium of the initiate from latent to realized potential is inevitably accompanied by a radical realignment of his emotional relationship with the imago of parental authority" (65). When Phaethon has told his story to its fatal conclusion, the therapist sums up pompously with words that might have come directly out of *The Myth of the Hero:* "It has been said that the myth is a public dream, dreams are private myths. Unfortunately we give our mythic side scant attention these days" (67).[30]

As the play ends, following the transformation of Philemon and Baucis into trees, the narrator and members of the cast chant in chorus the words: "Let me die the moment my love dies . . . Let me not outlive my own capacity to love . . . Let me die still loving, and so, never die" (83). In pantomime Midas appears, washes his face in the water, and is relieved of his fateful power. His daughter enters and embraces him; they kneel together in the pool as the other actors blow out candles floating in the water. It is easy to understand the popular appeal of this charming presentation for those who prefer their Ovid lite. The audience sees familiar—or, as the case may be, unfamiliar—stories rendered readily accessible to the modern sensibility through their contemporary idiom and perspective. No historical context or imaginative projection is required. Many viewers who attended performances shortly after the tragedy of September 11, 2001, were particularly moved, they reported, by the story of Ceyx and Alcyone, in which they detected a similarity to the experiences of those who lost loved ones in the World Trade Center.[31]

Ovid would no doubt have been amused by Zimmerman's comic juxtapositions and modernizations and by her skill and ingenuity in transposing his narratives into a new medium. But would Ovid have agreed with Zimmerman's pop-psychological view that Ceyx and Alcyone are initially "too much lost in each other, not individuated enough" and that as birds "they have more independence" and "a more mature relationship"?[32] And surely that great ironist would himself have smiled at the mawkish sentimentalism of the utterly non-Ovidian ending. However that may be, the enthusiastic response to Zimmerman's brilliant theatrical adaptation is a vivid symptom of the Ovid boom of the 1990s.

Other potentially fascinating plays based on Ovid's tales never got written. While in California shortly before his death, the German playwright Heiner Müller (1929–1995) bought an English translation of the *Metamorphoses* (apparently the Garth anthology of 1717) with the intention of writing a series of theatrical pieces based on its stories. Müller, already noted for his dramatizations and reworkings of themes from ancient Greek literature,[33] kept the volume with him constantly during the last months of his life but died before he was able to carry out his project. The prize-winning filmmaker and writer Alexander Kluge, who relates those facts, speaks in this connection of the "alliances across the ages" and the "world of re-narrative" that characterizes our age.[34]

It is safe to assume, on the basis of his other works, that any play by Müller based on themes from the *Metamorphoses* would have had a political thrust. German writers of recent decades have been less concerned with Ovid than were their Anglo-American counterparts, but when they did turn to the Roman poet, they often had a political or social-critical agenda. In his poem "Augustus Weather" ("Augustuswetter: Aufforderung zum Tyrannenmord nach zweitausend Jahren," 1999), Peter Horst Neumann uses the example of Augustus and Ovid, as the subtitle indicates, as an "exhortation to tyrannicide two thousand years later." The poem opens with the image of the emperor sleeping in the shade of a pine tree. "Ein schlafender Kaiser / ist ein guter Kaiser" ("A sleeping emperor is a good emperor").[35] But the poet urges his reader to aim well when the emperor awakens, for he has already exiled to Asia a poet who never returned. And to Ovid or Mandelstam or Max Herrmann-Neisse (an exile from Hitler's Germany included because he was Neumann's fellow countryman from Silesia) one could easily add another hundred names. So aim at the emperor's heart, he concludes, "as though it were still beating." Neumann, a professor of German literature at a German university, does not make it clear which contemporary ruler in the sequence following Augustus-Stalin-Hitler he has in mind, but the poem leaves us in no doubt about its insurrectionary message.

Joseph Brodsky (born 1940), though himself an exile, is less concerned with Ovid the exile than with the author of the *Metamorphoses*. Despite its title his "Letter to Horace" (1995), which resembles in tone the casual flippancy adopted by many other writers in the nineties, actually deals less with Horace than with Ovid. Of all the Romans, he reminds us, only "poor Ovid" paid any heed to his

Hyperborean ancestors, the primitive Slavic peoples.[36] Of all the Roman poets, he continues, he has more difficulty picturing Ovid than, say, Horace or
Propertius; Ovid he visualizes as being something between Paul Newman and
James Mason (433). For Horace, he thinks, Ovid must have appeared to be "just
a punk, an aristo, privileged from the cradle" (433). Brodsky assures us that he
would rather talk to Ovid, or Propertius for that matter, than to Horace.

Typically for the nineties, Brodsky finds Ovid greater as a poet than either
Virgil or Horace, for in the quality of his imagination "Naso beats you all" (434).
Although he had no system or philosophy, "his imagination couldn't get curbed,
neither by its own insights nor by doctrine" (452). Ovid was the pure poet: "His
game was morphology, and his take was metamorphosis" (454). With that statement Brodsky sums up the almost wholly aesthetic response to Ovid among the
novelists, playwrights, and poets of the decade, a response that expressed itself in
a variety of new "metamorphoses" ranging from philosophical and adventure
novels through trivial fictions to some of the finest translations and poetic adaptations that this generation has produced.

CONCLUSION

◢12◣

OVID IN THE NEW MILLENNIUM

The Ovid boom shows no signs of abating. In a thriller by the Swedish writer Arne Dahl published in 2003, *Upp till toppen av berget* (To the top of the mountain), a copy of the *Metamorphoses* provides a key clue to the mystery. On the eve of the millennium Ovid even made his way to Hollywood. Toward the beginning of Stanley Kubrick's much-touted film *Eyes Wide Shut* (1999), a Hungarian roué asks Alice, in a gesture toward seducing her, if she has ever read the Latin poet Ovid's work *The Art of Love* (prefacing his remark with the suggestive Ovidian gesture of sipping from her champagne glass). She quips in response, and with surprising acumen despite her tipsiness, that Ovid ended up "all by himself, crying his eyes out in some place with a very bad climate."[1] Nor is Ovid absent from poetry of the new millennium. Edward Hirsch's volume, *Lay Back the Darkness* (2003) contains several poems generally indebted to the *Metamorphoses*—notably three entitled "Self-Portrait as Eurydice" and others with Ovidian images—as well as one specifically attributed to Ovid. "After All the Orphic Enchantments (*Metamorphoses,* Books Ten and Eleven)" reviews, in one sustained (eight quatrains) sentence, Orpheus's adventures after his return from the underworld to his death at the hands of the Thracian women, only to wonder in conclusion if it was worthwhile to sacrifice his life to go back to the underworld and Eurydice's shade.[2] The Israeli poet Liat Kaplan contrasts the Kafkaesque "metamorphoses of tormented dreams," from which one awakens as a huge insect, with a more "civilized" kind: "Like Ovid

I understand only what lives, that is, / moves, rots, dries up, transforms itself, dies: becomes other."[3]

"Metamorphosis" has become a commonplace, so frequently does the word occur in titles ranging from works on psychology, political science, and philosophy—*Metamorphoses: Toward a Materialist Theory of Becoming, Metamorphoses of the Body, Miraculous Metamorphoses: The Neoliberalization of Latin American Populism,* or *Metamorphoses of Reason*—to such serious literary studies as Caroline Walker Bynum's *Metamorphosis and Identity* in the conceptualization of the Middle Ages (werewolves, alchemy, cosmology), Francisco Gentil Vaz da Silva's *Metamorphosis: The Dynamics of Symbolism in European Fairy Tales,* and Marina Warner's *Fantastic Metamorphoses, Other Worlds: Ways of Telling the Self,* which surveys manifestations of shape-changing in myth, folklore, and literature since the fifteenth century.[4]

Ovid has not been left out of this scholarly renaissance, which has recently produced *The Cambridge Companion to Ovid* (2002) and *Brill's Companion to Ovid* (2002) as well as two new introductions in German;[5] an English translation of Niklas Holzberg's important book, with the title *Ovid: The Poet and His Work* (2002); and R. J. Tarrant's long-awaited edition of *Metamorphoses* in Oxford Classical Texts (2004). Arthur Golding's classic 1567 rendition of the *Metamorphoses* has just been reissued in a scholarly edition.[6] Nor has Ovid escaped the attention of postmodern critics. Indeed, Philip Hardie maintains that "Ovid's texts go further than many others to meet the concerns of a certain dominant strand of current criticism and theory" because he "thematises these concerns in a way that makes it (too?) easy to detect something like the presence of a postmodernist critic already lurking within the ancient texts themselves."[7] Hardie himself builds on earlier applications of postmodern theory to Latin literature—such as Freudian-Lacanian ideas of repetition and loss and Derridan deconstructions of presence and absence—in his analysis of Myrrha's transformation into a myrrh tree, through which she is suspended between life and death. "Any and every instance of metamorphosis results in a state that is neither life nor death, but something in between. The product of every metamorphosis is an absent presence" (82).[8]

MILLENNIAL FICTIONS

The new millennium has already generated a prose analogue to the poetic anthology *After Ovid.* In *Ovid Metamorphosed* Philip Terry brings together nineteen internationally known writers who have contributed stories based not only on the *Metamorphoses* but also on the *Ars Amatoria,* the *Heroides,* and Ovid's life.[9] Like the poems in *After Ovid,* the stories are, with two exceptions, occasional pieces written specifically for this volume. Cees Nooteboom is represented by a segment of his novel *The Following Story* (Mussert's classroom discussion of Phaethon's death; see chap. 11 above). M. J. Fitzgerald's story "Antiquity's Lust" (on Tereus, Philomela, and Procne) is one of a still unpublished cycle of stories retelling Ovidian tales from the woman's point of view[10]—an enterprise akin to the feminist re-visions of classical myths in Germany by such writers as Christa Wolf (*Kassandra, Medea*) and Christina Brückner (*If only you had spoken up, Desdemona*).[11] Four of the pieces are only tangentially connected to the project: e.g., Gabriel Josipovici's sentimentalizing memoir of his mother's affection for the tale of Ceyx and Alcyone; and Catherine Axelrad's witty "Report on the Eradication and Resurgence of Metamorphic Illness in the West, 1880–1998)," which in a parody of medico-scientific jargon reviews several recent cases of "AME" (ancient metamorphic epidemic), such as Kafka's *Metamorphosis*, Garnett's *Lady into Fox*, Marcel Aymé's (non-Ovidian) children's tale in *Contes du chat perché*, and Marie Darrieussecq's *Truismes*.

Several of the stories amount to feminist updatings of the myths: Michèle Roberts reinscribes Hypsipyle's epistle (from *Heroides*) to a Jason who has just sped off in his little blue MG; Joyce Carol Oates relocates the brutal tragedy of Actaeon's offending male gaze to Cape Breton Island in 1923; Patricia Duncker sets Pluto's kingdom into a sleazy contemporary underworld of pornography and violence; and Margaret Atwood's sibyl, who forgot to ask Apollo for eternal youth, has evolved into a shriveled but successful business tycoon carried around in a three-foot-tall decanter. In another twist, Philip Terry ("Void") amusingly reworks Ovid's *Ars amatoria* for the advice column of a modern men's magazine. Paul West's "Nightfall on the Romanian Coast," in which Ovid in the underworld "blathers away in mental prose like a manure heap observing its own decomposition," turns into an exercise in heavy-handed bad taste ("Julia *mère* was ganged while I took notes"). Marina Warner mixes Ovid's Leto, Celtic history, and a talking wolf from fairy-tale land into a pointless mythic miscegenation ("Leto's Flight"), apparently meant to exemplify her own theories of myth and folklore. The most provocative contribution is A. S. Byatt's thoughtful meditation "Arachne," in which autobiography, art history, entomology, needlework, and literary spider lore (Emily Dickinson) are woven into a fascinating literary tapestry which emphasizes the moral ambiguity of Ovid's art (does he side with Arachne or Athene?), the precision of his imagination, and the perennial attraction of weaving for women artists.

Philip Terry ends his introduction with the exhortation that "the riches of Ovid should be transformed to reshape the present, waking us up to the fact that nothing in our world is ever as solid as it seems, that our dreams of shopping schemes, luxury apartments, holidays in the sun, sex shows and success are no more substantial than the cloud-capped towers, the gorgeous palaces and the solemn temples of myth" (18). The stories in his collection may well appeal to the residents of luxury apartments who holiday in the sun and visit sex shows. But they are too uneven in substance, style, and quality to attract readers who aspire to the solemn temples of myth. While several of the pieces can take their place alongside the better poems of *After Ovid* or the more successful scenes from Mary Zimmerman's *Metamorphoses*, others show clear signs of haste, calculation, and indifference to Ovid.

The new millennium also saw the publication of two remarkable Ovidian works in German: Durs Grünbein's *Das erste Jahr* (2001; The first year) and Yoko Tawada's *Opium für Ovid: Ein Kopfkissenbuch von 22 Frauen* (2000; Opium for Ovid: A pillow book of 22 women). The brilliant young poet and essayist Grünbein (born 1962) has created a striking work virtually unique in twentieth-century literature, since Ezra Pound first praised its significance, for its focus on and emulation of Ovid's *Fasti*.[12] Grünbein, who has also translated Seneca's *Thyestes* (2001), has stated that he is "indebted to Roman literature for the most important lessons about writing."[13] Various of his earlier poems betray the influence of Juvenal, Horace, and other Roman authors.[14] Like Ovid's *Fasti, Das erste Jahr*, Grünbein's journal and workbook for the year 2000, takes the calendar year as occasion for poems and reflections on the most varied topics, including incidents from his own life (with a sharply contoured account of the birth of his daughter and her early months), history, world literature from antiquity to the present, modern science, philosophy, and politics.[15] Tying it all together is a constant awareness of "the large relationships" ("die großen Zusammenhänge") that informed the great poems of the past from Virgil and Ovid to Dante (163). The complacent writers of the present, Grünbein censures, do not realize in their ignorance "that the world they describe is separated from Ovid's metamorphosis-cosmos only by the thinnest membranes" (188). "Future Ovids," he remarks in another context, "will have to concern themselves with the minute transformation-artists" (244), by which he means the epidemic viruses—AIDS, Ebola, Hepatitis B, and others—that are transforming the modern world. While Grünbein never mentions the *Fasti* in this fascinating volume, the model of Ovid's great calendar work is clearly ever present in the mind of this contemporary poet who is bound by such powerful ties to Roman antiquity.

Yoko Tawada, who was born in Tokyo in 1960, came to Germany in 1979 to continue her study of modern literature at the University of Hamburg. Residing permanently in Hamburg since 1982, she has won several important prizes for books written in German as well as Japanese. In 1998 she held the prestigious Tübinger-Poetik-Dozentur, for which she delivered a series of three lectures published under the title *Verwandlungen* (Metamorphoses)[16] and dealing with topics whose Ovidian implications are immediately evident: "Voice of a Bird, or the Problem of Foreignness"; "Script of a Tortoise, or the Problem of Translation"; and "Face of a Fish, or the Problem of Transformation."

Opium für Ovid differs from any of the works discussed in earlier chapters, to the extent that it not only uses Ovidian material in a modern context but also, as the subtitle suggests, combines Eastern and Western literary traditions.[17] The early eleventh-century *Pillow Book* (*Makura no soshi*), one of the classics of Japanese literature, comprises a potpourri of odd facts, stories, observations, whimsical lists (e.g., "rare things," "pleasing things"), and reminiscences jotted down in some 320 sections by Sei Shonagon, a court attendant to the Empress Sadako.[18] This Japanese classic suggests the form of Tawada's work, which is not so much a collection as a cycle of twenty-two scenes, not stories with a plot, connected by overlapping characters. These dreamy scenes, in which almost no men appear, offer portraits of the inner and outer lives of women—writers, editors, teachers, hairdressers, clothing designers, dancers, and others in their roles as wives and mothers—as they go about their affairs in contemporary Hamburg, occasionally crossing one another's paths, and rediscovering senses dulled by the demands of life and, sometimes, drugs. Having learned about life through books, these women are often confused or disappointed by their confrontation with reality. One is often reminded, though she is never mentioned, of Virginia Woolf—notably the ruminations of *Mrs. Dalloway* and the transformations of *Orlando.*

While the "plots" have little to do with Ovid's tales, each of the women is named for a figure from the *Metamorphoses,* beginning with Leda (whose story is mentioned at *Met.* 6.109) and ending with Diana. Some of them are further characterized by a trait based on their mythic models. Thus Daphne "stands in the posture of a tree and smiles" (30–31); when Ariadne wakes up, "she feels as though deserted by someone" (202); when Diana turns the beam of a flashlight onto her book, "moon-shaped light falls on a page" (217); Io sometimes dreams that she has been transformed into a cow (111). The hairdresser Thisbe, who reports the gossip from customer to customer, "resembles a slit in the wall. People on both sides of the wall don't want to talk with one another, they also don't want to get acquainted, but through the slit named Thisbe their curiosity about the other side grows" (184–85). Iphis goes to Thisbe for a men's haircut: "today she has finally decided to make a man of herself" (182). On another occasion in this self-referential work, Thisbe reports to the narrator that she has a customer whose neighbor knows a writer who has written a book that deals with twenty-two women (190).

There are two explicit references to Ovid. When Thetis stays awake all night reading, she explains her swollen eyes by lying that she cried after quarreling with a friend. "No one was to find out that during this night she had read the *Metamorphoses* from cover to cover" (122). The curious title, *Opium für Ovid,* is explained in the section about the aspiring film director Pomona, who has become drug-dependent because she takes drugs simply in anticipation of possible pain. "Dependency" has a broader symbolic meaning for the author. England, she reminds us, was once economically dependent on China for its tea supply. To free itself from that dependency, England adopted "a postcolonial strategy" (130). "The opium policy! England forced India to produce opium and sold it for much money to China. . . . Only opium or communism can rule a land as large as China." The author tells us that her own reasoning is precisely the opposite of Pomona's: rather than anticipating or denying her pain with drugs, she cultivates it almost greedily and transmutes it into the heady intoxication of art, which in turn becomes her antidote or "opium" against the colonizing power of Ovid, whose images tend to creep into her writing like a drug.

> I want to compose my pains myself, no dependence on a colonial power. If the one tablet transforms my skin into tree bark, I shall soften it again through an intoxication. An opium against Ovid. My opium war has not yet ended. If the intoxication is there, you no longer need a second person to tell you: you are so and so. (172)

In her hallucinatory inebriation the author experiences metamorphoses even without opium or Ovid: "In the state of intoxication I discover a remarkable gesture of everyday objects; they act as though they were not themselves, as though they were only containers for something else" (78). Her purse holds coins in its stomach; her window becomes the front side of an aquarium, through which she can gaze into a watery landscape. It gradually becomes clear that all the persons in these scenes, despite their Ovidian names and traits, are inventions of the nameless author, who uses them to explore and project various aspects of her own personality. When Scylla interrupts a conversation between the author and Latona, "it suddenly occurred to me that Latona and Scylla had never become acquainted; so the scene described here must be erased from the text" (36). The book, which exists for and from literature, ends with the child Diana, reading stealthily in bed, who thinks that one day she will be permitted to stay awake reading. "I shall read as long as I like, I shall read through whole nights, and the nights will become longer and longer, they will become so long that I shall never again have to get up" (218). Life is transformed wholly into art.

The German reviewers were almost unanimously enchanted by the gossamer prose and subtle sensibility of these delicate miniatures, but more than one found that that the work as a whole is artificially constructed and that the Ovidian parallels constitute a distraction. One might suggest, in response, that Tawada's work can be read as counter-Ovidian and that Ovid's presence is contrastive rather than constitutive: the self-sufficient individual does not require any identification with or justification through mythic figures. The unnamed author, who enters her narratives from time to time in the first person, firmly rejects all attempts to force her into a role, either Eastern or Western. When someone asks her why she never mentions Nabokov, "who also comes from the East," and suggests that such associations with "the giants of European literature" would be good for her reputation, she responds: "I don't want to have any predecessors or to produce any successors" (91). Ovid, too, belongs among these rejected predecessors. Her figures are precisely *not* postfigurations of the mythological women whose names they bear. Her metamorphoses are not adaptations but contemporary analogues. Imagination, her "opium against Ovid," is intoxication enough for the author, whose pillow book constitutes a catalog of metamorphoses of her own persona.

While the contributors to such anthologies as *After Ovid* and *Ovid Metamorphosed* are constrained by the exigencies of the genre to deal with the shorter tales from the *Metamorphoses*, three recent Ovidian novels, in a switch from the fictionalizations of the nineties, have turned back to the poet's life. The acknowledgments in Jane Alison's book show that this former Princeton classics major (born 1961) has done her homework thoroughly although *The Love-Artist* (2001) almost totally reinvents Ovid's life.[19] To escape the scandal of *The Art of Love* and to await the publication of *Metamorphoses*, Ovid goes for a vacation to the Black Sea—the eastern shore near Colchis and hence Medea territory. There he meets the mysterious foundling Xenia, whose very name suggests strangeness or foreignness and whose enchanting eyes and visions caused her to be handed over "for years each to a magus, an alchemist, and a pharmaka, so that her wild skills could be disciplined" (44). Now she is occupied as a healer with a lively side business in love potions.

Ovid takes her back to Rome, where in his absence the *Metamorphoses* have enjoyed a huge success. Augustus's granddaughter Julia, who hates her grandfather for his treatment of her mother and, detesting her own husband, regularly aborts her pregnancies, takes on Ovid as her secret protégé. Xenia, as she builds up a thriving practice of witchcraft among lower-class Romans, gradually becomes jealous of the unknown patroness, in whom she senses a competitor. Meanwhile, Ovid is working on his drama *Medea,* with which he hopes to demonstrate his seriousness as a poet and win his place alongside Virgil and Horace. Through reciprocal illumination, his Medea begins to take on characteristics of the real sorceress Xenia, while Xenia is transformed in Ovid's mind more and more into a Medea.

Through his vivid poetic images, Ovid determines the manner in which he and others see the world. As Ovid recites his verses to Xenia, she imagines that "she entered a world of stones that became as tender as skin, feathers that sprouted from fingertips, hair coarsening to brambles and twigs, flesh hardening again to lifeless stone, girls flung into the sky as stars" (64). Wherever the characters of the novel look on land, sea, or air, they see images from the *Metamorphoses*. But this transformation contains a degree of exploitation: Ovid becomes incapable of seeing human beings in their integrity and individuality. Corinna angrily accuses him: "*You are a crow! You watch, and wait, and then fly at me to snatch what you want to use.* He had pondered her words as he lay gazing at her, and had for a moment felt his nose becoming a hard beak, his skin turning to glossy black feathers" (67). This confusion of life and art, his inability to accept people, and especially women, as they are, and his tendency to reduce others to little more than material for his poetry, precipitates Ovid's tragedy.

Xenia, pregnant with twins, becomes insanely jealous of Julia. Julia, in turn, has been faking a pregnancy and reveals to Ovid that she plans to substitute his twins as her own—and then to reveal the deception to Augustus on his deathbed: that his heirs are the children of a debauched poet and a barbarian sorceress. Drugging Ovid, Xenia saturates the manuscript of his drama with a juice that will delete its text from the scrolls, thereby metaphorically murdering his intellectual child. But she refuses to fulfill in reality the Medean destiny that Ovid has tried to impose upon her. She writes a letter betraying Julia's plot to Augustus and then flees back to the Caucasus, where she bears her two children, leaving for Ovid nothing but a note with two lines from his *Medea*: "I gave you your life. Now you're wondering—will I take it, too?" (226; *servare potui: perdere an possim rogas?*).[20] Julia is sent into exile and Ovid is relegated to Tomis, where he is tormented by doubts regarding his future fame. (Xenia has refused to tell him what she knows with visionary certainty: that his work will endure forever.)

In her feminist re-vision of Ovid's life, Alison provides a lively, solid background, albeit saturated with magic, witchcraft, and the occult smacking too obviously of secondary sources: elements clearly calculated to appeal to New Age sensibilities. Stylistically, too, the prose lacks elegance and features, instead of genuine eroticism, too many thighs: sweating (35, 82), peach (91), white (121), bare (155), marble (173), strained (174), narrow (221). Although the prologue shows Ovid being sent off to exile and the epilogue depicts him briefly in Tomis, the novel makes little use of *Tristia* or *Epistulae ex Ponto*. Here the key works are the *Ars amatoria,* for which Ovid gained his reputation as a ladies' man, and the *Metamorphoses*. The book is filled with transformations—psychological ones, as when Ovid's love is transformed and Xenia's—and metaphorical ones:

So it was not just that his words would live on for a few hundred years; it was more than that. The bodily, expiring things of the world were transformed by him into words—which themselves would be taken up, millennia later, by other hands, other minds, and transformed once more into voluptuous bodies of color and marble. Sublimation. (146)

Lucien d'Azay's curious meditation *Ovide, ou l'amour puni* (2001; Ovid, or Love punished), falls formally somewhere between the novel and the scholarly monograph, but displays no trace of the tactful and tasteful restraint that characterized Émile Ripert's *Ovide: Poète de l'amour.*[21] D'Azay (born 1966) is the author of trendy travelogues—*A Sentimental Journey (à travers Chaillot et Passy)* (1995), *Florence* (1999), *Les cendres de la Fenice* (2000). Using standard secondary sources and a good command of the basic primary texts, his "récit biographique" (11) seeks to present an Ovid tailored for the contemporary European jet-setter—a French analogue to *Ovid Metamorphosed* or Mary Zimmerman's *Metamorphoses.*

D'Azay was inspired to his undertaking, he tells us, "in the marvelous month of September of the year 2000," when he received a stone from Constanţa, sent by a peripatetic friend. The narrative begins with an account, including an interior monologue based on the *Tristia* with frequent quotations of the Latin, of Ovid's arrival and living conditions in Tomis. D'Azay often interrupts the narrative to make comparisons: Ovid edits his lines aloud, "like Flaubert bawling" (31); the Getae are labeled with the English expression "white trash" (44). Tomitan discourse consists largely of small-town chitchat: "Pure province, wasn't it? Something like Berck, Coutances, or Harfleur" (43). Doubling back to the beginning, d'Azay recounts Ovid's life chronologically, but always in the same irritatingly knowing style. In Athens the rich young aristocrats devote themselves to "body-building" (72). The lawyers of Ovid's day are not yet known as *bavards* (chatterboxes), but their reputation is no better in the Forum than it is today in New York (89). Ovid is something of an *arriviste* with a nostalgia for purity, not unlike Balzac's Rastignac and Rubempré or Stendhal's Sorel. When he recites his poetry, the young women swoon as though "in the presence of the Beatles" (97).

In d'Azay's vision of ancient Rome the women no longer want to bear children and weave their robes, preferring ready-to-wear clothes from the Orient (141). Like mindless twentieth-century starlets, they wear boots (*calcei*), throw away their brassieres and bare their breasts beneath T-shirts (*tunica interior*), enlarge the décolletés of their *stolae,* prance "topless" on the beach, spend their days shopping and jogging, and practice yoga. Describing Maecenas's coterie, the author tells us that Ovid was politically to the left of the patron: "he was, let's say, a traditional leftist (a caviar leftist, to be sure), or rather: a bourgeois progressivist, whose slightly opportunistic vein did not permit him to be classed among the anarchist Tories of whom George Orwell speaks" (100). Unlike the older poets, who perceived signs of decadence and regretted the loss of the Old Roman virtues, the young men, though also disgusted by the regime, "preferred to sing *O sole mio* after the fashion of Albert Camus" (101). Messalla was "a Buddha of the *Urbs*," of lively mind and immense culture, who could be insolent "à la Mauriac" (103). Esoteric cults, which "rocked the spirits tenderly, like the ebb and flow of the ocean at Club Med" (195), "irresistibly" (at least to a mind like d'Azay's) evoke "le *New Age*" (197).

The smart allusions—to Péguy, Gide, Byron, Schubert, Joyce, Céline, Malraux, Sartre, Pirandello, and many others—become wearyingly predictable, as do the personal digressions. We are told that the author lives in Venice in a little house on the *fondamenta di Borgo* (12); that he learned Latin and Greek at the collège Saint-Lazare d'Autun and that, when the translations or papers were bad, his teacher would throw them at the students with the commentary "zéro, à recopier" (56); and that later he attended a school for officers of the reserve at Evreux (83). "Three times in my life, I confess, I have had recourse to this little treatise [*Remedia amoris*], which isn't too much, after all, in a life of an amateur seducer who is thirty-four years, one month, and four days old at the moment when he writes this phrase (17 October 2000). The relevant young women, all three of whom refused me, were named Eve, Mathilde, and Eve" (185).

The chapter on *Ars amatoria* (154–75) amounts to little more than a paraphrase, with the comment that its language displays a cynicism reminiscent of such young women's magazines as *Jeune & Jolie* (154). The discussion of the *Heroides* (136–46) hardly goes beyond a listing of the eighteen women and a few brief comments, based largely on secondary sources. The legends functioned like "jazz standards" (137): themes on which the poet extemporizes his variations in an elegiac tonality. The discussion of the lost play *Medea* (146–50) is based wholly on the passage at the beginning of *Metamorphoses* 7. The pages on the *Metamorphoses,* which are said to anticipate "Frankenstein and the 'je est un autre' of Rimbaud" (202), focus on the horror scenes and argue that Ovid had a genius for special effects and, in Hollywood, would have directed thrillers, horror films, westerns, and soft porn. "Twice a week Stephen Spielberg and Quentin Tarentino would have gone to take private lessons in his personal studios" (211). The passage concludes with a generalization of equal profundity.

It appears that our identity is never definitive; it is incessantly menaced by a metamorphosis. It is not even said that one becomes what one is. Such a character is never acquired; as long as one does not know oneself, one exists, like

Narcissus, who dies from having desired to know himself. Does it necessarily follow that essence precedes existence? There is sometimes a presentiment of existentialism in Ovid. (223)

Some sections are lifted almost verbatim from secondary works: the passage on Augustus and his wives, including all the references from classical sources (257–58), is taken from Régis Martin, *Les douze Césars: Du mythe à la réalité* (Paris: Les Belles Lettres, 1991, 129–31). Other passages amount to standard literary history rephrased in trendy theoretical jargon. The pages (287–90) recounting a vision experienced by Ovid shortly before his death constitute a paraphrase of *Heroides* 12 (Medea).

D'Azay claims to have consulted more than a hundred books and as many essays on the causes of Ovid's relegation (247). His researches are evident in such aperçus as: to send Ovid away from Rome was a punishment akin to condemning Woody Allen to life outside Manhattan (257). The farewell scene with his wife is portrayed as being "eminently Fellinian" (265). It is d'Azay's view that Ovid's crime was of a sexual nature. Ovid is supposed to have numbered among his mistresses a beautiful Oriental courtesan who was twice pregnant by him and who had knowledge of wondrous aphrodisiacs and astonishing sensual practices. When the aging Augustus heard about her, he became infatuated and hoped that she could rejuvenate his sexuality. One evening the courtesan invited Ovid to watch from a hiding place "a spectacle that would not fail to stupefy him" (260). Not aware of the circumstances, he recognized too late the old man whose perversions his ex-mistress, with a sinister smile, exposed before his eyes. His hope of being recalled to Rome was a futile illusion, for who could imagine that this "aged beatnik" would receive "a standing ovation for his comeback on the scene?" (262). After all, he was regarded (wrongly, d'Azay concedes) as a kind of "unbridled fornicator, an ex-sixty-eighter ahead of his time."

The book is rounded off by another letter from d'Azay's friend, who visits Ovid's monument at Constanţa, copies the epitaph (from *Tristia* 3.373–76) in Latin and Romanian along with a French translation, and describes in another facile juxtaposition of past and present the small plastic statues of Ovid that can be purchased there in the bars and shops. D'Azay's ultimate trivialization has succeeded through his glib analogies, ostentatious chunks of undigested erudition, and glitzy language, which teems with slang, Americanisms, and precious French vocabulary, in reducing Ovid to the level of a shallow postmodern contemporary. Nothing is missing in this portrait of an ancient ancestor of late twentieth-century Euro-trash but the black turtleneck sweater and dark glasses. The author has done the rest. We do not turn away from this postmillennial Ovid with a sense of gratification.

Like Churchill's Russia, Josef Skvorecky's delightfully imaginative *An Inexplicable Story, or The Narrative of Questus Firmus Siculus* (2002), which the author in his dedication calls a "jest" and a tribute to Edgar Allan Poe, might well be termed "a riddle wrapped in a mystery inside an enigma."[22] In this case the riddle is a play, or rather the fragment of a play, entitled *The Faithful Husband* and allegedly written by Ovid in his exile. In his play, we are given to understand, Ovid explained the mystery of his relegation: he had gone to bed with Livia, the wife of Augustus, in order to avenge himself on the emperor, who had earlier seduced Ovid's first wife Racilia. Ovid himself, we learn, did not die at Tomis. Following Augustus's death, Ovid's death by drowning was falsely reported so that he could safely be sent by friends in power to Vindobona (Vienna), a place of gentler exile, where he wrote his play. But when Ovid is spotted at a performance of the play in Vindobona by his enemy Marcus Vesanius, the butt of the poet's curse poem *Ibis,* he must again be removed for his own safety— this time to the court of Cunobelinus (Shakespeare's Cymbeline) in Britain, where presumably he dies.

The riddle and the mystery, which constitute only one aspect of the narrative, are never fully explained because both are handed down to us in seven highly fragmented and enigmatic scrolls containing the autobiography of one Questus Firmus Siculus, an adventurous young Roman who discovers that he is in fact Ovid's son through an extramarital affair of his beautiful mother Proculeia, the real "Corinna" of Ovid's *Amores.* Because the scrolls break off at crucial points, the full story never emerges clearly, and we are left with tantalizing hints at the riddle of Ovid's play and the mystery of his exile. The story continues with the enigma of Questus's destiny.

Following the death of the various principals, Questus, sailing on a steam-driven ship that he has invented, makes his way to Central America, where he sets down the account of his life. This manuscript, discovered centuries later by archaeologists excavating Mayan ruins in Honduras, is now presented in a translation edited with full scholarly apparatus (explanatory footnotes and a lengthy commentary) by Patrick Oliver Enfield (whose name constitutes an anagram of "POE"). Each successive edition of the work is enlarged by letters from readers, who point out similarities between the ancient manuscript and various modern works: a bedroom farce by Georges Feydeau, Poe's *Narrative of Arthur Gordon Pym,* and Jules Verne's *Le sphinx des glaces* (The sphinx of the ice-fields). One lengthy epistle from a German reader, filled with Gogolian irrelevancies, contains an additional bit of manuscript from the hand of Questus, which seemingly supports the validity of the larger narrative. In fact, the work, which in its spirit of playfulness resembles nothing so much as Bocheński's *Nazo poeta,* is in the last analysis not simply another fictionalization of Ovid's life, but also a comic parody of scholarly editions and academic procedures. In his author's note, which lies outside the complex fiction of edited manuscripts and addenda, Skvorecky (born 1924) reports charmingly on the friendship, dreams, and reading, extending over many years, that finally led him to intertwine such varied literary loves into his fascinating pastiche, which in its encapsulated organization and playful literary ironies, is highly Ovidian.

THE OVIDIAN SEISMOGRAPH ·

The Ovidian works from 1912 to the present reveal remarkably consistent patterns. With few exceptions, but with varying emphases, writers have been fascinated by three aspects: Ovid the man as the exemplary exile; Ovid the poet as the advocate of words over things; and the *Metamorphoses* as the fitting symbol of change. Exile has sometimes provided simply a metaphor for social alienation or voluntary expatriation, but the political history of the twentieth century often reified that metaphor for writers who were driven out of their countries by the Russian revolution in the 1920s, by National Socialism in the 1930s, and by a sequence of later catastrophes all over the world. Ovid as the poet of aestheticism holds little attraction for writers in exile, but precisely that role claims the attention of writers reacting against the politicization of art or, indeed, any suggestion of art's social responsibility. The *Metamorphoses,* finally, strike resonance in eras of social upheaval when the world seems to be undergoing radical change, as well as in periods obsessed more solipsistically with personal transformation. These aspects, either individually or in various mixtures, account for virtually all the modern metamorphoses of Ovid.

All three aspects are strikingly evident in the first two examples we considered, the Ariadne paintings of Giorgio de Chirico and *Ariadne auf Naxos* by Hugo von Hofmannsthal and Richard Strauss: exile in the figure of Ariadne, a figure drawn from Ovid's *Metamorphoses* as well as his *Heroides;* the priority of art in the figure of the composer in the opera and in de Chirico's almost willful play with variations in his Ariadne cycle; and metamorphosis in, respectively, Ariadne's transformation into stone and her spiritual elevation. In addition, those two foundational works expose the principal technique through which Ovid and his works have been made relevant for the twentieth century: the interpenetration of past and present, of myth and reality, both through de Chirico's location of his classical statue in a conspicuously contemporary environment and through the encounter of ancient tragedy and modern opera buffa in the opera.

The concentrations of works over the past century (see the appended chronology) expose several waves of Ovidianism. In the earliest wave, bracketed by the years 1912 and 1922, all three aspects emerge. Apart from de Chirico and Mandelstam, who experienced actual political exile, exile plays a relatively minor role for the high modernists. Some, like Joyce, found in that status an appropriate image for the writer's alienation from his society; but for others, such as Eliot and Rilke, exile receded in significance before the Tiresian consciousness, capable of integrating a fragmented culture, and the Orphic belief in the power of art to provide meaning in the face of social upheaval and cultural change. Metamorphosis as the characteristic of this new society becomes a keynote in major works of prose from Kafka's *Metamorphosis* to Virginia Woolf's *Orlando.*

After the 1920s and in the face of harsh political reality, Ovid fades into the background and, apart from sporadic appearances in shorter works over the next three decades, does not show up again in full force until the bimillennial celebrations of 1957–58. The modern appropriations of Ovid have been restricted mainly to poetry and fiction—appropriately, one might think, since Ovid produced his own major works in those genres. The bimillennial celebration produced three works for the theater in Romania (Scherg, Manoliu, Sălceanu), where national history created an audience interested in plays dealing with Ovid's life and exile. (In Hartmut Lange's *Staschek, oder das Leben des Ovid* the poet is peripheral to the life of the picaresque hero.) Only recently, with Achim Freyer in Vienna and Mary Zimmerman in the United States, have creative directors sought to bring the *Metamorphoses* to life on the stage.

Since 1957, and with increasing intensity, the three prominent aspects of Ovidianism have been evident in successive waves. The publicity surrounding the celebrations alerted many readers to Ovid's iconic status as the ur-exile. Among Romanians at home and abroad this awareness was coupled with a renewed appreciation of Ovid as a proto-Romanian and the earliest herald of their national religion, language, and culture. In the West, meanwhile, the exiled Ovid was co-opted as an image for the writer disenchanted with ideology of any sort. Gradually the fictional interest of the skeptical generation shifted to Ovid's life prior to his exile and to his inner life in the exotic and multicultural realm on the Black Sea. In the course of the 1980s a new wave brought the *Metamorphoses* into the foreground as the apt image for a society undergoing rapid change in the wake of the collapse of communism and in a globalized world.

From this process Ovid emerges as the exemplary "post"-poet. Constantly conscious of his own epigonal status vis-à-vis Virgil and Horace and of a life lived in the political and social stability following the civil wars, which enabled him to pursue a poetic career quite different from that of his predecessors, he foreshadowed the post-realism of high modernism, the postwar mentality of the exiles, and the postmodernity of the "Me!" generation. In fact, the waves of his popularity have continued since antiquity to alternate in a regular rhythm with the ascendancy of Virgil. During the entire nineteenth century and culminating with the bimillennium of his death in 1881, Virgil was the classical Roman poet par excellence while Ovid, considered worthy of no serious scholarly attention, was relegated to the schoolbooks. The reign of Virgil with his alleged patriotism and religiosity lasted into the twentieth century, when abruptly the cataclysmic social, cultural, and political upheavals accompanying World War I made his *pietas* and *amor patriae* less convincing to the early modernists. The skeptic Ovid emerged, for the first time in over a century, as the fitting icon for the age. By 1930, however, Ovid was swept away again by the resurgence of Virgil, the bimillennium of whose birth coincided with the rise of nationalism, imperialism, and local variations of *Blut und Boden* in many Western states. This *aetas Virgiliana* began to wane after World War II, but it was not firmly displaced until 1957, when the bimillennium of Ovid's birth was celebrated in many countries, introducing a new wave of Ovidianism that was enhanced in the 1980s and 1990s by the attention of such emerging constituencies as the feminists, the postmodernists, the urban satirists, the multiculturalists, and the aficionados of sex, violence, and the fantastic.

From the ancient *tenerorum lusor amorum,* the medieval *Ovidius Christianus* and *Ovide moralisé,* and the *Ovidius redivivus* and *Ovide travesti* of the Renaissance, Ovid has progressed by way of Ovid baroque'd and rococo'd to such recent manifestations as Ovid eroticized, nationalized, psychologized, and trivialized. Every age gets the Ovid it deserves. What sort of Ovid will the new millennium bring forth? Where, indeed, can it go beyond the frothy trivializations at the turn of the millennium? Will continued skepticism toward government and religion combined with an intensified solipsism sustain a new and perhaps more serious *aetas Ovidiana*? Or will the tragedy of September 11, terrorism, and wars in the Middle East produce a surge of patriotism and spirituality in the West that will look again to Virgil's *pietas* and *amor patriae* as its model? Classics of the past, and the manner in which they are received, function as sensitive seismographs for detecting the spiritual tremors of any age. Wherever our collective spirit may lead us, our spontaneous choice of literary icons from the past, long before the sociologists and cultural critics and philosophers have completed their surveys and analyses and theories, will provide a reliable chart of our course.

CHRONOLOGY

1898–1902	Jacob Burckhardt, *Griechische Kulturgeschichte*
1910	Ezra Pound, *The Spirit of Romance*
1911	Maurice Hewlett, *Ariadne in Naxos*
1912	Giorgio de Chirico, *Ariadne* cycle
	Paul Ernst, *Ariadne auf Naxos*
	Hofmannsthal/Strauss, *Ariadne auf Naxos*
	C. G. Jung, *Wandlungen und Symbole der Libido*
	Franz Kafka, *Die Verwandlung* (publ. 1916)
	R. C. Trevelyan, *The Bride of Dionysus*
1915	Victor Eftimiu, "Statuia lui Ovidiu"
1916	James Joyce, *A Portrait of the Artist as a Young Man*
	Osip Mandelstam, *Stone* (2nd ed.)
1919	Ezra Pound, *Canto 4*
1921	D. H. Lawrence, *The Lost Girl*
	Émile Ripert, *Ovide: Poète de l'amour*
1922	T. S. Eliot, *The Waste Land*
	David Garnett, *Lady into Fox*
	Hermann Hesse, *Piktors Verwandlungen*
	Osip Mandelstam, *Tristia*
	Paul Valéry, *Charmes*
1923	Rainer Maria Rilke, *Sonette an Orpheus*

1924	Adrian Maniu, "Elegie"
	Corneliu Moldavanu, "Ovidiu la Tomis"
1925	Robert Graves, "Ovid in Defeat"
	Edward Kennard Rand, *Ovid and His Influence*
1928	Virginia Woolf, *Orlando*
1931	Nicolae Iorga, *Ovidiu*
	Pablo Picasso, etchings for *Metamorphoses*
1933	Edgar Martini, *Einleitung zu Ovid*
1936	John Masefield, "Letter from Pontus"
1939	Bertolt Brecht, "Besuch bei den verbannten Dichtern"
	Constantin Salcia, "Pont Euxin"
1945	Hermann Fränkel, *Ovid: A Poet between Two Worlds*
1946	Gottfried Benn, "Orpheus' Tod"
	André Gide, *Thésée*
	Richard Strauss, *Metamorphosen*
1951	Benjamin Britten, *Six Metamorphoses of Ovid*
	Lalla Romano, *Le metamorphosi*
1952	George Balanchine, *Metamorphoses*
1953	William Carlos Williams, "Narcissus in the Desert"
1955	Leopold Ahlsen, *Philemon und Baucis*
	Georg Scherg, *Ovid*
1955	L. P. Wilkinson, *Ovid Recalled*
1957	Bimillennial Celebrations in Romania
	Petre Manoliu, *Ovidiu la Tomis*
1958	Bimillennial Celebrations in Italy and France
	Eckart von Naso, *Liebe war sein Schicksal*
	Grigore Sălceanu, *Ovidius*
1959	Josef Eberle, *Stunden mit Ovid*
1960	Vintila Horia, *Dieu est né en exil*
1961	Zbigniew Herbert, "Apollo and Marsyas"
1963	Ernst Fischer, *Elegien aus dem Nachlaß des Ovid*
1964	Geoffrey Hill, "Ovid in the Third Reich"
1965	M. Rejnus, *Die Wiederkehr des Ovid*
1968	C. H. Sisson, "Metamorphoses"
1969	Jacek Bocheński, *Nazo poeta*
1972	Italo Calvino, *Le città invisibili*
	Hartmut Lange, *Staschek, oder Das Leben des Ovid*
1974	C. H. Sisson, "Ovid in Pontus"
1975	E. L. Doctorow, *Ragtime*
	Seamus Heaney, "Exposure"

1978	David Malouf, *An Imaginary Life*
1979	Italo Calvino, "Ovid and Universal Contiguity"
1980	Derek Walcott, "The Hotel Normandie Pool"
1983	Derek Mahon, "Ovid in Tomis"
	Charles Tomlinson, *Poetry and Metamorphosis*
1984	Volker Ebersbach, *Der Verbannte von Tomi*
1985	*Helios:* "Contemporary Interpretations of Ovid"
	Women's Classical Caucus: "Reappropriating the Text"
1987	Achim Freyer, *Metamorphosen des Ovid*
1988	Christoph Ransmayr, *Die letzte Welt*
	Salman Rushdie, *The Satanic Verses*
1990	Feminist issue of *Helios*
1991	Julia Kristeva, *Le vieil homme et les loups*
	Cees Nooteboom, *Het volgende verhaal*
	Lawrence Norfolk, *Lemprière's Dictionary*
1992	Luca Desiato, *Sulle rive del Mar Nero*
	Antonio Tabucchi, "Sogno di Publio Ovidio Nasone"
1993	Allen Mandelbaum, trans., *Metamorphoses of Ovid*
1994	Mavis Cheek, *Aunt Margaret's Lover*
	Michael Hofmann and James Lasdun, eds., *After Ovid*
	David Slavitt, trans., *Metamorphoses of Ovid*
1995	Joseph Brodsky, "Letter to Horace"
	Anne Carson, "On Ovid"
	David Wishart, *Ovid*
1996	Ron Burns, "Murderer, Farewell"
	Waldtraut Lewin, *Die Frauen von Kolchis*
1997	Ted Hughes, *Tales from Ovid*
	Marin Mincu, *Il diario di Ovidio*
1998	Christopher Martin, ed., *Ovid in English*
	Mary Zimmerman, *Metamorphoses*
1999	Peter Horst Neumann, "Augustuswetter"
2000	Yoko Tawada, *Opium für Ovid*
	Philip Terry, ed., *Ovid Metamorphosed*
2001	Jane Alison, *The Love-Artist*
	Lucien d'Azay, *Ovide, or l'amour puni*
	Durs Grünbein, *Das erste Jahr*
2002	Liat Kaplan, "Metamorphoses"
	Josef Skvorecky, *An Inexplicable Story*
2003	Edward Hirsch, *Lay Back the Darkness*

NOTES

1. THE LURE OF ARIADNE

1. See Michael R. Taylor, *Giorgio de Chirico and the Myth of Ariadne* (Philadelphia: Philadelphia Museum of Art, 2002).

2. De Chirico's many paintings are not mentioned in Christa Lichtenstern, *Metamorphose: Vom Mythos zum Prozessdenken: Ovid-Rezeption, Surrealistische Ästhetik, Verwandlungsthematik der Nachkriegskunst* (Weinheim: VCH, 1992); or in Udo Reinhardt, "Griechische Mythen in der bildenden Kunst des 20. Jahrhunderts. Highlights zu Homers Odyssee und Ovids Metamorphosen," *Gymnasium* 106 (1999): 25–71.

3. Taylor, *Giorgio de Chirico*, 22. On the confused history of the sculpture identified variously as Cleopatra, the Sleeping Nymph, and finally Ariadne, see Leonard Barkan, *Unearthing the Past: Archaeology and Aesthetics in the Making of Renaissance Culture* (New Haven: Yale University Press, 1999), 233–47.

4. Taylor, *Giorgio de Chirico*, 67–76. Taylor also reproduces such examples as a nineteenth-century wax cast (38, fig. 25) and the *Reclining Ariadne* in the park at Versailles (plate 4), all in the conventional pose.

5. For a representative list of treatments in painting, sculpture, drama, opera, ballet, and other forms see Herbert Hunger, *Lexikon der griechischen und römischen Mythologie: mit Hinweisen auf das Fortwirken antiker Stoffe und Motive in der bildenden Kunst, Literatur und Musik des Abendlandes bis zur Gegenwart*, 8th ed. (Vienna: Hollinek, 1988), 69–74.

6. The story of Ariadne is mentioned briefly in many classical sources: e.g., Homer's *Odyssey* 11.321–25, and Hesiod's *Theogony* 947–49; and Plutarch relates it in passing in his account of Theseus in *Parallel Lives*. But the most extensive accounts occur in Catullus's *Carmen* 64.52–201 and 249–64; and in four works by Ovid: *Ars amatoria* 1.525–64, *Heroides* 10.1–152, *Fasti* 3.459–516, and *Metamorphoses* 8.169–82. On the popularity of the theme as *publica materies*, see Florence Vertucci, *Ovid's Toyshop of the Heart: Epistulae Heroidum* (Princeton: Princeton University Press, 1985), 244–45; and Jörg Maurer, *Untersuchungen zur poetischen Technik und den Vorbildern der Ariadne-Epistel Ovids* (Frankfurt am Main: Peter Lang, 1990), 149–54.

7. I take the biographical information principally from de Chirico's *Memoirs*, trans. Margaret Crosland (Coral Gables: University of Miami Press, 1971); James Thrall Soby, *Giorgio de Chirico* (New York: Museum of Modern Art, 1955); and Taylor's exhibition catalog.

8. Giorgio de Chirico, *Hebdomeros. Le peintre et son génie chez l'écrivain* (Paris: Carrefour, 1929).

9. De Chirico, *Memoirs*, 34.

10. Ibid., 24—27.

11. Ibid., 61.

12. From the extensive literature discussing the biographical relationship see Hermann J. Weigand, "Nietzsche's Dionysus-Ariadne Fixation," *Germanic Review* 48 (1973): 99—116.

13. This is not the place to deal with the complex question of Nietzsche's Ariadne image. See Adrian Del Caro, "Symbolizing Philosophy: Ariadne and the Labyrinth," *Nietzsche-Studien* 17 (1988): 125—57, which recapitulates and takes issue with many previous studies.

14. In the case of a classical philologist like Nietzsche, it is probably fruitless to search for a specific source—and pointless, since his remarks on Ariadne remain so general. Yet Nietzsche did study Ovid's *Metamorphoses* as a schoolboy, cited Ovid in his essays, and mentioned him frequently in his early letters. In contrast, he did not encounter Catullus until his university years; and then Catullus is mentioned only in connection with a seminar paper by another student.

15. Del Caro, "Symbolizing Philosophy," 136—37.

16. *Apollinaire on Art: Essays and Reviews, 1902—1918*, ed. Leroy C. Breunig, trans. Susan Suleiman (New York: Viking, 1972), 223.

17. Taylor, *Giorgio de Chirico*, 55, 188.

18. Giorgio de Chirico, *Il meccanismo del pensiero: Critica, polemica, autobiographica 1911—1943*, ed. Maurizio Fagliolo (Turin: Einaudi, 1985), 13—17.

19. On "transformation" (*Verwandlung*) in Nietzsche see Lichtenstern, *Metamorphose*, 123—36.

20. Taylor, *Giorgio de Chirico*, 46, suggests that in the later paintings of *Piazza d'Italia* the Ariadne figure appears, more positively, to represent the golden thread of art.

21. Here I disagree with Taylor (ibid., 81), who suggests that Homer's *Odyssey* and Plutarch's *Lives* were probably among his sources. In the *Odyssey* (11.321—25) Ariadne is not deserted by Theseus but killed by Artemis on the island of Dia; and for Plutarch, Ariadne is simply a passing episode in his lengthy account of Theseus's life and adventures—an account that includes several variants of the story.

22. E.g., the *Self-Portrait* of 1911 entitled *ET.QUID.AMABO.NISI.QUOD.AENIGMA.EST?*

23. E.g., *Il meccanismo del pensiero*, 20—23. That de Chirico had read these poets in the original and knew from memory the important lines at the end of the *Metamorphoses*—*parte tamen meliore mei super alta perennis / astra ferar, nomenque erit indelebile nostrum* ("in my better part, however, I shall be borne immortal beyond the high stars and my name shall be imperishable")—is suggested by his mistaken attribution to Ovid of the identical sentiment from Horace: *Non omnis moriar* ("I shall not wholly die," *Car.* 3.30.6) inscribed on a Doric column above Arnold Böcklin's grave near Florence—which continues: *multaque pars mei / vitabit Libitinam.* See "Arnoldo Böcklin," in *Il meccanismo del pensiero*, 166—71; here 171.

24. For a review of the multiple sources and a critical comparison of the versions by Catullus and Ovid, see Howard Jacobson, *Ovid's Heroides* (Princeton: Princeton University Press, 1974), 213—27.

25. Elisabeth Frenzel, *Stoffe der Weltliteratur. Ein Lexikon dichtungsgeschichtlicher Längsschnitte*, 9th ed. (Stuttgart: Kröner, 1998), 57; Barry B. Powell, *Classical Myth* (Englewood Cliffs, NJ: Prentice Hall, 1995), 250; and Silke Köhn, "Ariadne," in *Antike Mythen und ihre Rezeption: Ein Lexikon*, ed. Lutz Walther (Leipzig: Reclam, 2003), 52—58. That Catullus was presumably one of Ovid's principal sources is irrelevant for the history of the story's reception; Ovid, and not Catullus, provided the source of themes and images for most later writers. See Konrat Ziegler and Walther Sontheimer, eds., *Der kleine Pauly: Lexikon der Antike in fünf Banden* (Munich: Deutscher Taschenbuch Verlag, 1979), 4:387. In antiquity Catullus was never an author read in school like Ovid; his poems, virtually unknown during the Middle Ages, were rediscovered only about 1300. Accordingly, all the medieval representations, upon which the later tradition was based, were taken from Ovid, and especially from the ever-popular *Heroides*. Despite a later celebrity in the European Renaissance, with a few notable exceptions—Tennyson, Swinburne, Aubrey Beardsley, Ezra Pound, W. B. Yeats—"Catullus' presence in English poetry is also relatively limited, in

comparison with, say, Ovid's," according to Charles Martindale, "Foreword to Kenneth Quinn, *The Catullan Revolution*, 2nd ed., Bristol Classical Paperbacks (London: Duckworth, 1999), xvi–xvii; here xvii. Martindale goes on to point out that "only a small number of poems were regularly translated and imitated"—mainly the short love lyrics and *not* including, notably, *Carmen* 64. "Catullus thus partially fails one test by which one can judge whether an ancient poet is fully alive in the later culture." Even the revival of Catullan studies of the past fifty years has tended to focus on the brief poems.

26. Taylor, *Giorgio de Chirico*, 39.

27. Soby, *Giorgio de Chirico*, 13, 48–49; Taylor, *Giorgio de Chirico*, 25.

28. See Manfred Hoppe's afterword in: Hugo von Hofmannsthal, *Operndichtungen 2*, vol. 24 of *Sämtliche Werke*, ed. Rudolf Hirsch (Frankfurt am Main: Fischer, 1985), 86–87 (hereafter *Operndichtungen 2*).

29. For an account of the genesis as well as a full interpretation of the libretto and music of the opera, see Donald G. Daviau and George J. Buelow, *The Ariadne auf Naxos of Hugo von Hofmannsthal and Richard Strauss* (Chapel Hill: University of North Carolina Press, 1975).

30. I base my discussion on the German text in *Operndichtungen 2*, 7–48.

31. Karl J. Naef, *Hugo von Hofmannsthals Wesen und Werk* (Zürich: Niehans, 1938), 144–54; here 144. The centrality of the theme of transformation is widely recognized in Hofmannsthal criticism. See Daviau and Buelow, *Ariadne auf Naxos*, 148–54; Walter Jens, *Hofmannsthal und die Griechen* (Tübingen: Niemeyer, 1955), 102–4; and Christiane Chauviré, *Hofmannsthal et la métamorphose* (Paris: Éditions de l'Éclat, 1991), 39–47.

32. Quoted in *Operndichtungen 2*, 172.

33. Ibid., 204–7; here 205.

34. Hofmannsthal coined the phrase in the notes of self-interpretation entitled *Ad me ipsum* (begun 1916; first printed 1930); in his *Aufzeichnungen*, ed. Herbert Steiner (Frankfurt am Main: Fischer, 1959), 211–44; here 218. The passages relevant to *Ariadne* are reprinted in *Operndichtungen 2*, 226.

35. Hofmannsthal, *Aufzeichnungen*, 226.

36. *Operndichtungen 2*, 64.

37. Jens, *Hofmannsthal und die Griechen*, 108; Jens includes Hesiod even though the three verses that Hesiod devotes to Ariadne do not tell the same version of the story.

38. Daviau and Buelow, *Ariadne auf Naxos*, 92.

39. See Richard Exner, *Index nominum zu Hugo von Hofmannsthals Gesammelten Werken* (Heidelberg: Stiehm, 1976).

40. Hugo von Hofmannsthal, *Lustspiele 3* (Frankfurt am Main: Fischer, 1956), 297.

41. Hugo von Hofmannsthal, *Prosa 3* (Frankfurt am Main: Fischer, 1952), 473.

42. Hugo von Hofmannsthal, *Dramen 3* (Frankfurt am Main: Fischer, 1957), 457.

43. The novelty of the synthesis of opera buffa and opera seria has been noted by other critics: see Naef, *Hofmannsthals Wesen und Werk*, 146–47; and Jens, *Hofmannsthal und die Griechen*, 100.

44. Jens, *Hofmannsthal und die Griechen*, 6, 14.

45. Karl G. Esselborn, *Hofmannsthal und der antike Mythos* (Munich: Fink, 1969), 11–13. On Nietzsche's influence on the entire generation see Gotthart Wunberg, *Der frühe Hofmannsthal. Schizophrenie als dichterische Kultur* (Stuttgart: Kohlhammer, 1965), 23–25.

46. Hofmannsthal, *Aufzeichnungen*, 106.

47. Maurice Hewlett, *The Agonists. A Trilogy of God and Man* (New York: Scribner's, 1911), x.

48. R. C. Trevelyan, *The Bride of Dionysus. A Music-Drama and Other Poems* (London: Longmans, 1912).

49. Paul Ernst, *Ariadne auf Naxos: Ein Schauspiel in drei Aufzügen* (Leipzig: Poeschel & Trepte, 1912).

2. TRANSITIONS

1. Martin Schanz, *Geschichte der römischen Literatur*, 2nd ed., vol. 2/1 (Munich: Beck, 1899), 234.

2. Eduard Norden, *Die römische Literatur* (1910), 5th ed. (Leipzig: Teubner, 1956), 75.

3. Charles Thomas Cruttwell, *A History of Roman Literature* (New York: Scribner's, 1908), 305–7.

4. Wilhelm Sigismund Teuffel, *Geschichte der römischen Literatur*, 6th ed., vol. 2 (Leipzig: Teubner, 1910), 93.

234 Notes to Pages 19–25

5. L. P. Wilkinson, *Ovid Recalled* (Cambridge: Cambridge University Press, 1955; rpt. Bath: Chivers, 1974), 285–86.

6. Marion Giebel, *Ovid: Mit Selbstzeugnissen und Bilddokumenten* (Reinbek bei Hamburg: Rowohlt, 1991), 126. For the information in this section see also Hermann Fränkel, *Ovid: A Poet between Two Worlds* (Berkeley: University of California Press, 1945); Wilkinson, *Ovid Recalled;* Sara Mack, *Ovid* (New Haven: Yale University Press, 1988); Niklas Holzberg, *Ovid: Dichter und Werk* (Munich: Beck, 1997; *Ovid: The Poet and His Works,* trans. G. M. Goshgarian [Ithaca, N.Y.: Cornell University Press, 2002]); and Peter White, "Ovid and the Augustan Milieu," in *Brill's Companion to Ovid,* ed. Barbara Weiden Boyd (Leiden: Brill, 2002), 1–25.

7. Michael Dewar, "Ovid in the 1st–5th Centuries A.D.," in *Brill's Companion,* 384–412.

8. Ralph Hexter, "Ovid in the Middle Ages: Exile, Mythographer, and Lover," in *Brill's Companion,* 413–42; here 416–24.

9. All otherwise unattributed quotations are taken from *Tristia* 4.10.

10. Edgar Martini, *Einleitung zu Ovid* (Brünn: Rohrer, 1933), 1–3.

11. See Ronald Syme, *History in Ovid* (Oxford: Clarendon, 1978), 215–29 ("The Error of Caesar Augustus").

12. The most complete survey of the various theories can be found in J. C. Thibault, *The Mystery of Ovid's Exile* (Berkeley: University of California Press, 1964).

13. Vintila Horîa, "Ovid: Dichter der Verbannten," *Merian* (June 1966), 78–83.

14. Ludwig Traube, *Einleitung in die lateinische Philologie des Mittelalters,* vol. 2 of *Vorlesungen und Abhandlungen von Ludwig Traube,* ed. Franz Boll (Munich: Beck, 1909–20), 113. On the reasons for Virgil's popularity see Domenico Comparetti, *Virgilio nel medio evo* (1872); *Virgil in the Middle Ages,* trans. E. F. M. Benecke (New York: Macmillan, 1895).

15. Michael von Albrecht, *Geschichte der römischen Literatur: Von Andronicus bis Boethius, mit Berücksichtigung ihrer Bedeutung für die Neuzeit,* 2nd ed. (Munich: Saur, 1994), 644.

16. Ernst Robert Curtius, *Europäische Literatur und lateinisches Mittelalter,* 2nd ed. (Bern: Francke, 1954), 28.

17. See ibid., 68, for a list of such precepts; and Edward Kennard Rand, *Ovid and His Influence* (Boston: Marshall Jones, 1925), 131–37, on his stature as *ethicus* and *theologus.*

18. C. de Boer, ed., *"Ovide moralisé": Poème du commencement du quatorzième siècle,* published from 1912 to 1935 in five volumes of the Verhandelingen der Koninklijke Akademie der Wetenschappen, Afd. Letterkunde. I quote here from volume 21 of the Verhandelingen (Amsterdam: Johannes Müller, 1920), book 4, verses 3150–3584 (tale) and 3585–3731 (allegorization).

19. On the celebrity of Ovid see especially Giovanni Pansa, *Ovidio nel medioevo e nella tradizione popolare* (Sulmona: Caroselli, 1924). Still useful is Wilmon Brewer, *Ovid's Metamorphoses in European Culture,* 2 vols. (Boston: Cornhill, 1933–41), which amounts to a running commentary on the individual episodes of books 1–10 with sources, other classical treatments, and influence in art and literature down to the nineteenth century. Martini, *Einleitung zu Ovid,* 81–98, is of enormous bibliographical value.

20. Franco Munari, *Ovid im Mittelalter* (Zurich: Artemis, 1960), 35.

21. On Ovid in the Middle Ages see—in addition to Curtius, Rand, Pansa, Wilkinson, and Munari—Charles Marindale, ed., *Ovid Renewed: Ovidian Influence on Literature and Art from the Middle Ages to the Twentieth Century* (Cambridge: Cambridge University Press, 1988); Michelangelo Picone and Bernhard Zimmermann, eds. *Ovidius redivivus: von Ovid zu Dante* (Stuttgart: Metzler, 1994), 63–202; William S. Anderson, ed., *Ovid: The Classical Heritage* (New York: Garland, 1995); Walter Berschin, "Ovid in der biographischen Literatur des Mittelalters," in *Ovid: Werk und Wirkung,* Festgabe für Michael von Albrecht zum 65. Geburtstag, ed. Werner Schubert, 2 vols. (Frankfurt am Main: Peter Lang, 1999), 911–14; *Brill's Companion to Ovid,* ed. Philip Hardie; *The Cambridge Companion to Ovid* (Cambridge: Cambridge University Press, 2002); and Michael von Albrecht, *Ovid: Eine Einführung* (Stuttgart: Reclam, 2003), 279–95. Wilfried Stroh, ed., *Ovid im Urteil der Nachwelt: Eine Testimoniensammlung* (Darmstadt: Wissenschaftliche Buchgesellschaft, 1969), contains a collection of statements on Ovid from classical antiquity to the early twentieth century, along with a useful bibliography.

22. The translation is known today only through some 400 lines of a manuscript fragment and from a mid-sixteenth-century adaptation by Jörg Wickram.

23. Wilkinson, *Ovid Recalled*, 391–92.

24. On Ovid and Dante see Edward Moore, *Studies in Dante. First Series: Scripture and Classical Authors in Dante* (Oxford: Clarendon, 1896), 206–28.

25. On Ovid and Chaucer see E. F. Shannon, *Chaucer and the Roman Poets*, Harvard Studies in Comparative Literature 7 (Cambridge: Harvard University Press, 1929).

26. Rand, *Ovid and His Influence*, 150. See also Wilkinson, *Ovid Recalled*, 399–438; *Ovid: Werk und Wirkung*, 915–1020; and Hermann Walter and Hans-Jürgen Horn, eds., *Die Rezeption der Metamorphosen des Ovid in der Neuzeit: Der antike Mythos in Text und Bild*, Internationales Symposion der Werner-Reimers-Stiftung (Berlin: Mann, 1995).

27. Rand, *Ovid and His Influence*, 152–56.

28. Michael von Albrecht, "Vondels niederländischer Ovid—ein poetisches Testament," in his *Rom: Spiegel Europas. Das Fortwirken antiker Texte und Themen in Europa*, 2nd ed. (Tübingen: Stauffenberg, 1998), 179–203.

29. Sarah Annes Brown, *The Metamorphosis of Ovid: From Chaucer to Ted Hughes* (London: Duckworth, 1999); and Raphael Lyne, *Ovid's Changing Worlds: English Metamorphoses, 1567–1632* (Oxford: Oxford University Press, 2001).

30. E.g., *Ovid's Metamorphoses*, trans. Arthur Golding; ed. Madeleine Forey (Baltimore: Johns Hopkins University Press, 2002).

31. See Jonathan Bate, *Shakespeare and Ovid* (Oxford: Clarendon: 1993); and A. B. Taylor, ed., *Shakespeare's Ovid: The Metamorphoses in the Plays and Poems* (Cambridge: Cambridge University Press, 2000).

32. A. D. Nuttall, "The Winter's Tale: Ovid Transformed," in *Shakespeare's Ovid*, 135–49.

33. J. W. Velz, "The Ovidian Soliloquy in Shakespeare," *Shakespeare Studies* 18 (1986):1–24, analyzes in particular the influence of Medea's great soliloquy at *Met.* 7.11–71.

34. *Essays of John Dryden*, ed. W. P. Ker, 2 vols. (Oxford: Clarendon, 1926), 1:230–43.

35. Rand, *Ovid and His Influence*, 161; and Émile Ripert, *Ovide: Poète de l'amour, des dieux et de l'exil* (Paris: Colin, 1921), 227–54.

36. Michel de Montaigne, *The Complete Essays*, trans. Donald M. Frame (Stanford: Stanford University Press, 1958), 130 (1:26:"Of the Education of Children"). Later, to be sure, he admits that Ovid's works, "which once enchanted me, hardly entertain me at all now" (298; 2:10, "Of Books").

37. See Maria Moog-Grünewald, *Metamorphosen der Metamorphosen: Rezeptionsarten der ovidischen Verwandlungsgeschichten in Italien und Frankreich im 16. und 17. Jahrhundert* (Heidelberg: Winter, 1979).

38. Wilkinson, *Ovid Recalled*, 441–42.

39. E. M. Butler, *The Tyranny of Greece over Germany: A Study of the Influence Exercised by Greek Art and Poetry over the Great German Writers of the Eighteenth, Nineteenth, and Twentieth Centuries* (Cambridge: Cambridge University Press, 1935).

40. C. M. Wieland, *Poetische Jugendwerke*, ed. F. Homeyer, in *Gesammelte Schriften* 1/1 (Berlin: Weidmann, 1909), 310–32; here 313.

41. Immanuel Kant, *Beobachtungen über das Gefühl des Schönen und Erhabenen* (1764), in *Werke in zehn Bänden*, ed. Wilhelm Weischedel (Darmstadt: Wissenschaftliche Buchgesellschaft, 1968), 2:834.

42. Goethe, *Dichtung und Wahrheit*, bk. 10, in *Goethes Werke*, ed. Erich Trunz, 2nd ed. (Hamburg: Wegner, 1957), 9:413.

43. G. W. F. Hegel, *Vorlesungen über die Ästhetik*, part 2, sec. 2, chap. 1c, in *Werkausgabe*, vol. 14 (Frankfurt am Main: Suhrkamp, 1970), 39. On developments from Winckelmann to Hegel see Christa Lichtenstern, *Metamorphose: Vom Mythos zum Prozessdenken. Ovid-Rezeption, Surrealistische Ästhetik, Verwandlungsthematik der Nachkriegskunst* (Weinheim: VCH, 1992), 9–23.

44. Michael von Albrecht, "Goethe und die Antike, am Beispiel Ovids," in *Rom*, 645–59.

45. Friedrich Schlegel, *Geschichte der europäischen Literatur* (1803–1804), in *Kritische Friedrich-Schlegel-Ausgabe*, ed. Ernst Behler et al., vol. 11 (Paderborn: Schöningh, 1958), 133.

46. Theodore Ziolkowski, *The Classical German Elegy, 1795–1950* (Princeton: Princeton University Press, 1980), 149–57.

47. August Wilhelm Schlegel, *Geschichte der klassischen Literatur* (1802–1803), in *Kritische Schriften und Briefe*, ed. Edgar Lohner, vol. 3 (Stuttgart: Kohlhammer, 1964), 251.

48. Anne-Louise-Germaine de Staël, *De la littérature considerée dans ses rapports avec les institutions sociales* (Paris: Charpentier, 1887), 1:104 (chap. 6).

49. G. Otto Trevalyan, *The Life and Letters of Lord Macaulay,* 2 vols. (New York: Harper, 1875), 1:411–13.

50. Michael von Albrecht, "Metamorphose in Raum und Zeit. Vergleichende Untersuchungen zu Rodin und Ovid," in *Rom,* 517–68.

51. Theodore Ziolkowski, *Virgil and the Moderns* (Princeton: Princeton University Press, 1993), 4–6.

52. Robert Graves, "The Virgil Cult," *Virginia Quarterly Review* 38 (1962): 13–35; here 13.

53. For this reason I cannot share Brown's assumption, in *The Metamorphosis of Ovid,* 181, that there was "an 'embedded' Ovidianism" in the work of modernist writers; for any such assumption ignores the radical break that the nineteenth century represents and the individual effort required on the part of writers, as we shall see, to recapture Ovid for themselves and their own purposes.

54. Virginia Woolf, "Mr. Bennett and Mrs. Brown" (1924), in *Collected Essays,* 4 vols. (London: Hogarth, 1966), 1:319–37; here 320.

3. OVID *REDIVIVUS*

1. James Joyce, *A Portrait of the Artist as a Young Man* (New York: Viking, 1956).

2. Harry Levin, *James Joyce: A Critical Introduction,* rev. ed. (Norfolk, Conn.: New Directions, 1960), 61–62.

3. Donald Lateiner, "The Epigraph to Joyce's *Portrait,*" *Classical and Modern Literature* 4 (1983–84): 77–84; here 81.

4. Niall Rudd, "Daedalus and Icarus: From the Renaissance to the Present Day," in *Ovid Renewed,* ed. Charles Martindale (Cambridge: Cambridge University Press, 1988), 37–53; here 50–51.

5. Lateiner, "Epigraph," 79.

6. David Hayman, "Daedalian Imagery in *A Portrait of the Artist as a Young Man,*" in *Hereditas: Seven Essays on the Modern Experience of the Classical,* ed. Frederic Will (Austin: University of Texas Press, 1964), 31–54, deals with the images of labyrinth, minotaurs, and wings. But because Hayman always speaks vaguely of "the myth" (36) and Joyce's "Greek modes of thought" (34), not realizing that Ovid is the specific and principal source, he often goes farther in claiming parallels than the text allows.

7. Levin, *James Joyce,* 61.

8. I cannot agree here with Lateiner, "Epigraph," 82, who sees in the ending an assimilation of the two aspects into a "Martyr-Artist." Stephen has rejected precisely the "saintly" aspect of his name.

9. Consider, for instance, Ovid's claim at *Amores* 3.12.21–42 that many of the most famous myths are nothing more than the invention of the poets; or his assertion at *Ex Ponto* 4.8.55 that even the gods are created by the poets' verses: *di quoque carminibus, si fas est dicere, fiunt.*

10. Edgar M. Glenn, "Pound and Ovid," *Paideuma* 10 (1981): 625–34; here 626.

11. Ezra Pound, "Elizabethan Dramatists," *Egoist* 4 (1917): 154–56; here 155.

12. Ezra Pound, *The Spirit of Romance* (New York: Dutton, 1910), 6.

13. Glenn, "Pound and Ovid," 626.

14. Ezra Pound, *ABC of Reading* (New Haven: Yale University Press, 1934), 35.

15. Pound, "Elizabethan Dramatists," 155.

16. Ezra Pound, *Guide to Kulchur* (Norfolk, Conn.: New Directions, 1952), 149.

17. Pound, *ABC of Reading,* 44, 115.

18. Letter of 16 July 1922 to Harriet Monroe, *The Letters of Ezra Pound, 1907–1941,* ed. D. D. Paige (New York: Harcourt, 1950), 183.

19. Ezra Pound, *Selected Prose, 1909–1965,* ed. William Cookson (London: Faber, 1973), 53.

20. *Literary Essays of Ezra Pound,* ed. T. S. Eliot (London: Faber, 1954), 149–200; here 179.

21. Glenn, "Pound and Ovid," 628.

22. *Letters of Ezra Pound,* 90.

23. Ibid., 87.

24. J. P. Sullivan, "Ezra Pound and the Classics," in *New Approaches to Ezra Pound: A Co-ordinated Investigation of Pound's Poetry and Ideas,* ed. Eva Hesse (London: Faber, 1969), 215–41; here 220–23.

25. *Letters of Ezra Pound,* 231. See in this connection Ron Thomas, *The Latin Masks of Ezra Pound* (Ann Arbor: UMI Research Press, 1983).

26. Lillian Feder, "Pound and Ovid," in *Ezra Pound among the Poets,* ed. George Bornstein (Chicago: University of Chicago Press, 1985), 13–34; here 28. See Canto 98, for instance, where the phrase occurs twice.

27. Reinhold Schiffer, "Der zweimal verwandelte Dionysos: Zur Mythenrezeption bei Ovid und Pound," *Arcadia* 8 (1973): 235–47.

28. *The Cantos of Ezra Pound* (New York: New Direction, 1948), 13–16. Canto 4 was first published privately by John Rodker (London: Ovid Press, 1919) and subsequently reprinted in *Dial* 68 (June 1920): 689–92, and in Pound's *Poems 1918–1921* (New York: Boni and Liveright, 1921).

29. For details see Carroll F. Terrell, *A Companion to the Cantos of Ezra Pound* (Berkeley: University of California Press, 1980), 10–15. On Canto 4 see Mary Bernetta Quinn, *The Metamorphic Tradition in Modern Poetry* (New York: Gordian, 1966), 34–36; George Dekker, "Myth and Metamorphosis: Two Aspects of Myth in *The Cantos,*" in *New Approaches to Ezra Pound,* 280–302; here 292–93; Charles Tomlinson, *Poetry and Metamorphosis* (Cambridge: Cambridge University Press, 1983), 67–68; Feder, "Pound and Ovid," 25–26; and Ellen Brinks, "On Pound's Fourth Canto," *Paideuma* 19 (1990): 137–44, which includes a bibliography with additional titles.

30. Christine Bokke-Rose, "Lay Me by Aurelie: An Examination of Pound's Use of Historical and Semi-Historical Sources," in *New Approaches to Ezra Pound,* 242–79; here 257–59.

31. Pound, *Spirit of Romance,* vi.

32. W. B. Yeats, *A Packet for Ezra Pound* (1929; rpt. Shannon: Irish University Press, 1970), 2.

33. Lillian Feder, *Ancient Myth in Modern Poetry* (Princeton: Princeton University Press, 1971), 106–21; here 107.

34. Hugh Kenner, *The Pound Era* (Berkeley: University of California Press, 1971), 536.

35. David Roessel, "'Like Ovid in Thrace': D. H. Lawrence's Identification with a Roman Poet," *Classical and Modern Literature* 10 (1989–90): 351–57; here 352.

36. *The Letters of D. H. Lawrence,* ed. J. T. Boulton, 8 vols. (Cambridge: Cambridge University Press, 1979–2000), 2:521.

37. Roessel, "Like Ovid in Thrace," 356.

38. *Letters of D. H. Lawrence,* 3:241–42.

39. Ibid., 3:242.

40. D. H. Lawrence, *The Lost Girl* (New York: Thomas Seltzer, 1921), 350. It is a curious coincidence, but no more than that, that in Willa Cather's novel *A Lost Lady* (1923) Niel Herbert reads Ovid's *Heroides* over and over. But I cannot attribute to this passing reference the same thematic significance as does Erik Ingvar Thurin, *The Humanization of Willa Cather: Classicism in an American Classic* (Lund: Lund University Press, 1990), 251–64. It surely has none of the shaping power that Virgil's *Georgics* exert on *My Ántonia* (1918).

41. D. H. Lawrence, *Kangaroo* (New York: Viking, 1951), 15.

42. Freud did not coin the term "narcissism," which was used almost simultaneously in 1898–99 by P. Näcke and Havelock Ellis. Freud himself had introduced the word on several earlier occasions. But the essay of 1914 marks a significant point in the development of his thought and essentially legitimized the term in psychology. See the *Studienausgabe* of Freud's works, ed. Alexander Mitscherlich (Frankfurt am Main: Fischer, 1989), 3:37–68.

4. *ANNUS MIRABILIS OVIDIANUS*

1. "Émile Ripert: Le poète disparu," *Méditerranéen no. 5* (5 April 2000).

2. Ripert's introduction to his *Ovide. Poète de l'amour, des dieux et de l'exil* (Paris: Armand Colin, 1921), vii–xiv.

3. Ripert shares the anti-German animus that also characterized the work of his friend André Bel-lessort, *Virgile: Son Œuvre et son temps* (1920). See Theodore Ziolkowski, *Virgil and the Moderns* (Princeton: Princeton University Press, 1993), 32–33.

4. Gareth Reeves, *T. S. Eliot: A Virgilian Poet* (London: Macmillan, 1989); and Ziolkowski, *Virgil and the Moderns*, 119–29.

5. Both essays available in Eliot's *On Poetry and Poets* (1957; rpt. London: Faber, 1986), 53–71 and 121–31.

6. Frank Kermode, *The Classic: Literary Images of Permanence and Change* (1975; rpt. Cambridge: Harvard University Press, 1983), 15. Kermode quotes Eliot's statement from *Transatlantic Review* (Jan. 1924).

7. Included in his mother's letter of 4 April 1905 to Milton Academy in Massachusetts; *The Letters of T. S. Eliot*, ed. Valerie Eliot, vol. 1: 1898–1922 (New York, Harcourt, 1988), 8.

8. Letter from his mother, August 1920; *Letters of T. S. Eliot*, 1:398–99.

9. T. S. Eliot, *Selected Essays* (London: Faber, 1951), 292–304; here 296–97. Along with Ovid, Eliot includes Gautier, Baudelaire, Laforgue, Catullus, and Propertius in his list.

10. "London Letter," *Dial* 71 (October 1921): 452–55; here 453.

11. "A Prediction in Regard to Three English authors," *Vanity Fair*, 21 (Feb. 1924): 29.

12. I cite the text by line according to *The Complete Poems and Plays, 1909–1950* (New York: Harcourt, 1958), 37–55.

13. The centrality of metamorphosis in *The Waste Land* has often been noted and extensively discussed: e.g., Mary Bernetta Quinn, *The Metamorphic Tradition in Modern Poetry* (New York: Gordian, 1966), 130–47; Charles Tomlinson, *Poetry and Metamorphosis* (Cambridge: Cambridge University Press, 1983), 23–47; and Stephen Medcalf, "T. S. Eliot's *Metamorphoses*: Ovid and *The Waste Land*," in *Ovid Renewed*, ed. Charles Martindale (Cambridge: Cambridge University Press, 1988), 215–46.

14. See in this connection especially John B. Vickery, *The Literary Impact of The Golden Bough* (Princeton: Princeton University Press, 1973), 233–79; here 243–44.

15. Denis Donoghue, "The Word within a Word," in *"The Waste Land" in Different Voices*, ed. A. D. Moody (London: Edward Arnold, 1974), 185–201.

16. In the facsimile edition, 47; my attention was drawn to this note by Robert Langbaum, "New Modes of Characterization in *The Waste Land*," in *Eliot in His Time: Essays on the Occasion of the Fiftieth Anniversary of The Waste Land*, ed. A. Walton Litz (Princeton: Princeton University Press, 1973), 95–128; here 109.

17. Medcalf, "Ovid and *The Waste Land*," 240, suspects that Eliot saw the anthropological dimension in the coupling of the snakes as a manifestation of snake worship.

18. E.g., many of the contributions in *Eliot in His Time* are concerned extensively with the genesis of the poem.

19. First published in *Poems Written in Early Youth* (1950); quoted here from the facsimile edition of *The Waste Land*, ed. Valerie Eliot (New York: Harcourt, 1971), 95–97. See Medcalf, "Ovid and *The Waste Land*," 235; and Donald J. Childs, "*Metamorphoses*, Metaphysics, and Mysticism from *The Death of Saint Narcissus* to *Burnt Norton*," *Comparative and Modern Literature* 12 (1992): 15–29.

20. I do not find convincing the attempt of Sarah Annes Brown to posit an (unmentioned) myth of Pygmalion and Galatea in "A Game of Chess." See *The Metamorphosis of Ovid: From Chaucer to Ted Hughes* (London: Duckworth, 1999), 182–83.

21. See Medcalf, "Ovid and *The Waste Land*," 242.

22. See the anthology *Gods and Mortals: Modern Poems on Classical Myths*, ed. Nina Kossman (Oxford: University Press, 2001), 137–38.

23. Many scholars assume that the "stumps" refer to the amputated arms of Lavinia in *Titus Andronicus*. I am more persuaded by Medcalf's suggestion, in "Ovid and *The Waste Land*," 239, that the stumps allude to Philomela's tongue.

24. On this line see Tomlinson, *Poetry and Metamorphosis*, 42–46.

25. On the role of pagan ritual in *The Waste Land* see Lillian Feder, *Ancient Myth in Modern Poetry* (Princeton: Princeton University Press, 1971), 222–31.

26. He later substituted one written on February 9 for the twenty-first and added a twenty-sixth, writ-

ten on February 13. For the dates see the *Inhaltsverzeichnis,* the first volume of Rilke's *Sämtliche Werke,* ed. Ernst Zinn, 6 vols. (Frankfurt am Main: Insel, 1955–66).

27. See Theodore Ziolkowski, *The Classical German Elegy, 1795–1950* (Princeton: Princeton University Press, 1980), 234–53.

28. Regarding the sonnets in a historical European context see Walter Mönch, *Das Sonett: Gestalt und Geschichte* (Heidelberg: Kerle, 1955), 258–61.

29. See Theodore Ziolkowski, *The View from the Tower* (Princeton: Princeton University Press, 1998), 115–23.

30. Rainer Maria Rilke, *Briefe an Nanny Wunderly-Volkart,* ed. Niklaus Bigler and Rätus Luck, vol. 1 (Frankfurt am Main: Insel, 1977).

31. Letter of 9 Feb. 1922 to Anton Kippenberg; Rainer Maria Rilke, *Briefe,* ed. Ruth Sieber-Rilke and Karl Altheim (Wiesbaden: Insel, 1950), 741.

32. Mönch, *Das Sonett,* 258–61.

33. See Walter A. Strauss, *Descent and Return: The Orphic Theme in Modern Literature* (Cambridge: Harvard University Press, 1971), 9–12, 178; and Judith Ryan, *Rilke, Modernism and Poetic Tradition* (Cambridge: Cambridge University Press, 1999), 176–77.

34. "Über die biologischen Voraussetzungen des Imperium Romanum" (1915) and "Vom Wesen der ewigen Stadt" (1917). The second series was published in Schuler's *Fragmente und Vorträge aus dem Nachlaß,* ed. Ludwig Klages (Leipzig: Barth, 1940).

35. J. J. Bachofen, *Urreligion und antike Symbole,* ed. Carl Albrecht Bernouilli, 3 vols. (Leipzig: Reclam, 1926), 1:318–19.

36. Letter of 18 March 1915 to Marie von Thurn und Taxis-Hohenlohe; Rilke, *Briefe,* 483–84. See Hans Jürgen Tschiedel, "Orpheus und Eurydice: Ein Beitrag zum Thema: Rilke und die Antike," *Antike und Abendland* 19 (1973): 61–82; rpt. with "Nachtrag 1986" in *Rainer Maria Rilke,* ed. Rüdiger Görner (Darmstadt: Wissenschaftliche Buchgesellschaft, 1987), 285–318; here 299–300.

37. See the account of his lecture in the *Basler Nachrichten* (16 Nov. 1919); rpt. in Rainer Maria Rilke, *Schweizer Vortragsreise 1919,* ed. Rätus Luck (Frankfurt am Main: Insel, 1986), 229–33; here 232.

38. Ernst Zinn, "Ovids Arion: Eine Übertragung des jungen Rilke," in Zinn's *Viva Vox: Römische Klassik und deutsche Dichtung,* ed. Michael von Albrecht (Frankfurt am Main: Peter Lang, 1994), 379–94; here 386.

39. In Rilke's review of Walter Pater's *The Renaissance,* in *Sämtliche Werke* 5:601.

40. Tschiedel, "Orpheus und Eurydice," 286–95.

41. Rilke, *Sämtliche Werke,* 5:139–201; here 174.

42. Ibid. 5:257–78; here 268. Rilke published a revised version of the lecture in 1907.

43. See Ernst Zinn, "Rainer Maria Rilke und die Antike," in *Viva Vox,* 315–77; here 337.

44. Rilke, *Sämtliche Werke,* 2:364.

45. Ibid., 6:924.

46. "Über den jungen Dichter," in Rilke, *Sämtliche Werke* 6:1051; see also "Puppen," 6:1068.

47. Rilke, *Sämtliche Werke,* 2:56–57.

48. Letter of 25 December 1920; in Rainer Maria Rilke and Merline, *Correspondence 1920–1926,* ed. Dieter Bassermann (Zurich: Niehans, 1954), 148–53; here 151–52.

49. Ralph Freedman, *Life of a Poet: Rainer Maria Rilke* (New York: Farrar, Straus and Giroux, 1996), 480–81.

50. Undated letter to Gertrud Ouckama Knoop; Rilke, *Briefe,* 728.

51. Cited here and elsewhere from the text in Rilke, *Sämtliche Werke,* 1:727–73.

52. Ernst Leisi, *Rilkes Sonette an Orpheus. Interpretationen, Kommentar, Glossar* (Tübingen: Gunter Narr, 1987), 74, 123–26.

53. See Eudo C. Mason, *Rainer Maria Rilke: Sein Leben und sein Werk* (Göttingen: Vandenhoeck, 1964), 119.

54. Ibid.

55. Ibid., 123.

56. Paul Valéry, *Cahiers,* 29 vols. (Paris: Centre National de la Recherche Scientifique, 1957–61), 6:569.

57. Huguette Laurenti, ed., *"Ovide chez les Scythes": Un "beau sujet". Étude génétique d'un manuscrit inédit de Paul Valéry par le group Paul Valéry de l'I.T.E.M. (C.N.R.S.)* (Montpellier: Centre d'étude du XXe siècle—études valéryennes, 1997).

58. See the index to *Cahiers,* ed. Judith Robinson, 2 vols. (Paris: Gallimard, 1974).

59. Paul Valéry, "Naissance de 'La jeune Parque,'" in *Œuvres,* ed. Jean Hytier, 2 vols. (Paris: Gallimard, 1957), 1:1613.

60. I am aware that the serpent motif has also been associated with the tale of Psyche as related in Corneille's *Psyché,* from which the poem's epigraph is taken. But the allusion in the tale of Psyche is only metaphorical, while the serpent that bites the Young Fate as well as Eurydice is quite real.

61. Ziolkowski, *Virgil and the Moderns,* 68–74.

62. Osip Mandelstam, *Collected Critical Prose and Letters,* ed. Jane Gary Harris, trans. Jane Gary Harris and Constance Link (London: Collins Harvill, 1991), 112–16; here 112.

63. Quoted by Victor Terras, "Classical Motives in the Poetry of Osip Mandel'štam," *Slavic and East European Journal,* n.s. 10 (1966): 251–65; here 254.

64. Omry Ronen, "Osip Mandelshtam," in *European Writers of the Twentieth Century,* ed. George Stade, vol. 10 (New York: Scribner, 1990), 1619–49; here 1630, 1645.

65. For criticism I am indebted to Terras, "Classical Motives"; Clarence Brown, *Mandelstam* (Cambridge: Cambridge University Press, 1973), 270–75; Jane Gary Harris, *Osip Mandelstam* (Boston: Twayne, 1988); Petra Hesse, *Mythologie in moderner Lyrik: Osip E. Mandel'štam vor dem Hintergrund des "silbernen Zeitalters"* (Bern: Peter Lang, 1989), 109–13; and Alexander Podossinov, "Die Exil-Muse Ovids in russischer Dichtung des XX. Jahrhunderts (Mandelstam und Brodsky)," in *Ovid: Werk und Wirkung,* ed. Werner Schubert (Frankfurt am Main: Peter Lang, 1999), 1061–77.

66. Osip Mandelstam, *Stone,* trans. Robert Tracy (Princeton: Princeton University Press, 1981). Mandelstam's poems are conventionally cited by their number in the collected works.

67. Brown, *Mandelstam,* 309, sees here a quotation of Ovid's *Tristia* 3.10.34 (*ducunt Sarmatici barbara plaustra boves*), but the allusions to the Sarmatian tribes and their ox-drawn carts are so frequent that it seems unnecessary to pinpoint a specific source.

68. Mandelstam, *Stone,* 207.

69. Podossinov, "Die Exil-Muse Ovids," 1066.

70. Ronen, "Osip Mandelshtam," 1640.

71. *Complete Poetry of Osip Emilevich Mandelstam,* trans. Burton Raffel and Alla Burago, with an introduction and notes by Sidney Monas (Albany: State University of New York Press, 1973), 102–3.

72. Podossinov, "Die Exil-Muse Ovids," 1064.

73. Ibid., 1065.

74. Hesse, *Mythologie in moderner Lyrik,* 110.

75. Brown, *Mandelstam,* 274–75; Harris, *Osip Mandelstam,* 35–37. Pushkin seems to be a more likely and thematically useful source than Tibullus, as suggested by Terras, "Classical Motifs," 260.

76. Brown, *Mandelstam,* 283.

77. Hesse, *Mythologie in moderner Lyrik,* 112.

78. Robert Graves, *Welchman's Hose* (London: Fleuron, 1925), 11–13.

5. THE MODERNIZATION OF METAMORPHOSIS

1. See Otto Kern, "Die Metamorphose in Religion und Dichtung der Antike," in *Goethe als Seher und Erforscher der Natur,* ed. Johannes Walther, for the Kaiserlich Leopoldinische Deutsche Akademie der Naturforscher zu Halle (Leipzig, 1930), 185–204; here at 185, he says without citation or source that Pliny coined the term. But the earliest attributions in the *Patrologia Latina* and the various glossaries of Medieval Latin are to Lactantius, Hilarius, and other writers of late antiquity.

2. William S. Anderson, "Multiple Change in the *Metamorphoses,*" *Transactions of the American Philological Association* 94 (1963): 1–27.

3. Recent studies have shown, both specifically and by implication, that the idea of metamorphosis

enjoyed a resurgence in the Renaissance: e.g., Leonard Barkan, *The Gods Made Flesh: Metamorphosis and the Pursuit of Paganism* (New Haven:Yale University Press, 1986); Jonathan Bate, *Shakespeare and Ovid* (Oxford: Clarendon, 1993); and Maria Moog-Grünewald, *Metamorphosen der Metamorphosen: Rezeptionsarten der ovidischen Verwandlungsgeschichten in Italien und Frankreich im 16. und 17. Jahrhundert* (Heidelberg:Winter, 1979).

4. For the reference to Burckhardt I am indebted to Friedmann Harzer, *Erzählte Verwandlung: Eine Poetik epischer Metamorphosen* (Tübingen: Niemeyer, 2000), 7−8.

5. I cite the text according to Jacob Burckhardt, *Gesammelte Werke* (Basel: Schwabe, 1955−59), 6:7−19.

6. Kern, "Metamorphose in Religion und Dichtung der Antike," 195−97.

7. See Rätus Luck's notes to his edition of Rilke's *Schweizer Vortragsreise 1919* (Frankfurt am Main: Insel, 1986), 147−52.

8. The standard English translation by R. F. C. Hull is based on the fourth edition, revised by Jung and with a different title: *Symbols of Transformation,* 2nd ed. Bollingen Series 20 (Princeton: Princeton University Press, 1970).

9. Hull, *Symbols of Transformation,* 340, 425.

10. Ibid., 231.

11. See Harzer, *Erzählte Verwandlung,* 26−39 ("Metamorphose-Konzepte"); and Irving Massey, *The Gaping Pig: Literature and Metamorphosis* (Berkeley: University of California Press, 1976), 3−15.

12. See "Metamorphosis" in *The Encyclopaedia of Religion and Ethics,* ed. James Hasting, 13 vols. (New York: Scribner's, 1908−27), 8:593−94; and the entries "Shape Shifting" and "Transmigration" in *The Encyclopedia of Religion,* ed. Mircea Eliade, 16 vols. (New York: Macmillan, 1987), 13:225−29 and 15:21−26.

13. I take these useful distinctions from Harzer, *Erzählte Verwandlung,* 39−45.

14. Some scholars—e.g., Massey, *Gaping Pig,* 186−92—insist on a sharp distinction between metamorphosis and metaphor, arguing that metamorphosis assumes continuity between two different forms whereas metaphor provides a linguistic bridge between terms understood to be physically distinct. But in the context of metamorphosis the distinction can be quite useful: "metaphorical metamorphosis" designates a transformation with the *tertium comparationis* of a name; while "metonymic" displays no such common ground.

15. Harzer, *Erzählte Verwandlung,* 128−36.

16. This point needs to be stressed because it is sometimes misunderstood by scholars who know their Kafka better than their Ovid: see Stanley Corngold, *The Commentators' Despair: The Interpretation of Kafka's "Metamorphosis"* (Port Washington, N.Y.: Kennikat, 1973), 12.

17. Victor Erlich, "Gogol and Kafka: Note on 'Realism' and 'Surrealism,'" in *For Roman Jakobson: Essays on the Occasion of His Sixtieth Birthday,* ed. Morris Halle (The Hague: Mouton, 1956), 102−4; and Idris Parry, "Kafka and Gogol," *German Life and Letters,* n.s. 6 (1953): 141−45.

18. Hartmut Binder, "Leben und Persönlichkeit Franz Kafkas," in *Kafka-Handbuch in zwei Bänden,* ed. Hartmut Binder (Stuttgart: Kröner, 1979), 1:203−7.

19. See Kafka's "Brief an den Vater," in *Hochzeitsvorbereitungen auf dem Lande und andere Prosa aus dem Nachlaß* (New York: Schocken, 1953; licensed German edition S. Fischer), 171; and *Tagebücher* (New York: Schocken, 1949; licensed German edition S. Fischer), 139.

20. Letter of 25 Oct. 1915 to Kurt Wolff Publishers; in Franz Kafka, *Dichter über ihre Dichtungen,* ed. Erich Heller and Joachim Beug (Munich: Heimeran, 1969), 58.

21. I quote from the text in Franz Kafka's *Sämtliche Erzählungen,* ed. Paul Raabe (Frankfurt am Main: Fischer Taschenbuch, 1971), 56−99.

22. Heinz Politzer, *Franz Kafka: Parable and Paradox* (Ithaca: Cornell University Press, 1962), 65−82.

23. In his annotated bibliography, *Commentators' Despair,* Corngold cites 128 different interpretations that had appeared by 1970.

24. Gustav Janouch, *Gespräche mit Kafka* (Frankfurt am Main: Fischer, 1968), 43−44; also Kafka, *Dichter über ihre Dichtungen,* 60.

25. See Theodore Ziolkowski, *Dimensions of the Modern Novel: German Texts and European Contexts* (Princeton: Princeton University Press, 1969), 37−67; here 55−57. In later stories the valence of the image becomes more positive.

26. Some critics read the ending as precisely the opposite: as the family's degradation into the dehumanizing demands of the modern world of work, from which Gregor had sought to liberate himself. See the critique of this view by Hartmut Binder, *Motiv und Gestaltung bei Franz Kafka* (Bonn: Bouvier, 1966), 350–60. Carole Newlands has also made the provocative suggestion, in this sense, that the Samsa family represent the hounds pursuing Gregor as Actaeon (in her reader's comments on my manuscript).

27. See Kafka's comment in his letter of 6–7 Dec. 1912 to Felice Bauer, in *Dichter über ihre Dichtungen*, 56; and Politzer, *Franz Kafka*, 82.

28. Pierre Brunel, *Le mythe de la métamorphose* (Paris: Colin, 1974), 125–65, discusses Kafka's story in a chapter titled "Un mythe de la dégradation."

29. *Kindheit und Jugend vor Neunzehnhundert: Hermann Hesse in Briefen und Lebenszeugnissen, 1877–1895*, ed. Ninon Hesse (Frankfurt am Main: Suhrkamp, 1966), 108.

30. "Ein paar Basler Erinnerungen," quoted in *Hermann Hesse: Eine Chronik in Bildern*, ed. Bernard Zeller (Frankfurt am Main: Suhrkamp, 1960), 36.

31. Benjamin Nelson, "Hesse and Jung. Two Newly Recovered Letters," *Psychoanalytic Review* 50 (1963): 11–16. On the influence of psychoanalysis on Hesse's writing, see Theodore Ziolkowski, *The Novels of Hermann Hesse: Themes and Structures* (Princeton: Princeton University Press, 1965), 9–14.

32. "Gedanken zu Dostojewskijs Idiot," in Hermann Hesse, *Gesammelte Dichtungen und Schriften*, 7 vols. (Frankfurt am Main: Suhrkamp, 1952–57), 7:178–86; here 181–82. Unless otherwise noted, I cite Hesse's works according to this edition.

33. Ziolkowski, *Novels of Hermann Hesse*, 15–33.

34. First published in 1954 as a facsimile edition with Hesse's watercolor illustrations (Frankfurt am Main: Suhrkamp). An English translation, with a facsimile of the original, is available in *Pictor's Metamorphoses and Other Fantasies*, ed. Theodore Ziolkowski, trans. Rika Lesser (New York: Farrar, Straus and Giroux, 1982), 114–20.

35. "Goethe und Bettina" (1924); in *Gesammelte Schriften*, 7: 283–91; here 288–89.

36. Janouch, *Gespräche mit Kafka*, 43; also Kafka, *Dichter über ihre Dichtungen*, 59–60.

37. I base my biographical information on the first two volumes of David Garnett's autobiography, which cover the years through 1922: *The Golden Echo* (London: Chatto and Windus, 1953) and *The Flowers of the Forest* (London: Chatto and Windus, 1955).

38. Garnett, *Flowers of the Forest*, 245.

39. Ibid., 243–44.

40. Respectively, *The International Book Review* (Sept. 1923) and Heywood Broun in the *New York World* (6 May 1923).

41. I quote from the American edition, *Lady into Fox* (New York: Knopf, 1923).

42. For a study of the novel in the light of Woolf's affair with Vita, see Jean O. Love, "*Orlando* and Its Genesis: Venturing and Experimenting in Art, Love, and Sex," in *Virginia Woolf: Revaluation and Continuity*, ed. Ralph Freedman (Berkeley: University of California Press, 1980), 189–218.

43. Virginia Woolf, *Orlando: A Biography* (New York: Harcourt/Harvest, [n.d.]).

44. Nigel Nicolson, *Portrait of a Marriage* (New York: Atheneum, 1973), 225.

45. Virginia Woolf, *A Writer's Diary*, ed. Leonard Woolf (New York: New American Library, 1968), 123 (entry for 18 March 1928), and *passim*.

46. The latter aspect is treated by Harold Skulsky, *Metamorphosis: The Mind in Exile* (Cambridge: Harvard University Press, 1981), 195–222 ("Virginia Woolf's *Orlando*: Metamorphosis as the Quest for Freedom").

47. James King, *Virginia Woolf* (London: Hamish Hamilton, 1994), 70.

48. Virginia Woolf, *The Common Reader. First Series* (1925; rpt. New York: Harcourt/Harvest, [n.d.]), 24–39.

49. Virginia Woolf, *Jacob's Room and The Waves* (New York: Harcourt/Harvest, [n.d.]).

50. Theodore Ziolkowski, *Virgil and the Moderns* (Princeton: Princeton University Press, 1993), 106–9.

51. Virginia Woolf, *To the Lighthouse* (New York: Harcourt/Harvest, [n.d.]), 189. See Ziolkowski, *Virgil and the Moderns*, 104–6.

52. Sarah Annes Brown, *The Metamorphosis of Ovid: From Chaucer to Ted Hughes* (London: Duckworth, 1999), 201–15; here 203.

53. Ibid., 201–3.

54. Ibid., 204–7, Brown detects other associations between Ovid's and Woolf's Daphne scenes, but they are dependent upon the Apollo who is absent in Woolf's account.

55. Brown, *Metamorphosis of Ovid*, makes a case for other analogies: Salmacis and Hermaphrodite (207–10), Pygmalion (210–13), as well as Actaeon and Callisto (213–15). Although the first two have no textual basis, a certain similarity can be argued: the first might appeal to Woolf because of her interest in androgyny; and the second for her passion about creative artistry. But for reasons discussed above—the significant difference between metaphoric and metonymic metamorphosis—I find the Actaeon/Callisto analogy unpersuasive. Orlando is not transformed; and she does not suffer a violent death or transposition to the heavens.

56. Picasso's etchings have been frequently reprinted in various editions of the *Metamorphoses*, e.g., in the Insel Taschenbuch edition of Johann Heinrich Voss's classic translation of 1798 (Frankfurt am Main: Insel, 1990).

57. Udo Reinhardt, "Griechische Mythen in der bildenden Kunst des 20. Jahrhunderts: Highlights zu Homers Odyssee und Ovids Metamorphosen," *Gymnasium* 106 (1999): 25–71, esp. 48–69. Most of Reinhardt's examples are post-1945.

58. Reinhart Herzog, "Antike-Usurpationen in der deutschen Belletristik seit 1866 (mit Seitenblicken auf die Geschichte der klassischen Philologie)," *Antike und Abendland* 23 (1977): 10–27.

59. Ziolkowski, *Virgil and the Moderns*, 12–26.

60. T. H. Higham, "Ovid: Some Aspects of His Character and Aims," *The Classical Review* 48 (1934): 105–116; here 105.

6. The Ur-Exile

1. Letter of 12 Feb. 1946 to Hermann J. Weigand; Hermann Broch, *Briefe von 1929 bis 1951*, ed. Robert Pick (Zurich: Rhein-Verlag, 1957), 243.

2. Hans von Flesch-Brunningen, *Vertriebene: Von Ovid bis Gorgulaff* (Vienna: Elbemühl, 1933).

3. Bertolt Brecht, *Gesammelte Werke in 20 Bänden*, ed. Elisabeth Hauptmann (Frankfurt am Main: Suhrkamp, 1967), 9:663–64.

4. The fact that Lucretius was originally supposed to head the list is immaterial for the finished poem. See Tom Kuhn, "Ovid and Brecht: Topoi of Poetic Banishment," *Brecht Yearbook* 24 (1999): 162–75; here 173 n. 4. Kuhn proposes several commonalities between the two exiles.

5. Lion Feuchtwanger, "The Working Problems of the Writer in Exile," in *Altogether Elsewhere: Writers on Exile*, ed. Marc Robinson (Boston: Faber, 1994), 256–60; here 256.

6. Hartmut Froesch, "Exul poeta—Ovid als Chorführer verbannter oder geflohener Autoren," in *Lateinische Literatur, heute wirkend*, ed. Hans-Joachim Glücklich, vol. 1 (Göttingen: Vandenhoeck & Ruprecht, 1987), 51–64; here 54. Froesch is interested less in specific cases of reception and more in a morphology of exile writing generally.

7. Jo-Marie Claassen, *Displaced Persons: The Literature of Exile from Cicero to Boethius* (Madison: University of Wisconsin Press, 1999), 238–40. Claassen's epilogue, 252–58, takes a brief look at the modern reception.

8. Manès Sperber, "Auf der Brücke, die zu keinem Ufer führt: Die Zunft der schreibenden Emigranten," *Rheinischer Merkur*, 19 Dec. 1980, 28.

9. John Masefield, *A Letter from Pontus and Other Verse* (London: Heinemann, 1936), 1–17.

10. I base this paragraph on the survey by John C. Thibault, *The Mystery of Ovid's Exile* (Berkeley: University of California Press, 1964). See the summary and chronological list on pages 115–29.

11. Radu Vulpe, "Ovidio nella città dell'esilio," in *Studi Ovidiani* (Rome: Istituto di Studi Romani Editore, 1959), 39–62; Paul MacKendrick, *The Dacian Stones Speak* (Chapel Hill: University of North Carolina Press, 1975); John Richmond, "The Latter Days of a Love Poet: Ovid in Exile," *Classics Ireland* 2

(1995): 1–10 (www.ucd.ie/~classics/95); and Adrian Rădulescu, *Ovid in Exile*, trans. Laura Treptow (Iaşl: Center for Romanian Study, 2002).

12. I take the following examples from Kurt Smolak, "Der verbannte Dichter (Identifizierungen mit Ovid in Mittelalter und Neuzeit)," *Wiener Studien. Zeitschrift für Klassische Philologie und Patristik,* N.F. 14 (1980): 158–91.

13. I quote the text as appended to ibid., 189–91.

14. Ibid., 166–67.

15. B. Bischoff, "Eine mittelalterliche Ovidlegende," *Historische Jahrbücher* 71 (1952): 268–73; cited by Smolak, "Der verbannte Dichter," 167.

16. Paul Klopsch, *Pseudo-Ovidius De Vetula: Untersuchungen und Text* (Leiden: Brill, 1967).

17. Smolak, "Der verbannte Dichter," 172 n. 52.

18. John Dryden, "Preface to the Fables" (1700), in *Essays of John Dryden*, ed. W. P. Ker, 2 vols. (Oxford: Clarendon, 1926), 2:246–73.

19. Michael von Albrecht, "Der verbannte Ovid und die Einsamkeit des Dichters im frühen XIX. Jahrhundert (Zum Selbstverständnis Franz Grillparzers und Aleksandr Puškins)," in his *Rom: Spiegel Europas. Das Fortwirken antiker Themen und Formen in Europa,* 2nd ed. (Tübingen: Stauffenberg, 1998), 433–69.

20. Franz Grillparzer, *Sämtliche Werke,* ed. Peter Frank and Karl Pörnbacher, vol. 1 (Munich: Hanser, 1960), 72–73, 214–31.

21. E.g., *Tristia* 1.5.36, 2.470, and more generally 1.2 and 1.4. On shipwreck as a metaphor in poetry and thought, see Hans Blumenberg, *Schiffbruch mit Zuschauer: Paradigma einer Daseinsmetapher* (Frankfurt am Main: Suhrkamp, 1979).

22. I base my discussion on the translation by von Albrecht in "Der verbannte Ovid und die Einsamkeit des Dichters."

23. Alphonse de Lamartine, *Méditations,* ed. Fernand Letessier (Paris: Garnier, 1968), 51–53 ("Premières méditations poétiques," 15).

24. Charles Baudelaire, *Curiosités esthétiques: L'art romantique et autres oeuvres critiques,* ed. Henri Lemaitre (Paris: Garnier, 1986), 341.

25. Paul Verlaine, *Œuvres poétiques complètes,* ed. Y.-G. Le Dantec, 5 vols. (Paris: Éditions Vialetay, 1955–56), 3: 67–68.

26. Joseph Brodsky, "The Condition We Call Exile," in *On Grief and Reason: Essays* (New York: Farrar, Straus and Giroux, 1995), 22–34; here 23. Also in *Altogether Elsewhere,* 3–11.

7. THE ROMANIAN CONNECTION

1. I take the information in this section largely from Nicolae Lascu, "Ovidio nella tradizione e nella letteratura romena fino alle recenti celebrazioni Ovidiane in Romania," *Maia* 17 (1965): 177–88; Nicolae Lascu, *Ovidiu: Omul Şi Poetul* (Cluj: Deitura Dacia, 1971), 407–57; Gheorghe Carageani, "Ovidio e la Romania," *Annali Istituto Universitario Orientale, Napoli, Sezione Romanza* 40 (1998): 399–411; and (the only article in English with which I am familiar) Adriana Mitescu, "Ovid's Presence in Romanian Culture," *Romanian Review* 26 (1972): 54–57.

2. Edward Gibbon, *The Decline and Fall of the Roman Empire,* 2 vols. (New York: Modern Library, [n.d.]), 1:573 (chap. 18). On the history of Romania from prehistory to the late empire see Paul MacKendrick, *The Dacian Stones Speak* (Chapel Hill: University of North Carolina Press, 1975).

3. Vintila Horia, "Ovid: Dichter der Verbannung," *Merian,* June 1966, 78–83; here 80.

4. See Lascu, "Ovidio nella tradizione," 186, and Carageani, "Ovidio e la Romania," 405, for further examples.

5. Lascu, "Ovidio nella tradizione," 187–88.

6. Ovidiu Brimba, *Ovidio (la vita, l'ambiente, l'opera)* (Rome: Bulzoni, 1971).

7. Georg Scherg, *Ovid: Trauerspiel* (Bucharest: Staatsverlag für Kunst und Literatur, 1955).

8. John Wakeman, ed., *World Authors 1950–1970* (New York: Wilson, 1975), 676–77.

9. See the account by W. Granger Blair in the *New York Times*, 30 Nov. 1960, 11.

10. *Times Literary Supplement*, 2 June 1961, 345; and Moses Hadas in the *New York Herald Tribune*, 3 Sept. 1961, *Books*, 7. Peter G. Christensen, "Vintila Horia's Treatment of Ovid's Religious Conversion in *Dieu est né en exil*," *Journal of the American Romanian Academy of Arts and Sciences* 20 (1995): 171−85, provides a good survey of the critical and scholarly response.

11. Stephen Spender in *The New York Times Book Review*, 10 Sept. 1961, 5; and Robert Payne in *Saturday Review of Literature*, 4 Nov. 1961, 42.

12. Horia, "Ovid: Dichter der Verbannung," 81.

13. Vintila Horia, *Dieu est né en exil* (Paris: Fayard, 1960), 11. My references are to the original French edition, but the work has been translated into English: *God Was Born in Exile*, trans. A. Lytton Sells (New York: St. Martin's, 1961).

14. Horia subsequently elaborated this theme in "Ovid: Dichter der Verbannung," *Merian*, June 1966, 78−82.

15. Vasile Pârvan, *Getica, o Incercare de Protoistorie a Daciei* (Bucharest, 1926). The work, in Romanian, contains a lengthy résumé in French. Its principal findings, along with several of the illustrations, are also accessible in Vasile Pârvan's *Dacia: An Outline of the Early Civilizations of the Carpatho-Danubian Countries*, trans. I. L. Evans and M. P. Charlesworth (Cambridge: Cambridge University Press, 1928).

16. E.g., N. Herescu, "Ovide, le gétique," in *Atti del Convegno internazionale ovidiano*, 1:55−80, and his "Poeta Getes," in *Ovidiana: Recherches sur Ovide*, ed. N. I. Herescu (Paris: Belles Lettres, 1958), 391−95.

17. This aspect of Horia's novel has been fully treated by M. Bonjour, "*Dieu est né en exil* de Vintila Horia ou un Ovide Metamorphosé," in *Colloque: Présence d'Ovide*, ed. R. Chevallier (Paris: Belles Lettres, 1982), 441−454.

18. Jérôme Carcopino, "L'Exil d'Ovide, poète néopythagoricien," in his *Rencontres de l'histoire et de la littérature romaines* (Paris: Flammarion, 1963), 59−170.

19. Horia, "Ovid: Dichter der Verbannung," 79.

20. Vintila Horia, *Journal d'un paysan du Danube* (Paris: La Table Ronde, 1966), 71−73. Horia's journal has not previously been evaluated in connection with the novel.

21. Both in Latin and, as he tells us in his postscript, in the French translations by Émile Ripert and Jacques Chamonard.

22. The usual form is Zalmoxis, as employed by Herodotus (bk. 4.94−96). Horia takes the metathesized form from Strabo's *Geography* (7.3.5). See Mircea Eliade, *De Zalmoxis à Gengis Khan* (Paris: Payot, 1970; trans. Willard Trask as *Zalmoxis: The Vanishing God* [Chicago: University of Chicago Press, 1972]).

23. In his *Journal*, 81, Horia notes that an Arabic newspaper in Beirut reviewed his novel as a historical study and hailed Theodore's (utterly fictitious) letter from Rome as new documentary evidence for early Christianity.

24. On the religious aspect of the novel Christensen, "Horia's Treatment of Ovid's Religious Conversion," is especially good.

25. Robert Graves, in his novel *King Jesus* (1946), had already made brilliant use of these common ideas.

26. The religious aspect of Horia's novel has been fully treated by Kurt Smolak, "Der verbannte Dichter," *Wiener Studien*, n.s. 14 (1980), 58−61. But Smolak goes too far, in my opinion, when he seeks (179−184) to identify the 13th-century pseudo-Ovidian *De vetula* as a specific source for Horia's religious interpretation of Ovid. In the first place, the arguments for Horia's possible acquaintance with that esoteric text, which at the time was scarcely available, are not persuasive. In the second place, the analogies that Smolak cites—a manuscript left in a chest, a radical alteration in his personality, various doctrines of Christianity—are so general and vague that they can easily be explained in a more plausible manner.

27. M. Bonjour, "*Dieu est né en exil* de Vintila Horia ou un Ovide metamorphosé," 453.

28. Two English-language critics of the novel, neither of whom appears to be acquainted with the larger Romanian context or the appreciations by Smolak and Bonjour, ignore this aspect and therefore come to more negative evaluations of its merits: Betty Rose Nagle, "Ovid: A Poet between Two Novelists (Vintila Horia, *God Was Born in Exile*, and David Malouf, *An Imaginary Life*)," *Helios* 12 (1985): 65−73; and Phyllis B. Katz, "Ovid's Last World: An Age of Iron," *Classical and Modern Literature* 12 (1991−92):

127–37. Katz adduces J. M. Coetzee, *The Age of Iron,* as analogous to Horia's novel; but a closer parallel is evident in Coetzee's *Waiting for the Barbarians* (1980), in which also the representative of "civilization" is attracted into complicity with the "barbarians."

29. *Il diario di Ovidio* (Milan: Bompiani, 1997). Page numbers in parentheses refer to this work.

30. Marin Mincu, "La morte a Tomis," in *Metamorfosi,* Atti del Convegno Internazionale di Studi, Sulmona, 20–22 Nov. 1994, ed. Giovanni Papponetti (Sulmona: Centro Ovidiano di Studi e Richerche, 1997), 212–17; here 212.

31. They are not cited in Adrian Mitescu, "Ovid's Presence in Romanian Culture," *Romanian Review* 26 (1972): 54–57.

8. Interiorized Exile in the West

1. W. H. Auden, "I Like It Cold," *House and Garden,* December 1947, 110–11.

2. David Malouf, *An Imaginary Life* (New York: Braziller, 1978).

3. See Betty Rose Nagle, "Ovid: A Poet between Two Novelists (Vintila Horia, *God Was Born in Exile,* and David Malouf, *An Imaginary Life*), *Helios* 12 (1985): 65–73; and Marianthe Colakis, "David Malouf's and Derek Mahon's Visions of Ovid in Exile," *Classical and Modern Literature* 13 (1992–93): 229–39.

4. Itard's work, published originally in 1801, was translated into English by George and Muriel Humphrey under the title *The Wild Boy of Aveyron* (New York: Appleton-Century-Crofts, 1962).

5. Colakis, "Visions of Ovid in Exile," 230 n. 3, suggests as a possible source for the association of the wolf boy with Ovid's sojourn in Tomis Delacroix's painting, *Ovid parmi les Scythes,* which contains a boy with a wolf at his side.

6. In the *Oxford Book of Classical Verse in Translation,* ed. Adrian Poole and Jeremy Maule (Oxford: Oxford University Press, 1995), 389–90.

7. In Derek Mahon, *The Hunt by Night* (Winston Salem: Wake Forest University Press, 1983), 37–42.

8. For a comparison see Colakis, "Visions of Ovid in Exile."

9. C. H. Sisson, *Collected Poems 1943–1983* (Manchester: Carcanet, 1984), 135–44, 179, 295; and *Collected Translations* (Manchester, Carcanet, 1996), 285–95.

10. Sisson, *Collected Poems,* 179.

11. Seamus Heaney, *North* (London: Faber, 1975), 72–73.

12. Anne Carson, *Plainwater: Selected Prose and Poetry* (New York: Knopf/Random House, 1995), 32.

13. Ernst Fischer, *Elegien aus dem Nachlaß des Ovid* (Leipzig: Insel, 1963), 51–62.

14. Hartmut Lange, "Arbeiten im Steinbruch," in his *Theaterstücke 1960–72* (Reinbek bei Hamburg: Rowohlt, 1973), 7–13; here 9.

15. Ibid., 8.

16. I translate from Lange's *Theaterstücke 1960–72,* 307–41. See the discussion in Kurt Smolak, "Der verbannte Dichter (Identifizierungen mit Ovid in Mittelalter und Neuzeit)," *Wiener Studien: Zeitschrift für Klassische Philologie und Patristik* n.s. 14 (1980): 184–87.

17. Lange offers the theoretical justification for his conception of truly modern Communist art in his "Arbeiten im Steinbruch," 12.

18. I have been unable to obtain a copy of the radio play "Ovid's Return" (*Die Wiederkehr des Ovid*) by the Czech writer M. Rejnus, which was produced in 1965 by Westdeutscher Rundfunk and depicts Ovid as an anti-Augustan who is punished by exile for his political resistance. See Hartmut Froesch, "Exul poeta—Ovid als Chorführer verbannter oder geflohener Autoren," in *Lateinische Literatur, heute wirkend,* ed. Hans-Joachim Glücklich, vol. 1 (Göttingen: Vandenhoeck & Ruprecht, 1987), 51–64; here 59.

19. Volker Ebersbach, *Der Verbannte von Tomi,* in *Der Verbannte von Tomi: Historische Erzählungen* (Berlin: Der Morgen, 1984), 5–142.

20. Waldtraut Lewin, *Die Frauen von Kolchis* (Munich: dtv, 1996).

21. T. S. Eliot, "*Ulysses,* Order, and Myth" (1923); rpt. in *Forms of Modern Fiction,* ed. William Van O'Connor (1948; rpt. Bloomington: University of Indiana-Midland, 1959), 120–24.

22. Theodore Ziolkowski, *Fictional Transfigurations of Jesus* (Princeton: Princeton University Press, 1972), esp. 6–13.

23. The poem first appeared in Walcott's *The Fortunate Traveler* (1981); I quote from Derek Walcott, *Collected Poems, 1948–1984* (New York: Farrar, Straus and Giroux, 1986), 439–45.

24. Walcott is exploiting a device widely used by other modern writers, e.g., Thornton Wilder in *The Cabala* (1926), in which Virgil appears in a vision to a young American cultural pilgrim on his way home from Rome. See the chapter "Virgil *Redivivus*" in my *Virgil and the Moderns*, esp. 194–203.

25. I quote from Julia Kristeva, *Le vieil homme et les loups* (Paris: Fayard, 1991); the novel has appeared in English under the title *The Old Man and the Wolves*, trans. Barbara Bray (New York: Columbia University Press, 1994).

26. See Michael Wood's review of the English translation, *London Review of Books*, 26 Jan. 1995, 17–18.

27. *Dictionary of Literary Biography*, vol. 196: *Italian Novelists since World War II, 1965–95*, ed. Augustus Palotta (New York: Gale Group, 1999), 116–23.

28. Luca Desiato, *Sulle Rive del Mar Nero* (Milano: Rizzoli, 1992).

29. Luca Desiato, "Il doppio esilio di Ovidio," in *Metamorfosi*, Atti del Convegno Internazionale di Studi, Sulmona, 20–22 Nov. 1994, ed. Giuseppe Papponetti (Sulmona: Centro Ovidiano di Studi e Ricerche, 1997), 203–10.

9. Ovid in the Sixties and Seventies

1. Hermann Fränkel, *Ovid: A Poet between Two Worlds*, 1945; rpt. Sather Classical Lectures 18 (Berkeley: University of California Press, 1969), vii–viii.

2. Respectively in *Bookweek*, 26 Aug. 1945, 2; *Times Literary Supplement*, 25 Aug. 1945, 400; and *New York Times*, 2 Sept. 1945, 14.

3. See Johanna Niżyńska, "Marsyas's Howl: The Myth of Marsyas in Ovid's *Metamorphoses* and Zbigniew Herbert's 'Apollo and Marsyas,'" *Comparative Literature* 53 (2001): 151–69.

4. For other examples see Nina Kossman, ed., *Gods and Mortals: Modern Poems on Classical Myths* (Oxford: Oxford University Press, 2001). Gide is generally a Virgilian and read Virgil's works throughout his life, an influence we see from the early *Traité du Narcisse* (1891) to the late memoir of his wife Madeleine (1947). See Theodore Ziolkowski, *Virgil and the Moderns* (Princeton: Princeton University Press, 1993), 59–64.

5. Lalla Romano, *Le metamorfosi* (Turin: Einaudi, 1967), 13.

6. That Benn had long been familiar with this translation is proved by his quoting a line from it— "Schaut' er sich selbst in stygischer Flut" (from the section on Narcissus and Echo) as the epigraph to his early essay "Das moderne Ich" (1920).

7. Gottfried Benn to Friedrich Wilhelm Oelze, 31 August 1946; in Gottfried Benn, *Dichter über ihre Dichtungen*, ed. Edgar Lohner (Munich: Heimeran, 1969), 88.

8. Gottfried Benn, "Probleme der Lyrik," in *Gesammelte Werke in vier Bänden*, ed. Dieter Wellershoff (Wiesbaden: Limes, 1962), 1:494–532; here 503–5.

9. Benn, *Gesammelte Werke*, 3:191–93. The poem has been translated by Michael Hamburger in *Modern European Poetry*, ed. Willis Barnstone et al. (New York: Bantam, 1966), 143–44.

10. Harald Steinhagen, *Die Statischen Gedichte von Gottfried Benn* (Stuttgart: Klett, 1969), 107–52; here 109. Steinhagen is the standard source for the textual variants and genesis of the poem, along with a detailed analysis of its lyrical devices. For a discussion of Benn's poem in the context of his oeuvre see Hugh Ridley, "Gottfried Benn's *Orpheus' Death*," *Classics Ireland* 3 (1996): 1–7.

11. Michael Beck and Benedikt Simone, "Ovid und Benjamin Britten," in *Tradita et inventa: Beiträge zur Rezeption der Antike*, ed. Manuel Baumbach (Heidelberg: Winter, 2000), 531–48.

12. Ulrich Fleischer, "Zur Zweitausendjahrfeier des Ovid," *Antike und Abendland* 6 (1957): 27–59.

13. "Worte zum Gedächtnis Ovids," in Ernst Zinn, *Viva Vox: Römische Klassik und deutsche Dichtung*, ed. Michael von Albrecht (Frankfurt am Main: Peter Lang, 1994), 257–85.

14. L. P. Wilkinson, *Ovid Recalled* (Cambridge: Cambridge University Press, 1955; rpt. Bath: Chivers, 1974).

15. Respectively in *Times Literary Supplement,* 21 Oct. 1955, 620; *Manchester Guardian,* 21 Oct. 1955, 6; and *Spectator,* 25 Nov. 1955, 739.

16. Helmut Schelsky, *Die skeptische Generation: Eine Soziologie der deutschen Jugend* (Düsseldorf: Diederich, 1957).

17. Ibid., 84–85, 492.

18. Eckart von Naso, *Liebe war sein Schicksal: Roman um Ovid* (Hamburg: Wolfgang Krüger, 1958).

19. Published in the volume *King Log* (1968); in Geoffrey Hill, *New & Collected Poems, 1952–1992* (Boston: Houghton Mifflin, 1994), 49.

20. I base my discussion on the authorized German translation by Peter Lachmann with the unfortunate title *Der Täter heißt Ovid* (Vienna: Europa Verlag, 1975).

21. E. L. Doctorow, *Ragtime* (New York: Bantam, 1975).

22. See David Garrison, "Ovid's *Metamorphoses* in E. L. Doctorow's *Ragtime,*" *Classical and Modern Literature* 17 (1997): 103–15. While I fully agree with Garrison's initial generalization that the Ovid passage "elaborates in miniature the principle of transformation that informs both the *Metamorphoses* and *Ragtime*" (104), I am not convinced by his more specific analogies: that Evelyn Nesbit corresponds to the goddess Diana or that Coalhouse Walker's transformation to destructive rage resembles the stories of Actaeon and Tiresias. It goes too far and undermines the argument, I believe, to call *Ragtime* "a modern version of the *Metamorphoses*" (114).

10. OVID IN THE EIGHTIES

1. In a lecture delivered on several occasions and variously published. See Harry Levin, *Refractions: Essays in Comparative Literature* (New York: Oxford University Press, 1966), 271–95.

2. Hans Robert Jauß, "Der literarische Prozeß des Modernismus von Rousseau bis Adorno," in *Adorno-Konferenz 1983,* ed. Ludwig von Friedeburg and Jürgen Habermas (Frankfurt am Main: Suhrkamp, 1983), 95–130; here 195.

3. See, for example, Andreas Huyssen, *After the Great Divide: Modernism, Mass Culture, Postmodernism* (Bloomington: Indiana University Press, 1986); Arthur Kroker and David Cook, *The Postmodern Scene: Excremental Culture and Hyper-Aesthetics* (New York: St. Martin's, 1986); Rolf Günter Renner, *Die postmoderne Konstellation: Theorie, Text und Kunst im Ausgang der Moderne* (Freiburg: Rombach, 1988); and Peter Koslowski, *Die Prüfungen der Neuzeit: Über Postmodernität, Philosophie der Geschichte, Metaphysik, Gnosis,* ed. Peter Engelmann (Vienna: Passagen/Böhlau, 1989).

4. Clemens Heselhaus, "Metamorphose-Dichtungen und Metamorphose-Anschauungen," *Euphorion* 47 (1953): 121–46.

5. Leonard Barkan, *The Gods Made Flesh* (New Haven: Yale University Press, 1986), 18.

6. Philip Terry, Introduction to *Ovid Metamorphosed,* ed. Philip Terry (London: Chatto and Windus, 2000), 15.

7. See Jon Solomon, *The Ancient World in the Cinema,* rev. ed. (New Haven: Yale University Press, 2001), 17, 117, 128.

8. See additional examples of specific mythological metamorphoses—not all Ovidian and mostly not from the eighties—in *Gods and Mortals: Modern Poems on Classical Myths,* ed. Nina Kossman (Oxford: University Press, 2001).

9. C. H. Sisson, *Collected Poems 1943–1983* (Manchester: Carcanet, 1996), 135–44.

10. Italo Calvino, *Six Memos for the Next Millennium,* trans. Patrick Creagh (Cambridge: Harvard University Press, 1988). Calvino was not able to write the sixth lecture before his death.

11. Italo Calvino, "Ovid and Universal Contiguity," in Italo Calvino, *The Literature Machine. Essays,* trans. Patrick Creagh (London: Secker and Warburg, 1987).

12. For a discussion of the pattern and its function see Mario Barenghi's notes to *Le città invisibili* in Italo Calvino, *Romanzi e racconti,* ed. Claudio Milanini, vol. 2 (Milan: Mondadori, 1992), 1359–65; and Martin McLaughlin, *Italo Calvino* (Edinburgh: Edinburgh University Press, 1998), 100–109.

13. Calvino, *Romanzi e racconti*, 2:419–20. *Invisible Cities* has been translated by William Weaver (New York: Harcourt/Wolff, 1974).

14. I consider it extremely unlikely that Calvino was aware of Eckart von Naso's novel, *Liebe war sein Schicksal* (1958), in which Lalage is the bisexual friend who seduces Ovid's wife and later tries to seduce the impotent Ovid, and who betrays the affair to Ovid's lover Corinna/Arethusa.

15. Italo Calvino, "Un' antologia di racconti 'neri'" (1984), in *Saggi 1943–1985*, ed. Mario Barenghi, vol. 2 (Milan: Mondadori, 1995), 1689–95; here 1695.

16. Monika Schmitz-Emans, "Metamorphosen der Metamorphosen: Italo Calvino und sein Vorfahr Ovid: Calvinos Poetik und Ovids *Metamorphosen*," *Poetica: Zeitschrift für Sprach- und Literaturwissenschaft* 27 (1995): 433–69; here 444. I am less persuaded by Schmitz-Emans's arguments for the presence of Ovid in Calvino's works of the 1950s and 1960s.

17. James Harrison, *Salman Rushdie* (New York: Twayne, 1992), esp. 89–99.

18. Duncan F. Kennedy, "Recent Receptions of Ovid," in *The Cambridge Companion to Ovid*, ed. Philip Hardie (Cambridge: Cambridge University Press, 2002), 320–35; here 329.

19. Salman Rushdie, *The Satanic Verses* (New York: Holt/Picador, 1997).

20. Kennedy, "Recent Receptions of Ovid," 328–29.

21. Salman Rushdie, "Italo Calvino," in his *Imaginary Homelands: Essays and Criticism, 1981–1991* (London: Granta, 1991), 254–61; here 261.

22. Salman Rushdie, "Artist Crushed by the Myths of a Tyrant," *Independent on Sunday*, 13 May 1990; rpt. in *Imaginary Homelands*, 291–93; here 293.

23. See Kennedy, "Recent Receptions of Ovid," 323. Kennedy adduces such passages as examples for his persuasive argument that in Ransmayr's novel "history is troped as metamorphosis."

24. See Ronald Syme, *History in Ovid* (Oxford: Clarendon, 1978), 114–34 ("The Sons of Messalla").

25. I translate from the paperback edition: Christoph Ransmayr, *Die letzte Welt: Roman mit einem Ovidischen Repertoire* (Frankfurt am Main: Fischer Taschenbuch, 1991), here 127. *The Last World: with an Ovidian Repertory* is the translation by John Woods (New York: Grove Weidenfeld, 1990).

26. Michael Hofmann, *Times Literary Supplement*, 21 April 1989, 435.

27. See Phyllis B. Katz, "Ovid's Last World: An Age of Iron," *Comparative and Modern Literature* 12 (1992): 127–37.

28. Peter G. Christensen, "The Metamorphosis of Ovid in Christoph Ransmayr's *The Last World*," *Classical and Modern Literature* 12 (1991–92): 139–151, discusses conscious anachronism and modernization as techniques of the novel.

29. *Trachinia* occurs at *Met.* 11.269 as the kingdom of Ceyx in Thessaly.

30. I take the biographical information from Barbara Vollstedt, *Ovids "Metamorphoses," "Tristia" und "Epistulae ex Ponto" in Christoph Ransmayrs Roman "Die letzte Welt"* (Paderborn: Schöningh, 1998), 25–28. Vollstedt incorporates new information from an interview that she conducted with Ransmayr.

31. In *Das Wasserzeichen der Poesie* (Nördlingen, 1985), 10–13.

32. Vollstedt, *Christoph Ransmayrs Roman*, 28.

33. Ransmayr, "Entwurf zu einem Roman," reprinted in Thomas Epple, *Christoph Ransmayr: Die letzte Welt: Interpretationen* (Munich: Oldenbourg, 1992), 122–24.

34. Vollstedt, *Christoph Ransmayrs Roman*, 194–96, provides an extensive bibliography of the mainly positive, but sporadically negative reviews. See also Ulrich Schmitzer, "Tomi, das Kaff, Echo, die Hure— Ovid und Christoph Ransmayrs *Die letzte Welt*: Eine doppelte Wirkungsgeschichte," in *Mythen in nachmythischer Zeit: Die Antike in der deutschsprachigen Literatur der Gegenwart*, ed. Bernd Seidensticker und Martin Vöhler (Berlin: De Gruyter, 2002), 276–97, who appraises the critical reception.

35. In addition to Vollstedt and Schmitzer, see Michael von Albrecht, "Ransmayrs Roman *Die letzte Welt*," in his *Rom: Spiegel Europas. Das Fortwirken antiker Texte und Themen in Europa*, 2nd ed. (Tübingen: Stauffenberg, 1998), 696–721; and Jochen Gündele, *"Immer wieder anders und neu—*Christoph Ransmayrs Roman *Die letzte Welt* und das Werk Ovids: Ansätze zu einem Vergleich," in *Tradita et inventa: Beiträge zur Rezeption der Antike*, ed. Manuel Baumbach (Heidelberg: Winter, 2000), 601–14.

36. Von Albrecht and other scholars view the "Ovidian Repertoire" as an integral part of the novel and

not simply as "Ovid Light" or an appended "Reader's Digest," in the words of more skeptical reviewers. See Vollstedt, *Christoph Ransmayrs Roman,* 185.

37. Ibid., 190.

38. Von Albrecht, 697–98.

39. Notably Epple, *Christoph Ransmayr,* 92–98; Andrea Wanke and Armin Sieber, "*Die letzte Welt:* Konsumartikel, Kalligraphie oder einziger Trost?" in *"Keinem bleibt seine Gestalt": Ovids Metamorphosen und Christoph Ransmayrs Letzte Welt,* ed. Helmut Kiesel and Georg Wöhrle (Bamberg: Otto Friedrich-Universität, 1990), 29–38; Reinhold F. Glei, "Ovid in den Zeiten der Postmoderne: Bemerkungen zu Christoph Ransmayrs Roman *Die letzte Welt,*" *Poetica* 26 (1994): 409–27; Martin Kiel, *Nexus: Postmoderne Mythenbilder—Vexierbilder zwischen Spiel und Erkenntnis mit einem Kommentar zu Christoph Ransmayrs "Die letzte Welt"* (Frankfurt am Main: Peter Lang, 1996), 171–242; and Thomas Anz, "Spiel mit der Überlieferung. Aspekte der Postmoderne in Ransmayrs *Die letzte Welt,*" in *Die Erfindung der Welt,* ed. Uwe Wittstock (Frankfurt am Main: Fischer, 1997), 120–32.

40. Friedmann Harzer, *Erzählte Verwandlung: Eine Poetik epischer Metamorphosen* (Tübingen: Miemeyer, 2000), 174–98, offers the most detailed analysis of the theme of metamorphosis in Ransmayr's novel.

41. Antonio Tabucchi, *Sogni di sogni* (Palermo: Sellerio, 1992), 19–21.

42. John F. Miller, "Tabucchi's Dream of Ovid," *Literary Imagination: Review of the Association of Literary Scholars and Critics* 3 (2001): 237–47, persuasively suggests that the date is "based on Ovid's own reference to Tiberius' triumphal spoils in the entry for January 16 in his calendar-poem, the *Fasti* (1.645–48)."

43. See ibid., 241–42, for an account of the ancient symbolism of the butterfly.

44. The English translation by Nancy J. Peters, *Dreams of Dreams, and The Last Three Days of Fernando Pessoa* (San Francisco: City Lights, 1999) translates the word *ballonzolante* misleadingly, I think, as "hopping clumsily" (15).

11. Ovid in the Nineties

1. Douglas Coupland, *Generation X* (New York: St. Martin's, 1991).

2. Robert Jay Lifton, *The Protean Self: Human Resilience in an Age of Fragmentation* (New York: Basic Books, 1993), 1. In fact, Lifton refers to Homer and Joyce, not Ovid (5, 50).

3. I have seen this novel only in the English translation by Linda Coverdale: *Pig Tales: A Novel of Lust and Transformation* (New York: New Press, 1997). See the allusion, for instance, in Catherine Axelrad's satire, "Report on the Eradication and Resurgence of Metaphoric Illness in the West, 1880–1998," in *Ovid Metamorphosed,* ed. Philip Terry (London: Chatto & Windus, 2000), 237–43; here 242.

4. Alison Sharrock, "Womanufacture," *Journal of Roman Studies* 81 (1991): 36–49.

5. E.g., Sara Mack, *Ovid* (New Haven: Yale University Press, 1988); and Marion Giebel, *Ovid: Mit Selbstzeugnissen und Bilddokumenten,* rowohlts monographien (Reinbek bei Hamburg: Rowohlt, 1991).

6. Christa Lichtenstern, *Metamorphose: Vom Mythos zum Prozessdenken* (Weinheim: VCH, 1992); Alessandro Barchiesi, *The Poet and the Prince: Ovid and Augustan Discourse* (Berkeley: University of California Press, 1997); Sarah Annes Brown, *The Metamorphosis of Ovid: From Chaucer to Ted Hughes* (London: Duckworth, 1999); and Niklas Holzberg, *Ovid: Dichter und Werk* (Munich: Beck, 1997; trans. G. M. Goshgarian [Ithaca: Cornell University Press, 2002]).

7. See Glenn W. Most, "The Following Article," in *Ovid: Werk und Wirkung,* Festgabe für Michael von Albrecht zum 65. Geburtstag, ed. Werner Schubert, 2 vols. (Frankfurt am Main: Peter Lang, 1998), 2:1079–95.

8. I. Darlapp, "Cees Nooteboom: Die folgende Geschichte, und Thomas Mann: Der Tod in Venedig (ein Vergleich)," *Anregung* 42 (1996): 405–11.

9. Cees Nooteboom, *Het volgende verhaal* (Amsterdam: De Arbeiderpers, 1991).

10. A curious and symptomatic parallel can be drawn to a short novel written ten years earlier, Peter Handke's *Across (Der Chinese des Schmerzes,* 1983). There, too, the central figure is a high school classics teacher who leaves his job because of an existential crisis. In this case, however, his favorite poet, whose work he is engaged in translating, is Virgil (the bimillennial of whose death had been widely observed

in 1981). Unlike Mussert, who follows his classical archetype into a premature and lonely death, Handke's schoolteacher is eventually reintegrated into society in the spirit of Virgilian ethos. See Theodore Ziolkowski, *Virgil and the Moderns* (Princeton: Princeton University Press, 1993), 231–33.

11. Lawrence Norfolk, *Lemprière's Dictionary* (New York: Harmony Book, 1991). See Ulrich Broich, "Crossing the Borders between Fiction and Reality: Two Ovidian Novels from the 1990s," *Poetica* 35 (2003): 425–30, who deals with Norfolk and Ransmayr.

12. Interview with Lawrence Norfolk, *Bloomsbury Review,* March–April 1993, 14–16.

13. In *Classical Whodunnits: Murder and Mystery from Ancient Greece and Rome,* ed. Mike Ashley (New York: Carroll & Graf, 1997), 126–44.

14. David Wishart, *Ovid* (London: Sceptre, 1995), 1.

15. The often unlikely complexities of plot almost never go beyond the various hypotheses outlined three decades ago by John C. Thibault, *The Mystery of Ovid's Exile* (Berkeley and Los Angeles: University of California Press, 1964).

16. Mavis Cheek, *Aunt Margaret's Lover* (London: Hamish Hamilton, 1994).

17. Allen Mandelbaum, *The Metamorphoses of Ovid,* a new verse translation (New York: Harcourt, 1993), 3.

18. David R. Slavitt, *Virgil* (New Haven: Yale University Press, 1991), 171.

19. David R. Slavitt, *The Metamorphoses of Ovid,* translated freely into verse (Baltimore: Johns Hopkins University Press, 1994), 1.

20. See the editors' introduction, *After Ovid: New Metamorphoses* (New York: Farrar, Straus and Giroux, 1994), xi–xiii.

21. The story of Marsyas, embodying (literally!) the struggle between art and power, attracted writers from Communist Eastern Europe during the 1960s and 1970s. See Wolfgang Maaz, "Berlin: Kunerts Antike," in *Mythen in nachmythischer Zeit: Die Antike in der deutschsprachigen Literatur der Gegenwart,* ed. Bernd Seidensticker and Martin Vöhler (Berlin: De Gruyter, 2002), 229–54. Maaz mentions (236–37), in addition to Günter Kunert, Zbigniew Herbert, and Thomas Brasch.

22. Preface to *Ovid in English,* ed. Christopher Martin (London: Penguin, 1998), xiv–xv.

23. Ted Hughes, *Tales from Ovid* (New York: Farrar, Straus and Giroux, 1997), viii.

24. I am grateful to Carole Newlands for this interpretive suggestion.

25. For further observations on Slavitt, Hughes, and *After Ovid* see Brown, *Metamorphosis of Ovid,* 217–27; and John Henderson, "Ch-Ch-Ch-Changes," in *Ovidian Transformations: Essays on the Metamorphoses and Its Reception,* ed. Philip Hardie and others (Cambridge: Cambridge Philological Society, 1999), 301–23.

26. Respectively by *Time,* 3 Dec. 2001, and the online reviewer for "culturevulture.net," 7 Dec. 2001.

27. Mary Zimmerman, *Metamorphoses: A Play,* based on David R. Slavitt's translation of *The Metamorphoses of Ovid* (Evanston, Ill.: Northwestern University Press, 2002).

28. The story of Cupid and Psyche, one of the most popular tales from classical mythology, first occurs in the second-century work of Apuleius, the *Metamorphoses* or "Golden Ass."

29. In an interview with Bill Moyers on PBS, 22 March 2002.

30. Joseph Campbell, *The Hero with a Thousand Faces,* 2nd ed. (Princeton: Princeton University Press, 1968), 133–37, discusses the psychoanalytical implications of the myth of Phaethon.

31. Bill Moyers's observation in his interview with Mary Zimmerman.

32. Ibid.

33. E.g., *Philoktet* (1966), *Herakles* (1966), *Ödipus Tyrann* (1969), *Prometheus* (1974), *Medea* (1983). See Wilfried Barner, "'Modell, nicht Historie': Heiner Müller," in *Mythen in nachmythischer Zeit,* 257–72.

34. Alexander Kluge, "Risse" (acceptance speech for the Georg Büchner Prize), *Frankfurter Allgemeine Sonntagszeitung,* no. 43, 26 October 2003, Feuilleton 23, 26; here 26. Kluge's own rather idiosyncratic writings also suggest a loosely Ovidian structure and tone. His most recent thousand-page compilation titled *Die Lücke, die der Teufel läßt* (2003; The gap the devil leaves), for instance, consists of five hundred fantasies, fairy tales, horror stories, satires of contemporary political and social circumstances, culminating in a piece called "The Devil in the White House" and held together by a loosely associative principle of correspondences and irony not unlike the *Metamorphoses.*

35. Peter Horst Neumann, *Die Erfindung der Schere. Gedichte* (Bargfeld: Bücherhaus, 1999), 53. The following twelve-line poem, "In Tomi," which according to Neumann's note (76) was prompted by Ransmayr's *Last World*, relates that all strangers in that Black Sea town are called "Ovid" and that a whore named Echo presents the poet with Ovid's poem.

36. Joseph Brodsky, *On Grief and Reason: Essays* (New York: Farrar, Straus and Giroux, 1995), 428–58; here 429.

12. Ovid in the New Millennium

1. Stanley Kubrick and Frederic Raphael, *Eyes Wide Shut. A Screenplay* (New York: Warner Books, 1999), 18–19.

2. Edward Hirsch, *Lay Back the Darkness: Poems* (New York: Knopf, 2003), 9–10.

3. Liat Kaplan, "Metamorphoses," trans. Irit Sela, *Ariel: The Israel Review of Arts and Letters* 114 (2002): 17.

4. Rosi Braidotti, *Metamorphoses: Toward a Materialist Theory of Becoming* (Cambridge, Mass.: Polity, 2002); José Gil, *Metamorphoses of the Body*, trans. Stephen Muecke (Minneapolis: University of Minnesota Press, 1998); Jolie Demmers et al., eds., *Miraculous Metamorphoses: The Neoliberalization of Latin American Populism* (London: Palgrave, 2001); Alessandro Lazzari, ed., *Metamorphosen der Vernunft* (Würzburg: Königshausen & Neumann, 2003); Caroline Walker Bynum, *Metamorphosis and Identity* (New York: Zone, 2001); Francisco Gentil Vaz da Silva, *Metamorphosis: The Dynamics of Symbolism in European Fairy Tales* (New York: Peter Lang, 2002); Marina Warner, *Fantastic Metamorphoses, Other Worlds: Ways of Telling the Self* (Oxford: Oxford University Press, 2002).

5. Ulrich Schmitzer, *Ovid* (Hildesheim: Olms, 2001); and Friedmann Harzer, *Ovid* (Stuttgart: Metzler, 2002).

6. Arthur Golding, *Metamorphoses of Ovid,* ed. Madeleine Frey (Baltimore: Johns Hopkins University Press, 2002).

7. Philip Hardie, *Ovid's Poetics of Illusion* (Cambridge: University Press, 2002), 29.

8. For instance, Micaela Janan on Apollo and Hyacinthus in "The Book of Good Love," *Ramus* 17 (1988): 110–37; and Don Fowler, "Pyramus, Thisbe, King Kong: Ovid and the Presence of Poetry," in *Roman Constructions: Readings in Postmodern Latin* (Oxford: Oxford University Press, 2000), 156–67.

9. Philip Terry, ed., *Ovid Metamorphosed* (London: Chatto & Windus, 2000).

10. Two other stories from the cycle by M. J. Fitzgerald have appeared in print: "Eurydice," in Fitzgerald's *Rope-Dancer* (New York: Random House, 1985), 109–15; and "The Invention of Greek Statues" (on Andromeda), in *Literary Imagination: The Review of the Association of Literary Scholars and Critics* 3 (2001): 223–31.

11. Christine Brückner, *Wenn du geredet hättest, Desdemona: Ungehaltene Reden ungehaltener Frauen* (1983; rpt. Munich: Ullstein, 2000).

12. For this provocative suggestion I am indebted to Michael von Albrecht, *Ovid: Eine Einführung* (Stuttgart: Reclam, 2003), 290. Albrecht also perceives a debt to Ovid's *Fasti* in the organization of Ransmayr's *Last World* (see chap. 10).

13. Durs Grünbein, "Zwischen Antike und X," in *Mythen in nachmythischer Zeit: Die Antike in der deutschsprachigen Literatur der Gegenwart,* ed. Bernd Seidensticker and Martin Vöhler (Berlin: De Gruyter, 2002), 97–100; here 97.

14. Michael von Albrecht, "*Nach den Satiren:* Durs Grünbein und die Antike," in *Mythen in nachmythischer Zeit,* 101–16.

15. Durs Grünbein, *Das erste Jahr: Berliner Aufzeichnungen* (Frankfurt am Main: Suhrkamp Taschenbuch, 2001).

16. Yoko Tawada, *Verwandlungen,* Tübinger Poetik Vorlesung (Tübingen: Konkursbuchverlag, 1998).

17. Yoko Tawada, *Opium für Ovid. Ein Kopfkissenbuch von 22 Frauen,* 2nd rev. ed. (Tübingen: Konkursbuchverlag, 2001).

18. The Japanese classic has provided the model for another recent fiction, albeit set in contemporary

Japan and without the Ovidian associations, by the Australian writer Jan Blensdorf: *My Name Is Sei Shonagon* (New York: Overlook, 2003).

19. Jane Alison, *The Love-Artist* (New York: Farrar, Straus and Giroux, 2001).

20. This is one of the two extant lines of the tragedy. See L. P. Wilkinson, *Ovid Recalled* (rpt. Bath: Chivers, 1974), 116.

21. Lucien d'Azay, *Ovide, ou l'amour puni* (Paris: Les Belles Lettres, 2001).

22. Josef Skvorecky, *An Inexplicable Story, or The Narrative of Questus Firmus Siculus,* trans. Káča Poláčková Henley (Toronto: Key Porter Books, 2002). I am indebted to Carole Newlands for alerting me to this work.

INDEX OF OVIDIAN THEMES
(in cited works)

INDEX